TIBETAN AND ZEN BUDDHISM IN BRITAIN

This book analyses the transplantation, development and adaptation of the two largest Tibetan and Zen Buddhist organisations currently active on the British religious landscape: the New Kadampa Tradition (NKT) and the Order of Buddhist Contemplatives (OBC). The key contributions of recent scholarship are evaluated and organised thematically to provide a framework for analysis, and the history and current landscape of contemporary Tibetan and Zen Buddhist practice in Britain are also mapped out. A number of patterns and processes identified elsewhere are exemplified, although certain assumptions made about the nature of 'British Buddhism' are subjected to critical scrutiny and challenged.

David N. Kay has lectured on and conducted doctoral research into the development and adaptation of Tibetan and Zen forms of Buddhism in Britain at St Martin's College, Lancaster.

ROUTLEDGECURZON CRITICAL STUDIES IN
BUDDHISM
General Editors:
Charles S. Prebish and Damien Keown

RoutledgeCurzon Critical Studies in Buddhism is a comprehensive study of the
Buddhist tradition. The series explores this complex and extensive tradition
from a variety of perspectives, using a range of different methodologies.

The series is diverse in its focus, including historical studies, textual translations and commentaries, sociological investigations, bibliographic studies, and
considerations of religious practice as an expression of Buddhism's integral religiosity. It also presents materials on modern intellectual historical studies,
including the role of Buddhist thought and scholarship in a contemporary, critical context and in the light of current social issues. The series is expansive and
imaginative in scope, spanning more than two and a half millennia of Buddhist
history. It is receptive to all research works that inform and advance our knowledge and understanding of the Buddhist tradition.

THE REFLEXIVE NATURE OF
AWARENESS
Paul Williams

BUDDHISM AND HUMAN
RIGHTS
*Edited by Damien Keown, Charles
Prebish and Wayne Husted*

ALTRUISM AND REALITY
Paul Williams

WOMEN IN THE FOOTSTEPS
OF THE BUDDHA
Kathryn R. Blackstone

THE RESONANCE OF
EMPTINESS
Gay Watson

IMAGING WISDOM
Jacob N. Kinnard

AMERICAN BUDDHISM
*Edited by Duncan Ryuken Williams and
Christopher Queen*

PAIN AND ITS ENDING
Carol S. Anderson

THE SOUND OF LIBERATING
TRUTH
*Edited by Sallie B. King and
Paul O. Ingram*

BUDDHIST THEOLOGY
*Edited by Roger R Jackson and
John J. Makransky*

EMPTINESS APPRAISED
David F. Burton

THE GLORIOUS DEEDS OF
PURNA
Joel Tatelman

TIBETAN AND ZEN BUDDHISM IN BRITAIN

Transplantation, development and adaptation

David N. Kay

RoutledgeCurzon
Taylor & Francis Group

LONDON AND NEW YORK

First published 2004
by RoutledgeCurzon
11 New Fetter Lane, London EC4P 4EE

Simultaneously published in the USA and Canada
by RoutledgeCurzon
29 West 35th Street, New York, NY 10001

RoutledgeCurzon is an imprint of the Taylor & Francis Group

© 2004 David N. Kay

Typeset in Goudy by Taylor & Francis Books Ltd
Printed and bound in Great Britain by MPG Books Ltd, Bodmin

British Library Cataloguing in Publication Data
A catalogue record for this book is available from the British Library

Library of Congress Cataloging in Publication Data
A catalog record for this book has been requested

ISBN 0–415–29765–6

TO MY PARENTS AND MY WIFE, ANIMA

CONTENTS

CONTENTS

CONTENTS

ILLUSTRATIONS

Figures

PREFACE

This book is the end result of my doctoral research into contemporary forms of British Buddhism, conducted between 1993 and 2000 through the Department of Religion and Ethics at St Martin's College, Lancaster. The latter half of the twentieth century witnessed a growing interest in Buddhism as a religious option amongst British people and the increasing diversification of the British Buddhist landscape. The focus of my research from the outset was Tibetan and Zen forms of Buddhism owing to the fact that, whilst scholarly research into the nature and development of British Buddhism was making significant advances in some areas – notably the *Theravāda* tradition and the self-consciously 'Western' movement called the Friends of the Western Buddhist Order (FWBO) – the Tibetan and Zen traditions remained a neglected area. An exhaustive examination of all Tibetan and Zen groups that were active on the British Buddhist landscape during the 1990s was beyond the scope of the study; selection was necessary in order to yield material that would give a meaningful insight into the processes of transplantation, development and adaptation. The New Kadampa Tradition (NKT), which has its roots in the Tibetan *Gelug* tradition, and the Order of Buddhist Contemplatives (OBC), which is rooted in Japanese *Sōtō* Zen, were chosen because they were amongst the first wave of Tibetan and Zen groups to become established in Britain, each tracing their origins back to the early 1970s. After three decades of growth and development, these groups now represent the largest Tibetan and Zen Buddhist organisations, institutionally and numerically, that are currently active on British shores. The NKT and OBC are therefore significant to anyone who wishes to understand the nature and development of British Buddhism generally, and its Tibetan and Zen forms specifically. The present work aims to further this understanding and open up the scholarly discussion of Tibetan and Zen Buddhism in Britain by providing a detailed analysis of the transplantation, development and adaptation of the NKT and OBC. The variety of Tibetan and Zen traditions in Britain are surveyed as the immediate historical backdrop and broader institutional context of these groups, but the focus of the study is firmly upon the emergence and development of the NKT and OBC.

The book is divided into four parts. Part I surveys the emerging scholarly literature on British Buddhism, evaluates the key contributions, and organises these findings thematically to provide a framework for analysing the NKT and OBC. To contextualise these movements the landscape of contemporary Tibetan and Zen practice is mapped out and the history of these growing and diverse sectors of British Buddhism is charted. Part II examines the indigenous Tibetan context of the NKT before charting its emergence in Britain and outlining the contours of its sense of self-identity. The NKT, it is argued, is a movement that is rooted firmly within traditional *Gelug* exclusivism whilst simultaneously reflecting and reacting against the conditions of modernity. Part III outlines the historical and ideological growth of the OBC within the context of the biography of its Western founder and her relations with traditional Japanese *Sōtō* Zen. The influence of trans-cultural processes on the OBC's transplantation in Britain are acknowledged, but the widely accepted 'Protestant Buddhism' thesis is subjected to critical scrutiny. Part IV concludes the study by reflecting upon recent developments within the NKT and OBC, speculating about possible future directions, and returning to the framework adopted in the first chapter to structure a comparative discussion.

It is my hope that this work will be of interest to a number of related fields. It is my intention, first and foremost, to provide scholars who are involved in the emerging discipline of study that is centred around the transplantation and development of Buddhism in the West with an introduction to Tibetan and Zen Buddhism in Britain. The thematic survey of scholarly findings on British Buddhism should prove accessible to undergraduates, whilst the ethnographic data on the NKT and OBC aims to fill a gap in the literature for those more established in the field. I also hope that the book will have a wider application for those involved in the study of contemporary religion. A range of theories concerning the internal dynamics of new religious movements are utilised to make sense of the inner patterns and processes at work within the NKT and OBC, and scholars interested in the study of contemporary religious groups, their internal dynamics and their relationships with broader religious traditions will find this book a useful comparative resource. Finally, I hope that the book will be of interest to those who are its subjects: Western Buddhists themselves, particularly those practising within Tibetan and Zen traditions. The scholarly interest in Western Buddhism, and the manner in which Western Buddhists are represented, does not pass unnoticed within Buddhist communities. It is my sincere wish that the Buddhists who made this study possible will hear their voices within its pages and find the scholarly discussion of their traditions of practice both interesting and enriching.

ACKNOWLEDGEMENTS

The completion of this work has depended upon the support, generosity and kindness of many individuals and institutions. I am grateful to the Department of Religion and Ethics, St Martin's College, Lancaster, for the financial and academic support I received during the course of my doctoral studies. In particular, I would like to thank Dr Ian Harris for his expert advice, support and encouragement. I would also like to thank the staff of Harold Bridges Library, St Martin's College, Lancaster. I am indebted to the scholars and researchers who either read and commented on draft sections of my original thesis or who took the study forward through friendly discussion. In particular, I would like to thank Professor Geoffrey Samuel, Department of Anthropology, University of Newcastle, New South Wales, and Dr Sandra Bell, Department of Anthropology, Durham University, for their generous advice. Special thanks are due to my family and friends for the love and support they have given me over the years. I also owe a great debt to my wife, Anima, who has supported and encouraged me throughout with great patience, understanding and humour. Finally, but by no means least, I must express my sincere gratitude to the many Buddhist practitioners, both in England and abroad, who have been so generous with their time and support. Besides enabling me to complete this work, their openness and goodwill has enriched my life and broadened my horizons.

ABBREVIATIONS

COI	Community of Interbeing
CPMT	Council for the Preservation of the Mahayana Tradition
EST	English Sangha Trust
FM	*Full Moon*
FMJ	*Full Moon Journal*
FPMT	Foundation for the Preservation of the Mahayana Tradition
FWBO	Friends of the Western Buddhist Order
IMI	International Mahayana Institute
IZA	International Zen Association
Jap.	Japanese
JOBC	*Journal of the Order of Buddhist Contemplatives*
JSA	*Journal of Shasta Abbey*
JTHBA	*Journal of Throssel Hole Buddhist Abbey*
JTHP	*Journal of Throssel Hole Priory*
JZMS	*Journal of the Zen Mission Society*
NBO	Network of Buddhist Organisations
NKT	New Kadampa Tradition
NRM	new religious movement
OBC	Order of Buddhist Contemplatives
SGI	Sōka Gakkai International
Skt	Sanskrit
SSC	Shugden Supporters Community
THPN	*Throssel Hole Priory Newsletter*
TTP	Teacher Training Programme
WCF	Western Ch'an Fellowship
ZMS	Zen Mission Society

Part I

REVIEW AND CONTEXTUALISATION

1

BUDDHISM IN BRITAIN

Review and contextualisation

Introduction

Alongside the growing interest in Buddhism as a religious option amongst British people and the increasing diversification of British Buddhism in the latter half of the twentieth century, a substantial amount of scholarly research has been undertaken into the nature and development of Buddhism in a British cultural context. The literature reflects the diversity of practice and indicates the analytical complexities encountered in the study of the importation and transplantation of a religious tradition into a new cultural environment. Any study of contemporary British Buddhism must thus take as its point of departure the groundwork laid down by previous studies.

For the purposes of analysis, I have divided the following review of this literature into three separate but interrelated sections. The first section, 'Buddhism and British Culture', reviews the literature on the differing levels of Buddhism's relationship with British culture and the transformations resulting from this contact; the second, 'The transplantation process', examines the numerous other conditions besides cultural interactions that affect the transplantation of an incoming religious tradition; and the third, 'Policies and patterns of adaptation', examines the issue of the conscious and deliberate adaptation of Buddhism by Buddhist groups within a Western cultural context. Special reference will be made throughout these sections to Tibetan and Zen forms of Buddhism in Britain. Whilst there are discernable continuities between individuals and groups, Buddhism in Britain remains characterised by great and enduring diversity. The Tibetan and Zen traditions of Buddhism are very different culturally, historically, doctrinally and practically, and such traditional differences inevitably influence the way they react to and develop within new cultural contexts. This discussion will therefore underline areas of particular interest to the development of Tibetan and Zen forms of Buddhism in Britain.

The final part of this chapter contextualises the groups under analysis within wider religious landscapes. The contours of the British Buddhist landscape are briefly outlined and specific attention is given to the development and presence of Tibetan and Zen organisations. This will set the scene for the subsequent analysis of the New Kadampa Tradition (NKT) and the Order of Buddhist

Contemplatives (OBC), the largest organisations within their respective traditions that are currently practising in Britain.

Buddhism and British culture

The impact of Buddhism on British culture

One way in which scholars have considered the interaction of Buddhism with British culture is to assess the impact of Buddhism on British cultural life beyond the boundaries of religious communities themselves. Puttick argues that 'the influence of Buddhism on contemporary life is in excess of the numbers involved' (Puttick 1993: 6) and, in support of this, refers to eminent philosophers, scientists and psychologists whose theories have been influenced by the Buddhist *weltanschauung*.[1] This view is shared by Scott who considers that Buddhism's biggest role in the twenty-first century 'might not necessarily be in terms of its numeric advancement, but in this contribution to the wider climate, debates and culture' (Scott 1995a). There is some disagreement, however, about the extent of Buddhism's influence on British society. Waterhouse is dubious about such claims, commenting that we 'simply do not know how influential Buddhism has been' (Waterhouse 1997: 16). Notwithstanding the absence of research into the *extent* of the influence, the fact that Buddhism *has* influenced British culture is undeniable. The capability of events within the Buddhist community – such as the *Dorje Shugden* (*rDo rje shugs ldan*) dispute of 1996, and the allegations concerning sexual manipulation and the abuse of authority within the Friends of the Western Buddhist Order (FWBO) in 1997 – to generate headline coverage in Britain's broadsheet newspapers is but one indication of Buddhism's potential and actual penetration of secular British life. It should also be remembered that the impact of Buddhism on British cultural life should be seen within the broader context of the West's ongoing encounter with oriental thought generally. According to Clarke (1997), this encounter became increasingly amplified throughout the twentieth century, extending beyond the realm of 'popular religious quests' into wider fields of intellectual endeavour including inter-religious dialogue, philosophical enquiry, psychology, and scientific and ecological speculation.

The appeal of Buddhism

Another way in which the interaction of Buddhism with British culture has been discussed is through a consideration of the appeal of Buddhism as a religious option for British people. Scholars assessing the Western attraction to the Buddhist path sometimes distinguish between the experience of the Western Buddhist 'convert' on the one hand, and sociological accounts of membership of new religious movements (NRMs) on the other. It has been argued that westerners who turn to Buddhism do not fit the prevailing sociological models of

4

conversion to NRMs, which describe membership in terms of a 'deviant cult response' to personal and social discontinuities. Finney is critical of sociologists who discuss Zen Buddhism in America in these terms and argues that whilst such explanations may help elucidate the recruitment of *some* Buddhists, they provide only a partial and limited account (Finney 1991: 379). His account of Zen practitioners is more akin to Volinn's proposed model of membership of Eastern meditation groups in America, which is characterised by 'a going towards [rather] than a fleeing from [...] a going towards a sought after experience' (Volinn 1985: 148). Studies of Buddhism in Britain echo Finney's assessments of American Buddhists. Puttick, for example, describes British Buddhists as 'active seekers' as opposed to 'passive converts', and the research findings of other scholars all attest to the high educational levels of British Buddhists and the discriminating and reasoned manner in which they negotiate their spiritual paths. Waterhouse's (1997: 222–228) discussion of the importance of 'personal authority' to British Buddhists in the legitimation of their religious beliefs and practices is especially pertinent to this debate .

Sociological theories of NRM membership and recruitment are nevertheless considered to have some applicability to the Western Buddhist experience; hence Finney argues that prevailing 'deviance' explanations 'suffer not so much from being irrelevant as from being incomplete' (1991: 381). Studies of Buddhism in Britain have taken as axiomatic the view that changing social and cultural conditions in the host society over the last one hundred and fifty years have favoured the emergence of Buddhism, and that whilst the British experience may be characterised primarily by an active 'going towards' movement, there is also a fair amount of 'fleeing from' involved as well. That is, Buddhism's appeal can be explained in part by its perceived differences to and discontinuities with those elements of British culture and religion with which people have become dissatisfied or disillusioned.

There is general agreement that the most important cultural precondition paving the way for the successful growth of Buddhism in Britain has been the decline in the authority of the Christian Church. The initial appeal of Buddhism in Victorian Britain is placed by Clausen (1975) and Almond (1988) within the context of a 'period of doubt' whereby the rise of rationality, science, historiography and Darwinian evolutionary theory undermined the position of Christianity in Britain and Europe, prompting disillusioned Europeans to look elsewhere for intellectual and spiritual inspiration. Buddhism was appealing largely because of its perceived differences to Christianity including, amongst other things, the fact that it was non-theistic, non-dogmatic and emphasised spiritual autonomy above faith in an external saviour figure. Dissatisfaction with Christianity and the perception of Buddhism as a 'more inspiring, nourishing, and intellectually convincing alternative' (Puttick 1993: 6) are still cited as major reasons for the latter's appeal and growth. Peter B. Clarke discusses the appeal of non-Christian religions in terms of a growing intellectual and psychological inability to take the Judeo-Christian notions of God, sin and salvation seriously. He argues that new religious forms, including Buddhism, fulfil the modern desire for 'a non-hierarchical, non-sacramental, free-thinking, undogmatic and quasi-scientific approach to religion that is relevant [and] can be experimented with' (Clarke 1993: 3–4).[2]

Buddhism is also seen as a religion providing modern man with answers to the spiritual despair ensuing from rampant industrialisation, rationalism, secular-materialism and consumerism. Baxter explains Buddhism's success in terms of the alternative it offers to the perceived options of modern Western culture, namely 'the supernaturalist theistic religions on the one hand, and the assumptions of secular materialism on the other' (Baxter 1986: 176). Puttick (1993: 7) also considers that modern city life may have prompted an interest in Buddhism in the same way that emerging cosmopolitan communities boosted the early growth of Indian Buddhism.

Besides accounting for its success in terms of the 'alternative' it offers to features of British religion and culture that are regarded as alienating, some scholars emphasise how perceived compatibilities and continuities between Buddhism and more valued elements of British society have been an equally important condition.[3] With respect to the earliest encounters, for example, it is well documented how the appeal of Buddhism lay equally in its perceived *similarities* with aspects of Christianity for which British Victorians retained an affection, such as the figure of Christ and his moral code. According to Clausen, the fact that

> Buddhism, like Christianity, had an attractive personal founder who had led a life of great self-sacrifice [...] should not be underestimated among the reasons for the appeal of Buddhism in Victorian England and America.
>
> (Clausen 1975: 6)

The early appeal of Buddhism is also explained in terms of its perceived compatibility with both the rational/scientific outlook on the one hand, and the romantic outlook on the other. Baumann maintains that the earliest German Buddhists were predominantly rationalists who praised Buddhism 'as a scientific and analytical religion which did not contradict the findings of modern science' (Baumann 1997: 279). Whilst Buddhism facilitated the Western rationalist's critique of Christianity, for the romantic who was alienated from both traditional Christianity *and* the scientific alternative, it provided 'a source of spiritual renewal' (Batchelor 1994: 252). According to Batchelor, the rationalistic and romantic attitudes underlying the appeal of Buddhism in the Victorian period should also be seen as persisting 'psychological strata within the Western mind' (1994: xii) informing the existential engagement with Buddhism today. Modern Buddhist exegetes and practitioners from within a variety of contemporary traditions still appeal to the 'fit' between Buddhism and the rationalistic critique of Christianity, and modern developments in psychology, science and environmentalism are regularly cited as movements that are entirely compatible with the Buddhist framework.[4] Buddhism continues to appeal to westerners therefore because of its perceived continuities with valued currents in Western cultural life.

The attraction to Zen and Tibetan forms of Buddhist practice in the latter half of the twentieth century is often explained in terms of their perceived differences to and compatibilities with Western religion and culture. Ellwood (1979) argues that the growth of Zen in America after the Second World War expressed the widespread cultural alienation of Americans who sought discontinuity with their society and rebelled against it by embracing alternative faiths and cultures. Zen was an attractive alternative because of its perceived continuities with anti-structural ideals of spontaneity, experience and freedom. The growth of Zen since the 1960s is accounted for in terms of the social and religious unrest favouring the emergence of NRMs generally, although its perceived continuities with psychotherapy and the human potential movement are singled out by Layman (1976) as particularly significant. Counter-cultural trends are also considered central to the emergence of Tibetan Buddhism, which has been 'presented to westerners as a possible way forward in a dark and troubled world' (Campbell 1996: 28). The exotic sensuality of its rituals and symbology and the profundity of its religious philosophy make Tibetan Buddhism a 'vibrant alternative' to Western cultural, philosophical and religious traditions. At the same time, the appeal is explained in terms of the common ground between Western and Tibetan Buddhist traditions especially in the areas of science, medicine and psychological theory, and modern movements concerning the issues of gender, race, peace and the environment:

> any religious tradition from a different culture, in order to find relevance in the minds of new converts, would have to contain concepts or symbols which would be in some way recognisable, so that the meanings arising out of particular representations and texts would be different enough, but not so totally alien as to be dismissed out of hand. What is interesting about the Tibetan tradition for westerners is that it contains *both* features [...] the familiar philosophical base *and* the absolutely alien iconography.
>
> (Campbell 1996: 168)

The manner in which westerners have adopted Buddhism, involving the interplay between discontinuity *and* continuity with elements of Western religion and culture, raises questions about the nature of the religion being embraced. Rather than being predisposed towards Buddhism because it fulfils their spiritual needs, westerners interpret or 'read' Buddhism selectively in ways acceptable to them. The 'Buddhism' of westerners, therefore, is not so much a religion they have *converted to* as something they have *created* during the process of conversion. Batchelor describes this succinctly:

There are as many kinds of Buddhism as there are ways the fragmented and ever-changing European mind has to apprehend it. In each case 'Buddhism' denotes something else.

(Batchelor 1994: 274)

Chryssides also notes how the cultural and religious baggage westerners take into their new faith problematises the nature of 'Buddhism':

The religion to which they convert is [...] not a 'pure' form [...] but the immigrant religion overlaid with Western modes of thinking.

(Chryssides 1994: 71)[5]

This process is not unique to the reception of Buddhism in Britain but characterises the transplantation process of any religion into a new cultural context. Pye argues that the transplantation of religion

involves a complex relationship between tradition and interpretation, or in other words, an interplay between what is taken to be the content of the religion and the key factors in the situation which it is entering.

(Pye 1969: 236)

Closer scrutiny of the appeal of Buddhism to westerners thus leads us onto a deeper level of the interaction of Buddhism with British culture, a level where British culture impacts upon and transforms Buddhism. The dynamics of these subtle cultural relationships have been the subject of considerable research, which will now be explored.

The impact of British culture on Buddhism

In an article about the presence of Indian religions in the West, Hardy maintains that Western cultural history is 'the appropriate overall framework of reference for analysis' because these modern Indian religious movements 'are primarily mirrors in which we can (and must) see ourselves, and not invaders from an alien world' (Hardy 1984: 15). With respect to the development of Buddhism in Britain, scholars have found his observations equally applicable; 'Buddhism' should be considered not simply as an external phenomenon imported from abroad, but as something that has 'evolved from within our own culture' (Hardy 1984: 15).

Mellor's work on the development of Buddhism in Britain has most clearly articulated the assumptions of cultural translation theory. He considers Buddhism as a 'problematic category' for the analyst rather than as a label for a 'readily identifiable phenomenon of Eastern origin [...] merely transferred into a Western context' (1991: 73), because its transplantation into British society has occasioned 'a series of sophisticated religious and philosophical interactions' (1989: 339). As religions are always embedded in socio-cultural realities, they should be studied with reference to the cultural contexts in which their ideas and practices are expressed. The British religious and cultural context must thus be central to studies of British Buddhism. Mellor traces the development of Buddhism in England and locates it within the context of broader cultural and religious discourses such as those of theosophy, modernity and Protestant Christianity. English expressions of Buddhism, he maintains, have absorbed elements of the discourses that form part of their 'enunciative field' and consequently reveal continuities with wider Western religious and cultural trends. The continuities between English Buddhism and Protestant Christian religious discourse, such as the prevalent individualism and rejection of religious form as an 'empty category', are seen as particularly striking. Mellor acknowledges that the different Buddhist groups of his study relate to Protestant Christian discourse in very different ways, with, for example, the *Theravāda* British Forest Sangha representing a far more sophisticated position vis-à-vis Western individualism and religious ritual than the FWBO's wholesale acceptance of the former and rejection of the latter. Nevertheless, since both groups have absorbed elements of a Protestant Christian nature, he believes the specific character of Buddhism in England 'can be elucidated in the light of an awareness of the liberal Protestant trend' (1989: 340). Hence, rather than talking about the 'transference' of Buddhism from Eastern contexts to a British cultural context, he characterises this development as one of 'cultural translation':

> Buddhist groups in England are a 'significant cultural development' [...] not because they divert Western culture into new religious channels, but because they explore the existing channels in new ways.
>
> (Mellor 1991: 90)

In many ways, Mellor's thesis is an extension and refinement of previous analyses of the initial reception of Buddhism by Victorian Britain. Almond examines how Buddhism was 'created' rather than 'discovered' via a process of textualisation and imaginative interpretation.[6] He situates Victorian discourse about Buddhism within the broader context of discourse about the East and examines how it reflects the dynamics of 'orientalism', defined and analysed by Said as 'a Western style for dominating, restructuring, and having authority over the Orient' (Said 1978: 3). Victorian interpretations of Buddhism, Almond argues, passed through a 'conceptual filter' made up of Western images of the oriental way on the one hand, and Victorian concerns and values on the other:

> The Victorian world in all its diversity, confident of its cultural hegemony, was incorporated, and crucially so, in its interpretation of Buddhism.
>
> (Almond 1988: 141)

Bell is critical of accounts like Almond's that explain the nineteenth-century reception and rendering of Buddhism as a project dominated by westerners. The introduction of Buddhism into Britain, she argues, has always been a process of 'active collaboration between Britons and Asian Buddhists, collectively and individually' (Bell 1991: 11). She is also critical of Mellor's claim that the nature of British Buddhism can be elucidated in terms of Protestant Christian discourse, disagreeing in particular with his characterisation of the FWBO as a movement that is 'highly suspicious of ritual' (Bell 1996: 91).[7] The broadly Protestant character of British Buddhism is taken as axiomatic by a number of scholars, sometimes too uncritically. For example, Waterhouse's suggestion that Buddhism in Bath displays 'broadly Protestant tendencies' (1997: 240) is neither situated within a thorough survey of the available theoretical literature nor is it grounded within fieldwork itself beyond a number of passing remarks concerning the laicised orientation of the groups under study. A scholarly account of British Buddhism that subjects the Protestant thesis to critical scrutiny is long overdue, and this is an area that will be addressed within my analysis of the teachings and practices of the OBC.

Bell is in agreement, however, with Mellor's general theoretical statements about the relationship between Buddhism and British culture. Her article on change and identity in the FWBO analyses elements of the movement's ideology and organisational structure in light of the contemporary social theory of Giddens, who characterises the conditions of modern society as constitutive of 'high modernity'.[8] 'High modernity' refers to the 'post-traditional' character of modern society that has been brought about by the pace and scope of contemporary social change. In particular, it refers to the reflexivity that has been injected into modern life, whereby most aspects of pre-established social activity have become susceptible to 'chronic revision' in the light of new information. According to Giddens, the reflexivity of high modernity extends into the realm of personal identity because in the context of a post-traditional order, external authorities become suspect and unreliable and the 'self' becomes a 'reflexive project' that has to be 'routinely created and sustained in the reflexive activities of the individual' (1991: 52). Bell argues that within a society characterised by social and individual reflexivity, one would expect to find 'symbolic communities' that are dedicated to the project of personal self-discovery, and she analyses the FWBO as a vivid example of such a religious movement. The FWBO's philosophy and concomitant institutionalisation of personal growth

> chimes with several broad currents in Britain's atomised and pluralist, late twentieth century society; a society increasingly and generally more subjective and oriented to the inner life of the individual.
>
> (Bell 1996: 90)

Waterhouse (1997: 225) has also noted the affinity between contemporary Buddhist practice and features of modernity, in this case pointing to the importance of personal authority to British Buddhists who live in a modern society in which all external authorities have been challenged and undermined.

The cultural and religious baggage that westerners carry into their Buddhist practice and the ramifications this has for the nature of 'Buddhism' has also been an area of discussion with reference to Zen and Tibetan forms of Buddhism in the West. Scholars have noticed, for instance, how the 'Beat Zen' of the 1950s' American 'beat generation' was a highly selective reading that ignored the structured, disciplined, meditative and ritual aspects of Zen in order to provide 'both an expression and a legitimation of their dissatisfaction and their "hip" way of life' (Ellwood 1979: 145). Interestingly, the opposite mode of 'Square Zen', which entails the wholesale appropriation of Asian Buddhist forms by westerners, has been analysed as a style of practice that is equally informed by the cultural baggage of its proponents. Alan Watts argued this, adopting a Jungian approach towards the Western practice of Zen. To understand Zen fully, he argued, Western man 'must understand his own culture so thoroughly that he is no longer swayed by its premises unconsciously' (Watts 1958: 6). It is because westerners lack this understanding that Zen has taken the forms it has – 'Beat Zen' being the Zen of 'displaced' Christians seeking justification for caprice and social criticism, and 'Square Zen' being the Zen of 'unconscious' Christians seeking 'a more plausible authoritative salvation than the Church or psychiatrists seem to be able to provide' (Watts 1958: 11).

Jung's theories on the problems raised by westerners embracing Eastern religions are drawn upon extensively in Bishop's study of the fantasies of Tibetan Buddhism in the Western cultural imagination. Rather than approaching Buddhism as an abstract system, Bishop approaches the religion as 'a place within the imaginative terrain of the West' (Bishop 1993: 25). Analysing the West's relationship with Tibetan Buddhism from a modified Jungian perspective, he considers the nature of the depth imagination of the two cultures and the archetypal significance of Tibetan Buddhism for the West. He believes that Tibetan Buddhism 'has a great capacity to engage with the darkness and depths of the psyche' (1993: 19) but that its potential value has been undermined because its appropriation by westerners has been highly selective, involving the avoidance of the 'dark corners' of the Western psyche:

> Partisans of Tibetan Buddhism frequently seem blind to the dark side of this immense structure: to its oppressive and chaotic hierarchy, its historical justifications of gross inequalities of power, wealth, and human dignity [...].
>
> (Bishop 1993: 94)[9]

The transplantation process

As Mellor argues, an awareness of the subtle manner in which Buddhism interacts with the British religio-cultural context should be central to the study of

Buddhism in Britain. The value of this approach lies in the recognition that 'Buddhism', rather than being a simple signifier of phenomena existing 'out there' in the East, is in many ways a relative category rooted in the historical and cultural circumstances of the West. By considering Buddhism as a 'pre-determined intellectual formation' instead of something that is inseparable from its cultural expressions, the observer of contemporary Buddhism would over-simplify the transplantation process since he would remain unaware of 'the range of relationships between English Buddhism and both Western and Eastern culture' (Mellor 1991: 89). Awareness of the relationship between Buddhism and British culture also provides a basis for identifying and explaining continu-ities that may exist between different Buddhist forms in Britain, such as the emphasis of many groups on the value of lay practice.

However, an appreciation of religious and cultural relationships, though illu-minating, does not explain the total transplantation process. Cultural translation may be crucial to the successful transplantation of a Buddhist tradition in an alternative cultural context, but this can occur in varying degrees and with differing levels of awareness. It can, for example, occur at a largely unconscious level or it can be pursued self-consciously by Buddhist groups as part of their poli-cies of adapting and making Buddhism meaningful for westerners. Furthermore, it is by no means the only condition affecting the successful transplantation of Buddhism in Britain. Some of the most important factors and conditions that shape the transplantation process *as a whole* will now be outlined.

Material conditions

All studies of Buddhist groups in Britain emphasise the importance of material conditions to their successful transplantation and growth. At its most basic level this refers to a group's ability to attract committed supporters who will become financial sponsors, but it extends to the process of institutionalisation whereby an efficient legal, organisational and administrative structure is created 'in order to "crystallize" the more or less sporadic gatherings and to gain a lasting footing' (Baumann 1995: 63). Different Buddhist groups develop their own unique financial mechanisms, which often reflect the nature of their tradi-tion. The FWBO's emphasis on developing profitable businesses and Right Livelihood cooperatives, for example, reflects its lay orientation and concomi-tant desire to be financially self-sufficient, whilst the British Forest Sangha adopts a more traditional attitude – albeit an adapted one, since lay donations are not based on the ideology of merit-making – towards lay-monastic relations. The British Forest Sangha also receives financial support from supporters in the indigenous context of its tradition (i.e. from lay patrons in Thailand), as does Sōka Gakkai International (SGI) UK (i.e. from SGI's Japanese headquarters).[10] For groups that do not have the good fortune of receiving such support from within their indigenous traditions, the skilful mobilisation of available resources becomes all the more crucial to their success. This could involve developing fund-raising initiatives and exploiting the financial rewards of registering as a charity, on an organisational level, to making advantageous use of the state benefits system, on an individual level.

Studies also demonstrate the importance of clear institutional and administrative structures to the success of Buddhist groups. Mellor discusses how the emergence of the English Sangha Trust (EST) and FWBO, from within a British Buddhist context dominated by the London Buddhist Society, involved various attempts to control existing institutional sites and create alternative sites for the dissemination of Buddhist discourse. The establishment and growth of these alternative institutional structures not only facilitated further 'discursive separations' but also gave the EST and FWBO the credibility and authority to disseminate their own particular understandings of Buddhism. Waterhouse also illustrates how 'religious and agency authority structures operate alongside each other' (Waterhouse 1997: 214) within British Buddhist groups. This parallel structure is vital for dealing with religious matters on the one hand, whilst dealing with financial and organisational considerations on the other, as groups seek to make their 'religious goods' available to others. Towards this end, the larger Buddhist organisations seek to generate publications and often establish their own publishing companies.[11]

Trans-cultural processes

Recent research has indicated that in order to fully understand the transplantation process of Buddhist traditions in the West, the observer must also take important trans-cultural processes into consideration. The transplantation of certain Buddhist traditions in Western countries is affected significantly by the transformation those traditions have already undergone within indigenous contexts resulting from the impact of Western cultural, political and ideological forces in Asian countries – particularly in the South and Far East – since the late eighteenth century. The transformation of Buddhism in indigenous contexts resulting from its encounter with the West is referred to by scholars as Buddhist 'reformism' or 'modernism', and sometimes as 'Protestant Buddhism'.[12] These terms imply the incorporation by Asian Buddhists of scientific, rationalistic, humanistic and Protestant Christian values – such as anti-clericalism and anti-ritualism – into their traditional Buddhist frameworks. The transplantation process involves trans-cultural constituents whenever Buddhist forms that have been transformed in this way are then imported into the West. The nature of Buddhism in the West, then, may not only be conditioned by the religio-cultural baggage informing the Western converts' interpretation of Eastern Buddhist traditions. As some traditions – or strands within traditions – may have already been transformed through their encounters with Western forces, the transplantation process can take on greater complexity.

Trans-cultural processes have not, however, been central to the transplantation of all Buddhist traditions in the West because not all forms of Buddhism have been transformed by the forces of Westernisation and modernisation. In particular, Tibetan forms of Buddhism did not generally develop in a modernist direction prior to their transplantation in the West because Western and modernist forces had not penetrated so deeply into Tibetan culture. Even in the countries where these forces have been most pervasive, such as Sri Lanka or Japan, not all forms of Buddhism assimilate modernist elements in the same way or to the same degree, and many forms are not significantly affected at all by such forces. The transplantation process of Buddhist forms in the West, therefore, continues to be characterised by great diversity. Nevertheless, it is important to acknowledge the presence and importance of trans-cultural processes whenever these form part of the transplantation process. The impact of Buddhist modernism upon the transplantation process has been most clearly illustrated by Bell and Sharf with reference to the transplantation of South Asian *Theravāda* Buddhism and Japanese Zen Buddhism in the West. It is to their work, particularly the theories of Sharf, that I now turn.

Church (1982) notes that due to the Western colonial presence in South-East Asia, the adaptation process began even *before* Buddhism was introduced into Britain; furthermore, its arrival resulted both from the 'pull' factors of interested westerners and from the 'push' factors of socio-political circumstances in the East. Bell develops these points by arguing that the transplantation process has always involved 'the complex dynamic of cross-cultural processes' (Bell 1991: 2). She considers the emergence of British Buddhism within a broad context, arguing that its progress in the new Western context has always been 'contingent upon what was happening in the old' (1991: 42), and criticises Clausen's and Almond's accounts of the early reception of Buddhism in Britain because they overlook the reciprocal cross-cultural nature of the process. By restricting themselves to the British Victorians' rendering and 'reconstruction' of Buddhism, they ignore the fact that Asian Buddhist modernists 'both contributed to and were influenced by that rendering' (1991: 33), becoming 'equal and active participants in a two way process' (1991: 13). In this way, the Western scholarly 'reconstruction' of Buddhism and the indigenous South-East Asian *Theravāda* Buddhist reform movements evolved through a complex process of mutual influence and modification. Bell argues that this pattern continued to characterise the development of Buddhism in Britain throughout the twentieth century. In support of her thesis, she examines how the successful establishment of a monastic *Sangha* in Britain depended both upon its strong links with forest hermitages in Thailand and upon various modern reforms in indigenous *Theravāda* contexts. The lay meditation and nuns' movements in South-East Asian *Theravādin* countries, for example, are seen as important precedents that have enabled the British Forest Sangha to put down roots in Britain by emphasising lay meditation and innovating in the area of female ordination. Bell concludes that for *Theravāda* Buddhism to be successfully transplanted in Britain, certain conditions 'had to be met in both the indigenous setting and the host setting' (1991: 376). The transplantation process thus involves 'contingent patterns that flow in both directions between Asian and Western cultures as they interact' (1991: 2).

14

The 'intricacies of trans-cultural processes' to which Bell refers are also taken into account by Sharf, who traces the modern emphasis on inner expe-rience and meditation within the Buddhist reform movements of South-East Asia and, especially, of Japan. According to Sharf, the historical and cultural processes that gave rise to the re-creation of *Theravāda* Buddhism in a Protestant shape during the colonial period of South Asia can also be observed behind the modern construction of 'Protestant Zen' in Japan. The architects of Buddhist modernist discourse in Japan emerged out of the histor-ical and ideological ferment of the Meiji period (1868–1912). During this period Japan experienced dramatic social change resulting from rapid Westernisation, modernisation and industrialisation, and Buddhism became the subject of critique and persecution by a government intent upon modernising the country. In response, there arose a vanguard of modern Buddhist leaders who reformed Buddhism along modernist lines and defended it against government censure. The successful polemic of Meiji 'New Buddhism' was developed by apologists of Japanese Zen in their own way. This emergent modernist Zen discourse was also heavily influenced by the Kyoto school, a new Japanese philosophical movement that drew upon both Asian and Western resources and which maintained that Japanese culture and reli-gion is characterised by its direct or unmediated experience of reality. Sharf maintains that this emphasis on 'experience' can be traced directly back to the writings of Western scholars of the late nineteenth century who were also attempting to defend religion from the 'onslaught of Enlightenment values'.[13] By privileging experience, then,

> the Japanese, like their Western mentors, sought to naturalise the cate-gory 'religion' – if religious traditions were predicated upon an ineffable, noetic and mystical state of consciousness, then they could not be rejected as mere superstition, infantile wish-fulfilment, or collective hysteria.
>
> (Sharf 1995b: 45)

According to Sharf, the earliest proponents of Zen in the West, such as Shaku Sōen Rōshi (1859–1919) and his lay student D. T. Suzuki (1870–1966), were modernist Japanese intellectuals. Zen appeared in the West at the right historical moment because its purported anti-intellectualism, anti-ritualism and iconoclasm, and its emphasis on the unmediated experience of ultimate truth, confirmed and hardened the 'hermeneutic of experience' characterising Western scholarship of religion at the turn of the last century. Western scholar-ship of Buddhism was subsequently characterised by the assumption that the 'essential core' of the religion should be understood as 'a private, veridical, inef-fable experience inaccessible to empirical scientific analysis' (Sharf 1995a: 135). The 'Zen' that so appealed, then, was the modernist – or 'Protestant' – form emerging from the New Buddhism of the Meiji period; thus those aspects of Zen most attractive to the Occident – the emphasis on spiritual experience and the devaluation of institutional forms – were derived in large part from Occidental sources.

(Sharf 1995a: 140)

Sharf maintains that this version of Zen 'is not Zen at all, at least not the Zen practised by the "masters of old"' (Sharf 1995b: 51). The writings of Suzuki and others responsible for the Western interest in Zen do not represent traditional – i.e. pre-Meiji – Zen theory and practice, and their status and influence within the established Japanese *Rinzai* and *Sōtō* Zen sects has been negligible. Traditional Zen monasticism still flourishes in Japan and it 'continues to emphasize physical discipline and ritual competence, while little if any attention is paid to inner experience' (Sharf 1995c: 249).

The nature of the incoming tradition

Amongst the most important conditions influencing the transplantation process is the shape and nature of the incoming tradition; that is, the traditionally Buddhist forms and structures that have developed over the centuries in Buddhist countries quite independently of Western cultural contact and influence. Baumann acknowledges the role of indigenous features, observing how transplantation processes illustrate 'the close interrelation of dispositions of the host culture and particular preconditions of the imported religious tradition' (Baumann 1994: 58). The precondition he singles out as most important to a tradition's successful transplantation is its degree of flexibility with regard to its willingness to adapt within the new socio-cultural context. Flexible traditions are successful in new cultural contexts because they intentionally seek strategies of adaptation and creative innovation, whereas inflexible traditions which prioritise the conservation of traditional forms are less successful. The success of the NKT, as an 'inflexible' organisation that has emerged from the conservative strand of *Gelug* Buddhism, challenges this assertion, as does Bell's comment that

> It would [...] be wrong to conclude that the conservative nature of the *Theravāda* was an obstacle to its cross-cultural transmission; for [...] it was the absence of the symbols of *Theravāda* identity and their discourse concerning 'pastness' that thwarted the project in its earliest phase.
>
> (Bell 1997)

Baumann's distinction between flexible and inflexible traditions provides a potentially useful model for examining the development of Buddhism in Europe, a point reinforced by Waterhouse who notes that some schools of Buddhism 'lend themselves more readily to transmission across cultures than others' (Waterhouse 1997: 228). The illustrations he gives, however, raise practical and theoretical problems. Baumann characterises the traditions propagated by Europeans as 'flexible' because they generally 'aim to create a European or Western Buddhism' (Baumann 1994: 58), whilst those of ethnic migrant groups are 'inflexible' or 'stiff'. This is far too simplistic to be of any practical analytical value since European Buddhist forms themselves range widely across the flexible/inflexible spectrum. Furthermore, the distinction Baumann (1994: 58) makes between the 'dispositions of the host culture' and the 'preconditions of the imported religious tradition' collapses because the flexible nature of the 'imported' tradition here refers to nothing other than the disposition of Europeans to develop skilful methods of mediating the path.

Bell provides a more satisfying example of how the preconditions of an imported religious tradition can facilitate its transplantation into an alternative cultural context. Besides the importance of modern movements in indigenous contexts which create the conditions for Buddhism's successful development in Britain, she argues that the traditional character of Thai forest monasticism has made it a particularly suitable form of *Theravāda* Buddhism to import. This combines the strict adherence to the *Vinaya*, a very conservative form of legal authority, on the one hand, with the charismatic authority that arises out of the disciplined life, and which enables a degree of flexibility and adaptability, on the other. This synthesis equips the British Forest Sangha with 'the potential for resilience and continuity without compromising its ability to adjust to new conditions', indicating that forest monks may be 'the ideal transmitters of *Theravāda* Buddhism across cultures, particularly when they are Western forest monks making a return journey' (Bell 1991: 292).

Bell makes a similar point with reference to the transmission of Tibetan *Vajrayāna* Buddhism into Western cultural contexts which is, she maintains, facilitated by the 'shamanic' nature of the charismatic authority possessed by Tibetan Tantric teachers. She bases her ideas upon Samuel's distinction between the 'shamanic' and 'clerical' complexes within Tibetan Buddhism and, in particular, upon his contention that *lamas* in Tibet 'function as shamans, and they do so through the techniques and practices of *Vajrayāna* Buddhism' (Samuel 1993: 9). Bell argues that the success of the Tibetan *lama* Chogyam Trungpa Rinpoche (1939–87) as 'an expert cultural broker and innovator' in America derived from his status and expertise within the shamanic complex of Tibetan Buddhism:

> The shaman is [...] particularly well placed and equipped to negotiate the boundaries between different mundane worlds, such as those that are perceived to exist between traditional Tibetan society and modern American societies.
>
> (Bell 1998: 61)

Waterhouse examines how the transplantation and adaptation of all Buddhist traditions is inevitably shaped by indigenous processes, emphasising the importance of examining British Buddhist groups within the context of their 'root' traditions. She argues that British Buddhism will always be diverse because the diverging authority sources called upon by different schools to authenticate their practices in indigenous settings are transferred along with the schools to Britain and 'inevitably influence the changes which can be made and the ways in which they are legitimised' (Waterhouse 1997: 27). She also illustrates how indigenous forces of a different nature can affect the transmission of Tibetan Buddhism specifically through her examination of the impact, upon *Karma Kagyu* (*Karma bKa'brgyud*) Buddhists in Britain, of the dispute regarding the identity of the *Karmapa* which has destabilised the *Karma Kagyu* tradition at its highest levels. Disagreement and factionalism within the exiled *Karma Kagyu* Tibetan community, she observes, has generated discord between different *Karma Kagyu* centres in Britain. An understanding of the transplantation of *Karma Kagyu* Buddhism in Britain therefore requires an appreciation of indigenous religio-political disputes between high-level Tibetan representatives within this lineage. My discussion of the Foundation for the Preservation of the Mahayana Tradition (FPMT) and the NKT will illustrate that an appreciation of divisions within indigenous Tibetan Buddhist contexts is equally vital to our understanding of the transplantation of *Gelug* Buddhism in Britain. Conflict and division, of course, are aspects of incoming Buddhist traditions that could potentially hinder their successful transplantation in the West. The fact that these indigenous features have not retarded the development of Tibetan Buddhism in Britain so far is perhaps a reflection of the Western capacity to ignore the 'shadow' side of Tibetan spirituality.

Samuel also examines how indigenous forces shape the development of Tibetan forms of Buddhism in Western cultural contexts. International networks of Buddhist centres developed by Tibetan refugee *lamas* in the West, he argues, represent the extension and endurance of a traditional pattern within Tibetan Buddhism rather than being a modern, 'Western' development. In the pre-modern period, individual *lamas* working within a decentralised and entrepreneurial context would establish networks extending over long distances and travel between them in ways analogous to today's 'globe-trotting' *lamas*. Whilst acknowledging the considerable differences between traditional and modern networks, Samuel concludes that there is much 'continuity between patterns of Buddhist social organization in pre-modern Tibetan societies and those found among modern Tibetan-derived Buddhist groups' (Samuel 1996). Tibetan Buddhism's success in its new global context thus appears to have been facilitated by the suitability of Tibetan modes of social organisation within the conditions of modernity and globalisation.

Policies and patterns of adaptation

Analyses of the relationship between Buddhism and British culture discussed earlier describe the nature of British Buddhism mainly in terms of unconscious processes and inevitable transformations resulting from the importation of a religious tradition into a new, and ever-changing, cultural context. However, it has also been recognised that Buddhist groups are sensitive to the manner of their insertion into the British cultural environment, conscious as they are of the fact that the successful transmission of their tradition requires 'some form of cultural meditation, or significant perspectives on culture' (Mellor 1989: 21). One of the most important conditions affecting the successful transplantation of a Buddhist tradition is its attempt to make itself comprehensible and relevant within the new socio-cultural context through the adaptation of traditional forms and the creation of new ones. Buddhist groups are aware of this and develop deliberate, consciously worked-out policies and methods for the purposeful adaptation of Buddhism in Britain.

The extent to which groups are aware of the influence of British cultural and religious trends as they formulate their policies of adaptation appears to vary. Baumann discusses, for example, how 'unavoidable ambiguities' – inevitable misunderstandings which occur when foreign ideas are interpreted using concepts from the host culture – can be consciously adopted and supported by Buddhist groups as an adaptation strategy to facilitate their acceptance and growth (Baumann 1994: 42). Mellor also found that the British Forest Sangha is self-conscious and discriminating in its relationship with British culture and religion. By contrast, he maintains that the FWBO is 'firmly in line' (Mellor 1991: 78) with wider religio-cultural trends, in spite of its rhetoric that claims otherwise.[14] The consciously worked-out policies Buddhist groups develop towards the adaptation of Buddhism for a British cultural context, and the manner in which these are implemented, has also become a major area of concern within the academic discussion of British Buddhism.

Policies and patterns

The historical diffusion of Buddhism across cultures and the transformations resulting from its interaction (conscious or unconscious) with alternative socio-religious structures have occasioned considerable discussion within the study of the dynamics of religion.[15] It is often the case that both scholars *and* practitioners of British Buddhism appeal to these historical precedents when explaining and legitimising adaptations that are made in Britain. Green, for example, points to Buddhism's 'inherent flexibility and [...] ability to adapt readily to new sociocultural conditions' (Green 1989: 278), and Wilson justifies the synthesis of Buddhism and science with the view that the *Buddhadharma* is always 'adapted by a judicious assimilation of indigenous traditions' (Wilson 1987: 77). For Buddhist groups themselves, however, the logic of history and the claim that Buddhism is 'inherently' adaptable is not usually a sufficient basis for developing a policy of adaptation. The need for suitable forms of expression on the one hand and the demands of the tradition on the other have to be held in a creative tension. Buddhist groups are concerned to show that any adaptations of traditional forms are consistent with and are legitimated or authorised by their tradition, and that innovations remain authentically 'Buddhist'. Therefore studies of the policies of Buddhist groups towards adaptation have necessarily involved an analysis of the attitudes Buddhist groups adopt towards the concepts of tradition and authority.

Mellor considers British Buddhism as 'a creative development centred around the concepts of modernity and tradition' (Mellor 1989: 16). Drawing upon Weber's typology of authority and contemporary social theory, he explores the concept of tradition as a form of legitimation for religious activity, comparing this with the anti-traditional approaches of charismatic authority and modernism. Within the context of British Buddhism, the British Forest Sangha developed an approach based on traditional authority, taking the forest monastic tradition of Thailand as its 'pristine' or 'normative model for self-definition' (Mellor 1989: 355). The FWBO, by contrast, developed an anti-traditional, 'essentialist' approach based on Sangharakshita's charismatic authority which encourages rupture with Eastern traditions rather than continuity with them. These divergent attitudes towards the significance of traditional authority have, Mellor argues, engendered fundamentally different understandings of what Buddhism is and how it should be presented in the West. The British Forest Sangha emphasises continuity with the Thai tradition as a source of authority and as a constraining force on alterations to traditional forms, and so adopts a cautious approach towards adaptation. Innovations such as changes in monastic attire, ordination for women and the postulancy programme have been developed strictly within traditional *Theravāda* norms and in consultation with the representatives of the lineage in Thailand. The FWBO, by contrast, does not identify Buddhism with any one of its traditional manifestations but seeks instead to separate the 'essential principles' of Buddhism from its Eastern cultural forms and present it in a form that is self-consciously Western. This Buddhist 'essence' is articulated by Sangharakshita, whose claim to charismatic authority enables him to see his own understanding of Buddhism as authentic 'regardless of tradition, seen as peripheral', and to 'adapt Buddhism to Western circumstances in a radical manner' (Mellor 1989: 179). The separation of religious form from content and the internalisation of religious significance underpins the FWBO's dissolution of traditional lay/monastic distinctions and its de-emphasis of ritual action. The FWBO's radical emphasis on individualism, its rejection of religious form as an 'empty category', and its evolutionary perspective of history are seen by Mellor as indicative of the influence of Protestant Christian and modernist perspectives.[16]

Bell also considers adaptation within the British Forest Sangha and the FWBO in light of their approaches to traditional and charismatic authority. Her analysis is more subtle than Mellor's, however, because she recognises that there is a 'synthesis' of traditional and personal charismatic authority within the British Forest Sangha that both allows for innovation (e.g. the nuns' order) whilst ensuring the 'cautious manner' of its implementation. Waterhouse (1997) argues that because Mellor restricts his analysis of Buddhism to the level of public discourse, he is unable to recognise the significance of the *Theravāda* monks' charismatic authority in the lives of British lay Buddhists. Another reason why Mellor overlooks this is that his analytical centre of gravity lies firmly within British cultural patterns and their influences, whereas Bell adopts a cross-cultural perspective and so considers the nature of the incoming tradition (in this case the Thai forest monastic tradition) as a central factor in the transplantation and adaptation process.

Waterhouse explores the concepts of authority and adaptation through her case study of Buddhist groups in Bath:

> An understanding of the authority structures underlying contrasting forms of Buddhist practice is [...] fundamental to an understanding of the ways in which Buddhism is adapting [...].
>
> (Waterhouse 1997: 1)

Adaptations made by Buddhist groups, she argues, are tempered and legitimated by the authority sources of their 'root' traditions. Different Buddhist schools authenticate their practices with recourse to different authority structures and this ensures that whilst the adaptation process amongst British Buddhist groups may be similar, leading to 'changes which are broadly Protestant in nature' (Waterhouse 1997: 27), it is not identical. Waterhouse found that whilst British Buddhists situate themselves within particular schools and adhere to their traditional authority structures, they hold this in tension with the authority of their own personal experience which is particularly important for authenticating their religious practice. This emphasis has a traditionally Buddhist basis but should also be seen within the context of modernity wherein any authority 'is authoritative only in so far as the individual chooses that it should be so at any given time' (Waterhouse 1997: 225).

In her study, Waterhouse identifies four types of authority sources that are recognised by British Buddhists, observing that, whilst all acknowledge sacred texts and personal experience as authoritative, there is considerable disagreement in their attitudes towards the value of both tradition and faith in exemplary teachers. The perception that Buddhism is a rational-scientific system encouraging 'personal investigation of the truth' rather than 'blind faith' has since its earliest reception in Britain been a factor behind its appeal and growth. Waterhouse observes how,

> As an increasing number of forms of Buddhism become popular, the tension between faith in a teacher and personal experience becomes of more immediate concern.
>
> (Waterhouse 1997: 36)

21

The emergence of Tibetan and Zen forms of Buddhism in particular has raised the contentious issue of the role of faith within spiritual practice, because within these traditions the reliance of the disciple upon the wisdom and authority of the teacher is considered vitally important. The authoritative spiritual guide is regarded as the living representative and embodiment of ultimate truth, which, it is believed, has been transmitted to him via an unbroken lineage that can be traced directly back to the Buddha:

> the image of the unbroken transmission of wisdom is perhaps more central to Tibetan Buddhism than to any other psycho-spiritual or religious group, with the notable exception of Zen.
>
> (Bishop 1993: 100)

The dangers of uncritically importing the traditional authority structures of Tibetan and Zen forms of Buddhism into Western cultural contexts is an issue of considerable theoretical and practical interest. The central issue of concern is that the importance attached to faith and trust in the spiritual master carries with it the potential for abuse, a concern that has been borne out by a number of sexual and financial scandals within Buddhist organisations involving the abuse of authority by both Asian and Western teachers.[17] In response to these issues, the concept of spiritual authority has itself become an area of adaptation within Tibetan and Zen contexts. The authority of the teacher and the importance of developing faith are rarely questioned as vital constituents of the religious path, but there have been attempts to adapt both the institutional contexts of the master–disciple relationship and the attitudes of disciples entering such relationships. There is, for example, much discussion about the importance of carefully and deliberately examining teachers before making a commitment to them and how, even then, one should retain a 'healthy skepticism' (Collcutt 1988: 204).[18]

The question of authenticity

All Buddhist groups in Britain seek to make their teachings and practices comprehensible and relevant to British people and, to this extent, are involved in a project of adaptation. As Batchelor notes, adaptation is 'not so much an option as a matter of degree', and even the most conservative of Buddhist teachers at the traditional pole of the spectrum must make modifications 'simply in order to be understood in the modern West' (Batchelor 1994: 337). At the same time, Buddhist groups are concerned to show that their adaptation of traditional forms and their creation of new ones are authentic expressions of the *Buddhadharma*. Some groups, like the FWBO, eschew reliance on particular Eastern traditions, instead legitimating their adaptations with direct reference to the essential principles of Buddhism. Most groups share this emphasis on the 'essentials' of Buddhism, but appeal simultaneously to the sources of authority that operate within the particular Eastern traditions to which they are connected in order to legitimate any adaptations or cultural omissions. For all groups engaged in the project of adaptation, however, the question of authenticity is always a central concern.

The authenticity or inauthenticity of contemporary adaptations has also been a concern for certain scholars of Buddhism, a fact that is worth exploring further because of the methodological issues it raises. Green considers the adaptation of Buddhism in Britain in terms of Pye's study of the concept of 'skilful means' (Pye 1978). Based upon the central philosophical distinction between conventional and ultimate truths, this *Mahāyāna* Buddhist concept understands all forms of Buddhist teaching and practice as 'provisional devices' formulated in terms of the karmic conditions – intellectual, spiritual, socio-cultural, etc. – of their recipients. This concept is often referred to by contemporary Buddhist groups to sanction adaptations because it provides philosophical legitimation for the development of new forms in changing socio-cultural conditions. Pye argues that the concept lies behind Buddhism's strength as a 'cultural force' since it works creatively within alternative thought-structures towards the Buddhist purpose of enlightenment. According to Pye, Buddhism utilises other systems without losing sight of its own central meaning:

> the normative discernment of skilful means entails an interpretative activity within the tradition [...]
>
> (Pye 1978: 160)

It is this point that Green takes up as she attempts to assess adaptations within British Buddhism. Her spectrum model ranges from tradition-orientated groups that make no attempt to adapt, to groups whose various techniques of adaptation are regarded by Green as authentic expressions of skilful means – that is, interpretative activities *within the tradition* – to groups whose adaptations cannot be seen as genuine cases of skilful means because 'they have stepped outside of the tradition altogether, so that there is little truly Buddhist meaning left in them' (Green 1989: 283). Green includes the SGI amongst the contemporary groups that are 'selling out' to Western culture in this way, a claim that is by her own admission contentious and which has since been challenged by Waterhouse (1997: 26). Green is aware of the philosophical and epistemological problems of attempting to evaluate the authenticity of new or adapted forms of Buddhism. Such assessments raise the question of what constitutes the 'essence' of Buddhism, and she admits her suspicion of essentialist positions, arguing that 'it is notoriously difficult to isolate an essence when the particulars themselves are so varied' (Green 1989: 279). In the final analysis, however, Green herself accepts an essentialist perspective, arguing that a form of Buddhism that lacks the concepts of rebirth and *nirvāṇa* 'is no longer Buddhism', and unfavourably evaluating certain contemporary manifestations in light of it.

REVIEW AND CONTEXTUALISATION

In an article about the controversial Japanese cult *Aum Shinrikyō*, Pye outlines the methodological distinction between an operational definition of religion, which is 'the starting point for a non-evaluative description [...] a working definition for the purposes of study', and a normative definition, which 'establishes an evaluatory norm for the recognition of religion, and [...] is the starting point for an evaluatory appraisal' (Pye 1996: 262). He maintains that, provided the specialist can make this distinction, he can cross the boundaries of his discipline in extreme cases and engage in critical, evaluatory discussion without compromising his academic integrity. Whilst he argues that from the viewpoint of the historical and comparative study of religion, '*Aum Shinrikyō* is certainly a religion', he goes on to reject its claim to be a Buddhist religion. He finds the goal and teachings of *Aum Shinrikyō* to be un-Buddhist from the view-point of skilful means because – as with Green's view of certain British Buddhist groups – there is no evidence of 'the important regulatory feature of leading back towards central Buddhist conceptions' (Pye 1996: 267). He also finds the movement un-Buddhist from the perspective of the history of Buddhist ideas, arguing that

> without wishing to offer a normative definition about what authentic Buddhism must be like, the historian of religion can nevertheless provide some discerning differentiation.
>
> (Pye 1996: 268)

Unfortunately Pye does not develop this point beyond his comments about the eclecticism of *Aum Shinrikyō* and its 'opportunist scooping' of Buddhist ideas.[19]

According to the distinctions outlined by Pye, from the point of view of the academic study of religion, Green's assessments of British Buddhism and Pye's own evaluation of *Aum Shinrikyō* seem to be methodologically unsound. First, their appeal to the concept of skilful means to make a scholarly distinction between authentic and inauthentic expressions of Buddhism is problematic. Since skilful means is a religious concept from *within* the Buddhist tradition, its suitability as a paradigm for academic analysis must be regarded as highly questionable. Green and Pye's use of the concept in this way confuses the crucial distinction between the operational and normative perspective, a point well illustrated by Sharf:

> Historians of Buddhism must be particularly circumspect in wielding the hermeneutic of *upāya* [skillful means] [...] Scholars must be wary lest such patently 'theological' strategies come to substitute for critical historiographic and ethnographic reconstruction.
>
> (Sharf 1995c: 267–268)

Secondly, whilst rejecting both the feasibility and methodological advisability of establishing a normative definition of 'what authentic Buddhism must be like', both Green and Pye come very close to doing this. Other scholars have in similar ways maintained that there are criteria for assessing the validity of new interpretations of Buddhism in the West.[20] Unlike Green, Pye is careful not to offer a specific normative definition of Buddhism himself against which *Aum Shinrikyō* can be measured, but his claim that the academic specialist has a responsibility 'to point out the implausibility of particular claims when interpretation is strained beyond widely perceived coherence' (Pye 1996: 268) suggests he has specific criteria in mind. It is certainly the case that the provision of 'discerning differentiation' by a religious historian, whenever new Buddhist currents that depart from ancient traditions emerge, need not compromise his academic integrity. However, this is not the case here because Pye's assessment of *Aum Shinrikyō*'s Buddhist identity as 'implausible' and 'incoherent' indicates that a normative definition of Buddhism *is* informing his evaluation. Interestingly, the essentialist perspective underpinning Pye's treatment of Japanese Buddhism has been criticised elsewhere by Kamstra who maintains, as I have done here, that 'a historian of religion as such is not supposed to be engaged in essences of religion' (Kamstra 1980: 277).

Contextualising the NKT and OBC

It is beyond the confines of this book to present a detailed historical survey of the transplantation of Tibetan and Zen forms of Buddhism in Britain. The purpose of this section is simply to sketch the contours of the broader British Buddhist environment and the specifically Tibetan and Zen contexts in which the groups of this study have developed.

The British Buddhist context

The institutional growth of British Buddhism has been examined by Waterhouse (1997). She identifies two trends from the data: first, the marked increase in the number of groups practising Tibetan Buddhism since 1991, a development that can be attributed mainly to the energetic expansion of the NKT following its creation in that year; and secondly, the reduction in the number of groups identifying themselves as non-sectarian or multi-traditional. Estimates of the numbers of British Buddhists belonging to the larger organisations, and the difficulties of calculating such figures, are also discussed by Waterhouse. In 1997 there were between 2,000 and 3,000 members of the FWBO, over 6,000 formal members of the SGI-UK (up to 4,000 of whom were active) and between 2,000 and 3,000 active members of the NKT. These are the three main Buddhist movements operating in Britain at the moment, both in terms of institutional representation and active membership, and their dominance has become the subject not only of academic analysis but also of discussion amongst concerned members of the wider British Buddhist community.[21] In spite of the recent increase in the number of groups following Zen

Buddhist traditions, no single Zen organisation even closely approximates the average size of these groups. The largest, the OBC, had twenty-eight groups in 2000 (making up 28.6 per cent of all Zen groups) and, with an estimated numerical size of approximately one thousand British practitioners, is not even a third of the size of the larger organisations. Even an outside estimate of the total number of *all* British Zen Buddhists, a figure I would currently place at between 2,000 and 3,000, is still significantly lower than the estimated size of the larger Buddhist groups.

The groups at the centre of the present study represent the largest Tibetan and Zen Buddhist organisations, institutionally and numerically, that are currently active on the British Buddhist landscape. This fact alone, in light of the general absence of studies on Tibetan and especially Zen Buddhism in Britain, justifies an in-depth analysis of their historical and ideological development. It is profitable to study the NKT and OBC together because they illustrate how two very different traditions of Buddhism, Tibetan *Gelug* and Japanese *Sōtō* Zen, have transplanted and adapted themselves to the West. The growth and development of these groups displays points of similarity and contrast and, furthermore, exemplifies many of the processes that have characterised the development of other forms of Buddhism in Britain. An analysis of the NKT and OBC will therefore contribute significantly to our understanding of the nature of the transplantation and adaptation process as a whole. Before we turn our attention to outlining their growth and development it will be useful to take a closer look at their more immediate Tibetan and Zen Buddhist contexts.

Tibetan Buddhism in Britain

The distribution of Tibetan Buddhist groups by school in 1981, 1991 and 2000 is indicated in Figures 1.1 to 1.3.[22] The first Tibetan Buddhist school to establish itself in Britain was the *Karma Kagyu* branch of the *Kagyu* tradition. In 1967, the charismatic and unconventional *lama* Chogyam Trungpa Rinpoche, along with Akong Rinpoche, founded Samye Ling Tibetan Centre in Dumfriesshire. This was one of the first Tibetan Buddhist centres in the West, and it continues, under the direction of Akong Rinpoche and Lama Yeshe Losal, to promote a wide range of religious, cultural and humanitarian activities. Whilst it has developed a small network of local meditation groups, Samye Ling functions as a retreat centre for a much broader clientele, appealing to individuals of differing Buddhist and non-Buddhist orientations. The *Kagyu* school remained the dominant Tibetan tradition in Britain until the 1990s, when it began to be overshadowed by the *Gelug* through the energetic activities of Geshe Kelsang's NKT. The *Kagyu* nevertheless continues to be well represented today mainly by the Shambhala Study Groups, which follow the style of practice developed by Trungpa following his 1970 move to America and creation of Vajradhatu (now known as Shambhala International); by groups affiliated to the Dechen Community, which is headed by the English *lama* Ngakpa Jampa Thaye (David Stott) under the guidance of his Tibetan teacher Karma Thinley Rinpoche; by groups connected to Lama Chime Rinpoche, who established Marpa House in Saffron Walden in 1973; and most recently by groups connected to the Danish teacher Ole Nydahl.

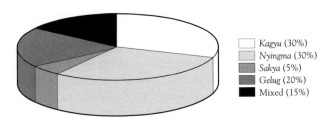

Figure 1.1 Tibetan Buddhist groups by school 1981 (total no. of groups = 20)

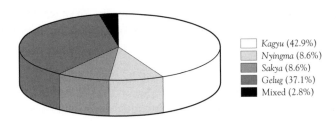

Figure 1.2 Tibetan Buddhist groups by school 1991 (total no. of groups = 35)

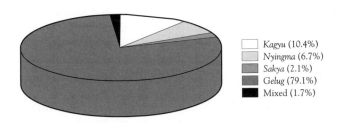

Figure 1.3 Tibetan Buddhist groups by school, 2000 (total no. of groups = 240)

REVIEW AND CONTEXTUALISATION

The first British centre for the study and practice of *Gelug* (*dGe lugs*) Buddhism was the Manjushri Institute in Ulverston, established in 1976 as part of the FPMT, an international network of centres founded by Lamas Thubten Yeshe and Zopa Rinpoche. Although their organisation became the major *Gelug* network in the West, its presence in Britain remained small, and in 2000 it was represented in only two localities. Its relatively marginal institutional representation can be explained largely in terms of a conflict that developed during the 1980s between students at the Institute and its FPMT-appointed Tibetan teacher Geshe Kelsang Gyatso on the one hand, and the central FPMT administration on the other. This resulted in the eventual appropriation, by Geshe Kelsang and his students, of the Manjushri Institute property and the creation of a separate network which in 1991 became known as the New Kadampa Tradition. In 1981, only one of the four *Gelug* groups in Britain was affiliated primarily with Geshe Kelsang, a representation that had risen to nine groups out of thirteen in 1991. The NKT expanded rapidly during the 1990s and it now dominates the Tibetan Buddhist landscape in Britain (making up 96.3 per cent of all *Gelug* groups and 76.2 per cent of all Tibetan groups). The only other significant *Gelug* representation in Britain comprises a number of groups connected to Geshe Damcho Yonten, the earliest of which, the Lam Rim Buddhist Centre in Gwent, was established in 1978.

The next best-represented Tibetan tradition in 2000 was the *Nyingma* (*rNying ma*) school. In terms of its institutional representation, the *Nyingma* in Britain has seen a fair amount of fluctuation, from having six groups in 1981 to having only three in 1991 before enjoying a renewed period of growth and, in 2000, being represented in sixteen different localities. This school has been represented mainly by groups connected either to the Tibetan *lama* and author of *The Tibetan Book of Living and Dying*, Sogyal Rinpoche, or by groups associated with the British *lama* Rigdzin Shikpo (formerly known as Michael Hookham). Sogyal Rinpoche began teaching in England in 1974 and established the Rigpa Fellowship in London in 1981 to unite his growing network of European and American centres within a single organisation. Rigdzin Shikpo has been director of the Longchen Foundation since it was created by Chogyam Trungpa in 1975 as a vehicle for disseminating *Nyingma Dzogchen* (*rDzogs chen*) teachings. *Dzogchen* teachings are also the focus of Namkhai Norbu Rinpoche's Dzogchen Community network, which has a small representation in Britain.

The *Sakya* (*Sa skya*) school has, of all the Tibetan Buddhist traditions in Britain, fared least well, and in 2000 was still represented in only five localities. All of these groups belong to the *Sakya* wing of the Dechen Community and are under the guidance of Ngakpa Jampa Thaye. The combined *Kagyu-Sakya* focus of the Dechen Community is a reminder that, whilst it may be convenient to distinguish between the different Tibetan schools for comparative purposes, in reality the boundaries between the schools are often more

28

fluid than the charts above suggest. In practice, the founding *lamas* of many of the groups in Britain, and consequently the groups themselves, combine teachings and practices taken from different Tibetan lineage-traditions. This reflects the traditional situation of Tibetan Buddhism, which, as Samuel makes clear, was much more diffuse, decentralised and differentiated than has commonly been understood:

> while it is customary to speak of the four main 'schools', 'orders', 'traditions' or even 'sects' of Tibetan Buddhism [...] these terms may imply a hierarchical structure and a degree of coherence and exclusivity which did not in fact exist.
>
> (Samuel 1996)

Zen Buddhism in Britain

Whilst Zen Buddhism currently represents only a small section of British Buddhism, it is nevertheless a varied and growing sector. Figures 1.4 to 1.6 indicate the distribution of Zen Buddhist groups by school in 1981, 1991 and 2000. They indicate that, whilst the Japanese *Sōtō* school has been the dominant tradition in terms of institutional representation, in recent years the Zen landscape has become more diverse, with substantial inroads being made by Chinese *Ch'an* and Vietnamese *Thien* schools, and with a significant increase in groups defining their lineage-tradition as mixed (most commonly a *Sōtō-Rinzai* combination). Although the Japanese *Rinzai* school has been a minority presence during this period, this was actually the first Zen school to become established in Britain, primarily through the activities of the lay scholar D. T. Suzuki and the founder and president of the Buddhist Society Christmas Humphreys (1901–83). Suzuki, who is described by Sharf as 'the single most important figure in the spread of Zen to the West' (Sharf 1995a: 116), was the first to provide a substantial body of accessible, English-language literature on Zen, an area which was still largely untouched by Western Buddhist scholarship at the turn of the twentieth century. Humphreys became Suzuki's agent in Britain, arranging for the British publication of his books and organising his visits to England during the 1930s and 1950s. He also became a proponent of *Rinzai* Zen himself, renaming his meditation class as the 'Zen Class' and composing a number of books that recycled Suzuki's modernist interpretation of Zen but which nevertheless reflected his own unique approach, described by Furlong as 'Christmas Zen' (Furlong 1987: 51).[23] For a long time the Zen Class represented the only organised Zen activity in Britain, although Humphreys' students were becoming increasingly exposed to alternative perspectives and many actively sought different ways of expressing their Zen practice, for example by pursuing a more traditional regime in Japan.

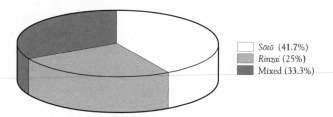

Figure 1.4 Zen Buddhist groups by school 1981 (total no. of groups = 12)

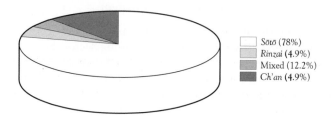

Figure 1.5 Zen Buddhist groups by school 1991 (total no. of groups = 41)

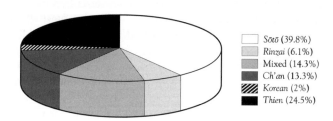

Figure 1.6 Zen Buddhist groups by school, 2000 (total no. of groups = 98)

The institutional flowering of Zen beyond the confines of the Buddhist Society began during the 1960s when a handful of alternative groups, such as Douglas Harding's Sholland Trust, were established in the south of England. Developments that occurred during the 1970s were more significant, inasmuch as they represented the beginnings of the earliest institutional Zen networks. In

1972, Dr Irmgard Schloegl and Peggy Kennett, two former members of Humphreys' Zen Class, returned to Britain having endured prolonged periods of training in Japan and established groups of their own. Whilst Schloegl's career as a *Rinzai* teacher began under the auspices of the Buddhist Society and with the full support of Humphreys, Kennett's career as a teacher of *Sōtō* began in conflict with the British Buddhist establishment which apparently never accepted her claims to be a Zen master. Her successful introduction of *Sōtō* in Britain was made possible by the prior development, both in Japan and in California, of a firm American following, and by the emergence in Britain of alternative sites of Zen activity, one of which, the Mousehole Buddhist Group in Penzance, provided an alternative avenue for her to organise visits and mobilise support. In 1972, she established Throssel Hole Priory in Northumberland as the British base of her Zen Mission Society (later renamed as the Order of Buddhist Contemplatives). Not only was this the earliest institutional establishment of *Sōtō* Zen in Britain, it was also the first site of organised Zen activity in the north of England as well as the first British monastic community in the Zen tradition.

During the next ten years, Schloegl and Kennett consolidated their presence as Zen teachers and gradually expanded their institutional representation. When Humphreys died in 1983, all Zen activities at the Buddhist Society came under Schloegl's direction. Whilst 'traditionalising' Buddhist Society activities, she retained certain features of Humphreys' approach, such as his emphasis on intellectual study as a preliminary to meditation practice, and current members of her network continue to feel a strong sense of continuity with 'Christmas Zen'. Schloegl ordained as a *Rinzai* nun in 1984 and is now known as Venerable Myoko-ni. Although it has the deepest roots in British society, her network is the smallest of those currently active, with a representation in only five localities. During the first decade of the OBC's British development, consolidation and stability were emphasised more than institutional expansion, the movement's main period of growth coming during the mid-1980s. In 1991, it was represented in twenty-three localities (making up 72 per cent of all *Sōtō* groups and 56.1 per cent of all Zen groups); by 2000, this had increased to twenty-eight groups (71.8 per cent of all *Sōtō* groups and 28.6 per cent of all Zen groups).

Two further Zen networks of Japanese origin also emerged during the 1980s. The first of these, the Zen Practice Centre Trust, grew out of a series of European tours made by the American teacher Genpo Merzel Sensei in the early 1980s. In 1984, Genpo Merzel, the second American Dharma-successor of Taizen Maezumi Rōshi (1930–96), left the Zen Centre of Los Angeles 'to devote himself completely to the international community of students he named "Kanzeon Sangha"'.[24] Maezumi Rōshi embodied three different lineages including both the *Sōtō* and the *Rinzai* branches of Zen, and hence the Kanzeon Sangha defines itself as a *Sōtō-Rinzai* combination. The growth of the British arm of the network has been slow and sporadic, but in 2000 it comprised ten local groups. The second network to emerge during this period was the

International Zen Association (IZA) (UK), which grew out of the 'missionary' activities of Jean Baby and Nancy Amphoux, two of the senior French disciples of the Japanese *Sōtō* teacher Taisen Deshimaru (1914–82). The IZA-UK is affiliated to the Association Zen Internationale, an international network that was created by Deshimaru in 1970 and which has its headquarters in the Loire Valley at the temple La Gendronnière. The growth of the IZA-UK has been steady, and in 2000 it was also represented in ten localities.

The 1990s saw a number of interesting developments with the emergence of two new networks of non-Japanese origin. The first of these, the Western Ch'an Fellowship (WCF), has its roots in the innovative Western Zen Retreats organised in Wales by Dr John Crook from around 1984. With an academic background in psychology, Crook believed that a Western form of Zen should combine traditional teachings and practices with Western psychological techniques and theories. In 1987, he became a disciple of the Chinese *Lin Chi* (Jap. *Rinzai*) master Sheng Yen (b. 1931), and from 1989 began to offer a programme of more orthodox *Ch'an* retreats alongside his Western retreats. From this time there was a proliferation of local *Ch'an* meditation groups around Britain and the gradual development of an organisational structure to unite them. The WCF became a constitutional reality in 1997 and it is now represented in thirteen localities. The second network to develop in recent years comprises groups dedicated to practising the teachings of Thich Nhat Hanh (b. 1926), a *Lam Te* (Jap. *Rinzai*) master in the *Lieu Quan* school of the Vietnamese *Thien* (Jap. Zen) tradition. During the 1960s, Thich Nhat Hanh was active in the Buddhist peace effort in Vietnam and founded the Tiep Hien Order ('Order of Interbeing'), a self-consciously eclectic movement 'based on the principles of Engaged Buddhism which emphasises social responsibility and peacework'.[25] He later settled in Bordeaux, France, and since the early 1980s has taught widely in Europe and America. The Order of Interbeing subsequently developed into an international organisation with groups and practice centres in over twenty countries. Although there have been disciples of Thich Nhat Hanh in Britain since the early 1980s, there was no significant institutional growth until the early 1990s. In 1993, this emerging network of individuals and groups became known as the 'Community of Interbeing' (COI), and by 2000 there were twenty-four groups following Thich Nhat Hanh's teachings on mindfulness and social engagement. The non-sectarian Amida Trust, which was founded in 1987 by David Brazier, also has a loose affiliation with Thich Nhat Hanh and the COI. This organisation, which specialises in the interface between Buddhism and Western psychotherapy and 'in developing humanitarian projects on Buddhist principles to help overcome suffering in the world',[26] was represented in five localities in 2000. The late 1990s also witnessed a growing interest in Korean Zen, although early attempts to establish a network of groups and centres have so far been unsuccessful.

Whilst this book is primarily concerned with the practise of Buddhism by westerners, it should be noted that there are a number of Asian-based temples in Britain which define themselves, at least in part, as Zen or *Ch'an* in orientation.[27] The expression of Buddhism within Asian immigrant and refugee communities represents a phenomenon very different – religiously, culturally and sociologically – to the practise of Buddhism by British 'converts'. Nevertheless, whilst British and Asian Zen Buddhist groupings are generally distinct, they do, as with other religious communities in Britain, occasionally intersect and overlap.[28]

Asian-based temples function primarily as religious and cultural focal points within the immigrant Chinese, Vietnamese and Korean communities, and they are to be found, predictably, in the major urban areas where these Asian groupings are clustered (London, Manchester and Birmingham). Weller observes that, whilst the role of Buddhism amongst the Chinese in Britain must be acknowledged, to use the classification of 'Buddhist' with reference to them is problematic in view of the 'often overlapping and intermingling complexity of Buddhist, Taoist and Confucian belief and practice found among many ethnic Chinese families and individuals' (Weller 2001: 33). This observation is equally applicable to the ethnic Vietnamese and Korean communities. It would therefore be difficult to assess how many ethnically 'Zen Buddhists' there are in Britain because religion within these communities is not experienced in such clear-cut, sectarian terms. Nevertheless, it is worth noting that the numbers of Buddhists connected to the ethnic-based temples in Britain – who thus engage in practices with at least a Zen component – are, on average, much higher than the numbers of British practitioners engaged in institutional Zen.[29]

There are a small number of British people connected to a number of the ethnic-based temples, and these should be mentioned in a survey of British Zen Buddhism. One of the main reasons why the British representation in these temples is so small is that the temples have not made any real attempts to draw British people into their activities, since they function primarily as religio-cultural centres for their specific ethnic communities. Furthermore, any British individual interested in the temples' activities faces considerable cultural and linguistic barriers, since the activities will almost certainly be conducted in an idiom that is foreign to them. Finally, the nature of the religiosity within these temples is unlikely to be attractive to most British people with an interest in Zen. Most temples combine Zen with Pure Land Buddhism, which emphasises devotional chanting and praying with an attitude of faith, and this does not seem to appeal to Western Buddhists. Also, the admixture of non-Buddhist elements (e.g. Confucianism and Taoism) with popular religiosity (e.g. ancestor worship) is unlikely to resonate with British practitioners who are interested in Buddhism primarily as a soteriological, philosophical and meditational system. British Buddhists do not tend to participate, therefore, in the regular meetings of Asian Buddhists at the temples for chanting and praying. Their interest and activity, rather, takes the form of book-borrowing (as at the Chinese temple Fa Yue in Dudley, West Midlands) or meditation (as at the Korean temple Yon-Hwa-Sa in Kingston-on-Thames, Surrey). This suggests that the phenomenon of an ethnically defined 'religious parallelism' may be a feature of some Asian-based temples in Britain. This term was coined by Numrich (1992) who found that within immigrant *Theravāda* temples in America there exist parallel congregations that meet separately and which have very different understandings and expressions of Buddhism.

Part II

THE NEW KADAMPA TRADITION

2

THE NEW KADAMPA
TRADITION
Background and cross-cultural context

Introduction: contextualising the NKT

The NKT's historical and institutional roots in Britain go back much further than 1991, the year when its Tibetan founder, Geshe Kelsang Gyatso (b. 1931), announced its official creation. The emergence of the NKT must, in particular, be considered against the context of another contemporary Western *Gelug* movement called the Foundation for the Preservation of the Mahayana Tradition (FPMT). Geshe Kelsang (see Figure 2.1) was originally brought to Britain to teach at an FPMT centre called the Manjushri Institute, but he split away from this organisation to develop a parallel network of his own that he later unified and gave a distinct identity as the NKT. As well as providing the immediate historical backdrop necessary for understanding the development of the NKT, the FPMT represents an alternative way of articulating and marketing Tibetan Buddhism for Western consumption. Though similar in many ways, these international Buddhist networks are also very different, and a comparative analysis will help illuminate the nature of Tibetan, and particularly *Gelug*, Buddhism both in Britain and in the West generally. The emergence and development of the FPMT, and the nature of Geshe Kelsang's relationship with it, will be examined in the next chapter.

Although Tibetan Buddhism in Britain remains a significantly neglected area, what has been written by observers so far indicates that this field of enquiry has often displayed a Western theoretical bias. This term refers to the tendency of observers to focus narrowly on the Western-convert appropriation and experience of Buddhist traditions to the exclusion of important historical and cross-cultural factors. Accounts of Tibetan Buddhism in Britain, for example, have tended to concentrate on the motivation and participation of westerners, and those which examine the Tibetan traditions themselves have focused mainly on their brief histories in the West, ignoring the continuing importance of broader historical and cross-cultural contexts.[1] This bias is also rife in the perceptions of many Western Buddhist practitioners themselves, whose understanding of the traditions they espouse is often simplistic, idealistic and uninformed about how broader historical and 'oriental' contexts continue to exert a normative influence on their development in the Occident. Many

Figure 2.1 Geshe Kelsang Gyatso, founder of the NKT

Source: Reprinted with permission from Tharpa Publications.

Western Buddhists who are critical of the NKT, for example, have referred to it as a 'new cult movement' led by a 'fanatical leader' or 'rogue geshe' who has departed from acceptable standards of *Gelug* behaviour. Such views betray a Western bias inasmuch as they idealise *Gelug* Buddhism and erroneously imply that no reference to the broader *Gelug* context is required in order to understand the NKT. This book aims to provide a much-needed theoretically balanced analysis of a high-profile contemporary Tibetan Buddhist movement. The emergence, development and self-identity of the NKT will be situated throughout within its appropriate historical, cultural and ideological contexts.

The NKT's public participation in a controversial campaign mounted against the Dalai Lama during 1996 resulted in harsh criticism from many British Buddhists, media agencies and even academics. Since the Dalai Lama commands widespread respect and admiration in the West, both as a religious leader and as a champion of an oppressed nation, it is unsurprising that public allegations of human rights abuses by *him* have met with hostility. It is arguable that the censure elicited, however, has also been informed by the idealistic and 'one sidedly bright' (Bishop 1993: 73) images of Tibetan Buddhism that characterise the Western imagination. The great difficulty many British Buddhists have had in coming to terms with the campaign and the media's portrayal of the NKT at the time as a dangerous and 'cultish' organisation, as opposed to a movement that is representative of certain currents *within* Tibetan Buddhism, resonates with the findings of Bishop, who claims to have consistently encountered 'a bewilderment and sometimes a hostility whenever Tibetan Buddhism is mentioned in tones which are less than sacrosanct' (1993: 46). Bishop considered his study to be a corrective to the critically imbalanced one-sidedness of Western images that deny Tibetan Buddhism's 'dark and messy aspects'. The examination of the NKT here proceeds in a similar vein, bringing a much-needed historical and cross-cultural perspective to bear upon the idealised fantasies that have been manifested both in the attitudes of NKT members and in the criticisms levelled at the movement from external sources.

The NKT cannot be fully understood by an examination that is restricted to its origins and development in Britain alone; nor can it be appreciated by situating it within a simplified or idealised Tibetan Buddhist context. Rather, its historical and ideological development must be situated within the broader context of *Gelug* Buddhist history during both the pre-modern period and in exile.[2] The emergence of the NKT onto the British Buddhist landscape represents the manifestation, in a Western context, of classical and contemporary divisions within the *Gelug* tradition with regard to: (i) policies about inter-traditional relations; and (ii) the related issue of *Dorje Shugden* reliance. Some discussion of these indigenous forces must precede our analysis of the transplantation process of *Gelug* Buddhism in Britain because many aspects of the NKT's emergence can only be understood within such a cross-cultural perspective. There are, of course, many other factors influencing the transplantation process, but these can be considered throughout the analysis.

Divisions within the *Gelug* tradition

The *Gelug* (meaning 'virtuous') tradition is one of the four main traditions of Tibetan Buddhism. It can be traced back to the popular teacher *Tsong Khapa* (*Tsong kha pa*) (1357–1419) and his disciples, who were originally known in the early fifteenth century as the *Gandenpa* (*dGa' ldan pa*) (that is, 'those from the monastery of *Ganden*'). It is believed that *Tsong Khapa* revived and continued the work of *Atiśa*, the Indian *ācārya* who founded the *Kadam* (*bKa' gdams*) order in the eleventh century.[3] Indeed, the *Gelug* order was also known as the 'New Kadam' order. The *Gelug* became politically dominant in central Tibet in the seventeenth century through the institution of the Dalai Lamas. Though not the formal head of the *Gelug* order – this position being reserved for the abbot of *Ganden* monastery, known as the *Ganden Tripa* (*dGa' ldan Khri pa*) – the Dalai Lama, as the order's highest incarnate *lama* and as the political head of Tibet, became its most influential and authoritative figure.

It is important to understand that, historically, the *Gelug* tradition has never been a completely unified order. In fact, internal conflict and division have been enduring features of *Gelug* history, and it has taken philosophical, political, regional, economic and institutional forms that have often interacted.

Furthermore, during periods when effective leadership has been exercised by the institution of the Dalai Lama, the authority of this figure has never been total and undisputed within the *Gelug*. As a political leader, the Dalai Lama is responsible for the welfare of the Tibetan state and must be sensitive not only to the interests of the *Gelug* school but also to the broader constituency – which includes other religious schools and aristocratic families – upon which his position rests. As a consequence, his relationship with the *Gelug* monastic establishment, represented mainly by the Three Seats (i.e. *Sera*, *Drepung* and *Ganden*, the three main monasteries of the *Gelug* school), has often been a source of tension and conflict:

> 'Religion' (and the religious segment) [...] was not the homogeneous entity it is typically implied to be, even within the Gelugpa Sect, and the great Gelugpa monasteries were often at odds with the Dalai Lama's government.
>
> (Goldstein 1990: 231)

Central to our understanding of the NKT are the historical and contemporary divisions within the *Gelug* tradition that have arisen from conflicting interpretations of the position of the *Gelug* school in relation to other Tibetan Buddhist schools. The appropriate policy that should be adopted in relation to other schools of Tibetan Buddhism has been a bone of contention amongst *Gelug* Buddhists since early on in the history of the tradition. Dreyfus discusses how sectarian differentiation in Tibet developed between the fourteenth and seventeenth centuries, against the backdrop of a politically tumultuous social context wherein emergent schools 'would be pitted against other religious groups competing for political influence and economical support' (Dreyfus 1997: 36). He traces the emergence of the *Gelug*, as a distinctly separate school, to *Tsong Khapa*'s successors rather than to *Tsong Khapa* himself, who developed his nascent following amidst a more eclectic, ecumenical and catholic atmosphere in which doctrinal differences 'were not yet understood to reflect deep sectarian divisions, but rather were taken as differences between teachers and lineages both inside and outside of a given school' (1997: 35). Dreyfus's discussion thus sheds light upon the beginnings of an important division within the *Gelug* school, between those who retained *Tsong Khapa*'s ecumenical and open approach and others, like *Tsong Khapa*'s disciple *Kedrubje* (*mKhas grub rje*) (1385–1438), who became 'quite active in enforcing a stricter orthodoxy, chastising [...] disciples for not upholding Dzong-ka-ba's [*Tsong Khapa*'s] pure teachings' (1997: 36).

From this time, as is the case with most religious traditions, there have been those within the *Gelug* who have interpreted their tradition 'inclusively', believing that their *Gelug* affiliation should in no way exclude the influence of other schools which constitute additional resources along the path to enlightenment. Others have adopted a more 'exclusive' approach, considering that their

Gelug identity should preclude the pursuit of other paths and that the 'purity' of the *Gelug* tradition must be defended and preserved. To many observers and practitioners, 'exclusivism' is dismissed as an unhealthy and restrictive attitude and is often seen as synonymous with 'sectarianism', which in this context means the bigoted and narrow-minded pursuit and defence of a particular sect's interests, doctrines and identity.[4] For the purposes of this study, it is important to recognise that whilst 'exclusivism' and 'sectarianism' share a similar emphasis on boundary maintenance and purity, they are not synonymous. Conservative and closed orientations may often result in bigoted, intolerant and even violent behaviour between Tibetan Buddhist schools – this fact is amply attested to by accounts of Tibet's religio-political history – but exclusively orientated individuals and factions do not always, or necessarily, engage in such hostilities. It should also be remembered that when traditions come into conflict, religious and philosophical differences are often markers of disputes that are primarily economic, material and political in nature.

The distinction Samuel makes between 'clerical' and 'shamanic' forms of Tibetan Buddhism, as represented by the fifteenth century *Gelug* formulation and the nineteenth century *Rimed* (*Ris-med*) (non-sectarian) movement, helps to illuminate the contours of the exclusive/inclusive polarisation running throughout *Gelug* history. The categories 'clerical' and 'shamanic' describe two fundamentally different modalities or orientations within Tibetan religious teachings, rituals and practices: the former is characterised by scholarship, philosophical analysis, celibate monasticism, structure, hierarchy and centralisation; the latter by communication with alternative modes of reality through *Vajrayāna* (Tantric) ritual, by celibate and non-celibate *lamas* operating in less structured and decentralised contexts, both for the achievement of enlightenment and for the performance of shamanic services for the laity. The original *Gelug* formulation was clerical in that *Tsong Khapa*, the 'reformer' of the monastic order, narrowed down and organised 'all that was essential within Tibetan Buddhism' (Samuel 1993: 543) into a single, structured and linear path emphasising the gradual and philosophical understanding of the enlightened state within an academic and monastic context. Due to its clerical orientation, the *Gelug* school tended to be exclusive of other systems, thereby encouraging traditional distinctions and sometimes sectarian intolerance.[5] The *Rimed* movement, by contrast, was shamanically orientated. It did not constitute an organised monastic order, nor did it have a definite doctrinal position, but was carried by *lamas* of the *Sakya*, *Nyingma* and *Kagyu* traditions who each promoted 'the specific lineages and practices of their own *gompa* as well as the general Rimed practices' (Samuel 1993: 538). *Rimed lamas* 'were less universally committed to the clerical path of monastic renunciation' and were encyclopaedic, seeking to bring together and transmit 'the numerous diverse traditions of Tantric yogic practice that had developed in Tibet over the preceding ten centuries' (Samuel 1993: 540–541). These practices were not regarded as 'exclusive alternatives', but as a body of partial descriptions and approaches, each of which might help to provoke the central insight of the shamanic vision. Rather than presenting a unique method for attainment, they made as many different methods as possible available, in a way that was quite unprecedented within Tibetan Buddhism.

(Samuel 1993: 541)

In maintaining the validity of all paths, this movement was thus radically inclusive, helping 'to break down the sectarian divisions that had developed between different traditions, each progressively entrenched within its own institutional monastic base' (Samuel 1993: 542). Modern forms of the non-Gelug orders have all been significantly shaped by Rimed, and, according to Samuel, there is 'every reason to suppose that this process will continue and be strengthened in years to come' (Samuel 1993: 274).

Whilst the Gelug formulation and the Rimed movement can be contrasted theoretically in terms of the distinction between clerical and shamanic forms of religion, in practice the situation is more complicated. Samuel maintains that the Gelug tradition and Rimed movement are actually synthetic positions which combine and reconcile both elements of Tibetan religious life:

both contain shamanic and clerical elements, but the Rimed approach is weighted towards the shamanic side, and the Gelugpa approach towards the clerical.

(Samuel 1993: 547)

The Rimed movement thus included great scholars, whilst the Gelug tradition produced famous Tantric meditators. Just as the Gelug tradition has, 'for all of its clerical emphasis, offered a range of possibilities involving different mixes of clerical and shamanic Buddhism' (Samuel 1993: 344), both exclusive and inclusive positions concerning inter-traditional relations have co-existed within the school and have characterised each stage of its history. We need only examine a few notable examples of this recurring tension here, though, to highlight the appropriate context for understanding the NKT.

The inclusive orientation which has continually manifested itself in all schools has, within the Gelug, traditionally characterised the Dalai Lamas, particularly the Great Fifth (1617–82),[6] the Great Thirteenth (1876–1933) and the current Fourteenth Dalai Lama (b. 1935).[7] These are all renowned for having received religious instruction from lamas of other Tibetan traditions such as the Sakya and the Nyingma. The Great Fifth and Great Thirteenth were even identified as Terton (gTer ston), or Nyingma 'Discoverers of Hidden Treasure', and the current Dalai Lama has gone to great lengths to promote inter-faith activity, considering it praiseworthy 'when someone practices all the Sakya, Gelug, Kagyu and Nyingma teachings through listening, thinking and meditation according to his own level of realization'.[8] The political policies of the Dalai Lamas have also been informed by this inclusive orientation. It can be discerned, for example, in the Great Fifth's leniency and tolerance towards opposing factions and traditions following the establishment of *Gelug* hegemony over Tibet in 1642;[9] in the Great Thirteenth's modernist-leaning reforms, which attempted to turn Tibet into a modern state through the assimilation of foreign ideas and institutions (such as an efficient standing army and Western-style education); and in the Fourteenth Dalai Lama's promotion of egalitarian principles and attempts to 'maintain good relations among the various traditions of Tibetan religion in exile' (Samuel 1993: 550).

This inclusive approach has, however, repeatedly met opposition from others within the *Gelug* tradition whose orientation has been more exclusive. The tolerant and eclectic bent of the Fifth Dalai Lama, for example, was strongly opposed by the more conservative segment of the *Gelug* tradition. These 'fanatic and vociferous Dge-lugs-pa churchmen' (Smith 1970: 16) were outraged by the support he gave to *Nyingma* monasteries, and their 'bigoted conviction of the truth of their own faith' (Smith 1970: 21) led them to suppress the treatises composed by more inclusively orientated *Gelug lamas* who betrayed *Nyingma*, or other non-*Gelug*, influences.[10] Similarly, the Thirteenth Dalai Lama's political reforms were thwarted by the conservative element of the monastic segment which feared that modernisation and change would erode its economic base and the religious basis of the state. His spiritually inclusive approach was also rejected by contemporaries such as Phabongkha Rinpoche (1878–1943). As the *Gelug* agent of the Tibetan government in *Kham* (*Khams*) (Eastern Tibet), and in response to the *Rimed* movement that had originated and was flowering in that region, Phabongkha Rinpoche and his disciples employed repressive measures against non-*Gelug* sects. Religious artefacts associated with *Padmasambhava* – who is revered as a 'second Buddha' by *Nyingma* practitioners – were destroyed, and non-*Gelug*, and particularly *Nyingma*, monasteries were forcibly converted to the *Gelug* position.[11] A key element of Phabongkha Rinpoche's outlook was the cult of the protective deity *Dorje Shugden*, which he married to the idea of *Gelug* exclusivism and employed against other traditions as well as against those within the *Gelug* who had eclectic tendencies.[12]

As with his predecessors, the current Dalai Lama's open and ecumenical approach to religious practice and his policy of representing the interests of all Tibetans equally, irrespective of their particular traditional affiliation, has been opposed by disgruntled *Gelug* adherents of a more exclusive orientation. This classical inclusive/exclusive division has largely been articulated within the exiled Tibetan Buddhist community through a dispute concerning the status and nature of the protective deity *Dorje Shugden* (see Figure 2.2). An outline of the main features of this controversy provides another important backdrop to the historical emergence of the NKT in Britain.

Figure 2.2 The protector-deity *Dorje Shugden*
Source: Reprinted with permission from Tharpa Publications.

The *Dorje Shugden* controversy

Dorje Shugden belongs to the class of beings within the Tibetan Buddhist pantheon known as *Chos skyong* (Skt. *Dharmapāla*), 'protectors of the religious law', or 'Dharma-protectors'. Dharma-protectors are deities who have vowed to serve and protect the Buddha's teachings and its practitioners, and they have been an important feature of the religious lives of all Tibetan Buddhist traditions. Whilst different traditions might give greater prominence to some protective deities over others, most deities are generally recognised by all and considered to be divided into two main branches. First, there are 'the powerful, high-ranking deities known as the *'jig rten las 'das pa'i srung ma*, i.e. the gods and goddesses who have passed beyond the six spheres of existence' (Nebesky-Wojkowitz 1956: 3). These supramundane deities are regarded as manifestations of enlightened beings, or Buddhas. Secondly, there is the much lower class known as the *'jig rten pa'i srung ma*, the mundane or worldly deities

> who are still residing within the spheres inhabited by animated beings and taking an active part in the religious life of Tibet, most of them by

assuming from time to time possession of mediums who act then as their mouthpieces.

(Nebesky-Wojkowitz 1956: 3)

The division between the supramundane and the worldly protectors is a fluid, rather than a rigid, system. By virtue of the merits they acquire by protecting Tibetan Buddhism, all the deities within the class of *'jig rten pa'i srung ma* will eventually pass into the rank of the *'jig rten las 'das pa'i srung ma*. Whilst the ascent into this supramundane class is said 'to be a progress of infinite slowness, if judged by human standards of time', the number of *'jig rten pa'i srung ma* increases rapidly by contrast

> due to the circumstance that many harmful spirits of the class called *nag phyogs gi bdud* [a term referring to unconverted deities and spirits of the dead] are still being conquered and changed into protectors of the Buddhist creed by appropriate ceremonies of the Tibetan Buddhist priesthood.
>
> (Nebesky-Wojkowitz 1956: 5)

In accordance with their role as protectors and defenders of the Buddhist religion, the iconography and ritual worship of protective-deities often uses violent, martial, and bloodthirsty language and imagery. Most protective-deities, of both the mundane and the supramundane classes, are depicted in a wrathful or ferocious form, and the majority of attributes they carry 'are arms destined to destroy the enemies of the Buddhist creed, the priests who break their religious vows and renegades' (Nebesky-Wojkowitz 1956: 15). There are, however, significant differences in the ways in which mundane and supramundane protectors are believed to serve and protect the Dharma. Since mundane protectors, as unenlightened beings, experience ordinary human emotions like anger and jealousy, they are thought to be partial towards the propitiating individual or group. In this context, the term 'enemies of Buddhism' can refer to beings who are 'perceived by the person or group as threatening' (Dreyfus 1998: 266), such as rival religious schools or impure practitioners within one's own tradition. Supramundane protectors, by contrast, are impartial because they have the wisdom and compassion of the Buddha. They can never be enlisted for the personal advantage of an individual or group and the violence they unleash is 'strictly motivated by compassion and aims at benefiting the beings who are its target, much like the actions of bodhisattvas described in the *Mahāyāna* literature'. In this context, the 'enemies of Buddhism' include beings whose actions 'threaten Buddhism as well as their own spiritual welfare' (Dreyfus 1998: 266).

Within the *Gelug* tradition, conflicting accounts have emerged about the protective deity *Dorje Shugden* and these have caused considerable intra-traditional conflict for many years. Whilst there is a consensus that this protector practice originated in the seventeenth century, there is much disagreement

45

about the nature and status of *Dorje Shugden*, the events that led to his appearance onto the religious landscape of Tibet, and the subsequent development of his cult. Two dominant accounts can be discerned.

One view holds that *Dorje Shugden* is a *'jig rten las 'das pa'i srung ma* (an enlightened being) and that, whilst not being bound by history, he assumed a series of human incarnations before manifesting himself as a Dharma-protector during the time of the Fifth Dalai Lama. According to this view, the Fifth Dalai Lama initially mistook *Dorje Shugden* for a harmful and vengeful spirit of a *trulku* (reincarnate *lama*) of *Drepung* monastery called *Dragpa Gyaltsen*,[13] who had been murdered by the Tibetan government because of the threat posed by his widespread popularity and influence. After a number of failed attempts to subdue this worldly spirit by enlisting the help of a high-ranking *Nyingma lama*, the Great Fifth realised that *Dorje Shugden* was in reality an enlightened being and began henceforth to praise him as a Buddha. Proponents of this view maintain that the deity has been worshipped as a Buddha ever since, and that he is now the chief guardian deity of the *Gelug* tradition. These proponents claim, furthermore, that the *Sakya* tradition also recognises and worships *Dorje Shugden* as an enlightened being.[14] The main representative of this view in recent years has been Geshe Kelsang Gyatso who, like many other popular *Gelug lamas*,[15] stands firmly within the lineage-tradition of the highly influential Phabongkha Rinpoche and his disciple Trijang Rinpoche.

Opposing this position is a view which holds that *Dorje Shugden* is actually a *'jig rten pa'i srung ma* (a worldly protector) whose relatively short lifespan of only a few centuries and inauspicious circumstances of origin make him a highly inappropriate object of such exalted veneration and refuge. This view agrees with the former that *Dorje Shugden* entered the Tibetan religious landscape following the death of *trulku Dragpa Gyaltsen*, a rival to the Great Fifth and his government.[16] According to this view, however, the deity initially came into existence as a demonic and vengeance-seeking spirit, causing many calamities and disasters for his former enemies before being pacified and reconciled to the *Gelug* school as a protector of its teachings and interests. Supporters of this view reject the pretensions made by devotees of *Dorje Shugden*, with respect to his status and importance, as recent innovations probably originating during the time of Phabongkha Rinpoche and reflecting his particularly exclusive and sectarian agenda. The present Dalai Lama is the main proponent of this position and he is widely supported in it by representatives of the *Gelug* and non-*Gelug* traditions.

Scholarly English language accounts of *Dorje Shugden* reliance seem to corroborate the latter of the two positions emerging from within the Tibetan tradition, suggesting that the status and importance of this protective deity has undergone a process of gradual elevation from around the time of Phabongkha Rinpoche. Nebesky-Wojkowitz presents *Dorje Shugden* as 'a divinity of comparatively recent origin' (1956: 134) and as one of the main *Gelug* protectors operating in the worldly spheres.[17] Dreyfus also maintains that the rare references to the deity in texts between the seventeenth and twentieth centuries indicate that *Dorje Shugden* 'was a minor though troublesome deity in the Ge-luk pantheon throughout most of the history of this tradition' (1998: 244). Furthermore, Mumford shows that modern-day *Gelug* and *Sakya* Buddhists in Nepal continue to regard the deity, in his dual capacity as 'a protector of both the kin group and the Buddhist dharma', as a popular *'jig rten pa'i srung ma*:

> He is extremely popular, but held in awe and feared among Tibetans because he is highly punitive.
>
> (Mumford 1989: 125–126)

Whilst *Dorje Shugden* is 'supposed to have made progress towards Buddhahood' (Mumford 1989: 127), he thus remains intimately involved in mundane realities, his cult taking both a localised and a universalised form.

Lama Chime Radha Rinpoche describes *Dorje Shugden* as 'a deity who came to prominence relatively recently' (1981: 31). Within certain sections of the *Gelug* tradition throughout the twentieth century, reliance upon this deity became increasingly central and his status was gradually elevated. According to Dreyfus, this process was intimately bound up with the immense popularity and influence of Phabongkha Rinpoche within the *Gelug*, his strong personal devotion to the deity and the sectarian orientation that he came to adopt in his later years. During the early period of his life, Phabongkha's orientation was inclusive, but he adopted a more exclusive and purely *Gelug* approach following a number of signs that his eclectic and open-minded outlook – which included the receiving of *Nyingma Dzog-chen* (or 'Great Perfection') teachings – was displeasing *Dorje Shugden*. His teaching tour of *Kham* in 1938 was a seminal phase, leading to a hardening of his exclusivism and the adoption of a militantly sectarian stance. In reaction to the flourishing *Rimed* movement and the perceived decline of *Gelug* monasteries in that region, Phabongkha and his disciples spearheaded a revival movement, promoting the supremacy of the *Gelug* as the only pure tradition. He now regarded the inclusivism of *Gelug* monks who practised according to the teachings of other schools as a threat to the integrity of the *Gelug* tradition, and he aggressively opposed the influence of other traditions, particularly the *Nyingma*, whose teachings were deemed mistaken and deceptive. A key element of Phabongkha's revival movement was the practice of relying upon *Dorje Shugden*, the main function of the deity now being presented as 'the protection of the Ge-luk tradition through violent means, even including the killing of its enemies' (Dreyfus 1998: 248). According to Dreyfus, the violent imagery used by Phabongkha in his invocations to *Dorje Shugden* are 'more than the usual ritual incitements contained in manuals for propitiation of protectors' and may have concerned 'the elimination of actual people by the protector' (1998: 249–250). It is also clear that, for Phabongkha, the 'enemies' of the *Gelug* refers less to the members of rival schools than to members of the *Gelug* tradition 'who mix Dzong-ka-ba's tradition with elements coming from other traditions, particularly the Nying-ma Dzok-chen' (Dreyfus 1998: 250). The mission of *Dorje Shugden* in this context, then, 'is less to fight other schools than to prevent Ge-luk practitioners from mixing traditions and even visiting retribution on those who dare to go against this prescription' (Dreyfus 1998: 250).

Reliance upon *Dorje Shugden* as a guardian of *Gelug* orthodoxy and exclusivism was thus promoted widely by Phabongkha during the 1930s and 1940s, and in this way a formerly marginal practice became a central element of the *Gelug* tradition. The rise in the popularity and importance of the deity was also accompanied by the gradual elevation of his ontological status. The first step in this process appears to have been the development of a prophetic tradition which states that

> the guardian-deity *rDo rje shugs ldan*, 'Powerful Thunderbolt', will succeed *Pe har* as the head of all *'jig rten pa'i srung ma* once the latter god advances into the rank of those guardian-deities who stand already outside the worldly spheres.
>
> (Nebesky-Wojkowitz 1956: 134)

It seems that during the 1940s, supporters of Phabongkha began to proclaim the fulfilment of this tradition and to maintain that the Tibetan government should turn its allegiance away from *Pehar*, the state protector, to *Dorje Shugden*.[18] The next stage in the status elevation process was Phabongkha's claim that *Dorje Shugden* had now replaced the traditional supramundane protectors of the *Gelug* tradition such as *Mahākāla*, *Vaiśrāvana* and, most specifically, *Kālarūpa* ('the Dharma-King'), the main protector of the *Gelug* who, it is believed, was bound to an oath by *Tsong Khapa* himself. This stage was reflected in the exalted way Phabongkha now addressed *Dorje Shugden* as 'the Protector of the Tradition of the Victorious Lord Mañjuśrī (i.e., Dzong-ka-ba)' and as 'the Supreme Protective Deity of the Ge-den (i.e. Ge-luk) Tradition' (Dreyfus 1998: 247). He now maintained that whilst *Dorje Shugden* 'assumes the pretense of being a worldly boastful god', he is in fact 'beyond the world' (Phabongkha Rinpoche, quoted in Dreyfus 1998: 240), that is a fully enlightened being. This claim seems to have enabled Phabongkha to legitimate *Dorje Shugden's* 'spectacular promotion in the pantheon of the tradition' (Dreyfus 1998: 247) without sacrificing the partiality and prejudice of the deity's violent action which was so vital to his vision of *Gelug* revival and survival. The view that *Dorje Shugden* 'is ultimately a fully enlightened buddha who merely appears as a mundane deity' (Dreyfus 1998: 255) was promoted even more forcefully by Trijang Rinpoche (1901–81), a devoted disciple of Phabongkha's who also became a hugely influential *Gelug lama*. Trijang Rinpoche was appointed Junior Tutor to the Dalai Lama in 1953, and his later pre-eminence as the main source of teaching for the *Gelug* tradition-in-exile 'further strengthened the position of Pa-bong-ka's lineage as embodying the central orthodoxy of the tradition' (Dreyfus 1998:

254). Whilst Trijang's view of other schools was more moderate than Phabongkha's, with the devotional element taking precedence over the sectarian in *Dorje Shugden* propitiation, he continued to regard the deity as a severe and violent punisher of inclusively orientated *Gelug* practitioners.

Whilst certain sections of the *Gelug* school were unconvinced by and disagreed with the elevation of *Dorje Shugden*'s importance and status under Phabongkha and Trijang Rinpoche, there was no open conflict or controversy. There was, as Dreyfus observes, 'enough room in the tradition to accommodate several views', and other prominent *lamas* such as Ling Rinpoche, the Senior Tutor to the Dalai Lama, 'offered an alternative to those who did not completely share Tri-jang's orientation'. The issue of relying upon *Dorje Shugden* did not become a subject of open dispute and contention until the mid-1970s, until which time the *Gelug* tradition seemed 'strong and united in its admiration of its great teachers, the Dalai Lama and his two tutors' (Dreyfus 1998: 255).

The young Fourteenth Dalai Lama was introduced to the practice of *Dorje Shugden* reliance by Trijang Rinpoche prior to the exile of the Tibetan Buddhist community in 1959. After some years in Dharamsala, the Dalai Lama became aware that his practice was in conflict, first with the state protector *Pehar*, and later with the main protective goddess of the *Gelug* tradition and Tibetan people *Palden Lhamo* (*dPal ldan lha mo*), who, as a *'jig rten las 'das pa'i srung ma* (an enlightened protector), objected strongly to *Dorje Shugden*'s pretensions.[19] He did not, however, voice his doubts about the merits of *Dorje Shugden* reliance until 1978 following the publication of a sectarian text by the *Gelug lama* Zimey Rinpoche (1927–96). This text, which is variously known as *The Yellow Book* or *The Oral Transmission of the Intelligent Father*,[20] enumerates a series of stories that Zimey Rinpoche had heard informally from Trijang Rinpoche about 'the many Ge-luk lamas whose lives are supposed to have been shortened by Shuk-den's displeasure at their practicing Nying-ma teachings' (Dreyfus 1998: 256). The text asserts the pre-eminence of the *Gelug* school which is symbolised and safeguarded by *Dorje Shugden*, and presents a stern warning to those within the *Gelug* whose eclectic tendencies would compromise its purity. This publication provoked angry reactions from members of non-*Gelug* traditions, setting in motion a bitter literary exchange that drew on 'all aspects of sectarian rivalry' (Kapstein 1989: 231).[21]

The Dalai Lama's reaction to the *Yellow Book* was extreme. Besides feeling personally betrayed by Zimey Rinpoche, he considered the book to be 'an attack on his role as the Dalai Lama, a rejection of his religious leadership by the Ge-luk establishment, and a betrayal of his efforts in the struggle for Tibetan freedom' (Dreyfus 1998: 257). He intervened in the dispute by publicly rejecting Zimey Rinpoche's 'awful book' as an 'insidious act of carelessness'[22] which could only damage the common cause of the Tibetan people because of its sectarian divisiveness. In a series of talks, he sought to undermine the status elevation of *Dorje Shugden* by reaffirming the centrality of the traditional supramundane protectors of the *Gelug* tradition and by maintaining that 'there is no need of a protector other than these for the Gelugpas'.[23] He also vehemently rejected *Dorje Shugden's* associated sectarianism, emphasising that all the Tibetan traditions are 'equally profound dharmas' and defending the 'unbiased and eclectic'[24] approach to Buddhist practice as exemplified by the Second, Third and Fifth Dalai Lamas. The dispute strongly reinforced his suspicions that *Dorje Shugden* reliance was in conflict with *Pehar* and *Palden Lhamo*, the deities who represent the interests of Tibetans generally, and he imposed partial restrictions on *Dorje Shugden* propitiation. Reliance on *Dorje Shugden* in private was acceptable so long as he was not propitiated as 'the Lord of the Dharma Protectors', but the practice was considered 'improper for a member of staff who was working for me and the Tibetan Government'[25] and was not to be publicly promulgated by the collective religious bodies like the monasteries and their colleges. The issue of relying on the protective deity *Dorje Shugden* thus became a major source of tension and division within the Tibetan Buddhist community-in-exile, and within the *Gelug* tradition in particular. The Dalai Lama's pronouncements were resisted by many individuals and groups, such as the re-established *Ganden Shartse* monastery in Mundgod (South India), for whom *Dorje Shugden* reliance was a central part of their spiritual lives.[26] Many of these, of course, as sympathisers and apologists of the Phabongkha tradition, were already critical of the Dalai Lama's inclusive orientation and impartial religious policies.[27]

These tensions continued to simmer beneath the surface of the Buddhist community-in-exile until the spring of 1996, when this conflict of authority erupted in a very public way following the renewed attempts of the Dalai Lama to subdue *Dorje Shugden* propitiation amongst government employees and *Gelug* monasteries in India. Within a matter of weeks, this protracted Tibetan Buddhist dispute, described by Batchelor as 'a well-guarded Tibetan secret' (1996: 119), had become the subject of heated debate between both Tibetan and Western Buddhists, and it was even making broadsheet newspaper headlines in Britain. So much attention was generated by this arcane conflict in Britain mainly because of the NKT's decision to enter the dispute in an uncharacteristically proactive and public way. The recent development of the *Dorje Shugden* dispute, and the NKT's participation in it, will be examined in Chapter 4.

The *Dorje Shugden* dispute has both religious and political dimensions, although the two are closely related. The first religious dimension concerns the broader *Gelug* debate between inclusive and exclusive interpretations of the *Gelug* tradition, the contours of which were outlined earlier. During the twentieth century, in contradistinction to the open and eclectic approach to spiritual practice adopted by inclusively orientated figures such as the Great Fifth, Great Thirteenth and Fourteenth Dalai Lamas, *Dorje Shugden* came to represent *Gelug* purity, supremacy and exclusivism. This religious debate also has strong political undercurrents. Whilst the conservative elements of the *Gelug* monastic establishment have often resented the inclusive and impartial policies of the Dalai Lamas towards rival Tibetan Buddhist traditions, the Dalai Lamas have in turn rejected exclusivism on the grounds that it encourages sectarian disunity and thereby harms the interests of the Tibetan state. In rejecting *Dorje Shugden*, the present Dalai Lama is thus speaking out against an orientation towards *Gelug* practice and identity that he considers spiritually harmful and, especially during Tibet's present political circumstances, nationally damaging.

Another important doctrinal issue concerns the question of whether *Dorje Shugden* devotees are relying upon – or 'taking refuge' in – an unreliable and capricious worldly deity or an enlightened Buddha. The distinction, from the viewpoint of the practitioner's spiritual welfare, is vital. To take refuge in a worldly deity is to abandon taking refuge solely in the Buddha 'and thus to abandon the very definition of being a Buddhist' (Williams 1996: 130). In a talk given to a gathering of Tibetan and Western disciples in 1986, the Dalai Lama thus explained that if one places worldly protectors and, in particular, *Dorje Shugden* amongst the ranks of the merit field, 'there is the danger of losing one's refuge'.[28]

On a specifically political level, it has been suggested that the Dalai Lama, in rejecting *Dorje Shugden*, is speaking out against a particular quasi-political faction within the *Gelug* tradition-in-exile who are opposed to his modern, ecumenical and democratic political vision, and who believe that the Tibetan government

> should champion a fundamentalist version of Tibetan Buddhism as a state religion in which the dogmas of the Nyingmapa, Kargyupa [sic] and Sakyapa schools are heterodox and discredited.
>
> (Sparham 1996: 12)

According to this interpretation, the Dalai Lama's wish to reform Tibetan politics-in-exile by establishing a modern and democratic system is being resisted by an ultra-conservative wing of the *Gelug* tradition. This faction is afraid that a democratically run assembly would erode the influence that the *Gelug* monastic segment has traditionally wielded over Tibetan affairs and implement a modern, pluralist and secular political vision that is fundamentally at odds with its own.[29] According to Sparham, *Dorje Shugden* has become a political symbol for this 'religious fundamentalist party'. Consequently, the Dalai Lama's rejection of *Dorje Shugden* should be interpreted not as an attempt to stamp out a religious practice he disagrees with, but as a political statement:

> he has to say he opposes a religious practice in order to say clearly that he wants to guarantee to all Tibetans an equal right to religious freedom and political equality in a future Tibet.
>
> (Sparham 1996: 13)

Dreyfus considers that whilst the political dimension of the *Dorje Shugden* practice forms an important element of the dispute, it does not provide an adequate explanation for it. Locating the dispute firmly within the religious context of the debate between exclusively and inclusively orientated *Gelug* adherents, he argues that *Dorje Shugden* is 'less the spirit of the Ge-luk political resentment against a strong Dalai-Lama than the spirit of a religious resentment against a perceived threat to the integrity of the Ge-luk tradition' (Dreyfus 1998: 269). He also maintains that to understand the Dalai Lama's extreme reaction to the *Yellow Book* and *Dorje Shugden* propitiation during the 1970s, we must first understand the ritual basis of the institution of the Dalai Lama. This complex ritual system, developed originally by the Great Fifth and reiterated by the present Dalai Lama, rests upon 'an eclectic religious basis in which elements associated with the Nying-ma tradition combine with an overall Ge-luk orientation' (Dreyfus 1998: 269). The purpose of the system is to portray the Dalai Lama's rule as a re-establishment of the early Tibetan empire by re-enacting its perceived religious foundation. This involves the promotion of teachings and practices, such as the devotion of *Padmasambhava*, that are central to the *Nyingma*, 'the Buddhist school that for Tibetans has a close association with the early empire' (Dreyfus 1998: 260). The present Dalai Lama has endeavoured to implement this ritual system in exile by developing the *Nyingma* side of his religious repertoire, by introducing *Nyingma* rituals at his personal *Namgyel* monastery and by encouraging the collective worship of *Padmasambhava*. This final measure, which he regards as an important means of restoring 'the synergy that existed between this figure and the Tibetan people, thus strengthening the power of the gods appointed by Guru Rin-bo-che [*Padmasambhava*] to protect Tibetans from dangers' (Dreyfus 1998: 262), has been resisted by more exclusively orientated segments of the *Gelug* who have boycotted the ceremonies. Within this context, the Dalai Lama opposes the *Yellow Book* and *Dorje Shugden* propitiation because they defy his attempts to restore the ritual foundations of the Tibetan state and because they disrupt the basis of his leadership, designating him as an 'enemy of Buddhism' and potential target of the deity's retribution.

3

THE EMERGENCE OF THE NKT
IN BRITAIN

Introduction

In addition to an appreciation of the broader Tibetan Buddhist context of the
NKT and the historical and cross-cultural forces that have shaped its development in the West, it is also important to situate this organisation within the
context of another contemporary Western *Gelug* movement: the Foundation for
the Preservation of the Mahayana Tradition (FPMT). This chapter outlines the
origins of the FPMT in the 1970s and examines the schism that gave rise to a
separate network of Buddhist centres headed by Geshe Kelsang Gyatso in the
mid-1980s. The teachings and orientation of Geshe Kelsang are analysed and
contextualised, and the crystalisation and creation of the NKT as a distinct
Buddhist network with a clear ideological vision in 1991 is charted. This will
set the scene for a more detailed examination of the main elements of the
NKT's sense of self-identity in Chapter 4.

Gelug Buddhism in the West: the FPMT

The FPMT is one of the longest-running international networks of Tibetan
Buddhist centres and certainly the largest organisation promoting the teachings
of the *Gelug* tradition in the West. FPMT sources trace its origins back to 1965
when the Tibetan founders of the organisation, Lamas Thubten Yeshe and
Thubten Zopa Rinpoche, first came into contact with westerners interested in
the Buddhist spiritual path. Lama Thubten Yeshe was born in 1935 near Lhasa
and entered the *Je* college of *Sera* monastic university at the age of 6, where he
lived and studied the subjects of the *geshe* (*dge bshes*) curriculum until the
Chinese annexation of Tibet in 1959. With thousands of other Tibetan
refugees, he escaped to India and resumed his monastic studies in the Indian
settlement camp of Buxaduar. It was here that he met Lama Zopa Rinpoche (b.
1946), a young reincarnate *lama* from Nepal. Although he was recognised as the
reincarnation of a Nepalese *Nyingma lama*, Lama Zopa entered one of the
Tibetan monasteries associated with the famous Tromo Geshe Rinpoche
(1865–1937) and ordained as a *Gelug* monk. In exile, Lama Zopa continued his
studies under Geshe Rabten,[1] who later sent him to study with Lama Thubten

Yeshe, an old student of his from *Sera Je*. A close teacher–disciple relationship quickly developed between the two of them.

Samuel (1996) has observed how the conversion of westerners to Tibetan Buddhism was not, in the early years, a deliberate policy pursued by the Tibetan government-in-exile. It was a development, rather, that depended upon westerners forging links with individual *lamas* independently of the Dharamsala administration. In 1965, Lamas Yeshe and Zopa met their first Western disciple, a wealthy woman of Russian descent called Zina Rachevsky. She became an enthusiastic disciple of the *lamas* and, in 1969, the three of them founded the Nepal Mahayana Gompa Centre (now known as Kopan monastery) on land purchased by Rachevsky at the top of Kopan hill in Kathmandu. Rachevsky later passed away in retreat and was unable to witness the international expansion of a movement that she had helped to begin and which continues to honour the role she played in bringing *Gelug* Buddhism to the West.

In the late 1960s and early 1970s, Kathmandu was one of the most popular sites along the 'hippy trail' for those westerners who, dissatisfied and disillusioned with their own cultural and religious traditions, sought exotic alternatives and new spiritual experiences in the East. The Kopan meditation courses led by Lamas Yeshe and Zopa became very popular, and they opened Tushita Retreat Centre in Dharamsala to provide for the overflow of serious meditators. Lama Zopa also opened a school, the Mount Everest Centre for Buddhist Studies, for Sherpa children in the Solu Khumbu region of Nepal to receive a closely supervised monastic education.

In 1974, the International Mahayana Institute (IMI) was established at Kopan monastery when fourteen Western monks and nuns received ordination. Most Western students, however, were not ordained, returning instead to their home countries. These students soon realised the need for their own Western Dharma centres and started meetings and meditation groups. In 1974, the *lamas* gave their first tour of the West, boosting the development of their fledgling network. Ordained members of the IMI were assigned posts in the new centres to help them become established, and Lama Yeshe invited Tibetan *geshes* to become resident teachers in the larger ones. Kopan monastery remained the spiritual and organisational hub of the movement, as well as being a place for Tibetan *geshes* to acclimatize to Western ways by teaching students and learning some English.

At the end of 1975, Lama Yeshe called his emerging international network the Foundation for the Preservation of the Mahayana Tradition. He also created an infrastructure to coordinate and unite its member centres by establishing the Council for the Preservation of the Mahayana Tradition (CPMT), a body comprising senior students and directors of the FPMT's centres who would meet annually to discuss projects and formulate guiding principles on the basis of his talks. He also established the Central Office to facilitate communication between the *lamas* and the centres and amongst the centres themselves, and to implement the decisions of the CPMT. By the late 1970s, then, the FPMT had evolved from being a loose federation of scattered groups into an organisation with an emerging infrastructure, a council to discuss its direction and develop policies, and an administrative headquarters, carrying the authority of the *lamas*, to coordinate and direct its various departments.

The idea for a centre in Britain first developed in around 1974 amongst Lama Yeshe's British students. The growing interest, generated initially through introductory Buddhist seminars and newsletters, was consolidated when Lamas Yeshe and Zopa visited Britain in 1975 as part of their second world teaching tour. In 1976, a mock-gothic mansion called Conishead Priory in Ulverston, Cumbria, was discovered, and its size – and perhaps more importantly its price of £70,000 – made it the ideal choice for a residential Buddhist centre. The priory was purchased and Manjushri Institute was registered as a charitable organisation, with Lama Yeshe as its Spiritual Director and the promotion of 'the Buddhist Faith and human growth, meditation and spiritual development in accordance with Buddhist principles throughout the United Kingdom'[2] as its stated objectives. The first event held at the priory was a twenty-three day meditation course given by the *lamas* that was attended by seventy students, twelve of whom stayed on afterwards to form the nucleus of an early community.

The most pressing task for the Institute's nascent community was the restoration of the building and surrounding gardens, which were in a severe state of disrepair and neglect. The centre developed a variety of business initiatives, such as a cafe, a printing press and a mail-order bookshop, as well as generating capital by renting out unused parts of the building in which other groups could conduct workshops on Buddhist and non-Buddhist subjects such as yoga, wholefood cooking, T'ai ch'i and psychotherapy. In addition to the immediate practical and financial concerns, the centre also needed to develop a viable management structure and find a style of community living that was workable. One of the early community members recalled that

> The initial, or big, problems at the beginning were, 'What does it mean? What kind of community are we trying to create here?' People used to anguish over this [...] Literally under one roof we had monks, nuns, lay people, lay married people, and children. And that's just crazy. But it hadn't really been thought out. It was early days. All these people were thrown together.

In spite of the inevitable teething problems, however, the community was united by its common interest in the Buddhist teachings. Initially, the education programme was the responsibility of an IMI nun who would lead *pūjās* and arrange courses by visiting teachers, but by 1977, the Institute had its own resident teacher, a Tibetan monk called Geshe Kelsang Gyatso.

Snellgrove's observation that the success of Tibetan Buddhism in the West derives largely from the physical presence of Tibetan *lamas* is pertinent to our understanding of the FPMT (Snellgrove 1987: 520). The successful development of FPMT Dharma centres was, and continues to be, greatly assisted by the presence of Tibetan *lamas* whom Lama Yeshe – and now Lama Zopa – would install as resident teachers.[3] In 1976, Lamas Yeshe and Zopa Rinpoche visited Geshe Kelsang Gyatso in Mussourie, India, and invited him over to Manjushri Institute. Born in Tibet in 1931, Geshe Kelsang Gyatso was a contemporary of Lama Yeshe's, studying for his *geshe* degree at *Sera Je* monastery before coming into exile. He was, by all accounts, a very well-respected scholar and meditator within the exiled Tibetan *Gelug* community. Manjushri Institute was a centre for which Lamas Yeshe and Zopa had grand designs, and they apparently sought the advice of the Dalai Lama when choosing Geshe Kelsang to fill the responsible position of overseeing its spiritual development. He accepted the invitation and moved into Conishead Priory in 1977 along with his translator to oversee the 'General Programme' of Buddhist studies.

Following the first international CPMT meeting, held at Manjushri Institute in 1978, Lama Yeshe decided to move Wisdom Publications, the publishing arm of the FPMT, from Delhi to Ulverston to take advantage of the Institute's energy, facilities and manpower. Over the next four years, books by both Lamas Yeshe and Zopa Rinpoche and by Geshe Kelsang emerged from the Cumbrian base. Lama Yeshe also decided, in 1979, to set up a Geshe Studies Programme at Manjushri Institute, and he installed another Tibetan *lama*, Geshe Jampa Tekchog, to direct it. In 1982, Geshe Tekchog moved on to become the abbot of the FPMT's first monastery, Nalanda, in France, and Geshe Konchog Tsewang replaced him as the Geshe Studies teacher. This was the first, and the most successful, Geshe Studies Programme instituted within the FPMT, and its creation at the priory precipitated an influx of IMI members from around the world. The ten-to-twelve-year programme, which was recognised and validated by the Dalai Lama,[4] was modelled on the traditional *geshe* degree, although it was abbreviated and modified for westerners, being open to lay practitioners, monks and nuns. A parallel educational structure thus developed at the Institute, with the Geshe Studies Programme on the one hand, and Geshe Kelsang Gyatso's General Programme on the other. The courses offered by the different *geshes* complemented each other but differed in one important respect: only Geshe Kelsang's General Programme included courses on Tantric Buddhism, and attendance upon these required the reception of a Tantric empowerment.[5] The Institute also organised extended visits over the summer months by other well-known Tibetan *lamas*, such as Song Rinpoche (1905–84), Geshe Rabten, Geshe Lhundup Sopa and the Institute's Spiritual Directors Lamas Yeshe and Zopa. By the end of the 1970s, then, Lama Yeshe's vision of Manjushri Institute as the spiritual and educational hub of the FPMT had crystalised. According to a disciple of his from this time, Lama Yeshe intended the Institute to 'become the central monastery of the FPMT [...] one of the early jewels of the FPMT crown'. The Institute was intended to be 'the pioneer among the western centres [...] the model on which FPMT centres would pattern themselves'.[6]

Another important development towards the end of the 1970s was the creation of a second British FPMT centre called Manjushri London. The centre itself was founded in 1978, and the first meeting was inaugurated by Geshe Kelsang Gyatso and Geshe Damcho Yonten from Lam Rim Buddhist Centre in Wales. In 1981, Lama Yeshe provided Manjushri London with a resident teacher, Geshe Namgyal Wangchen, and in 1982, the centre obtained its own property near Finsbury Park. This enabled the London centre, which had emerged as a branch of Manjushri Institute, to develop its own momentum and to grow, offering a teaching programme and planning a city outreach policy. Again, the presence of the Tibetan *lama* was crucial to the centre's success.

Geshe Kelsang Gyatso

The continuity of Geshe Kelsang's teaching with that of mainstream *Gelug* Buddhism has been observed by Waterhouse in her discussion of the NKT (Waterhouse 1997: 151). The doctrinally conservative nature of his teachings and the traditionally structured and direct style in which they are presented in his texts reflects his background within the rigorous scholastic and academic training system of *Sera Je* monastic university. His strongly 'clerical' orientation also reflects the approach of Trijang Rinpoche and Phabongkha Rinpoche, the two main *Gelug lamas* through whom he traces the lineage of his teachings. The clerical orientation of Phabongkha Rinpoche has been succinctly described by Samuel:

> P'awongk'a Rimpoch'e was not an originator of new teachings or approaches. His significance for the Gelugpa was as a transmitter and codifier of the Gelugpa tradition. He stood for a strict and pure continuation of the tradition of Tsongk'apa as it had developed in the great Gelugpa monasteries of central and east Tibet.
>
> (Samuel 1993: 545)

This characterisation of Phabongkha Rinpoche could equally be applied to Geshe Kelsang himself, for whom the faithful transmission and continuation of the tradition as it was taught to him has been much more important than adapting the teachings or innovating new ones for westerners. His allegiance to the protective deity *Dorje Shugden*, also traced back through Trijang Rinpoche and Phabongkha Rinpoche, forms another key element of his clerical and exclusive outlook. The clerical and exclusive character of Geshe Kelsang's thought, however, has not been static and fixed throughout his career. His concern with the conservation and preservation of the tradition of *Tsong Khapa* became increasingly urgent during his time in the West, and his exclusivism hardened and intensified. This was expressed through the growing prominence of *Dorje Shugden* reliance in his centres; a narrowing down of legitimate authority; an increase in structured study; an emphasis upon boundary maintenance and purity; and the eventual creation of the NKT in 1991, an event marking the public separation of his growing network of Dharma centres from the Tibetan Buddhist – and, more specifically, the *Gelug* – mainstream.

Since the teachings and practices outlined in Geshe Kelsang's texts are mostly in line with the presentations of other Tibetan *Gelug* teachers, there is no need to discuss them in detail here. Our analysis of his thought will therefore concentrate not on the content of the teachings, but on the clerical style in which they are articulated and the degree of inclusivism or exclusivism that can be discerned behind them. In order to understand Geshe Kelsang's thought, we must situate him within two main contexts: the indigenous Tibetan Buddhist context of the *Gelug* tradition on the one hand, and its Western transplantation and development on the other. When he came to Britain as the resident teacher of Manjushri Institute, he did so as a clerically orientated Tibetan *geshe* who, through the line of Phabongkha Rinpoche, had inherited a particularly exclusive version of *Gelug* Buddhism, symbolised and safeguarded by *Dorje Shugden*. At the time of his arrival and settlement in the West, the nature of Phabongkha's exclusivism and the practice of relying upon *Dorje Shugden* were being heatedly contested within the exiled Tibetan community, with the Dalai Lama taking a decidedly anti-Phabongkha and anti-*Shugden* stance. Information about the controversy filtered through to the West and, unlike Lamas Yeshe and Zopa Rinpoche who assimilated the Dalai Lama's recommendations, Geshe Kelsang became more firmly entrenched in his position as an apologist of the Phabongkha tradition. Alongside these indigenous forces, the increasingly clerical and exclusive orientation of his teachings was influenced by factors arising during the transplantation process itself. Institutional conflicts and power struggles, of the kind that have accompanied the development of other Buddhist organisations in Britain, clearly had a profound effect on him. His ability to witness at close quarters the way in which westerners have approached their Buddhist practice, and also the manner in which other Tibetan *Gelug* teachers have presented *Tsong Khapa's* tradition in the West, also led to shifts in the emphasis and orientation of his thought.

The sources available for examining the early thought and orientation of Geshe Kelsang are his initial publications: *Meaningful to Behold* (1980); a commentary to *A Guide to the Bodhisattva's Way of Life* (*Bodhicaryāvatāra;*), the classical *Mahāyāna* Buddhist treatise by the eighth-century Indian scholar *Śāntideva*; and *Clear Light of Bliss* (1982), a commentary to the generation and completion stages of Secret Mantra or Tantra.[7] Geshe Kelsang's reliance upon the commentaries and texts of *Tsong Khapa* and other prominent *Gelug* figures, his prayers of homage and request to the lineage of *Gelug gurus*, and his commitment to the *Prāsaṅghika Madhyamaka* school of philosophy all single him out as a representative of the Tibetan *Gelug* tradition. These elements of his presentation have remained constant throughout his teaching career and can be discerned in all of his publications up to the present time. The way in which he has understood and articulated his relationship with the religio-political world of Tibetan Buddhism and the contemporary *Gelug* sect has, by contrast, undergone significant changes during his time in the West. During the early period of his thought, Geshe Kelsang situated himself firmly within the context of the *Gelug* sect by invoking the authority of its two most influential figures: the Dalai Lama and the abbot of *Ganden* monastery (a position held at that time by Ling Rinpoche (1903–83)). *Meaningful to Behold* was thus dedicated 'to the long life of His Holiness the Fourteenth Dalai Lama' (Kelsang Gyatso 1980: viii), whilst *Clear Light of Bliss* included a foreword by 'Yong-dzin Ling Rinpoche, Ninety-seventh Holder of the Throne of Ganden' (Kelsang Gyatso 1982: vi–vii). During the later period of his thought, Geshe Kelsang's perception of himself and his centres vis-à-vis the contemporary *Gelug* sect changed dramatically, and he came to believe that he could only uphold the tradition of *Tsong Khapa* purely by separating from the degenerate world of Tibetan, and specifically *Gelug*, Buddhism. This shift was reflected in a number of revisions he made to the later editions of his texts following his creation of the NKT, such as the omission of the above references to modern *Gelug* authority figures.

Samuel has observed that whilst there is a considerable range of variation between the styles of *Gelug lamas* teaching in the West, on the whole they have tended to be more conservative and traditional than their Tibetan contemporaries emerging from within the *Rimed* movement, who have been more unconventional and willing to make 'original and creative adaptations of their Tibetan training' (Samuel 1993: 349). Figures like Geshe Rabten and Geshe Ngawang Dhargyey, whose teachings emphasise the clerical and traditional *Gelug* training they received in Tibet, contrast sharply with *Rimed* representatives like Sogyal Rinpoche, Tarthang Tulku and, most famously, Chogyam Trungpa Rinpoche, whose shamanic orientation enabled him, in Bell's terms, to become 'an expert cultural broker and innovator' (Bell 1998: 61). The style of Geshe Kelsang's early texts places him firmly at the clerical end of *Gelug* Buddhism. Both texts present a concise, straightforward, and academic exposition of the teachings and practices he received during his training in Tibet. With regard to the presentation of the teachings, an awareness of and sensitivity to his Western context can be discerned; for instance, he compares a Tantric trainee who lacks *bodhicitta* with 'a person who uses pound notes to light his cigarette or a Rolls Royce to cart manure' (Kelsang Gyatso 1980: 91). This does not extend, however, to changing the substantive content of the teachings. He acknowledges that westerners may find certain aspects of Buddhist doctrine, practice and cosmology difficult to accept, but he is unwilling to adapt or deliteralise such problematic areas to make them more acceptable. The emphasis is upon westerners making the effort to appreciate and assimilate the teachings rather than adapting them to fit their rationalistic sensibilities.

Meaningful to Behold and *Clear Light of Bliss* incorporate both inclusive and exclusive elements. Geshe Kelsang's early inclusivism is indicated by references to practices that are 'recommended by the lamas of all four traditions of Tibetan Buddhism' (Kelsang Gyatso 1980: 43) and by his veneration of the great *lamas* of other schools, such as 'the fully enlightened Indian master Guru

Padmasambhava' (Kelsang Gyatso 1980: 101). Both texts also include an extended notes section and bibliography that refer the reader to other authors, both of Gelug and non-Gelug schools and of other non-Tibetan traditions (e.g. Theravāda and Zen), for wider reading and edification. The General Diploma taught by Geshe Kelsang also recommended a wide selection of books, and these were stocked by the Manjushri Institute bookshop.

Such inclusive features notwithstanding, the early texts indicate that Geshe Kelsang's primary orientation was exclusive. For example, he encourages students to commit themselves to their chosen practice and to follow it exclusively. His critique of students who 'jump from one meditation to another' (Kelsang Gyatso 1980: 197) may be an allusion both to the Tibetan practitioners within the Rimed movement who follow multiple lineages of practice, and to the Western trainees encountered at Manjushri Institute who adopted a similar approach to their Buddhist training.

To understand how Geshe Kelsang's exclusive orientation was reflected in Clear Light of Bliss, it is useful to compare aspects of his commentary on the Gelug tradition of Mahāmudrā with a recently published commentary by the Dalai Lama entitled The Gelug/Kagyu Tradition of Mahamudra (Dalai Lama and Berzin 1997). Although the textual basis of both commentaries is the same, and in spite of the fact that Geshe Kelsang and the Dalai Lama both received the lineage of teachings from Kyabje Trijang Rinpoche, certain aspects of their discussion are quite different in emphasis. According to Samuel, the more 'clerical' elements of the Gelug tradition have opposed Dzogchen because of 'its tendency to use positive imagery to describe the state of Enlightenment' (Samuel 1993: 464), a tendency that derives largely from the greater emphasis placed within the Nyingma upon Yogacara conceptualisations of the path rather than the Madhyamaka. By reconciling and affirming the value of the different conceptualisations of enlightenment found within Gelug and Dzogchen teachings, the Dalai Lama situates himself firmly at the shamanic and inclusive end of the Gelug tradition. He is particularly concerned to show that there is no ultimate contradiction between the gradual, logical and rationalistic approach of the Prāsaṇghika Madhyamaka school of philosophy, as transmitted by the Gelug tradition, on the one hand, and the more imaginative, immediate and experiential approach of the Dzogchen system of the Nyingma tradition on the other. Geshe Kelsang's commentary, by contrast, is more clerical and exclusive. In it he maintains that 'pure' practitioners within all the Tibetan Buddhist traditions uphold the Prāsaṇghika Madhyamaka view of emptiness, and that without this view, 'there is no chance of their attaining liberation or enlightenment, no matter how much they meditate' (Kelsang Gyatso 1982: 192). There is no explicit mention here of Nyingma Buddhism, but the hardline approach taken towards the Prāsaṇghika Madhyamaka school clearly rules Dzogchen out as a valid or legitimate path to enlightenment. Coupled with this is his emphasis upon the importance of refuting 'mistaken or misleading teachings' (Kelsang Gyatso 1982: 153). According to Geshe Kelsang,

The ugly, unfortunate result of not understanding pure Dharma and of following misleading teachings that pretend to be pure Dharma is sectarianism. This is one of the greatest hindrances to the flourishing of Dharma, especially in the West. Anything that gives rise to such an evil, destructive mind should be eliminated as quickly and as thoroughly as possible.

(Kelsang Gyatso 1982: 154)

The view of sectarianism presented here contrasts sharply with that of the Dalai Lama who, in his commentary, stresses the importance of adopting an attitude of impartiality and respectful belief in the value of 'all the Buddhist lineages of Tibet – Sakya, Kagyu, Nyingma and Gelug – and likewise respect for Bon [the indigenous religion of Tibet] and all the other religions and spiritual traditions we find in the world' (Dalai Lama and Berzin 1997: 261). The Dalai Lama even goes so far as to say that Buddhist practitioners can broaden and deepen their understanding and practice of whatever is their main tradition by studying and practising 'as widely as [they] can the various traditions of Buddhism' (Dalai Lama and Berzin 1997: 261).

Problems at the priory

During the late 1970s, a situation of conflict developed between Lama Yeshe and Geshe Kelsang Gyatso when the latter decided to open up a Buddhist centre in York under his own spiritual direction rather than under the auspices of the FPMT. Lama Yeshe and the CPMT objected to this development because they felt that Geshe Kelsang was creating the potential for disharmony and was 'splitting the energies' that he should have channelled into the Institute alone. Their concerns were based upon the experience of Chenrezig Institute in Australia, whose teacher, Geshe Loden, had recently split away from the FPMT to develop his own Buddhist network. Although Geshe Kelsang maintained that the 'opening of the Centre in York caused not one moment of confusion or disharmony',[8] he was asked to resign so that a more suitable *geshe*, one committed totally to FPMT objectives, could take over as resident teacher. This prompted a response from the Institute's students, many of whom had developed a stronger connection with Geshe Kelsang, their daily teacher, than with Lamas Yeshe and Zopa, who visited the priory only rarely. They petitioned Geshe Kelsang to continue teaching them and it was on this basis that he decided to stay.

This marked the beginning of a rapidly deteriorating relationship between Geshe Kelsang and his students at the Institute on the one hand, and Lama Yeshe and the FPMT administration on the other. Lama Yeshe's project of defining and implementing an efficient organisational and administrative structure within the FPMT carried the potential for friction at a local level. The organisation's affiliated centres had initially been largely autonomous and self-regulating, but towards the late-1970s were increasingly subject to central management and control. The problems at Chenrezig Institute resulted from this centralising trend, and in turn they reinforced for the FPMT administration the importance of developing a clear organisational structure.

The conflict that was to develop between the FPMT and Manjushri Institute might have been avoided altogether if the centre had been under the direction of a student with a strong commitment to Lama Yeshe's vision. The management committee at the Institute, however, had since 1981 been made up principally of Geshe Kelsang's close students who were known as the 'Priory Group'. The Priory Group became dissatisfied with the FPMT's increasingly centralised organisation. Directives from Central Office came across as distant and authoritarian and they were often in conflict with how the Priory Group perceived the Institute's interests at a local level. The FPMT's designs to use Conishead Priory as an asset to provide funds for projects elsewhere within the FPMT network, for example, and the legal-financial liability Manjushri Institute had for Wisdom Publications were considered to be particularly unreasonable strains which threatened the Institute's existence. These formed part of a more general malaise with the situation, however, summarised by one NKT disciple, a member of the original Priory Group, in the following way:

> This was what was so difficult in the early years, the feeling that people here didn't really have any control over what was going on. And yet, year by year, we were left to run the place. We were here holding the place up, building it with our hands, trying to financially keep it going, keep the central heating running [...] And yet someone else, who had no connection, could say to us, 'Right this is going to happen there, or that lama's leaving and this one's coming and you've got to pay for this translator to fly in'. People got fed up with being told what to do by somebody else who didn't seem to have any particular awareness or connection. On one hand we were running a very viable and big centre, one of the earliest centres in the West. And at the same time there was the feeling that someone else was telling us what to do. And that just didn't work.

The Priory Group thus became increasingly unresponsive to directives coming from Central Office. By 1983, its desire for limited autonomy had evolved – with the backing of a large section of the Institute's community – into a campaign for full-blown independence. The FPMT administration opposed the Priory Group's drive for self-determination, rejecting its objectives as a 'narrow' distortion of the Institute's original purpose within Lama Yeshe's 'universal' and interconnected network. One FPMT student from that time described the conflict thus:

> The whole dispute took off with, essentially, Geshe Kelsang saying, 'I'm staying here for the concerns of my students who have asked me to

stay; my students who have put in all this energy in creating this building, all this effort', and Lama Yeshe saying, 'Look, what I'm about is creating a world-wide organisation for the preservation of the Mahayana tradition in all countries under the auspices of the Dalai Lama and I want you to be part of this team working for the same thing. And I don't want you to go out on a limb. And what you have in England is a centre which I see as part of something much bigger; it is a part of a bigger plan. It isn't just a monastery; it's part of a bigger whole, it's part of my mandala.' This was the whole essence of the dispute.

Lama Yeshe's attempts to reassert his authority over the Institute in 1983 were unsuccessful, and an open conflict of authority developed between the Priory Group and the FPMT administration. Geshe Kelsang and his students were now intent upon securing fundamental alterations in the nature of the Institute's relationship with the FPMT, and ultimately in separating the two altogether. Towards this end, they put pressure upon Lama Yeshe – in his capacity as Spiritual Director of the Trust – to authorise certain constitutional modifications that would give the Priory Group greater legal representation with respect to the Institute's future development. Lama Yeshe reluctantly agreed to this and, in February 1984, meetings between representatives of both 'sides' were arranged and mediated by the Office of His Holiness the Dalai Lama in London. These meetings resulted in an agreement to resolve the dispute and improve communication between the Institute and the FPMT. Subsequently, the existing Trustees of the Institute – mainly FPMT representatives – resigned and a new set, representing both 'sides' equally, were appointed. According to the agreement, the new Trustees were to pursue talks that would separate Wisdom Publications from the Institute and produce a new constitution enabling the Institute to remain within the FPMT whilst ensuring the autonomy it desired.

The dispute between the Institute and the FPMT, however, was never resolved. In the wake of Lama Yeshe's death in March 1984, the FPMT administration quickly lost interest in what became seen as a fruitless case. The Institute was no longer, from the FPMT's perspective, the dynamic and spiritual hub of the organisation that it once was. This was partly because the conflicts there had prompted many of Lama Yeshe's closest students to move away to different parts of the network, but there were other reasons. Most of the monks and nuns within the IMI, for example, had already moved away from the Institute to continue their studies in the newly created Nalanda monastery and Dorje Palmo nunnery in France. Furthermore, although the legal-financial connection still needed to be severed, Wisdom Publications had, for pragmatic reasons, already moved its offices away from the Institute to London in 1982. These developments appear to have provided the Priory Group with extra legitimation for their claim to self-determination, whilst also enabling the FPMT administration to prioritise the development of the rest of its network and, in many ways, to consign Manjushri Institute to its past. From this time, then, Manjushri Institute began to develop primarily under the guidance of Geshe Kelsang and without reference to the FPMT.

The meetings between the appointed Trustees continued for many years, but they could not agree upon a constitution that suited all parties. The determination of Geshe Kelsang and the Priory Group to separate from the parent organisation was uncompromising, and this was a position that only hardened during the following years. In 1991, through the successful exploitation of a legal loophole, the assets of Manjushri Institute finally fell under the sole control of the Priory Group. Within a year, the Institute had a new name, Manjushri Mahayana Buddhist Centre, and a new constitution that embodied the objectives of the NKT, Geshe Kelsang's new Buddhist movement. These objectives, as will become clear, are very different from those of Lama Yeshe and Lama Zopa as they were established in the Institute's original Trust Deed and as they continue to be manifested throughout the FPMT network.

The conflict that developed between Manjushri Institute and the FPMT needs to be understood within two related contexts. First, the dispute has a practical and institutional dimension. Tensions inevitably arise within international Buddhist organisations when local 'Dharma communities', such as the Manjushri Institute, are centrally governed. These tensions are likely to be most acute during the early years of the network's development, when the nature and shape of authority structures within the institution are originally being hammered out and implemented. Furthermore, whilst arising initially from organisational developments, these conflicts have, in the case of the Institute and the FPMT, precipitated further shifts. The subsequent development of the structures of both the FPMT and the NKT was significantly influenced by this conflict. The main lesson the FPMT seemed to learn concerned the importance of effective communication within a centralised organisation. The dispute prompted 'a deep analysis of the dynamics of a worldwide Dharma organisation, inter-personal relationships and long – and short – range communication'.[9] The FPMT's publications began to include articles outlining the lines of communication and authority within the organisation, and during the following years the *Handbook for the FPMT* was drafted to explain the purpose and shape both of the network and of its member centres.[10] Similarly, the structure and organisation of the NKT was later developed – either consciously or unconsciously – in light of the Institute's struggles with the FPMT. The proud boasts of NKT students today about the decentralised nature of the organisation and the autonomy given to its centres should all be understood within this context.

The second, and equally significant, context within which the dispute should be placed is cross-cultural. Samuel has noted that international networks of Buddhist centres are liable to fragmentation and break-up because they are total entities 'composed of sub-units of markedly different type and structure' (Samuel 1996). The resident *geshes* are important 'sub-units' within the FPMT, and as long as Tibetan teachers continue to be brought into the organisation there will always be the potential for disruption because there is, as we have seen, 'more than one way of being a *geshe*' (Samuel 1993: 337). The problems the FPMT administration had in getting the Tibetan teachers in its centres to accept the 'Geshe Agreement' during the late 1970s illustrate this. Not all of the *geshes* shared Lama Yeshe's vision of *Gelug* Buddhism in the West or understood themselves to be part of it. This was the case with Geshe Loden, the teacher at the Chenrezig Institute in Australia, who opted out of the organisation in 1979 and subsequently established his own network of centres. It was also the case with Geshe Kelsang who, at the time of the Madhyamaka Centre dispute, refused to sign a Geshe Agreement with which he had been presented, claiming that 'I have had nothing to do with the FPMT before or after 1979'.[11] Whilst the FPMT's structures now ensure a degree of stability, senior students within the organisation have informed me that, even today, it is misleading to think of its teachers as 'FPMT *geshes*'. These *lamas* come to the West with various personal agendas and ideological perspectives and 'probably consider themselves to be autonomous, within the limits of the contract they are these days requested to agree to'.[12]

Lama Yeshe and Geshe Kelsang represented very different positions within their indigenous *Gelug* context in terms of the classical division between 'inclusive' and 'exclusive' orientations. Their differing orientations were carried with them from Tibet into exile, and later informed their conflicting visions of how *Gelug* Buddhism should be presented in the West. Although Lama Yeshe never encouraged the abolition of religious differences and followed the tradition of *Tsong Khapa* strictly, his orientation was more inclusive than exclusive. His Buddhistic interpretation of Christmas, published as *Silent Mind, Holy Mind* (1978), provides a good illustration of how he, like the Dalai Lama, went 'beyond the traditional confines that so often separate religions'.[13] His inclusivism was also expressed through the global, ecumenical and liberal nature of his Dharma network. According to Samuel's distinction, Lama Yeshe was more 'shamanic' than 'clerical' in that he never completed his *geshe* degree and favoured non-traditional methods of presenting teachings that were often frowned upon by his more conservative peers. By contrast, Geshe Kelsang was more exclusive and clerical in orientation. The founding of Madhyamaka Centre independently in 1979 provided the earliest indication that he did not share Lama Yeshe's inclusive vision, and his early teachings were exclusive in tone. Also, whereas Lama Yeshe was flamboyant and unconventional, in a style reminiscent of the Tibetan 'crazy *siddhas*', Geshe Kelsang has always favoured traditional and academic styles of behaviour and presentation.

Lama Yeshe's and Geshe Kelsang's differing ideological perspectives provided the conditions for the organisational dispute between the Institute and the FPMT to escalate. Geshe Kelsang was already predisposed to support his students in their struggle with the FPMT administration because the organisation was inspired by a vision that he did not totally agree with. This indicates how practical and organisational conflicts can be exacerbated when communities contain Tibetan *geshes*, and especially when strong *guru*–student bonds have been established, such as at Manjushri Institute where Geshe Kelsang was the only resident teacher to bestow Tantric empowerments. The statements he made during the dispute reflected his differing ideological position. His criticisms of Lama Yeshe and the FPMT, for example, would often be couched in terms of the destruction of the 'purity' of the Dharma. According to Geshe Kelsang, the creation of the central governing organisation of the FPMT by Lama Yeshe had 'mixed the Dharma with politics' and thereby destroyed it.[14] The notion of 'purity' was to become one of the defining characteristics of Geshe Kelsang's presentation of Buddhism in Britain through the NKT. Whilst it would be inaccurate to suggest that the same degree of exclusivism characterising his vision of Buddhism in the West today also characterised his vision in 1983, the purity/impurity polemic he employed during the dispute does indicate a leaning towards the clerical and exclusive pole. This orientation lent support to the unfolding conflict and, in turn, it appears to have been hardened by it.

This was a very difficult period both for the students living at the Institute and also for those within the FPMT administration, and it has clearly left some deep emotional scars. One of the main problems the students had at the time of the dispute was that of divided loyalties. Even though the dispute was primarily organisational and did not necessarily entail any breaking of spiritual bonds between the students and the *lamas*, to support Geshe Kelsang or Lama Yeshe still implied a rejection of the other on some level. Another problem the students experienced was that of reconciling the contradiction between their images of Tibetan *lamas* as 'highly realised' beings and the apparent state of conflict that had developed between them. The mental anguish experienced by many of the Institute's students at the time of the dispute clearly resulted largely from the same kind of idealistic images and fantasies of Tibetan Buddhism that Bishop has observed within Western Dharma communities. Students today are often unwilling to admit that there was actually any conflict between Geshe Kelsang and Lama Yeshe at all, and they will tend to talk of the conflict as one that was solely between the Western students. The way in which these students have rationalised the conflict is another reflection of the Western inability to deal with contradiction and ambivalence within the Tibetan Buddhist system.

Geshe Kelsang's network takes shape

From 1984, the Manjushri Institute continued to develop independently of the FPMT framework. Although Geshe Konchog Tsewang continued to teach Geshe Studies to students there, the main source of authority at the Institute was Geshe Kelsang. Of the two, it was Geshe Kelsang who had always taken the greater interest in the running and direction of the Institute, and most of the students there – though close to both *geshes* – were closer to him. According to students who were there during this period, there were no dramatic changes at the Institute, which continued to develop along much the same lines as before.

Although it was now self-governing, no longer referring to the overarching FPMT framework, life at the Institute continued to reflect the kind of approach that had been established within other FPMT centres. The students at the Institute may have felt stifled by the FPMT's organisation, but most continued to share Lama Yeshe's liberal, progressive and inclusive vision of bringing *Gelug* Buddhism to the West. The *Manjushri Institute for Buddhist Studies Handbook* (1984), printed shortly after the split from the FPMT, indicated how little life at the Institute had changed. This painted a picture of a community practising *Gelug* Buddhism under the guidance both of its resident *geshes* 'and of visiting fully qualified Buddhist masters'. The booklet advertised courses in 'related subjects' like yoga and Western psychology, and boasted that the Institute library 'has more than 3,000 books: over a third are on Buddhism and the others cover aspects of religion, philosophy and psychology'. The only obvious difference between this and earlier publications emerging from the Priory Press was that the Institute was described as 'a free association of individuals' rather than as a member of the FPMT. Whilst the booklet acknowledged that the Institute was founded by Lama Thubten Yeshe, it did not mention the FPMT organisation or suggest that the Institute belonged, or had ever belonged, to a larger Dharma network. The revisionism characterising the presentation of the NKT today can thus be traced back to this time.

Over the subsequent years, Geshe Kelsang's exclusive orientation appears to have hardened. We can only speculate about the reasons for this, but the rift with the FPMT certainly seems to have been a contributory factor. Some students also suggest that the successive deaths of major *Gelug* lineage-holders in the early 1980s, particularly those of Trijang Rinpoche (d. 1981), his root-*guru*, and Song Rinpoche (d. 1983), heightened Geshe Kelsang's awareness of the fragility of *Tsong Khapa's* tradition in the modern era and gave him a growing sense of his own responsibility in preserving it. He thus began to encourage a more exclusive developmental model in his centres, encouraging them to practise only Buddhist, and specifically *Gelug*, teachings. This was not always favourably received within the centres, as the following explanation of the process by a member of Vajravarahi Centre in Preston indicates:

Our first centre was a bit of a mixed bag because there were people who were just interested in Buddhism and people interested in different kinds of meditation and esoteric ideas who would come along. And they were trying to bring all these things in [...] And it was all a bit of a mish-mash. And then we got an instruction from Manjushri Institute. Geshe-la thought it would be better if we decided to concentrate our efforts just on being a Buddhist centre and promoting the Buddha's teachings. So that caused a little bit of a stir. There were some people who said, 'Well, that's not very religious.' They thought it was sectarian, keeping all these other things out, when they weren't doing any harm. But looking back on it it was definitely the right thing

to do because all these other things just dilute your energy. If you want
to achieve enlightenment you've got to concentrate on one thing.

The increasingly focused approach encouraged by Geshe Kelsang in his centres
did not at this stage entail an absolute commitment to him at the expense of
other *lamas*, and visiting Buddhist teachers were still welcomed. These were
mainly highly regarded *Gelug lamas* such as Geshe Lhundup Sopa and Geshe
Rabten, although famous non-*Gelug* Buddhist teachers such as Ajahn Sumedho
and Thich Nhat Hanh also visited the Institute on occasion. This indicates
perhaps how Geshe Kelsang's increasing *Gelug* exclusivism needed to be
balanced against the material needs of the Institute, which generated a significant proportion of its capital by organising external courses. It also suggests that
the hardening of his approach was not easily assimilated by the Institute's
students. The history of the Institute was rooted within that of the FPMT, and
the approach that characterised this organisation had left an enduring legacy
amongst its students. Many students at the Institute, for example, still liked to
travel to India and Nepal to meet different *lamas* and receive various Tantric
empowerments, a pursuit that was common amongst FPMT students and was
encouraged by the organisation. Geshe Kelsang discouraged this because he felt
that it distracted from the education programmes at the Institute, but in spite of
his voiced objections many students saw no contradiction and continued to go.
Over the years he would become increasingly exasperated with the enduring
FPMT style of practice within the Institute. This situation was an obstacle to
the successful implementation of his own approach, and illustrates the point
made by Waterhouse that religious authority 'has to be recognized as well as
claimed' (Waterhouse 1997: 30). Due to its history and the orientations of its
students, the development of Manjushri Institute was thus quite different from
that of Geshe Kelsang's other centres. His students outside of the Institute did
not share its FPMT legacy to the same degree, were more focused upon his spiritual direction, and were thus more receptive to his increasing exclusivism. It
was within these centres, particularly the Madhyamaka Centre in York, that the
distinguishing features of the NKT's emerging identity were originally developed and implemented.

Madhyamaka Centre was founded in 1979 in Hebden Bridge, West Yorkshire,
but it was moved to York shortly afterwards. The group was led by an experienced lay Buddhist who was one of Manjushri Institute's original community
members. He taught basic, practical Buddhism which drew heavily upon his
personal experience and the teachings of different traditions. Geshe Kelsang was
not automatically embraced as the centre's spiritual guide but was regarded in the
same light as the other *Gelug* teachers who visited the centre, such as Geshe
Ngawang Dhargyey, Song Rinpoche and Tsenshap Serkong Rinpoche
(1914–83). The character of the group changed and its status became more
defined, however, from 1983 onwards. Growing interest generated by an
extended three-month visit to York by Geshe Kelsang and sustained by the

popular teaching visits of Neil Elliott, an enthusiastic monk from Manjushri Institute, had enabled the group to secure its own premises. When Madhyamaka Centre became residential, Elliott was invited to become its resident teacher, and a sizeable community emerged under his guidance. Elliott is described by students from this period as a complex, extroverted and 'all-pervasive' character, and by all accounts he was a powerful, charismatic and inspirational teacher. He was also a very committed disciple of Geshe Kelsang. Through him the loci of spiritual authority was shifted heavily towards Geshe Kelsang, and the openness of the centre was gradually replaced by a more focused and committed approach. Elliott also wanted the centre to grow and expand and he attracted many newcomers, a number of whom shared his desire for expansion. A noticeable division eventually began to develop between these young, highly motivated and strongly committed students and the centre's older students, who preferred the more open style of teaching and practice presented by its original teacher. In 1986, the group actually split along these lines when Elliott received permission from Geshe Kelsang to move Madhyamaka Centre to Kilnwick Percy Hall, a mansion in Pocklington on the outskirts of York. The older students objected to this, feeling that a move out of the city would make the centre inaccessible, and most severed their connections. When Madhyamaka Centre moved to its new home in 1986, it did so as a young, energetic and committed unit.

The growth of Madhyamaka Centre reflected Geshe Kelsang's developing thought, but it was unique amongst his centres due to the scale of its development. The move to Pocklington enabled the centre to develop a large lay and monastic community with a full-time teaching programme equal to Manjushri Institute in size and scale but surpassing it in terms of the discipline and commitment of its students to Geshe Kelsang. Manjushri Institute and Madhyamaka Centre continued to develop quite independently of each other, and students from the Institute have recalled how they were always impressed on the occasions the communities did come together by the energy, seriousness of purpose, and levels of devotion the Madhyamaka students exhibited. Unlike the Institute, Madhyamaka Centre provided Geshe Kelsang with the conditions under which he was able to express his particular vision of Buddhism. According to one of its current students, before the NKT had officially begun, the centre 'was a kind of proto-type of the NKT'.

The personality, conviction and charisma of Elliott was central to the development of Madhyamaka Centre and, subsequently, to the growth and expansion of the NKT. Geshe Kelsang relied upon his Western 'heart disciple' and future spiritual successor to develop a style of practice that expressed his understanding of Buddhism in a way that was attractive and appropriate for Western students. Many of the distinguishing features of the NKT today, such as its study programmes and its energetic will to expand, were originally inspired by him in York, becoming normative for all of Geshe Kelsang's centres in 1991. Most notable amongst these was the centre's reliance upon the protective deity *Dorje Shugden*.

Dorje Shugden reliance in Geshe Kelsang's centres

Dorje Shugden reliance at Manjushri Institute was originally introduced not by Geshe Kelsang, but by Lama Yeshe when the Institute was first created. Whenever a new FPMT centre was set up, Lama Yeshe provided a Dharma-protector practice most suitable to it, and he gave Manjushri Institute the practice of *Dorje Shugden* because of the connection that was thought to exist between this deity and the tradition of *Tsong Khapa* and *Mañjuśrī*. Although he nominated a particular protector for each centre, Lama Yeshe, like other *lamas*, marginalised the importance of protector practices for westerners generally, in recognition of the fact that many have found this peculiarly 'Tibetan' dimension of Tibetan Buddhism either difficult to integrate or tangential to their main practices of mind-transformation. Protector practices have always, therefore, been kept quite low-key within the FPMT, for the most part limited to the private sphere of practice for those with Tantric commitments. This approach reflects that of the Dalai Lama who, when questioned about the relevance of protector practices for westerners in 1984, maintained that too much emphasis was placed on these deities in Tibet and that their usefulness is limited to practitioners experienced and adept in Tantric visualisation practices (Cabezon 1988: 63).

When Geshe Kelsang first arrived at Manjushri Institute, he maintained the centre's commitment to the *Dorje Shugden pūjā* and he did so in the customarily discreet manner of other FPMT centres, performing it in his room with only the ordained *Sangha* members present. He was already a committed *Dorje Shugden* devotee, like numerous other *Gelug geshes* who were from the monastic college of *Sera Je* (or, especially, *Ganden Shartse*) or who had connections with Trijang Rinpoche or Song Rinpoche, the main propagators of this practice in the modern era.[15] It is well known, for example, that Geshe Rabten, another graduate of *Sera Je*, had a strong commitment to *Dorje Shugden*, and that Lama Zopa Rinpoche also received the Life Entrustment initiation into the practice from Song Rinpoche. It is considered highly inadvisable to break these commitments, and so there was nothing unusual about *Gelug lamas* continuing to propitiate *Dorje Shugden* even after the Dalai Lama had spoken out against it in 1978, especially since his original comments against the practice had allowed for its continuation in private.

Lamas Yeshe and Zopa Rinpoche first came to the West before the Dalai Lama had spoken out against *Dorje Shugden* reliance and it is unlikely, in light of the FPMT's stated objectives to develop in line with his authority, that the practice would have been introduced otherwise. As the Dalai Lama's views slowly filtered down to the level of Western Dharma-circles, the FPMT began to implement his advice by de-emphasising *Dorje Shugden* and strongly promoting *Palden Lhamo*, the chief guardian goddess of the *Gelug* and patron-deity of Tibet. By contrast, in the early 1980s, Geshe Kelsang began to open the practice out to the wider community of Manjushri Institute. He transferred the monthly protector *pūjā* to the main *gompa*, making it open to those who felt inclined to attend, and he requested Song Rinpoche, who visited the Institute in around 1983, to offer the *Dorje Shugden* Life Entrustment initiation to a restricted group. Most students at this time did not experience the opening up of the protector practice by Geshe Kelsang as a symbolic event with implications on an ideological level, and when Song Rinpoche warned that it was inappropriate to take the initiation unless one was committed to the *Gelug* tradition, this was not understood as restrictive. The open and inclusive style of Buddhist practice still characterised the approach of the Institute's students. Also, to most students the protector *pūjā* was a loud and colourful ritual, which enabled them to spend time near the *geshes* but which was otherwise largely incomprehensible because the lengthy ritual was done in Tibetan and no commentary to it was offered. Nevertheless, the fact that Geshe Kelsang was beginning to promote this practice openly may indicate how *his* thought was developing. It is highly probable, given the traffic of Tibetan *lamas* passing through the Institute, that Geshe Kelsang soon became aware of the Dalai Lama's views on *Dorje Shugden*. The promotion of the practice at this time was not necessarily a direct challenge to the Dalai Lama's pronouncements, but it does indicate how his authority was regarded by Geshe Kelsang in a way that was different – perhaps less absolutist – to the way in which it was regarded by the FPMT. It is also significant that he started to encourage this practice within the community just as the conflict with the FPMT, an organisation which he considered to be destructive of the 'pure Dharma', was gathering momentum. The invitation to Song Rinpoche to grant the Life Entrustment may also be significant, because this *lama*, as well as being regarded as one of the most highly realised teachers within the *Gelug*, was also one of its most clerical and exclusively orientated.

In the spring of 1986, Geshe Kelsang decided to teach and grant *Dorje Shugden* initiations publicly at Manjushri Institute and at Madhyamaka Centre, where they had already been introduced by Neil Elliott. Students at the Institute and in York were pleased that they were going to finally receive a translation and commentary to a practice they had been doing for years in Tibetan and about which they understood very little. The teachings reflected the exclusivism associated with *Dorje Shugden* reliance inasmuch as Geshe Kelsang reinforced the warning that initiation into the practice required a single-pointed commitment to the *Gelug* tradition. Again, not all the students at the Institute appear to have experienced this as a significant movement towards exclusivism, integrating the practice without changing their generally inclusive orientation. Others did recognise the increasing exclusivism and embraced it, whilst some felt uncomfortable with it and did not. There was, of course, least ambiguity and resistance to the practice in the centres focused primarily upon Geshe Kelsang and which were already developing in an exclusive way. The practice was embraced with particular enthusiasm by the highly motivated students of Madhyamaka Centre who quickly fused it with their strongly committed approach to Buddhist activity. It is no coincidence that Madhyamaka was the first of Geshe Kelsang's centres to establish a separate 'Protector *gompa*'.

Geshe Kelsang's decision to encourage *Dorje Shugden* reliance on a wider level was resisted by some students who had (through their connections with other *lamas*) become acquainted with the Dalai Lama's specific objections to the practice. It was also resisted by the Office of the Dalai Lama in Dharamsala, which wrote to advise Geshe Kelsang of the Dalai Lama's position with regard to this practice and which sent copies of the talks he had given in India throughout the late 1970s and early 1980s for distribution amongst the students intending to receive the *Dorje Shugden* initiation. Geshe Kelsang, however, decided not to heed the advice and delivered his teachings to students who had not received copies of the Dalai Lama's talks. In addition to this, he appears to have expelled from the Institute those students who tried to publicise the controversy surrounding the protector practice. Consequently, the majority of students who adopted the *Dorje Shugden* practice at this time were unaware of its contentious dimensions. From this period until 1996, awareness of the controversy surrounding the practice was kept to a minimum within Geshe Kelsang's centres due to a policy of silence adopted by him and his senior students, whereby information would be withheld and discussion discouraged.

His decision to directly disagree with the Dalai Lama on this issue was not unprecedented. It was expressive, rather, of the classically recurrent conflict within the *Gelug* tradition with respect to inclusive and exclusive orientations, and of the specific manifestation of this conflict in the modern era around *Dorje Shugden* propitiation. Geshe Kelsang was in no way a lone dissenter on this issue; the position he adopted represented that which was held by a sizeable segment of the Tibetan *Gelug* community-in-exile. Not only was his connection with *Dorje Shugden* very strong but he was also committed (like many *Gelug lamas*) to its associated exclusivism, a perspective antithetical to the inclusive and eclectic approach encouraged by the Dalai Lama.[16]

The students who became aware of this conflict reacted to it in different ways. Some were unable to reconcile it with their idealised images of the Dalai Lama's authority within a homogenous *Gelug* system. Others, by contrast, had a more grounded understanding of the Tibetan system and were able to assimilate the disagreement whilst retaining their devotion for both Geshe Kelsang and the Dalai Lama. Also, at this stage Geshe Kelsang's exclusivism had not reached the extremes that characterise it today. He and his centres were still self-consciously *Gelug* in their identity and they continued to receive visiting teachers of the *Gelug* tradition, although these were decreasing in frequency. Furthermore, his centres – with the possible exception of the Madhyamaka Centre – continued to venerate the Dalai Lama and support Tibetan cultural and political activities. In the years leading up to the creation of the NKT in 1991, however, the character of Geshe Kelsang's centres would undergo further shifts that many of his students would find increasingly difficult to assimilate.

The dispute with the Office of the Dalai Lama appears to have led to a further hardening of Geshe Kelsang's exclusivism. The content of the Dalai Lama's talks, in particular, would have been anathema to Geshe Kelsang. In these talks, not only does the Dalai Lama undermine the practice of *Dorje Shugden*, but he also discredits Phabongkha Rinpoche, the main *lama* through whom Geshe Kelsang traces his lineage, *and* encourages an 'unbiased and eclectic' approach to Buddhist practice. The combination of these perspectives appears, in light of the subsequent shifts encouraged in his centres, to have strained Geshe Kelsang's personal devotion for the Dalai Lama to breaking point.

The crystalisation of the NKT

Early in 1987, Geshe Kelsang began a three-year meditative retreat in Dumfries, Scotland. He invited a *geshe* from *Ganden Shartse* monastery in South India, Geshe Losang Pende, to teach the General Programme in his absence, whilst Geshe Konchog Tsewang continued to run the Geshe Studies Programme. During this period, Geshe Kelsang's centres continued to receive visiting Tibetan *Gelug* teachers, including Jamyang Rinpoche and Geshe Tamdrin Gyatso (b. 1922), another *Ganden Shartse* graduate whom Geshe Kelsang had installed as resident teacher at his Spanish centre, Instituto Dharma. The visit of Lama Zopa Rinpoche to Manjushri Institute in 1988 is significant, indicating the ongoing devotion of the students to this *lama* and their desire to leave the negativity of the schism with the FPMT in the past. More significant to our understanding of the development of Geshe Kelsang's thought and the direction of his centres, though, are the visits in 1988 and 1990 of Venerable Choyang Duldzin Kuten Lama, the oracle of *Dorje Shugden*.

As is the case with most protective deities, *Dorje Shugden* is believed to take possession of more than one human medium. The most popular and famous human mouthpiece for this deity (both in Tibet and in exile) was probably the figure known as Venerable Kuten Lama (b. 1917). As a young monk, Kuten Lama studied in a branch monastery of *Ganden Shartse*, in the region of *Phagri*, that had been founded by Geshe Palden Tendar, whilst also making occasional visits to a monastery established by Tromo Geshe Rinpoche. Both of these figures were closely associated with the cult of *Dorje Shugden*, especially the latter, who despite living as a solitary Tantric hermit and thus representing the shamanic modality of Tibetan religiosity, nevertheless adopted an attitude of sectarian intolerance towards non-*Gelug* traditions. From the age of 17, Kuten Lama began to experience a number of violent seizures, and after a period of careful observation and examination by the high *lamas* of *Ganden Shartse* (including Trijang Rinpoche, Song Rinpoche and Zimey Rinpoche), it was finally determined that the possessing being was *Dorje Shugden*.[17] It was at this point that he became known as Kuten Lama, '*kuten*' meaning 'the body that holds the *Dharmapāla*'. For the next twenty years, he served as the oracle of the *Dharmapāla*, for both monastic and lay Buddhists who sought divine assistance. From 1950, he resided in *Lhasa* before fleeing into exile in 1959, accompanied by Zimey Rinpoche and guided safely away from danger through oracular divination. Kuten Lama first settled in a refugee camp in Buxaduar before moving to Mundgod in the south of India, taking up residence at the re-established *Ganden Shartse* where he continued to fulfil the important spiritual function of oracular divination for the exiled Tibetan community.

During his trips to Britain, Kuten Lama visited all of Geshe Kelsang's centres – at this time there were about a dozen – in order to enhance their commitment to *Dorje Shugden* and to perform special rituals 'dedicated for the success of each centre and for the spread of the Dharma in the West'.[18] His visits are significant for a number of reasons. First, as well as being the oracle of *Dorje Shugden*, Kuten Lama also happens to be Geshe Kelsang's uncle. An understanding of the centrality of *Dorje Shugden* reliance to Geshe Kelsang would be incomplete if, alongside exclusively orientated interpretations of *Gelug* Buddhism, the importance attached to continuity in Tibetan kinship systems was not also acknowledged as an important determining factor.[19] Secondly, Kuten Lama's association with the re-established *Ganden Shartse* monastery, a connection that is also noticeable in Geshe Kelsang's choice of *geshes* to visit and teach in his centres, is significant. The links with *Ganden Shartse* connected Geshe Kelsang to the main source of resistance within the exiled *Gelug* community in India to the Dalai Lama's pronouncements on *Dorje Shugden* reliance. Thirdly, Geshe Kelsang's period of retreat was also a time in which he worked out and gradually introduced into his centres the foundations that characterise the NKT today. It is unlikely that he would have embarked upon the process of constructing and implementing a distinct identity for his centres without employing the assistance of oracular divination.

The first major development that took place during Geshe Kelsang's retreat was his introduction of the 'Teacher Training Programme' (TTP) at the Manjushri Institute, a course of study that reflected the programmes being taught by Neil Elliott at Madhyamaka Centre. It required the kind of focused approach that Geshe Kelsang expected from his York students but which some students at the Institute seemed to lack due to their more open and inclusive orientation. By introducing the programme, he expressed his growing exasperation with his Manjushri students and an intention to bring them into line with the style of practice found elsewhere. One long-standing disciple at the Institute reflected that the introduction of the TTP entailed 'going from a passive to an active involvement', whilst another explained how 'there was a hardening up of expectations and commitments' at the Institute.

The TTP differed from earlier programmes taught by Geshe Kelsang at the Institute in terms of scope, duration and the level of commitment required. Originally designed as a seven-year course, it embraced a wider range of subjects and texts than the General Diploma and included topics that had previously been the preserve of the Geshe Studies Programme. Thus, whilst students were encouraged to attend other teachings to deepen their understanding and receive oral transmissions, there was actually little need to attend the Geshe Studies Programme. The TTP also differed from earlier study programmes in that it revolved around commentarial materials produced exclusively by Geshe

Kelsang in the form of published texts and unpublished transcripts. Whilst there was continuity at Madhyamaka Centre in terms of the structure and discipline of the TTP, students there recalled the textual emphasis as a novel development. The publication of teachings had always been a feature of Geshe Kelsang's life in Britain and, in 1985, Tharpa Publications was set up by a disciple of his primarily for this purpose. This activity became particularly important to him at this time and was to play a central part in his unfolding vision of the NKT.[20] By giving his study programmes a textual basis, Geshe Kelsang not only provided accessible materials to enhance the focus and commitment of his students, but also laid down structures through which spiritual authority could later be concentrated exclusively in him.

Three new texts by Geshe Kelsang were published between 1984 and 1988: *Buddhism in the Tibetan Tradition: A Guide* (1984), *Heart of Wisdom: A Commentary to the Heart Sutra* (1986), and *Universal Compassion: A Commentary to Bodhisattva Chekhawa's Training the Mind in Seven Points* (1988). In terms of orientation and style, these texts were contiguous with his earlier publications. The inclusion of notes and bibliographies referring to other *Gelug* authors indicated his continuing inclusivism and self-identity as a member of the contemporary *Gelug* sect. The commentaries continued to be organised and presented in a traditionally clerical way according to highly structured textual outlines. The wish to contextualise the teachings through Western-based analogies and examples was still very much in evidence, but Geshe Kelsang continued to show little interest in the project of adaptation. In certain respects, his teachings became, if anything, even more uncompromising and literalistic than before. For example, compared to Geshe Rabten and Geshe Ngawang Dhargyey's *Advice from a Spiritual Friend: Buddhist Thought Transformation* (1977), a commentary upon the same mind-training exercises as outlined in *Universal Compassion*, Geshe Kelsang's book placed a greater emphasis upon ideas like karma and rebirth, the six realms of existence, and the notion that, through meditating on taking and giving, physical illnesses like cancer can be cured. Two themes that were beginning to characterise Geshe Kelsang's presentation during the mid-to-late-1980s, and which later became defining features of the NKT, can also be discerned in *Universal Compassion*: an emphasis upon spreading Buddhism, and the importance of relying upon Dharma-protectors. Unlike the discussion of *Geshe Chekhawa* in *Advice from a Spiritual Friend*, Geshe Kelsang presented this famous *Kadampa geshe* as a missionary figure who spread the study and practice of mind training throughout Tibet. Since *Geshe Chekhawa's* root text on mind training encourages *Mahāyāna* trainees to make offerings to protective deities in order to be free from any interference when practising, it is of no surprise to find comment upon such practices in both *Advice from a Spiritual Friend* and *Universal Compassion*. There is a noticeable difference, however, in the emphasis placed upon protector-deity reliance in the two commentaries, with Geshe Kelsang going into more detail about its function and importance.

At this stage in the development of Geshe Kelsang's network, students were not required to rely on him exclusively. Many students clearly did, but he had not yet made it an absolute requirement within his centres. His perspective had yet to harden further, and the decisive shift appears to have taken place shortly after he came out of retreat in 1990 when he began to introduce new and radically exclusive policies within his centres. He had come to believe by this time that he had a central role to play in the preservation of *Tsong Khapa's* tradition in the modern age. The substance of the various reforms he implemented, therefore, was that the students within his centres were now to rely exclusively upon him for their spiritual inspiration and welfare. He was gravely concerned that the purity of *Tsong Khapa's* tradition was being undermined by the lingering inclusivism of his Western students, many of whom continued to seek spiritual inspiration from non-*Gelug* sources. This was something about which he had been outspoken for some years, but he now acted more forcefully in his opposition to it by discouraging his students both from receiving guidance from teachers of other traditions and from reading their books. Consequently, the library at Manjushri Institute, which was well known for its vastness and diversity, and which had been a testimony to the inclusive orientation of the Institute's students, was gradually purged. This began with non-*Gelug* books being removed, but as Geshe Kelsang's vision crystalised, even books by *Gelug* teachers became unacceptable to him and the library disappeared altogether. He thus became convinced that the Tibetan *Gelug* tradition as a whole no longer embodied *Tsong Khapa's* pure teachings and that he and his disciples must therefore separate from it. From this point onwards, Tibetan *Gelug lamas* would no longer be invited to teach within his network. This perceived degeneration extended to include its highest-level *lamas*, and so even veneration of the Dalai Lama was now actively discouraged.

Owing to the extent of their exclusivism, these measures were resisted throughout Geshe Kelsang's network. In particular, the removal of pictures of the Dalai Lama from the *gompas* and shrines of Geshe Kelsang's centres was found particularly disturbing. One NKT disciple recalled how

> There was a time when centres were not encouraged to have pictures of the Dalai Lama. We used to have pictures of the Dalai Lama and so on a lot in the centres [...] A lot of people had a great affection for the Dalai Lama, and respect. They asked about it, and some people were unhappy about it. It was explained that the Dalai Lama is not our guru. We have received no teachings from him [...] Geshe Kelsang is our root guru. There was some unhappiness.

By this stage, however, the authority of Geshe Kelsang was at its pinnacle and he was unambiguous and uncompromising about the reforms he wanted to implement. Furthermore, the reforms, though extreme, resonated with the exclusive approach to practice that was already being adopted by most of his centres. There was, predictably, most resistance to the reforms at the Manjushri Institute, particularly amongst the students who were closest to Geshe Konchog Tsewang. However, these students were a minority whose numbers dwindled even further when, following his retreat, Geshe Kelsang became outspoken against the Geshe Studies Programme and made the pursuit of his new programmes compulsory. As it was no longer possible for students to follow the programmes of both *geshes*, the basis of Geshe Konchog's teaching programme at the Institute was undermined, and in 1991 he retired to *Gyuto* monastery in Assam, India.

It is worth considering at this point the possible influences upon Geshe Kelsang that may have prompted him to adopt such a radical position following his retreat. It is evident that his outlook had become increasingly exclusive throughout the 1980s, but the reforms he introduced in 1990 were discontinuous in terms of their degree. Until this time, he may have disapproved of the inclusive approach to spiritual practice adopted by Western students but he did tolerate a certain level of openness. Also, though critical of certain strands within his tradition, he still self-consciously identified his centres as 'Gelug' and as part of a broader grouping of Tibetan and Western elements loosely united by their doctrine and devotion to the Dalai Lama.

The Dalai Lama's decision in the late 1980s, to make his views about *Dorje Shugden* reliance publicly known, may have contributed to Geshe Kelsang's decision to break away completely from the *Gelug*, prompting him to reassess his relationship with the Dalai Lama and to defend his own position.[21] According to one NKT disciple, *Dorje Shugden* reliance became increasingly important in Geshe Kelsang's centres

> in response to the fact that things were appearing in print, in certain English language publications, which seemed to present one, or a view of this protector practice, which was regarded as not quite fair, distorted.

Unsurprisingly, then, one of the first texts published by Geshe Kelsang following his creation of the NKT in 1991 was *Heart Jewel* (1991), his commentary to *Dorje Shugden* reliance, now promoted as the 'essential' practice of the NKT.

Geshe Kelsang's teaching tour of North America, following his return from retreat in 1990, is seen by some students as *the* significant formative event that led to his adoption of a radically exclusive position. During his tour of America he visited centres of other *Gelug lamas*, such as the centre under Geshe Lhundup Sopa's guidance in Wisconsin, and was very shocked by what he observed. He found that there was a widespread tendency amongst Western students to combine the teachings and practices of different Tibetan traditions and that, following the advice of the Dalai Lama, Tibetan *Gelug lamas* themselves were tolerating and sometimes encouraging this. In particular, the observation that *Dzogchen* techniques were being combined with *Gelug* practices appears to have provoked a particularly strong reaction from Geshe Kelsang. As a clerically and exclusively orientated *lama*, Geshe Kelsang would have been most vehemently opposed to the influence upon the *Gelug* of the *Nyingma*, the tradition which is furthest from *Tsong Khapa*'s structured system both philosophically and in terms of its meditational technique.[22]

To summarise, the creation of a text-based programme of study formed part of the gradual hardening of Geshe Kelsang's approach and indicates that he was beginning, during the time of his retreat, to conceive of a distinct structure and identity that would unite his various centres. But it was not until some time after he had returned from his retreat in 1990 that he introduced the radically exclusive reforms that characterise the NKT today. It appears to have been his tour of America that cemented this way forward, convincing him that the purity of *Tsong Khapa*'s tradition was under threat from all sides and that its preservation in the modern world required extreme measures. The purpose and character of his emerging 'New Kadampa Tradition' had thus been defined and largely implemented by the end of 1990. It should also be noted that there were important practical and material conditions that enabled his vision to be implemented. Earlier studies indicate that the success of Buddhist organisations depends largely upon their control of influential institutional sites for the propagation of Buddhist discourse, and this is equally true here. As noted earlier, the Manjushri Institute legally remained part of the FPMT until late 1990, when the assets of the Institute finally fell under the control of the Priory Group. The flowering of Geshe Kelsang's ideological vision in 1990 therefore dovetailed with the Priory Group's successful attempts to secure the institutional basis of Manjushri Institute. Once the material basis had been secured, the ideological vision embodied within the NKT could unfold unimpaired.

The creation and announcement of the NKT

In the spring of 1991, Geshe Kelsang Gyatso announced the creation of the 'New Kadampa Tradition', an event celebrated in the pages of *Full Moon* magazine as 'a wonderful new development in the history of the Buddhadharma'.[23] The NKT was created to unite the centres already under his spiritual direction – at that time there were approximately eight residential centres and twenty non-residential branches – within a common organisation. This organisation would enable the centres to 'cooperate in spiritual matters on a more formal basis' whilst providing them with 'a distinct identity within the wider Buddhist world'.[24] He also created the Education Council of the NKT, the purpose of which was to provide spiritual assistance for NKT centres, ensure the purity and authenticity of their education programmes, coordinate special events, and oversee the setting of examinations. It was also to provide resources for the promotion and opening of new centres throughout the world, especially outside the United Kingdom, by operating the New Centres Development Fund, the fund-raising arm of the NKT.

Geshe Kelsang announced the creation of the NKT to his centres by sending them a letter inviting them to become members of his 'world-wide family' and outlining the conditions of affiliation. One disciple described how

> Geshe Kelsang sent a letter to all the centres asking them if they wanted to be part of the tradition. If they did then Geshe Kelsang wanted them to accept a couple of things, such as that Geshe Kelsang would be the Spiritual Director; that when Geshe Kelsang dies it will be Gen Thubten Gyatso; that the study programme would be the NKT study programme; that each centre would appoint a Director and Education Programme Coordinator.[25]

In 1992, these conditions were formalised when the NKT became a charitable organisation and its member centres adopted a common constitution, reflecting their shared and exclusive endeavour to preserve and promote

> the pure tradition of Mahayana Buddhism derived from the Tibetan Buddhist meditator and scholar, Je Tsongkhapa, introduced to the West by the contemporary Tibetan Buddhist lama, Geshe Kelsang Gyatso Rinpoche, and embodied in the three study programmes: the General Programme, the Foundation Programme and the Teacher Training Programme.[26]

By the close of 1992, then, the NKT was established ideologically, structurally and legally, its centres being united by their 'shared devotion to our precious Founder' and 'a strong commitment to practising the pure Dharma he has taught us'.[27]

Although most of his centres accepted the terms of affiliation, there was a degree of resistance amongst the students of some, and at least one centre – the Amitayus Centre in Nantwich, Cheshire – decided to sever its association with Geshe Kelsang completely due to its inability to accept his new and radical exclusivism. Most NKT students recall the creation of the organisation in positive terms, however, stressing that the new and exclusive emphasis upon the authority of Geshe Kelsang and his study programmes gave the centres an energy and focus that was previously lacking, eliminating the confusions, conflicts and disagreements that are inherent to a more open and inclusive approach. One disciple explained that the creation of the NKT

> caused some bad feeling and people left in a huff, but in the end it was the right decision. For example, we're setting up a centre in Blackburn now and we're not having half the problems that we had in Preston, because in a way you're a bit more blinkered. And in some ways that's a

good thing because it stops you from straying off into blind alleys. Having seen what went on in Preston I know what to avoid, what's important, and so we're just concentrating on that and it does save a lot of aggravation.

The creation of the NKT in 1991 certainly marked a 'new development in the history of the Buddhadharma' inasmuch as it drew together within a single organisation, with a distinct identity and structure, the individual units that looked primarily towards Geshe Kelsang for spiritual guidance. As our prior examination of the early history of the organisation in Britain makes clear, though, the 1991 declaration was in many ways simply the culmination of a line of development that can be traced back to the early 1980s. Furthermore, to fully understand both the early history and the later identity of the NKT – the distinctive features of which are examined in the next chapter – we must situate them within the broader historical and cross-cultural context of *Gelug* Buddhism, the divisions between exclusive and inclusive *Gelug* orientations, and specifically the manifestation of this debate through the practice of *Dorje Shugden* propitiation.

4

THE IDENTITY OF THE NKT

Introduction

The focus of this chapter is the self-identity of the NKT. A preliminary discussion about the dynamics of history and identity construction within new religious movements (NRMs) provides a framework for analysing the multiple 'histories' that exist on an individual and public group level within the organisation. The organisation's rhetoric of decentralisation is contextualised against the history of institutional conflict detailed in the previous chapter. Key elements of the NKT's sense of self-identity, such as its emphasis on purity and exclusivism, are examined in detail, and the extent to which they affect the movement's orientation towards expansion, adaptation and engagement is considered. The NKT's reliance upon the controversial protective deity *Dorje Shugden* is also discussed, and its high-profile participation in a dispute concerning this practice that erupted in 1996 both in India and in the West is outlined. In conclusion, the NKT is presented as a contemporary Buddhist movement that is rooted firmly within traditional *Gelug* exclusivism but which simultaneously reflects and reacts against the conditions of modernity.

History and identity construction in the NKT

The dynamics of history construction in NRMs have been examined by Coney (1997). A history, she argues, is not a complete version of events or narrative whole but, rather, a socially negotiated and partial representation of the past that is subject always to revision and modification. History construction involves the highly selective ordering and reordering of social memory and the equally important process of collective forgetfulness, or 'social amnesia'. Emerging new religions, in fact, contain diverse individual, public and 'small group' histories, which appeal to each other for legitimation and reinforcement or compete for dominance. Specific elements of the history of a movement are remembered, concealed or forgotten for a variety of reasons, both accidental and deliberate. Memories can be retrieved and evoked through structures intended to facilitate recall such as myth, artefact and ritual, or they may vanish due to the turnover of a group's membership. They can also be consciously erased through the realignment and control of the group's leadership as it strives to repress an 'uncomfortable Other' or iron out discontinuities 'in favour of a strong, continuous storyline':

> Most often, what is forgotten is forgotten because it no longer fits in with the current version of events, especially one constructed by an elite group. Sometimes, indeed, unwelcome memories are systematically destroyed by leaderships.
>
> (Coney 1997)

Leaderships exclude memories by expelling individual malcontents or by simply not referring to unwelcome historical facts until they 'cease to be part of the group repertoire of memories'. Changing the name of the leader or group also allows memories associated with previous designations to fade whilst promoting the creation of new memories. The project of deliberately excluding histories, however, is not always completely successful because repressed memories 'can return to haunt the margins of a discourse and continue, despite their apparent absence, to influence its structure'. Alternatively, competing versions of events may only become temporarily submerged within the dominant account and may later 'rise again to the surface of the collective memory'.

The NKT is a religious movement in which the dynamics of history construction, as outlined by Coney, are well exemplified. Multiple 'histories' exist on an individual and public group level both inside and outside the movement. As the pre-history of the group is rooted in conflict and schism, the social organisation of memory and forgetfulness, especially by the group's leadership, is particularly striking. Accounts of current and former members either reinforce or contradict and compete with each other. They diverge widely over points of historical detail and often interpret the same events and processes in very different ways, reflecting a wide range of personal experience, depth of involvement, bias, opinion and loyalty. At the level of public discourse, the history and identity of the NKT has also, during the course of its development, undergone considerable realignment. Of course, such revision and reconfiguration of the past is commonplace within religious movements that are more concerned with issues of identity and ideology than with notions of historical veracity.

It is important that the observer looking at the NKT today accounts for the substantial pre-history of the movement's emergence in Britain, examining carefully the forces that influenced Geshe Kelsang's thought and the direction of his centres in the years preceding the NKT's announcement in 1991. Otherwise, there is a danger that the pre-history of the group might be (mis)placed within a narrative of continuity; that is, understood as if the features characterising the organisation today were *always* part of its outlook. Such anachronistic readings of the group's history are not uncommon among both NKT disciples and non-NKT Buddhists alike, who often place the group's emergence into a simplified teleological narrative, albeit for quite different personal and ideological reasons. Other disciples retain a greater awareness of the complexities of the group's historical emergence in spite of the leadership's attempts, at the public level of discourse, to eradicate certain 'unwelcome memories' of discontinuity and conflict by presenting an overarching narrative of continuity.

Individuals who are most likely to place the NKT's emergence within an overarching narrative of continuity fall within two main groupings: on the one hand, certain long-standing students within the Foundation for the Preservation of the Mahayana Tradition (FPMT) whose dealings with Geshe Kelsang and the Manjushri Institute terminated in the early 1980s; and, on the other, current NKT disciples whose involvement does not pre-date the formation of the organisation in 1991. Both groupings tend to lack an adequate awareness of the historical development of Geshe Kelsang's emergent network during the 1980s, and their very different backgrounds and personal experiences ensure that their assessments are poles apart.

The conflict between Geshe Kelsang and the FPMT in the early 1980s provoked feelings of anger and disappointment amongst many FPMT students, feelings that remain unabated today. These students often explain the emergence of the NKT in terms of the desire for power and prestige that, they believe, motivated Geshe Kelsang first to attempt to 'seize control' of the Institute and eventually to 'steal' it from its mother organisation. The origin of this drive for power is variously explained – as a result, for example, of the excessive devotion he received, upon arriving in England, from naive and undiscriminating Western practitioners; or as a product of his 'extreme envy' of Lama Yeshe, who was formerly a junior student to him in *Sera Je* monastery but who had now become the key personality behind a growing worldwide network of centres. The emergence of the NKT is thus described as the growth of a 'personality cult', orchestrated by a 'totally unscrupulous rogue geshe' through the 'cynical manipulation' of students and the 'transference of [their] loyalty and devotion' via the practice of *guru* devotion.[1]

Current disciples of Geshe Kelsang whose association with him is relatively recent also tend to place the NKT's emergence within a narrative of continuity that bypasses its actual historical development. These disciples, who usually have little or no awareness of the early history of the organisation, assume that since Geshe Kelsang is an 'enlightened being', the creation of the NKT had always been his intention. They tend to explain the years preceding 1991 as a period in which he carefully and deliberately planned, prepared and laid the foundations for the later organisation. This approach to the NKT's historical development reflects the dominant narrative that has been publicly promoted by the leadership of the organisation. The 'official' version of the NKT's history has been reluctant to admit that Geshe Kelsang's thought has undergone considerable development and change during his time in the West. It has also, in Coney's (1997) terms, repressed the 'uncomfortable Other' of the Institute's conflict with the FPMT, ironing out the discontinuities in favour of 'a strong, continuous storyline'. Promotional literature produced by the organisation has tended to concentrate mainly on the organisation's post-1991 development, keeping discussion of its early history brief and in line with its current identity, whilst making no references at all to the FPMT. The renaming of the Institute as Manjushri Mahayana Buddhist Centre in 1991 also facilitated the NKT's project of consciously forgetting its FPMT roots. These attempts to write the FPMT out of its group history is an aspect of the NKT's identity that current FPMT members, particularly those who had actively supported the early development of Manjushri Institute, find particularly objectionable.

The attempts of the NKT's leadership to eradicate unwelcome memories of discontinuity, conflict and schism by promoting a simplified, continuous and sanitized group history have been only partially successful. Whilst the accounts of recently recruited disciples reflect this dominant public-level narrative, it is not always replicated by longer-standing NKT students, many of whom were disciples of Geshe Kelsang at the time of the Institute's secession from the FPMT. Having been involved with the organisation throughout every stage of its early history, these students have a greater understanding of the complexities of its emergence and, in spite of their awareness of the 'official' storyline, tend not to collapse these into a simplified teleological narrative. Although their accounts are naturally biased against the FPMT, a continuing appreciation and respect for the memory and legacy of Lama Yeshe seems to have instilled a reluctance to gloss over their FPMT roots. These students also appreciate that Geshe Kelsang's vision of Buddhism in the West continued to develop significantly during the years following the split, and that the creation of the NKT had *not* always been his intention. A senior NKT teacher thus maintained that before 1991,

> we would have said we were '*Gelugpas*', or belonged to the *Gelugpa* order of Tibetan Buddhism. But Geshe Kelsang decided it was better to make a distinction between our own way of doing things and the way of doing things of the *Gelugpa*.

The NKT's organisational structure

A senior member and long-standing monk of the NKT explained the organisation's structure of authority in the following way:

> The NKT hierarchy is Geshe Kelsang; and then there's a successor, someone who will be the spiritual director of the NKT after Geshe Kelsang passes away; and then there's everybody else, all on the same level really.

Within the NKT, much emphasis is attached to the value and importance of lay religiosity, and in this respect the organisation reflects the broadly 'Protestant' character of its Western cultural context. Except at the very highest levels of the organisation, positions of responsibility, teaching and leadership are as likely to be filled by lay practitioners as they are by monks or nuns. The democratised and laicised nature of the organisation is one of the ways in which Geshe Kelsang is believed to have adapted *Gelug* Buddhism, the most clerical and strictly monastic of all the Tibetan traditions, for the West. Within the NKT, the appropriateness of lay practice applies not only to the *Sūtra* stages of the path, but also to Tantric practice, the form of practice that, according to *Tsong Khapa*, should not be undertaken without a solid grounding of academic study and celibate monastic discipline. The democratised nature of the movement is also reflected in the fact that men and women are regarded as completely equal and are both equally likely to assume positions of leadership and responsibility.[2] One NKT monk informed me that Geshe Kelsang deliberately emphasises the *Bodhisattva* vows rather than the vows of monastic ordination in order to cut across the traditional hierarchies – including gender-based distinctions – that are considered irrelevant to Buddhist practice in the West.

Although there are no formal hierarchies within the movement beyond the leader and his nominated successors, NKT centres nevertheless operate according to clear and centrally defined organisational and administrative structures. There is a uniform set of designated roles and responsibilities that, according to NKT guidelines, ensures the smooth and successful running of centres. The division of labour is predicated upon the complete separation of the spiritual and secular, an organisational model which reflects Geshe Kelsang's emphasis on preserving the 'purity' of the teachings by not mixing them with worldly, financial or political affairs. There are three basic positions of responsibility: the resident teacher and the education programme co-ordinator, who jointly oversee the centre's spiritual growth, and the administrative director, who takes care of its legal, financial and material concerns.

When discussing the organisation of the NKT, disciples of Geshe Kelsang dwell at length upon its decentralised and reflexive nature. The organisation is described as a loose federation of independent centres which are 'continuously changing in flavour and character' and which 'have no fixed structure or shape and are in no way exclusive'.[3] Geshe Kelsang is believed to 'encourage looseness and reject centralisation', and so the NKT is not understood as 'a rigid structure, a "movement" in the strict sense of the word', because there is 'no central organisation controlling [the centres]'.[4] These views are interesting in light of the fact that, doctrinally, ideologically and organisationally, the NKT is one of the most uniform and centrally administered organisations on the British Buddhist landscape. Comments about its decentralised and non-controlling nature clearly need to be understood against the background of the earlier conflict between the Manjushri Institute and the FPMT. When praising Geshe Kelsang's vision of the NKT, the organisational feature most often singled out is the fact that whilst his affiliated centres are united spiritually through their shared constitution, they remain legally and financially independent. One student explained how 'all the centres that are under the banner of the NKT are autonomous, which in the previous organisation they hadn't been'. This organisational structure also means that within the NKT 'there's no mixing of politics and religion, or money and religion'. The mixing of religion, politics and money was one of the main charges that Geshe Kelsang levelled against Lama Yeshe during the earlier dispute. As we have seen, the NKT has striven to consciously forget this conflict by writing the FPMT out of its historical narratives. The way in which the NKT understands and articulates itself organisationally nevertheless represents an example of how repressed memories 'can return to haunt the margins of a discourse' and continue to influence its structure.

Purity and impurity

Waterhouse rightly observes that a fundamental element of the NKT's self-identity is 'the notion of the purity of Geshe Kelsang's lineage and the importance of maintaining that purity in practice' (Waterhouse 1997: 151). According to the literature of the organisation, Geshe Kelsang united his centres as the NKT 'in acknowledgment of their pure lineage from Je Tsongkhapa',[5] and the explicit constitutional aim of the organisation is to preserve and promote this pure lineage as it has been handed on by Geshe Kelsang via the organisation's three-tier study structure. This is based exclusively upon the teachings contained in his texts, believed by members of the NKT to embody the pure lineage in its entirety. According to the teacher at Tushita Centre, Blackburn,

> The NKT is pure Buddhadharma; it isn't invented in any way, it's just as if Buddha Shakyamuni revealed it [...] So I guess you could say from that point of view that there is nothing better to be found. And that is the defining characteristic of the NKT: it's pure Dharma, everything else is a distraction. That's the core of it, the important thing about it. Everything else is just the icing on the cake.

The lineage represented by Geshe Kelsang is considered to be 'pure' because it has not been mixed with or diluted by the teachings of other traditions. One disciple explained the notion of purity as follows:

> You may have one pure tradition and another pure tradition. If you mix them what you get is a mish-mash without any purity and you have destroyed two traditions. So we're very strict on keeping the purity of the tradition. There is nothing invented and nothing taken away. It's completely pure so we can rely on it.

Geshe Kelsang is believed to have faithfully represented the teachings he received from his root *guru*, Trijang Rinpoche, who in turn faithfully transmitted the teachings of his root *guru*, Phabongkha Rinpoche, 'and so on all the way back to Buddha Shakyamuni'.

Critique of contemporary Buddhist practice

Conceptions of time and history within the Buddhist tradition describe an oscillating system involving alternating periods of improvement and degeneration (Nattier 1991). There is a consensus within the textual sources that the universe is currently in the lower reaches of an extended period of decline. Within the Buddhalogical framework, this decline is attributed both to the failings of Buddhists themselves and to the actions of those outside the Buddhist community (e.g. the persecution of Buddhism by secular authorities). According to Nattier, the anticipation of the disappearance of Buddhism within a finite number of centuries has, within much of South, South-East and Inner Asian Buddhism, led to the adoption of

> a fierce conservatism, devoted to the preservation for as long as possible of the Buddha's teachings in their original form [...] Thus the impulse to preservation (and, accordingly, the tendency to deny any change that may actually have taken place) is both understandable and expected.
>
> (Nattier 1991: 137)

The view of time and history presented by Geshe Kelsang and the NKT is traditional in its depiction of a universe oscillating between periods of relative progress and decline. Most attention is given to a specifically *Gelug* framework, which sees *Tsong Khapa* as 'the Second Buddha' (Kelsang Gyatso 1992: 166) appearing to reform and restore the pure teachings of Buddha *Śākyamuni* at a time when they had fallen into decline. History subsequent to *Tsong Khapa* is seen as one of progressive degeneration again, and modern practitioners are encouraged to view their spiritual guide as 'like a second Buddha for us, showing us the path and leading us to liberation and enlightenment' (Kelsang Gyatso 1992: 179).

When discussing the 'internal' causes for the decline and demise of Buddhism, the scriptures most commonly single out factors like the lack of diligent meditation, carelessness in transmitting the teachings, the appearance of false Dharma and the excessive association with secular society. There is no doubt that for Geshe Kelsang and the NKT, the decline of Buddhism in the modern world can be attributed to failings such as these within the Buddhist community. The organisation has, in fact, been outspoken in its criticism of the groups it holds responsible for the modern degeneration of Buddhism, and the two main groupings singled out are Western Buddhist practitioners on the one hand, and the contemporary *Gelug* sect of Tibetan Buddhism on the other.

Although Geshe Kelsang's use of the doctrine of decline is traditional in many respects, the emphasis that he has placed upon the modern degeneration of Buddhism is unusual. Other *Gelug lamas* have not dwelt upon this image to the same degree,[6] or used it so explicitly as part of an overall critique of contemporary Buddhist, and specifically *Gelug*, belief and practice. Geshe Kelsang's use of the image of degeneration is not surprising in light of the strand of Gelug Buddhism that he represents, a current that has defined itself as a bastion of purity against other elements within the tradition that corrupt the teachings with their open eclecticism. His exaggerated perception of the widespread decline of Gelug Buddhism has instilled a 'fierce conservatism' and urgency into the NKT's self-identity as an embodiment and protectorate of Tsong Khapa's pure tradition.

From an NKT perspective, the responsibility for the modern degeneration of Buddhism lies, in part, with Western practitioners, whose habitually open and eclectic orientation towards spiritual practice is believed to have damaged the transformative power of the various Buddhist traditions in the West. The tendency of westerners to 'pick and mix' traditions and create 'a sort of western soup' is regarded by one NKT practitioner as 'the biggest threat [to Buddhism] that westerners have'. The inclusivism of westerners is also believed to pose a specific threat to the continued existence of Tsong Khapa's pure tradition. Geshe Kelsang's books and study programmes are thus believed to have been 'specially written for people in degenerate times'[7] because their structured, systematic and focused nature skilfully responds to the 'handicap' of the Western mind which 'is fickle and finds it difficult to accept tradition' and is 'always wanting to choose bits from here and there, to be eclectic'.[8]

NKT students are often aware of and sensitive towards criticisms levelled against the organisation from outside which reject its approach as unhelpfully restrictive, and can offer well-versed and articulate defences of their more focused orientation. In turn, though critical of Western Buddhist practice generally, they rarely single out specific organisations as embodiments of impure practice. This is partly out of a concern not to speak ill of other Buddhists and partly out of a self-professed ignorance of other Buddhist traditions, a common trait amongst NKT students and a natural consequence of the exclusive approach encouraged by Geshe Kelsang.

The one tradition about which Geshe Kelsang has been explicitly outspoken, however, is the modern Gelug sect of Tibetan Buddhism. During his teachings at the NKT Spring Festival of 1995, he maintained that contemporary Gelug Buddhism was in a state of 'serious degeneration'. This critique is echoed by practitioners throughout the organisation who regularly define the NKT's purity in contradistinction to the impurity of modern Gelug Buddhism. The excessive involvement of monks in Tibetan political affairs and the preponderance of worldly and materialistic motivations are often cited as causes of degeneration. The tendency of Gelug practitioners to 'mix their tradition with other traditions' and the absence of a balanced combination of intellectual study and meditational practice within the sect are also emphasised.

The creation of the NKT in 1991 was thus a schismatic event, marking the formal separation of Geshe Kelsang and his network of centres from the degenerate religio-political world of Tibetan Gelug Buddhism. It was prompted by his radically exclusive belief that the Gelug sect itself had now become a major threat to the continuation of *Tsong Khapa*'s tradition in the modern world, and that he could protect the purity of the teachings only by severing all connections with it. In terms of his criticisms of *Gelug* belief and practice, Geshe Kelsang is firmly rooted within the exclusively orientated strand of the *Gelug* tradition, particularly as it was represented by Phabongkha Rinpoche. However, the fact that *Gelug* exclusivism went to the extreme of establishing a new and independent religious movement can be seen either as an innovation or as a departure from tradition.

Within the NKT, statements declaring the organisation as a modern and 'Western' form of Buddhism abound. In defining the movement in this way, the organisation is not simply maintaining that it represents Buddhism adapted for westerners; it is also striving to underline its separation from the Tibetan *Gelug* sect and emphasise the point that the West – via the NKT – is now the guardian and custodian of the pure tradition of *Tsong Khapa* in the modern world. From an NKT viewpoint, Geshe Kelsang has played a unique role in the transmission of *Tsong Khapa*'s pure teachings, and the organisation and study structures he has created in the West are now believed to protect and preserve a tradition that is all but lost in its indigenous Eastern context. Geshe Kelsang has also underlined the separation between himself and the wider *Gelug* sect through making a number of revisions to the later editions of his earlier publications. Dedications to the long life of the Dalai Lama found in editions of *Meaningful to Behold* prior to the creation of the NKT, for example, are omitted from the fourth edition published in 1994. Revisions made to the list of *Mahāmudrā* lineage *gurus* in the second edition of *Clear Light of Bliss*, published in 1992, are equally revealing. In the first edition, the lineage breaks into two branches from the time of *Panchen Losang Chogyen* (1570–1662) before recombining in Phabongkha Rinpoche, who is followed by Trijang Rinpoche and Ling Rinpoche, the 'current holder of the throne of Ganden' (Kelsang Gyatso 1982: iv). In the second edition, by contrast, a simplified lineage is presented which excises one of the two earlier branches and omits Ling Rinpoche altogether, replacing his name with that of 'Dorjechang Kelsang Gyatso Rinpoche' (i.e. Geshe Kelsang). Long-standing disciples of Geshe Kelsang have not been able to offer a clear explanation as to why he has made these revisions. One possible explanation for the simplification of the lineage has been offered by Paul Williams. He suggests that by retaining the lineage branch which includes the names of several Panchen Lamas, Geshe Kelsang may be creating a lineage and identity that is more closely aligned with the Panchen Lamas and their perceived rivalry with the central government of the Dalai Lamas.[9] Geshe Kelsang's reasons for omitting Ling Rinpoche from the lineage, and for dropping the reference to his position within the *Gelug* hierarchy as the *Ganden Tripa* as well as all references to the Dalai Lama, are more obvious.[10] These omissions enabled him to dissociate himself from the two main authority figures within the *Gelug* monastic system whilst promoting himself as the principal authentic disciple and direct lineage descendent of Trijang Rinpoche and Phabongkha

Rinpoche. These changes must also be seen against the backdrop of the unfolding *Dorje Shugden* dispute of the 1970s and 1980s. Ling Rinpoche, who was from *Drepung* monastery, was not a devotee of *Dorje Shugden*, and at the time of the dispute he naturally sided with the Dalai Lama. Geshe Kelsang was delivering the oral teachings on which *Clear Light of Bliss* is based at the Institute in 1980 at around the same time that the dispute was unfolding in India, and he was probably unaware of these developments as the first edition of the text was under preparation. His exclusion of Ling Rinpoche from the lineage in the second edition, his omission of references to the Dalai Lama, and the direct close association he draws between himself and Trijang Rinpoche thus represent a reaction to the *Dorje Shugden* dispute and reflect a reformulated understanding of the pure lineage and of his role as its present holder.

There are a range of attitudes within the NKT concerning the relative merits of their tradition vis-à-vis other Buddhist schools. Students at the more liberal end of the spectrum acknowledge the existence of other pure lineages and traditions. Whilst the predominant view of the contemporary *Gelug* sect is very negative and critical, even here more moderate views are represented within the NKT. One student attempted to soften the NKT's critique of the *Gelug* by emphasising that Geshe Kelsang

> has always made it clear that this [i.e. the degeneration of Tibetan *Gelug* Buddhism] is only according to common appearance, to what you can see when you go around the monasteries. We don't know what people are doing privately.

At the other end of the scale, there is a sector of the NKT's membership which does consider that the NKT is now the only pure tradition of Buddhism in the world. One of the most extreme representatives of this position described his understanding of the NKT in the following way:

> Spiritually times are becoming rapidly degenerate. It's almost as if the gangplank is being widened a little bit for people to get on the last ship. The NKT is without doubt that final flickering of the candle flame and is the only pure Dharma. This is the only place you can get it, via the NKT. The only place you can get pure Dharma teachings in their entirety. I avoid comparing Buddhism with Christianity like the plague, but it is like Noah's Ark to me. That's the only way I can describe it. This is a select club, really, and the only one worth joining.

Two traditional images that are drawn upon extensively in the construction and articulation of the NKT's self-identity are, first, the disciplined orthodoxy of the eleventh-century *Kadam* order of *Atiśa* and, secondly, the later reforming activity of *Tsong Khapa*. *Tsong Khapa's* reforming activity is mobilised in that Geshe Kelsang is considered to have done in the twentieth century West what

Tsong Khapa did in fifteenth-century Tibet: revitalise, re-establish and repackage the pure teachings of the Buddha in a time of widespread degeneration and decline. Geshe Kelsang himself has drawn this parallel between himself and the founder of *Gelug* Buddhism, and this has encouraged others within the NKT to do the same. Geshe Kelsang's former successor Gen Thubten Gyatso, for example, identified *Tsong Khapa* and Geshe Kelsang as the two great reforming figures since the time of the historical Buddha, appearing during different periods of degeneration to restore his pure doctrine and give it a new and meaningful presentation:

> People call Je Tsongkhapa the Second Buddha, not because he replaced Buddha Shakyamuni but because he restored the essential doctrine of Buddha and showed how it could be practised in impure times. From this viewpoint, we have to say that Geshe Kelsang Gyatso is the Third Buddha, because he has once again restored the essential purity of Buddha's doctrine and shown how to practise it in extremely impure times.[11]

The title 'New Kadampa Tradition' is thus appropriated and used to indicate that the modern *Gelug* sect itself has degenerated and become a source of contamination. Traditionally, this title has functioned as a synonym for '*Gelug*', but Geshe Kelsang employs it to evoke only the discipline and purity of both the early Tibetan *Kadam* masters and *Tsong Khapa* and therefore in contradistinction to the contemporary, and by implication corrupt, *Gelug* sect. Outside the corrupt world of Tibetan Buddhism, Geshe Kelsang is believed to have created a 'Western Pure Land'. Practitioners who are fortunate enough to encounter his teachings regard the establishment of the NKT as the dawning of a 'golden age' for Buddhism.

NKT exclusivism

The importance of cultivating a mind of faith and devotion in a qualified *guru* or *lama* is a fundamental element of all Tibetan Buddhist belief and practice, especially in personal Tantric practice where the *guru* may be explicitly combined and identified with the *yidam* (meditational deity). Teachings on *guru* devotion and *guru-yoga* naturally form an important part of the texts composed by Geshe Kelsang, and his general presentation of this concept is rooted firmly within traditional Tibetan outlines of the *guru*–disciple relationship. His teachings on this subject have, nevertheless, changed and developed during his time in the West and they now incorporate a number of unusual features. The main shift in his thought occurred with the creation of the NKT. Discussions of the *guru*–disciple relationship appearing in his publications from this time reflect an exclusivism that did not characterise his earlier presentation and which is uncommon within traditional Tibetan contexts.

Geshe Kelsang's texts list the traditional qualities that should be possessed by the ideal spiritual teacher, and he encourages students to check these qualifications thoroughly before relying upon someone as a spiritual guide. This attitude of critical enquiry should be retained throughout a person's spiritual career (Kelsang Gyatso 1982: 144). Since the creation of the NKT in 1991, this teaching on the importance of personal authority in negotiating the Buddhist path has been overshadowed by an emphasis upon developing 'unwavering faith and confidence' in the *guru* and upon having faith in the teachings 'even if we do not fully understand them' (Kelsang Gyatso 1993a: 78). The exclusive emphasis on the authority of Geshe Kelsang is also reflected in the texts. The earlier view that practitioners 'must depend upon the advice of experienced guides – fully qualified spiritual masters – and meditate according to their instructions' (Kelsang Gyatso 1982: 180) was replaced following the NKT's creation with the narrower claim that they must 'rely upon a qualified Spiritual Guide and practise precisely according to his or her instructions' (2nd edn: 190). According to Geshe Kelsang, the student must now 'be like a wise blind person who relies totally upon one trusted guide instead of attempting to follow a number of people at once' (Kelsang Gyatso 1991b: 17).

The emphasis Geshe Kelsang placed in his earlier texts upon adopting an exclusive approach to one's spiritual tradition was continued following the creation of the NKT. However, this teaching now took place within the organisational and ideological context of the NKT, and it was combined with the new teaching that one should rely exclusively upon only one trusted spiritual guide. Whereas the injunction about committing oneself to a single tradition was previously an attempt to encourage students to practise only the teachings of *lamas* within the *Gelug* tradition of Tibetan Buddhism, it now became an injunction to practise only within the NKT:

> Experience shows that realizations come from deep, unchanging faith, and that this faith comes as a result of following one tradition purely – relying upon one Teacher, practising only his teachings, and following his Dharma Protector.
>
> (Kelsang Gyatso 1992: 31)

Similarly, whilst the teaching that students should only rely upon teachers who 'share the same lineage and view as our principal Spiritual Guide' (Kelsang Gyatso 1992: 102) is not an uncommon view within Tibetan Buddhism, where *lamas* will often encourage students to study under others who have a similar orientation to themselves, this teaching carried a very specific and untraditional meaning within the context of the NKT. Since students within the organisation have only one spiritual guide, the teaching is in practice an injunction to study only under Geshe Kelsang and teachers who have trained under him. Even the most exclusively orientated *Gelug lamas*, such as Phabongkha Rinpoche and Trijang Rinpoche, do not seem to have encouraged such complete and exclusive reliance in their students as this.

Waterhouse found that sectarian statements between Buddhist groups, including statements made about the NKT, often stem from divergent attitudes towards authority sources and, in particular, from disagreements over the role of 'faith' within practice. Sectarian criticism of the NKT is not limited, however, to those individuals and groups who are sceptical about the role of faith in NKT Buddhist practice. Western Buddhists practising in the Tibetan tradition are often critical of the NKT, not because of its emphasis on faith in the spiritual guide but because of the *exclusivity* of its reliance on Geshe Kelsang. Some regard the NKT as a narrow distortion of the history and practice of *Tsong Khapa's* original *Gelug* formulation. According to one critic,

> *Tsong Khapa* studied Buddhism from all the schools. Consequently, the *Gelugpa* lineage has *Nyingma* and *Sakyapa* teachings in it, going far back [...] Buddhism is a rich tradition because of its diversity. Yes, it may be good to stay rooted in one tradition. But you should stay in your tradition *and* go elsewhere. This is the safer way to practise.

Waterhouse disagrees with the criticism that NKT students blindly follow their teacher, arguing that members of the organisation actually balance the authority of Geshe Kelsang for their practice against their own personal experience of the truth of the teachings. Students do assert that their faith in Geshe Kelsang is not uncritical but is based on sound reasons and experiential confirmation 'just as Buddha had directed his disciples'.[12] Nevertheless, much significance is undoubtedly attached throughout the organisation to the cultivation of pure faith and commitment, and many students appear to develop a deep faith in Geshe Kelsang very quickly, some maintaining that even before seeing or meeting him in person 'I knew for sure that that I had found my Spiritual Guide and my tradition'.[13] Practitioners within the NKT, then, are clearly not uniform in their attitudes towards authority sources; most combine both types of authority identified by Waterhouse, with some attaching greater significance to personal experience and others to faith in the spiritual guide. Perhaps the most common approach is the line encouraged by Geshe Kelsang himself in his more recent publications, wherein practitioners are encouraged to substitute critical enquiry for wholehearted faith and commitment once they have decided upon their spiritual guide and tradition.

In order to obtain spiritual realisations and to ensure that the pure tradition of *Tsong Khapa* remains in the world, NKT students are encouraged to 'practise purely'. This means that they must not mix their spiritual practice – their study, meditation, or *sādhana* recitation and visualisation exercises – with worldly or political activities or with other, non-NKT spiritual teachings. The books and *sādhanas* prepared by Geshe Kelsang upon which all NKT practice is based, and the infrastructure of the NKT organisation itself, are considered to have placed a boundary around *Tsong Khapa's* pure tradition, the survival of which depends entirely upon a widespread diligence in boundary maintenance. As part of the emphasis on pure practice, students within the NKT are discouraged from attending teachings or reading books by other Buddhist teachers and authors. According to Geshe Kelsang,

> If we follow these spiritual programmes we will steadily progress towards enlightenment, but if we try to do everything ourself and read many different books from many different traditions we will just get confused.[14]

The exclusive reliance on Geshe Kelsang encouraged within the NKT is transferred to his texts with the claim that they are 'scriptures, an emanation of the mind of the holy being'.[15] Promoting his books as the spiritual guide is also an effective way in which Geshe Kelsang makes himself available to students throughout the growing NKT network, wherein direct and personal contact with the *lama* – which, as we have seen, has been vital to the growth of Tibetan forms of Buddhism in the West – is very rare.

Most NKT students agree with the exclusive approach encouraged by Geshe Kelsang and believe that, to make progress spiritually, they must rely purely upon one teacher and one tradition. The prescription against reading non-NKT literature, however, is not universally followed by all members. One student continues to read books by other teachers but avoids the confusions and contradictions this is believed to create because 'what I do now is I filter them as I'm reading them'. Another maintained that, whilst he relies mainly on Geshe Kelsang, 'sometimes it's good to have a second opinion'. Other students are stricter in their exclusivism than this and completely bracket out all non-NKT materials from their range of spiritual resources. In explaining their reasons for doing so, however, they often assert that this in no way involves the forfeiture of their personal authority. One student described how she has 'never felt any inclination to look, study or even read a book on any other tradition', and another maintained that 'Geshe-la's books are such a nice parcel, why would you want to look anywhere else?'.

If the objective of an NKT student is to become a pure container for Geshe Kelsang's teachings, the aim of an NKT teacher is to function as a pure 'channel' in transmitting the teachings to others. The ideal teacher is someone who, whilst developing a range of effective presentational techniques, faithfully passes on the content of the teachings without colouring them in any way with their own personal ideas, preconceptions or prejudices. One NKT teacher described his role as 'a talking book' in the following way:

> It's a bit like a parrot in a way, teaching a parrot to talk [...] We're a telephone in a way, or loud speakers, and Geshe-la's teachings come through your mouth. We only say what we've read, so it's not as if we're doing very much really except presenting Geshe-la's ideas.

Other teachers emphasise the importance of becoming an effective 'conduit' by 'getting yourself out of the way'. The importance of faithfully transmitting Geshe Kelsang's texts helps to explain the emphasis in the Foundation and Teacher Training Programmes on thorough textual study, discussion and memorisation exercises. The NKT handbook on teaching skills states that every NKT teacher 'must give exactly the same explanation, otherwise the NKT will disintegrate'.[16]

Whilst personal experience of the teachings is considered important, the dominant view within the NKT is that the main qualification of a teacher is their purity of faith and discipleship. According to one NKT teacher, an individual's lack of experience or 'realisations' is not an obstacle because 'all you need to become a teacher is to have faith in Geshe Kelsang and know your Dharma a little bit'. The *guru-yoga* of *Tsong Khapa*, a practice which involves visualising and absorbing with the *guru* in the aspect of *Tsong Khapa*, is thus regarded as the core component of an NKT teacher's preparations, enabling him or her to teach in an almost oracular fashion as a mouthpiece for Geshe Kelsang. According to Gen Thubten Gyatso, 'there is only one teacher in the NKT, Geshe Kelsang; all the other NKT Teachers are his emanations'.[17] A consequence of this view, one student explains, is that 'giving teachings is like receiving them'.[18]

The missionary imperative

The NKT's self-identity as a source of pure Buddhism in a world of decline and degeneration has instilled a missionary drive within the organisation. The purpose of the NKT, as it has been conceived by Geshe Kelsang, is to ensure the continuation of *Tsong Khapa*'s pure tradition by spreading it all over the world through the creation of Dharma centres and the training of teachers. NKT students in Britain who have encountered Geshe Kelsang's 'doctrine of good fortune' have a responsibility to 'help spread his precious teachings to every corner of the world',[19] by establishing and teaching in centres overseas, by sponsoring and translating his books into non-English languages, or just by supporting the growth of new centres financially.

According to NKT literature, whilst Buddha *Śākyamuni*, *Tsong Khapa* and Geshe Kelsang 'have all introduced the same Dharma into the world', the uncommon contribution of the latter has been 'to lay down the structures to ensure that this precious Dharma will spread throughout the world'.[20] The publishing activity of the organisation is regarded as another key mechanism of growth. Since one of the most common ways in which people are attracted to the NKT is through reading Geshe Kelsang's books, it is considered imperative to publish them in every language and 'get them into every book shop in the world'.[21] Much emphasis is also placed on equipping NKT teachers with effective presentational techniques. Training in teaching skills within the organisation originally took the form of occasional short courses run by Gen

Thubten Gyatso, but it has now been integrated as a regular component of the Teacher Training Programme. A number of passages in Gen Thubten Gyatso's *Notes on Teaching Skills* are revealing about the organisation's missionary ambitions. NKT teachers should 'not worry about converting people at the beginning' but should concentrate instead on building up a supportive environment and a friendly rapport with their group, because

> If we feel that the Teacher understands us and is sympathetic to us, we will naturally feel close to him or her, and keep coming back.

The will to grow and expand is another element of the NKT's self-identity that has met with criticism from non-NKT Buddhists. Ken Jones (1996) is critical of the 'unhealthy' dominance of the Friends of the Western Buddhist Order (FWBO), Sōka Gakkai International (SGI) UK and the NKT on the British Buddhist landscape, characterising these movements as 'forceful and extrovert organisations where recruitment of new members is a major activity'. Others have claimed that the methods of recruitment outlined in *Notes on Teaching Skills* are deceptive and that a deliberate aim of group meditation within the organisation is to 'induce a pleasant trance-like state, in which the critical faculties are dimmed' so that the meditator 'becomes increasingly suggestible to group doctrine'.[22] Geshe Kelsang's response to such criticisms is that every organisation 'tries to attract more people with appropriate publicity' and that Gen Thubten's advice 'is free from any intention to trick or manipulate people'.[23]

The NKT has become sensitive to outside criticism on the subject of expansion and maintains that its emphasis on spreading NKT Buddhism is not 'empire building' but stems from a pure motivation to benefit others. The growth of the NKT, according to one student, 'is not something I see coming from the NKT's side':

> The NKT don't just get a map of the world and stick a pin in it and say, 'We'll send a teacher there' [...] I think there is a policy to support growth. But it's not like missionary activity, because the whole essence of Buddhism is that it is requested.

It is clear that the rapid expansion of the NKT since 1991, both in Britain and around the world, has been the result of a combination of both pull and push factors, as this student suggests. However, her characterisation of the organisation's proselytisation style as low-key clearly understates the 'push' element of the equation. Indeed, during 1995, a map of the world replete with pins indicating the presence of teachers and centres *was* displayed in Manjushri Centre to celebrate the global expansion of the NKT and to encourage students to contribute to the organisation's fundraising endeavours. The transplantation of NKT Buddhism around the world was energetically reported and the progress towards the eventual goal of creating an NKT centre in every British town was charted within the pages of *Full Moon* magazine up to 1997.

Following the creation of the NKT in 1991, the number of NKT centres began to rise dramatically, and there are currently over four hundred centres – the bulk of which are non-residential – represented in thirty-six countries. The overseas growth of the NKT has been concentrated mainly in North America and Spain, although inroads have also been made into South America, Australia and the rest of Europe. The number of NKT centres around the world provides a fair reflection of the pace and the extent of the movement's growth. They are not necessarily an accurate indicator, however, of the NKT's size in terms of its membership. According to NKT sources in July 1996, the number of individuals who regularly attended NKT activities did not exceed more than 3,000 people worldwide.

Engagement and dialogue

Owing to its emphasis on maintaining the purity of the teachings by not mixing them with worldly or political concerns, the NKT has displayed little interest in engaged Buddhist activities. The organisation is believed to have a beneficial influence on society, but the main way in which this is achieved is through the growth of Dharma centres, since 'the experience of pure Dharma is the only effective method to solve human problems'.[24] NKT centres are characterised as 'Bodhisattva communities' which are slowly transforming the wider world into a 'Bodhisattva society' by making the pure tradition of *Tsong Khapa* available. Students who have attempted to stir the NKT into a more direct form of social engagement than this have met opposition from others within the organisation. An article in *Full Moon* encouraging centres to practise 'sustainable Dharma'[25] prompted a critical response from another student who, in the following issue, maintained that training the mind and purifying karma is more important than 'rearranging the furniture of samsara'.[26]

During the first seven years of its development, the NKT displayed no interest in interfaith activities or dialogue with other Buddhist groups.[27] This deliberate distancing and separation from other groups was another consequence of the great emphasis attached to preserving the purity of the tradition. When asked about the reasons behind the organisation's decision not to participate in forums of dialogue such as the Network of Buddhist Organisations (NBO) (UK), students replied that such activities would be 'a distraction from the main aim of attaining enlightenment for the benefit of all living beings' and that, even though Buddhists engaging in dialogue may think they are talking about neutral issues, the eventual result of interaction with other Buddhist teachers and traditions would be the degeneration of the teachings. Having experienced cross-Buddhist dialogue in the past, one senior teacher within the organisation had come to believe very strongly that such activities were confusion-creating and even un-Buddhist:

Insofar as an organisation helps to get the Dharma across, pure Dharma, that's fine. But if it's something else, to build bridges between Buddhist societies and so forth, the question is, 'Well what does that do?'. I don't see any need to forge some kind of links as if there's something to be learned from that. There's nothing to be learned from that actually. All the methods to solve problems are found in the Dharma.

Adaptation within the NKT

The NKT's public-level policy towards adapting Buddhism for the West is stated in the preambles to the texts of its founder, who is, of course, the legitimating source of authority behind all adaptations. These claim that Geshe Kelsang

> bridges perfectly the ancient wisdom of the Buddhist faith as practised in his birthplace, Tibet, and the concerns and everyday preoccupations of people in the West.
>
> (Kelsang Gyatso 1993b: backflap)

Geshe Kelsang is considered 'ideally placed' to present Buddhism in a form accessible to westerners because his traditional scholarship and deep meditative experience of the teachings combine with 'a thorough understanding of our Western way of life' (Kelsang Gyatso 1993c: x). The 'essence' of the teachings, it is claimed, is exactly the same as *Śākyamuni* Buddha's and *Tsong Khapa's*, but it has been presented in a form suited to Western thinking and living. To underline this essentialist perspective, a distinction is often drawn by Geshe Kelsang and his followers between 'Tibetan' Buddhism and the Buddhism represented by the NKT, which is variously defined as 'Western', 'Kadampa' or simply 'Mahayana' Buddhism.

The main adaptation instigated by Geshe Kelsang is the emphasis he has placed upon translating the traditional Tibetan texts and *sādhanas*, as well as his own English-language commentaries, into the vernacular of his devotees around the world. Prior to the creation of the NKT, Tibetan language classes were offered in the larger centres within his network and *pūjās* were performed using the Tibetan script and accompanied by traditional musical arrangements. Since 1991, the study and ritual use of Tibetan has been gradually phased out and the musical style has also been modernised. Geshe Kelsang is also believed to have adapted traditional patterns of Tibetan Buddhist practice through his emphasis on sexual equality, the importance of lay practice and the role of the Dharma centre as opposed to the monastery, and by de-emphasising the use of oracular divination. The style of his books and the study programmes he has devised are also cited as major adaptations for the West. The author himself claims that his publications are 'aimed specifically at the twentieth century reader, which makes them much easier to understand and relate to than does a traditional presentation'.[28] Practitioners within the organisation readily reiterate this point and praise his texts as modern, accessible, and compatible with the customs and culture of the West. There is no doubting that Geshe Kelsang's presentation of the traditional *Gelug* doctrine is clear, comprehensive and well structured, and that his followers experience it as such. The style of his presentation since creating the NKT, however, retains all of the clericalism, literalism and conservativism of his earlier publications. Although he continues to use Western analogies and illustrations, some of the statements emerging from within the organisation concerning the 'modernised' and 'Westernised' nature of his presentation – such as the claim that his books address the pace of life on the streets of New York City – seem somewhat exaggerated.

As an alternative to the traditional methods of study within *Gelug* Buddhism, the NKT study programmes represent a more significant adaptation. Unlike the traditional *geshe* degree, which was open only to male monastics, the NKT programmes are open to all, including committed lay and female practitioners. The study of the *Vinaya* has not, as a consequence, been included as a subject on the programmes, and the more technical and analytical dimensions of the *geshe* degree have also been omitted. The exclusive reliance upon commentarial materials produced by Geshe Kelsang is also unusual. The lively tradition of combative and dialectical argumentation and debate within the *Gelug* monastic system has also been eclipsed by a milder emphasis on group 'discussion', the purpose of which is the mutual reinforcement of NKT doctrine and identity.

The NKT's conscious rejection of the 'Tibetan' designation and attendant claim to represent a 'Western' form of Buddhism reflects two aspects of its self-identity: first, it forms part of both its critique of the degeneration of Tibetan *Gelug* Buddhism and its self-identity as a bastion of *Tsong Khapa*'s pure tradition in the modern world; and secondly, it reflects the belief that Geshe Kelsang has adapted culturally alien forms of practice for the West. In a number of significant ways, as we have seen, the NKT does indeed represent an adapted form of Buddhism. However, as Waterhouse has pointed out, in respect of its doctrine, practices, mythology, symbolism and iconography, the Buddhism that is represented by the NKT remains recognisably 'Tibetan' in feel and character (Waterhouse 1997: 178). This traditional character of the NKT stems from the fact that alongside its concern to make Buddhism accessible to westerners, there is an equal if not greater emphasis upon conserving the pure tradition of *Tsong Khapa*. Through writing his books and founding the NKT, Geshe Kelsang is believed to have transmitted a pure lineage to the West and to have created the structures to ensure its continuation in the future. NKT disciples are keenly aware of their responsibility to maintain the purity of this tradition, and the antipathy towards 'mucking the Dharma up' ensures that the project of adapting Buddhism for the West is treated with caution. The relative conservatism of Geshe Kelsang's presentation is also often compared with that of other Tibetan *lamas* in the West who are considered to have over-adapted, and thereby destroyed, the purity of their respective traditions. Chogyam Trungpa is some-times singled out as an example of a *lama* whose 'skilful' adaptation of Buddhism for the West went too far. One student explained how Geshe Kelsang's commit-ment to maintaining the purity of his lineage tempers the project of adaptation within the NKT:

> In a sense it's all very conservative, with a small 'c'. There's no radical re-writing to make it available and attractive to new-age Californians [...] Geshe-la isn't on that end of the spectrum.

An interesting aspect of the NKT's approach is that an aim of Geshe Kelsang's main adaptations is conservation. This dynamic of *conservation through adaptation* is rooted in his critique of contemporary Tibetan *Gelug* practice and of Western eclecticism and the belief that he has re-established the pure tradi-tion of *Tsong Khapa* in the West. The adaptation of using the English language and of abandoning the study and ritual use of Tibetan, for example, not only makes the practice of Buddhism by westerners easier but also reinforces the belief that *Tsong Khapa*'s pure tradition is now located and conserved in the West through the NKT's English-language publications and will be transmitted to future generations primarily by westerners. In a similar way, the NKT study programmes were not only formulated to make the study and practice of Buddhism structured, systematic, and therefore clear and accessible to west-erners. The explicit objective of the programmes is the protection and preservation of *Tsong Khapa*'s pure tradition. By focusing upon one teacher and restricting the practice of Highest Yoga Tantra to that of the meditational deity *Vajrayoginī*, the programmes counteract the dangerous tendency of Western practitioners to follow multiple teachers, mix spiritual lineages and accept more Tantric commitments than they can realistically handle. Practitioners within the NKT commonly formulate the Buddhist path in terms of the dictum 'one *guru*, one *yidam* and one Dharma-protector'. This represents a point of contrast with Buddhist practice within the wider Tibetan Buddhist world and within Western-based organisations like the FPMT. Geshe Kelsang considers the open and inclusive approach to Buddhist practice adopted elsewhere to be incompat-ible with the continuation of the pure tradition of *Tsong Khapa*, and it is for the purpose of protecting and preserving this tradition that he formulated the NKT study programmes.

Dorje Shugden reliance

A key component of the NKT's self-identity – indeed, its 'essential practice' – is its emphasis upon *Dorje Shugden*. In line with the Phabongkha tradition, Geshe Kelsang presents *Dorje Shugden* as the principal protector of *Tsong Khapa*'s tradi-tion, maintaining that he has now replaced the traditional supramundane protectors such as *Mahākāla* and *Kālarūpa*. He also affirms the enlightened nature of the deity, portraying *Dorje Shugden* as an emanation of Buddha Mañjuśrī. Phabongkha's combination of this protective deity with *Gelug* exclusivism is also continued by Geshe Kelsang, who has emphasised that *Dorje Shugden's* protection and blessings will only be received by students who practise Kadampa Buddhism purely, without mixing.

Whilst the view of *Dorje Shugden* within the NKT represents a traditional strand of *Gelug* thought and practice, Geshe Kelsang has also veered from the traditional position in significant ways. The *extent* of his exclusivism has gone much further than that of Phabongkha and Trijang Rinpoche, and this has had an important effect upon the way in which *Dorje Shugden* is understood. Whilst Phabongkha's revival movement was spearheaded *within* the *Gelug* school, Geshe Kelsang's view of the decline of 'pure' *Gelug* practice led him to adopt a more radical position and to opt out of the *Gelug* altogether. He claims that the NKT has only been able to re-establish and propagate the pure tradition of *Tsong Khapa* throughout the West through the power of the deity:

> The Dharmapala has renewed Kadampa Buddhism. But, for specific reasons, he changed the place where Kadam Dharma will flourish.[29]

Whilst his exclusivism is more extreme than that of his predecessors, the sectarian excesses of Phabongkha have not been replicated in Geshe Kelsang's public-level teachings. In this respect he is closer to Trijang Rinpoche who prioritised the devotional element of the practice. The traditionally violent imagery is retained in the NKT's ritual invocations, which request *Dorje Shugden* to 'subdue immediately all traitors, enemies and obstacles who cause harm or injury' (Kelsang Gyatso 1993d: 32, 60). Such references to the 'enemies of Buddhism' here, however, must be seen within the context of Geshe Kelsang's commentary, which does not ascribe the same kind of violent partiality to *Dorje Shugden* that was present in Phabongkha's texts (Kelsang Gyatso 1991a: 96). Phabongkha's punitive characterisation of the deity does not form a part of Geshe Kelsang's presentation either. The *Dorje Shugden sādhana* does contain passages wherein the practitioner restores broken commitments by confessing to having 'mixed and polluted' the pure teachings with 'incomplete or false teachings' (Kelsang Gyatso 1993d: 41–42), but there are no passages akin to those in Phabongkha's texts which state that the deity will cause madness or shorten the lives of those with inclusive tendencies.

The final way in which Geshe Kelsang's presentation of *Dorje Shugden* differs is in terms of the deity's ontological status. Phabongkha and Trijang Rinpoche both promoted *Dorje Shugden* as a fully enlightened being who assumes the appearance of a worldly and boastful deity. A sectarian element to a protector practice, we will remember, only makes sense if the deity is regarded as a mundane and therefore partial being. This being so, Trijang Rinpoche's de-emphasis of the sectarian element is understandable in light of the increased emphasis he gave to *Dorje Shugden's* enlightened nature. Geshe Kelsang takes the elevation of *Dorje Shugden*'s ontological status another step further, empha-sising that the deity is enlightened in both essence *and* appearance:

> Some people believe that Dorje Shugdan is an emanation of Manjushri who shows the aspect of a worldly being, but this is incorrect. Even Dorje Shugdan's form reveals the complete stages of the path of Sutra and Tantra, and such qualities are not possessed by the forms of worldly beings.
>
> (Kelsang Gyatso 1991a: 94)

For such an unequivocal affirmation of the enlightened nature of the deity to remain doctrinally consistent, there is no room for a sectarian element.

As Geshe Kelsang's uncle and the oracle of *Dorje Shugden*, Kuten Lama has been an important figure in the NKT. Oracular divination seems to have been influential in Geshe Kelsang's decision to create the NKT, and the visits of the oracle around the period of the organisation's formation certainly galvanized the energy of the centres and enhanced their commitment. His subsequent visits from *Ganden Shartse* monastery in India were also big events, and he attracted large gatherings of NKT disciples wherever he went. Oracular divination, nevertheless, was never a regular feature of the NKT's spiritual activities and has not received any detailed coverage in Geshe Kelsang's texts. There are a number of possible explanations for the generally marginal position occupied by the oracle in the organisation. A pragmatic reason is that Kuten Lama's monastic base is in South India and this made him inaccessible to the daily life of the Western-based NKT. The self-identity of the NKT as an independent and 'Western' Buddhist movement offers a second explanation. The organisa-tion's relationship with Kuten Lama, and through him with the re-established *Ganden Shartse* monastery, problematised its self-proclaimed separation from the degenerate religio-political world of Tibetan Buddhism, and as a consequence the profile of the oracle within the NKT was kept low. The fact that whilst Kuten Lama was allowed to give religious discourses in NKT centres during his 1996 visit no translation from the Tibetan was provided underlines the point that the ongoing relationship with the oracle posed an ideological complication for the organisation. Thirdly, one senior student ascribed Kuten Lama's low profile to Geshe Kelsang's attempt to make Buddhism more accessible to the West by gradually dispensing with the 'culturally exotic' phenomena of oracular divination altogether. Finally, the oracle may have been marginalised by Geshe Kelsang because his presence raised a doctrinal ambiguity for the NKT. According to traditional Tibetan teachings, none of the high-ranking supra-mundane protective deities 'would condescend to interfere with more or less mundane affairs by speaking through the mouth of a medium' (Nebesky-Wojkowitz 1956: 409). The notion of oracular divination may thus have been problematised for Geshe Kelsang in light of his portrayal of *Dorje Shugden* as a fully enlightened being.

The controversy surrounding *Dorje Shugden* reliance had been a potential threat to the NKT's stability ever since the practice was popularised during the mid-1980s. Geshe Kelsang and his network of centres have received criticism from other westerners practising in the Tibetan tradition who, having become aware of the contentious dimensions of the practice, have most commonly sided with the Dalai Lama. The dispute first threatened to become public in Britain in 1985 when the Buddhist Society's journal *The Middle Way* published a book review by the *Nyingma* teacher Michael Hookham that commented upon the contentious dimensions of *Dorje Shugden* reliance.[30] This article appeared in print at around the same time that Geshe Kelsang was beginning to raise the profile of *Dorje Shugden* reliance in his main centres, and Manjushri Institute remonstrated indignantly with the Buddhist Society about its negative portrayal of the practice. In 1995, the dispute resurfaced again in the form of a lengthy polemical debate on the Internet.[31] The discussion by NKT Buddhists of the *Dorje Shugden* teachings and empowerments granted at the NKT Spring Festival by Geshe Kelsang provoked criticism from Western representatives of various Tibetan Buddhist traditions who, following the line of the Dalai Lama, objected to the propagation of the practice because of its associated sectarianism. The ensuing exchange in effect re-enacted the earlier Dharamsala dispute as defences of the treatises composed by the opposing sides of that earlier conflict were articulated in a way that, interestingly, even imitated the style of traditional Tibetan polemics.

Following the dispute between Geshe Kelsang and the Dalai Lama over the *Dorje Shugden* issue in 1986, the leadership of the movement adopted a policy of silence with respect to the contentious dimensions of the practice, withholding information and discouraging any discussion of it. The importance attached within the NKT to following the teachings of only one *guru* and to remaining within the boundaries of one's spiritual tradition also effectively insulated many members from hearing about the controversy from external sources. Awareness within the NKT about this issue up until 1996 was consequently very limited, partial and rarely well informed. Those who were aware that the practice was contested amongst the different Tibetan traditions often dismissed such disagreements as irrelevant distractions and maintained that, since they formed part of the degenerate world of 'Tibetan' Buddhism, they were 'not an issue for the NKT'. The policy adopted by the NKT's leadership to withhold information and limit awareness about *Dorje Shugden*'s contentious nature has also provoked external criticism. Many outside the organisation, like the critic quoted below, argue that Geshe Kelsang has acted unethically by allowing many of his disciples to commit themselves to a controversial practice without being in possession of all the information they require to make a reasoned and informed choice:

> The hub of the whole issue for me is the fact that anyone can worship whatever they want, but they should be doing this with some knowledge about it. If the practice is controversial, then new practitioners should be made aware that it is controversial.

Crisis and response: the *Dorje Shugden* affair

The recent history of the NKT has been characterised by conflict and contro-versy resulting from its participation in a Western-based campaign mounted against the Dalai Lama concerning his opposition to *Dorje Shugden* reliance amongst *Gelug* refugees in India. This conflict of authority, which had been simmering beneath the surface of the exiled Tibetan community since the late 1970s, erupted publicly in the spring of 1996 when the Dalai Lama began to voice his opposition to *Dorje Shugden* reliance with a greater sense of urgency. He began to state in more explicit terms that continued reliance on this protector not only harms the individual propitiator but also endangers the person of the Dalai Lama and undermines the political cause of Tibet. His government-in-exile thus initiated a programme to subdue *Dorje Shugden* propi-tiation amongst government employees and *Gelug* monasteries. In response, *Dorje Shugden* supporters in India created an organisation, the Dorje Shugden Devotees Charitable and Religious Society, to protest against the Dharamsala administration and to canvas international support for their campaign. The Dalai Lama's pronouncements, they claimed, actively suppressed their spiritual traditions and violated their right to the freedom of religious expression. The suggestion that the Dalai Lama himself might be guilty of human rights abuses against people who have suffered greatly at the hands of the Chinese generated interest beyond the Tibetan community, and the dispute was taken up by Indian media agencies.[32] The interest of the British media was also awakened when British Buddhists joined the fray, taking the dispute with the Dalai Lama onto the streets during his visit to England in 1996. Leading articles on the campaign appeared in the *Guardian*, the *Independent* and the *Daily Telegraph*, alongside BBC television and radio coverage.

The cause of *Dorje Shugden* supporters in India, and the reputation of devo-tees around the world, was taken up by sympathetic westerners who formed a pressure group, the Shugden Supporters Community (SSC), and mounted a campaign to coincide with the Dalai Lama's European tour of 1996. The campaign generated media attention through issuing news releases and press packs, including documentary 'evidence' of the Dalai Lama's undemocratic actions and human rights abuses.[33] It also organised public demonstrations both before and during his visits to England and Switzerland and participated in debates on various Internet discussion forums. The NKT played a leading role in this campaign. Geshe Kelsang encouraged his disciples to participate in the SSC demonstrations in June outside the Office of Tibet and the Buddhist Society in London. Furthermore, he also made the uncharacteristic decision to grant newspaper and BBC radio interviews himself in which he passionately condemned the Dalai Lama's pronouncements. For these activities, the NKT received harsh criticism and the SSC was presented by the media as a front for the NKT to pursue a 'smear campaign' aimed at sabotaging the Dalai Lama's morally impeccable image in the West without implicating itself.[34] The NKT and SSC rejected this charge, claiming they were separate groups with overlapping interests.[35] According to NKT sources, the weekly attendance of 3,000 people at NKT activities made it a tiny contingency of the SSC, which represented 'the union of many groups and individuals who worship Dorje Shugdan throughout the world (4 million people altogether)'.[36]

The NKT withdrew from the campaign completely and the office of the SSC ceased to function shortly after the Dalai Lama's return to India. Geshe Kelsang's students maintained that they had done all they could to further the cause of Tibetan *Dorje Shugden* worshippers and now felt that the campaign had to be fought mainly in India. The organisation's rhetoric of eschewing political involvement was invoked and the issue was dropped as quickly as it had been taken up. The Western manifestation of the dispute thus simmered down, although the potential for it to be reignited would remain as long as *Dorje Shugden's* Western followers and the Dalai Lama were irreconciled. This, of course, depended largely upon events within the Tibetan exile community, where the conflict between the staunch *Dorje Shugden* faction of the *Gelug* and the administration of the Dalai Lama showed no signs of abating. The most recent developments in the *Dorje Shugden* controversy, as played out both in India and in the West, and the extent of the NKT's involvement in them, will be discussed later. We will concentrate here on the significance for the NKT of the initial outbreak of the dispute in 1996.

The eruption of the *Dorje Shugden* controversy in 1996 was the first time this dispute, along with the deep-seated divisions it exposes, had been expressed publicly and in a Western context. The significance of this was analysed by commentators mainly in political terms, in that images of conflict and disunity harm the Tibetan cause whilst any suspicion raised about the Dalai Lama's moral character plays directly into the hands of the Chinese. It is also seen as significant in terms of its detrimental impact both on the 'peace-loving' image of Buddhism in the West and on the Western Buddhist community itself, which generally holds the authority of the Dalai Lama in the highest esteem. I want to focus here, however, upon the significance of the NKT's involvement in this dispute in terms of its stability, public image and self-identity.

On one level, the organisation's participation in the campaign was a pragmatic response to counteract the potentially negative effect of the Dalai Lama's pronouncements on its internal stability and future growth. The public manifestation of the dispute was the first time that the majority of NKT members, many of whom had commitments to practise *Dorje Shugden* reliance daily, became aware of its controversial nature. This situation of heightened awareness demanded that the organisation's leadership adjust its policy and publicly defend its 'essential practice' and reputation. Speaking to the *Independent* (15 July 1996), Geshe Kelsang thus stated that

> If [the] Dalai Lama [is] right, then up to now, this practice we have done for 20 years, everything [is] wasted: time lost, money lost, everything lost. That is the big issue.

The raised awareness about this controversy did not appear to cause great fragmentation within the NKT's membership. NKT disciples were generally receptive to the main criticisms of the Dalai Lama by the SSC campaign – namely that his pronouncements against *Dorje Shugden* rejected his root *guru* Trijang Rinpoche and abandoned his spiritual lineage – because they resonated with the NKT's central emphasis upon faithfully following the pure lineage-tradition of one's spiritual guide. Criticisms of the Dalai Lama's eclecticism and 'mixing of politics with Dharma' were equally well assimilated by students who had adopted the NKT view that Geshe Kelsang alone has revealed the Buddha's path completely unmixed with other paths. The majority of NKT students therefore supported the SSC campaign and many participated in it actively by writing letters of protest or by attending street demonstrations.

A number of students were clearly distressed about being in conflict with the Dalai Lama. For some, the respect and admiration they felt for him could not be reconciled with the proactive stance Geshe Kelsang had taken. Others severed their connections with the NKT completely after reappraising their spiritual loyalties in light of information that was now circulating in the public domain on the history and nature of the controversy. Most of those who were upset or troubled by the dispute, however, seemed to successfully resolve their concerns and remain committed NKT practitioners. Some did this by marginalising the importance of the controversy and by prioritising their spiritual practice. A degree of discomfort was evident even amongst the students who were most active and supportive of the SSC campaign. One student interpreted the Dalai Lama's actions as a 'skilful means', designed to turn people towards the NKT, the only source of pure Buddhism remaining in the world:

> My understanding is that the Dharma is dead, as far as Tibet is concerned and the rest of India is having the same problem [...] So the Dalai Lama is acting like a doctor in a hospice, nursing it to its death [...] He has thrown down the challenge and given people the opportunity to focus in on what is left of the Dharma, which is essentially the NKT.

The NKT's involvement in the dispute also had ramifications for its public image given the general popularity enjoyed by the Dalai Lama amongst Buddhists, non-Buddhists and media agencies. As Waterhouse observes, the organisation is 'very good at marketing its product' (1997: 142). It advertises its teachings and classes using various forms of media, including the local and national press. The attention attracted during the *Dorje Shugden* dispute, however, bore little resemblance to the positive, promotional kind to which the organisation had hitherto been accustomed. The SSC and the NKT were successful in their attempts to court the British media, but the publicity they generated backfired on them, and their allegations against the Dalai Lama were never really taken seriously. A brief analysis of the media coverage of the *Dorje*

Shugden dispute in Britain echoes the findings of previous research into journalistic bias towards 'new religions' in America and Australia, the key points of which are summarised by Richardson:

> the media are often not an objective, passive medium in social conflicts, but instead promote an ideologically dominant status quo, [a] hegemonic approach to issues [...] media become actively involved in creating an unfavourable and deviant image of social movements and their members (especially leaders) [...] on many occasions media appear to function as 'moral entrepreneurs' [...] and as institutions of social control that marginalise, delegitimise and discredit oppositional movements.
>
> (Richardson 1996: 290)

The British media were generally dismissive of the claims being made against the Dalai Lama by the SSC and much critical attention was directed towards the NKT itself. Articles in the *Guardian* and the *Independent* negatively portrayed the NKT as a 'cultish' movement that demands 'slavish devotion' to Geshe Kelsang and which cynically manipulates both its followers and the state support system in order to fund its expansion drive. The *Daily Telegraph* (17 July 1996) also bluntly expressed its a priori disapproval and rejection of the NKT's claims. Bias expressed by the British media may thus have had an adverse effect on the NKT's future growth in spite of the adage that 'there is no such thing as bad press'.

According to Geshe Kelsang's students, the main reason for the NKT's participation in the campaign was to put pressure on the Dalai Lama to lift his ban on *Dorje Shugden* reliance and re-establish religious freedom in the exiled *Gelug* community in India. The SSC maintained that it was staging protests in the West on behalf of Tibetan worshippers of *Dorje Shugden*, described as 'spiritual brothers and sisters', and NKT students joined the campaign out of a sense of 'spiritual solidarity'. When rationalised in this way, the NKT's activity seemed to represent a reversal of its self-proclaimed separation and independence from the religio-political world of Tibetan Buddhism. However, Geshe Kelsang's students insisted during the campaign that the NKT's participation in no way indicated a substantive change in its self-identity, emphasising that once the Dalai Lama lifted the ban, the *temporary* alliances established with *Dorje Shugden* supporters in India and around the world would terminate and the NKT would 'get back to normal'.

These claims notwithstanding, the NKT's participation in the campaign indicated a relationship with *Gelug* Buddhism that was more complicated than its rhetoric of discontinuity and separation suggested, and again the importance of adopting a cross-cultural approach to understanding Tibetan forms of Buddhism in the West is underlined. The NKT's activity threw into relief the *ideological* continuities that exist between the NKT world-view and the perspective of *Dorje Shugden* worshippers in India. It also betrayed the *actual* links between the NKT and the exiled *Gelug* community, which at that time endured through the figure of Kuten Lama. As the oracle of *Dorje Shugden*, Kuten Lama indirectly linked the NKT with *Gelug* Buddhists in India because he served both groups. This connection to the exiled *Gelug* community must be acknowledged as an important impetus behind the NKT's participation in the campaign. The visit of Kuten Lama to England during 1996 illustrates this because his presence was seen by some as that of an 'exile', making the campaign more relevant to NKT students whose real responsibility to *Dorje Shugden* devotees in India was made apparent.

As noted earlier, Kuten Lama was a popular figure in the NKT despite his marginal involvement at the level of religious discourse and practice. Consequently, his decision (upon returning to India towards the end of 1996) to sever his connection with the NKT and affirm his support for the Dalai Lama was met by Geshe Kelsang's students with shock and sadness. This development was, like the resignation and disrobing of Gen Thubten Gyatso earlier in the year, a significant blow to the organisation.[37] However, on another level this development partially resolved the ambiguity in the NKT's self-identity caused by its complicated relationship with the *Gelug* tradition of Tibetan Buddhism. In separating himself from the NKT, the oracle simultaneously severed the organisation's links to the exiled *Gelug* community, thereby bringing the NKT's self-proclaimed separation and independence from *Gelug* Buddhism to completion in all but an ideological sense. The same point could also be made about the declaration of Geshe Kelsang's expulsion from *Sera Je* monastic university, issued in the autumn of 1996, for his 'blatantly shameless mad pronouncements' against the Dalai Lama. Geshe Kelsang responded to this vitriolic declaration by reaffirming the NKT's complete independence from the Tibetan *Gelug* tradition in exile:

> I am not upset. I had already stopped my affiliation with Sera-Je twenty years ago and have no intention of renewing it. So I feel this doesn't make any sense.[38]

There was also a perception within the NKT that the oracle's renunciation of the movement actually resolved a further *doctrinal* ambiguity concerning the NKT's central practice of *Dorje Shugden* reliance. Although NKT students were shocked by Kuten Lama's renunciation of their organisation, they also rationalised the separation philosophically. Their opinions on this issue revealed an awareness of the traditional teaching that high-ranking or supramundane protectors (like *Dorje Shugden*) do not condescend to interfere with worldly affairs by speaking through human mediums. The marginal position of Kuten Lama within the context of the NKT's spiritual activities also made it easier for students to relativise his importance within the framework of the organisation. We observed earlier that *Dorje Shugden*'s ontological status underwent a gradual process of elevation from the time of Phabongkha Rinpoche. It may well be the case that the gradual apotheosis of *Dorje Shugden* has finally come to fruition within the NKT.

A rejection of modernity?

A number of scholarly accounts of British Buddhism maintain that the conditions of modernity are reflected in contemporary Buddhist practice. In particular, it has been argued that the reflexive nature of individual identity and the importance of personal authority that characterise post-traditional British society are reflected in Buddhist practice on both an individual and a social level. According to Waterhouse, these processes can be observed within the NKT insofar as members of this organisation (like practitioners within other contemporary Buddhist groups) balance the authority of their own personal experience against the traditional authority structures that are offered. To acknowledge the NKT's 'fit' with modernity, however, provides only a partial explanation of the nature of this movement. Certain aspects of its organisational and ideological structures lend themselves to quite a different interpretation, suggesting that the NKT may actually represent an alternative, critical and reactionary response to modernity.

This way of understanding the movement was first suggested to me by a former follower of Geshe Kelsang who had renounced her discipleship at the time of the NKT's formation, finding the radical new exclusivism of the organisation unacceptable. She had made sense of her own experience of the organisation by drawing upon her expertise as a sociology lecturer and had found Robert Lifton's *The Protean Self: Human Resilience in an Age of Fragmentation* (1993) particularly insightful. Lifton's book offers an examination of how people behaved, experienced and expressed themselves in the late twentieth century, focusing upon their varied responses to the unpredictability, uncertainty and fragmentation of modern society. Lifton maintains that personal identity, or the 'self', has responded to historical dislocation and social uncertainty in two main ways: through either proteanism or fundamentalism. Lifton's concept of the 'protean self' refers to the self's resilience under modernity, its fluidity and many-sided ability to engage effectively, in a spirit of exploration, experiment and improvisation, with the restlessness and flux of contemporary society. With respect to the holding of ideas, the protean self is sceptical and distrustful and 'tends to settle for a pluralistic spirituality that allows for doubt and uncertainty and includes a stress on personal responsibility' (1993: 127). Fundamentalism or totalism, by contrast, represents an opposite response to the same historical forces, reacting against modernity, proteanism and 'the fear of chaos' through 'the closing off of the person and constriction of the self-process' and the demand for 'absolute dogma and monolithic self' (1993: 10–11). Religious and political fundamentalist movements of the late twentieth century, Lifton maintains, 'are generally called forth by a perception that sacred dimensions of self and community are dying or being "killed"' (162). Fiercely defending their 'sacred, literalized text in a purification process aimed at alleged contaminants', such movements generally condemn pluralism and cultural complexity, distrust intellectual and spiritual suppleness, and seek to eliminate spontaneity and unpredictability. Obsessed with chaos and the loss of control, they immerse the self in 'all-or-none ideological systems and behavior patterns', creating a 'mentality of absolute certainty' (161) and providing a protecting, sheltering canopy against protean experimentation, fragmentation and despair.

The disaffected disciple mentioned above interpreted the NKT as a fundamentalist movement that caters to individuals who are 'tortured by choice and confusion', but whose organisational and ideological exclusivism 'in which everything is decided for the member' is fundamentally at odds with her own personal, protean quest:

> What it has to offer to the West is a lack of confusion, and westerners are tormented by confusion. Geshe Kelsang believes that there must be no confusion in the religion whatsoever [...] To me, that seems no different to fundamentalist Christianity [...] To me, my religion is about where does the confusion come from and [what does it] indicate. Confusion is part of the growth process. And if you remove confusion you have a childish religion [...] I wish to be an adult [and] deal with my own confusions as an adult [...] I don't want somebody else sorting out my confusion by not letting me read books that might contradict it.

Although this account reflects the highly subjective feelings and memories of a disaffected disciple, the theoretical framework through which she has made sense of her experiences is in many ways pertinent to our understanding of the NKT. This movement, like those outlined by Lifton, emerged from a perception that the 'pure tradition' was degenerating and dying out in the modern world. The perceived cause of this was, at least in part, precisely the kind of protean inclusivism and pluralism that modern fundamentalist groups stand in opposition against. Geshe Kelsang is believed to have re-established the pure tradition through his English-language commentarial texts and the NKT study programmes. These books present a narrow, simplified and literalised reading of the Tibetan *Gelug* tradition and are, in turn, relied upon literally and exclusively by many devotees out of a concern to preserve the pure lineage. The homogenous organisational structure, the concern to establish a uniformity of belief and practice throughout the movement, and the emphasis on following one tradition coupled with a critique of more open and eclectic approaches towards spiritual practice all resonate with Lifton's characterisation of modern fundamentalism.

Evidence for the mode of being described by Lifton as the 'fundamentalist self' can also be found amongst the accounts of individual NKT members. These are often critical of the dislocated and individualistic nature of contemporary society and portray the NKT as a favourable alternative and counterbalance to the conditions of modernity. According to one student, Dharma centres are crucial during a time 'when traditional concepts of community and society seem to be breaking down, when relationships are becoming increasingly disharmonious, when crime and hostility are rising'.[39] Another maintained that

> Living in a community fulfils social needs I think all of us have and which are almost impossible to fulfil in an increasingly fragmented and individualistic society.[40]

The primary metaphor that is used within the organisation for describing the NKT is that of the family. This image fosters cohesion within and commitment to the group and powerfully evokes the traditional qualities that are considered lacking within modern society. The NKT is presented as a global family, its members are 'the sons and daughters of the same father [Geshe Kelsang]', and events such as the spring and summer festivals are 'family reunions'. Manjushri Centre is the 'mother centre' of the organisation, and when residential centres create satellite groups they become 'parents' and perhaps even 'grandparents'. This manner of self-presentation represents a point of contrast with the FWBO, which has been critical of the collective mentality of the group, including the traditional family structure, as a constraining force on the development of the individual. Bell characterises the FWBO as a 'symbolic community' (1996: 88) and Mellor refers to it as 'a community of individuals' (1989: 321), with both emphasising how this organisation is concerned primarily with individuality and personal self-discovery.

One disciple's view that the NKT provides 'a true refuge for those lost in the wilderness of this uncertain world'[41] is mirrored by the conversion stories of others within the movement. These sometimes take the form of a reaction to historical and social uncertainties:

> You just need to watch the news or go outside and look at the environment. It's getting worse isn't it? Countryside is destroyed. That makes me want to turn to something, and that something is Dharma. You can't escape the terrible things. There's nothing much you can do so you want to turn to something.

A more common life-trajectory presented by NKT practitioners, however, describes a journey from the uncertainties of spiritual pluralism – that is, of 'drifting in and out' of various Buddhist schools but finding only confusion – to an encounter with the NKT which offers the certainty of spiritual progress via a pure tradition, a structured path and an exclusive form of commitment:

I know for myself that having a teacher, a study program, and a specific daily practice has helped me tremendously. In many ways, I've made more progress in the last year than in the nearly 30 previous years of self study.[42]

These accounts chime with the fundamentalist conversion narratives outlined by Lifton:

Fundamentalism announces to the self that its restless protean search for larger meanings and, above all, for immortality systems is over [...] Conversion delivers one from chaos [...] personal perceptions of chaos, along with anxiety over one's own elements of proteanism, can lead directly to fundamentalist conversion.

(1993: 170–172)

In creating the NKT, Geshe Kelsang was reacting to the perceived degeneration of Tibetan *Gelug* Buddhism on the one hand, and the spiritual inclusivism (or protean openness) of Western practitioners on the other. His critique of contemporary *Gelug* practice represents a traditional position of *Gelug* exclusivism that has a long history in Tibetan Buddhism, in both the pre-modern and the modern periods. His critique of Western inclusivism also emerges from the transportation of this traditional approach to the modern West. In light of these historical and cross-cultural continuities between the NKT and exclusively orientated strands of *Gelug* Buddhism, it would be foolish to interpret the organisation simply as a late twentieth-century reaction to the vagaries of modernity. Lifton's theories nevertheless remain helpful to our understanding of the NKT and its members. Geshe Kelsang's traditional exclusivism, as we have seen, has certainly been hardened by his experiences and observations of the modern West. Furthermore, the notion of the 'fundamentalist self' sheds light on why some people convert to this form of Buddhism and how the organisation functions for them. A number of the NKT's longer-standing disciples themselves believe that the appeal and success of the organisation derives from a felicitous convergence between Geshe Kelsang's very conservative and traditional presentation of Buddhism on the one hand, and the desire amongst westerners for a meaningful alternative to spiritual pluralism on the other. One student explained how Geshe Kelsang's conservatism resonates with the psychology of many westerners today, a psychology that no longer shares the exploratory and experimental disposition of westerners during the late 1960s and early 1970s:

Now westerners have a different mentality. They don't have the same emotional turbulence or experience as they had twenty years ago. Nowadays, then, Dharma is very conservative. 'Back to basics' is right for this generation. When the first lamas came over to the West, they were usually outrageous characters, such as Lama Yeshe and Akong Rinpoche. They were the hippies of their culture, and we were the hippies of our's. The next generation, though, are more traditional and conservative.

The view of the NKT presented here is of a contemporary Buddhist move-ment that is rooted firmly within traditional *Gelug* exclusivism but which simultaneously reflects and reacts against the conditions of modernity. The capacity of Tibetan forms of Buddhism to function in this way for westerners has also been observed by other scholars. Tucker's sociological study of Manjushri Institute during the early 1980s, for example, argued that American studies characterising Tibetan Buddhist groups as 'monistic movements' – that is, as movements which embrace the relativism and subjectivism underpinning modern culture – may have over-simplified the reality. The community at Manjushri Institute, she discovered, contained dualistic elements: whilst reflecting modern relativism and subjectivism through its emphasis on such things as scientific methods, individual responsibility and personal authority, the belief system and learning process being advocated was ultimately fixed, absolute and non-negotiable. She concluded that educated westerners are attracted to Tibetan Buddhism because it addresses their concerns about subjec-tive reality, relativism and moral ambiguity in an apparently open and scientific manner whilst actually offering them 'a secure but credible form of absolutism' (Tucker 1983: 222). Bishop's (1993) archetypal analysis, which interprets the concern of westerners with issues of order, guidance and continuity as an expres-sion of the perceived chaos and absence of authority in their own culture, also points to the reactive nature of Tibetan Buddhism in the West.

The FPMT revisited

The conflict with the Manjushri Institute during the early 1980s was a substan-tial setback for the FPMT. The dispute deprived the organisation of one of its most vital nerve centres at a time when Lama Yeshe's global vision was being consolidated. The eventual appropriation by Geshe Kelsang and his disciples of valuable FPMT assets and the differing vision to which they have been put are also considered by many FPMT students as offensive to Lama Yeshe's memory. Nevertheless, the network had the resources to recover quickly from the dispute. It was, in any case, overshadowed by the death of Lama Yeshe, the FPMT's founder and director, in March 1984. The passing of Lama Yeshe continues to be linked, in the minds of many FPMT students, to the 'inauspi-cious' behaviour of the Manjushri Institute.

Just as the NKT's self-understanding was influenced by the conflict between the Institute and the FPMT, the FPMT's organisational structure as outlined in the *Handbook for the FPMT* was clearly shaped by the same event differently interpreted. Directives laid down for the internal running of FPMT centres reflected the contentious dimensions of the earlier conflict. Centre directors thus have a responsibility 'to carry out Lama Yeshe and Lama Zopa Rinpoche's vision' and 'promote awareness of the FPMT within the centre's community'. Permission must be sought from Central Office to open new centres and it is understood that any new branches 'would be a part of the FPMT and as such subject to all the FPMT policies and conditions'. The legal constitutions of FPMT centres should reflect the fact that each centre 'is a part of the FPMT and shall be protected from becoming a part of another organisation, under another Spiritual Head'.

Lama Zopa Rinpoche inherited the role of Spiritual Director of the FPMT in 1984, and one of the most pressing tasks he faced was that of finding his predecessor's reincarnation. After conducting traditional divinations and consulting the Dalai Lama, he finally announced that Lama Yeshe had taken rebirth in the West in the form of a Spanish boy called Osel Hita Torres. In 1991, at the age of 7, Lama Osel (re-)entered Sera Je monastic university in South India to begin a course of study combining traditional Tibetan monastic and modern Western elements that would groom him for (re)assuming his position at the helm of the FPMT.

In the meantime, the FPMT continues to grow and develop under the guidance of Lama Zopa Rinpoche in a way that is considered to be faithful to Lama Yeshe's original 'big vision'. The vision of an interconnected network, developing in a self-conscious and reflexive way, wherein each centre shares a common purpose and sense of responsibility for the whole, is still very much in place. Projects originally implemented or conceived of by Lama Yeshe, such as his plan to build a large statue of the Buddha Maitreya in Bodhgayā, are still given priority within the FPMT. The growth of the organisation has taken place under the guidance and patronage of eminent Tibetan geshes and lamas, and particularly the Dalai Lama, who continues to represent its highest source of inspiration, authority and legitimation. The FPMT remains self-consciously Gelug in identity and strong links are maintained with Tibetan communities-in-exile, especially Sera Je. Support is offered for Tibetan cultural and political causes, and rather than seeing this as purely 'political', the FPMT endorses such activity as the work of Dharma. In terms of its relationship with other groups in the West, the FPMT is a firm advocator of the Dalai Lama's inclusive and inter-faith approach. Jamyang Centre has thus been very supportive of pan-Buddhist initiatives such as the NBO and the Western Buddhist Teachers Conferences in Dharamsala. FPMT Dharma centres also provide 'temporal benefits' such as massage and yoga therapy, and projects such as the Maitreya Leprosy Centre in Bodhgayā and the FPMT hospice centres in Australia also aim to actualise Lama Yeshe's wish that his network should impact beneficially upon its wider society. Such engagement in social welfare activity is also in line with the explicit recommendations of the Dalai Lama, and newsletters from Jamyang Centre include messages from him encouraging the FPMT to develop its work in the social domain, using the Buddha's message and techniques, in areas like education, health and community problems. The variegated FPMT network is thus very different from the NKT, which has separated and defined itself against broader Tibetan currents, has shown little interest in dialogue or social engagement, and which emphasises the creation of Dharma centres for Buddhist education and propagation only, according to the spiritual direction of a single teacher. It could be argued that the FPMT is substantially older than the NKT and that, in time, the latter will become more like the former in terms of its shape and range of activities. In light of the very different ideological visions propelling the two organisations, though, such a convergence seems unlikely. Indeed, in at least one respect, that of educational structure, the opposite seems to be the case. Throughout the FPMT's development, individual centres and *geshes* have enjoyed a significant amount of latitude and autonomy in terms of their spiritual programmes. The organisation has, however, recently attempted to introduce a greater degree of centralisation, standardisation and uniformity into its educational activities.

The NKT's exclusive and focused vision generates rapid expansion; thus, it quickly became a network that in terms of the number and distribution of its member centres far exceeded the FPMT. We must exercise caution, however, when making such comparisons. The FPMT does not share the same energetic will to expand that drives the NKT; rather, it follows a different model of growth that emphasises the consolidation of existing centres more than the generation of new ones. The FPMT's rate of growth in terms of centres established around the world is thus much slower than that of the NKT. In 1984, there were 33 FPMT centres and 8 other projects represented in 13 countries, and there are currently 135 centres, study groups and other projects represented in 31 countries. In terms of the numbers of individual students active around those centres, however, the NKT still has a long way to go before it matches the size of the FPMT. In 1988 – when it had only 41 centres and 6 other projects in 14 countries – FPMT sources estimated that up to 20,000 students were connected to the network.

With respect to the development of *Gelug* Buddhism in Britain, however, the NKT overshadows the FPMT in terms of both the distribution of its centres and the number of its practitioners.[43] The conflict with the Manjushri Institute may not have caused any lasting damage to the development of the FPMT internationally, but the loss of this institutional power base has seriously impaired its growth in Britain. Following the split, the FPMT in Britain was left with the comparatively small Manjushri Centre in London. It continued to develop as the FPMT's British base, and in 1990 it changed its name to Jamyang Meditation Centre in order to distinguish itself clearly from the Institute. Since 1994, Geshe Tashi Tsering (b. 1958), a *lharampa geshe* from *Sera Me* monastic university, has been Jamyang's resident teacher. In 1995, Jamyang entered a new chapter of its history by purchasing much larger premises, the Kennington Courthouse in South London, and since then students have been renovating the building and extending Jamyang's teaching programme and city outreach activities. The move to the Courthouse is indicative of how the FPMT's fortunes in Britain are changing, and it is likely that as Jamyang's activities increase it will become the basis for the creation of further satellite centres. In fact, the FPMT in Britain had already moved beyond a single locality base in 1988 when Shen Phen Thubten Choeling, a retreat centre in Herefordshire, was donated to the London centre; furthermore, a third FPMT centre was inaugurated in Leeds early in 1997.

Part III

THE ORDER OF BUDDHIST CONTEMPLATIVES

5

THE ORDER OF BUDDHIST CONTEMPLATIVES

Background and early development

Introduction: contextualising the OBC

This chapter outlines the early stages of the transplantation of Japanese *Sōtō* Zen Buddhism in Britain by detailing the emergence and development of the OBC, the first Zen movement to firmly establish itself on British shores. The biography of its Western founder, Peggy Kennett (see Figure 5.1), and her relations with the Japanese *Sōtō* sect are discussed, and the emergence and early development of the OBC in America and Britain is charted. The early ideological development of the OBC is examined through an analysis of the writings of Kennett and the assimilation of her teachings within the movement. The relevance of the widely accepted 'Protestant Buddhism' thesis to an understanding of the nature of the OBC is also considered, a critical appraisal of which is long overdue within the academic study of contemporary forms of Buddhism in the West.

To understand the transplantation of Japanese *Sōtō* Zen via the OBC we must contextualise it against the indigenous tradition because, as will become apparent, Kennett's interpretation of *Sōtō* Zen is in many respects representative of the traditional Japanese approach. Besides the normative influence of incoming indigenous traditions, however, the transplantation process is affected by conditions in the host culture and also by trans-cultural processes. To understand the important role played by conditions in the host culture, we must be sensitive in the first instance to the manner in which Kennett's cultural baggage – as an educated English woman, a disaffected Anglican and a passionate believer in sexual equality – shaped her interpretation and presentation of *Sōtō* Zen. The reception of Kennett's presentation by Western sympathisers of a similar cultural hue – that is, her resonances with and appeal to practitioners within the OBC compared to the strong, and often negative, reactions of her critics – must also be considered throughout. To appreciate the influence of trans-cultural processes on the development of the OBC, we must return in Chapter 6 to those modern developments in Zen which resulted from the impact of Western cultural and political forces in Japan.

Figure 5.1 Rev. Master Jiyu-Kennett, founder of the OBC
Source: Reprinted with permission of Shasta Abbey.

The emergence of the Zen Mission Society

I do not intend to simply reproduce the biography of Peggy Teresa Nancy Kennett (1924–96) here because extended discussions of her life can be found elsewhere.[1] The focus, rather, will be upon the aspects of her life that were formative to her thought as a Zen teacher and which help to illuminate the nature and development of her religious movement. Kennett recalls her school days as an important formative time, tracing her beliefs in sexual equality, her disenchantment with Christianity and her initial interest in Buddhism back to this period. After the Second World War, she entered higher education, studying medieval music at Durham University and obtaining a fellowship at Trinity College of Music, London. Although she claims to have 'converted' to Buddhism as a child, she remained a committed Christian into adulthood, believing that her deep calling was to become an Anglican priest. The Anglican Church's policy on female ordination and the sexism Kennett encountered as a church organist contributed further to her growing sense of disillusionment and she eventually renounced Christianity, becoming actively involved with Buddhism, which she believed afforded greater respect and opportunity for women. Her initial interest was in *Theravāda* Buddhism, at that time the most prominent form of Buddhism in England, and she became involved with the London Buddhist Vihara. Kennett also became a member of the Buddhist Society in 1954, and she studied and lectured at the society and even wrote for *The Middle Way* on the subject of music and Zen. Her strong personality would later clash, however, with some of the society's more prominent members, including its founder and president Christmas Humphreys.

During the 1950s, Zen was very much on the upswing within the Buddhist Society. Kennett's attentions gradually shifted away from *Theravāda* Buddhism and she became an enthusiastic member of Humphreys' popular Zen Class. She met and was 'greatly impressed' (Oliver 1979: 180) by D. T. Suzuki, and her view of Zen Buddhism, like that of Humphreys, was strongly tinged by Suzuki's modernist interpretation. More important than her meetings with Suzuki, however, was her introduction, in 1960, to Kōho Keidō Chisan (1879–1967), the chief abbot of *Sōjiji*, the head temple of the *Sōtō* sect in Japan. Kōho Chisan was touring Europe and America and Kennett helped to arrange his visit to England. Their encounter resulted in his extension of an invitation to her to become his disciple at *Sōjiji*, an offer she readily accepted. His tour of the West must be contextualised against the historical and social changes that forced the *Sōtō* sect to reform itself, to open up to the modern world, and to instigate missionary activity, both in Japan and in the West. These 'push' factors combined with important 'pull' factors, including the calls of Japanese emigrants abroad for a priestly representation and the growing Western interest in Zen.

When it comes to reconstructing the trajectory of Kennett's life in the East, we are heavily dependent upon her own diaries from this period. These were revised and edited following her return to the West and were eventually published in two volumes as *The Wild, White Goose* (1977a and 1978). These texts reflected Kennett's progress through the Japanese *Sōtō* system, initially as a trainee in one of its principal monasteries and later as a temple priest. We must remember, however, that as an autobiographer, Kennett was concerned less with historical accuracy than with providing legitimation and identity for herself and her movement. The autobiographical aims and purposes behind *The Wild, White Goose* will be examined in detail later; for the present, we will concentrate upon abstracting the facts from what is largely, to use Kennett's own words, 'a work of fiction' (Kennett 1977a: xi).

Kennett had arranged to visit Malaysia for three months en route to Japan to give lectures and to receive an award for setting a Buddhist hymn to music. She was surprised to discover upon her arrival in January 1962 that arrangements had been made for her to be ordained into the Chinese *Lin-Chi* school. Before leaving for Japan, she received *bhiksuni* ordination from the Venerable Seck Kim Seng, the Chinese abbot of Cheng Hoon Temple in Malacca, receiving the name *T'su-Yu* ('True Friend'). Upon arriving in Japan in April 1962, she was received by Kōho Chisan and admitted into *Sōjiji*, her ordination name changing to its Japanese equivalent of *Jiyu*. The circumstances of Kennett's spiritual career in the East were thus very unusual; few westerners have, like her, 'been formally ordained in both Rinzai and Soto Zen' (Rawlinson 1997: 363), and her admittance into *Sōjiji* as a Western woman in an all-male Japanese monastery was highly irregular.

A major theme of Kennett's diaries concerns the tribulations of her *Sōjiji* experience. Besides being plagued, throughout her time in Japan, by malnutrition and ill health, she 'had to overcome a great deal of prejudice and opposition as a woman and a foreigner' (Morgan 1994: 140). Although the difficult conditions depressed and almost overwhelmed her, she eventually accepted them as aspects of her 'personal *kōan*', the daily realities within which enlightenment must be found. Pursuing her training in this vein led Kennett to undergo a number of unusual religious experiences, culminating with the profound *kenshō* (experience of enlightenment) that, she claims, opened a new and expanded dimension of being to her. This experience also qualified Kennett to begin her ascent through the *Sōtō* priestly ranks. She underwent the ceremony of Chief Junior (*shusōshō*), assuming the role of an elder monk who leads and supervises other monks, and later received the Dharma transmission (*denbō*) from Kōho Chisan, becoming his 'true descendant' within the *Sōtō* lineage and having her understanding publicly authenticated. Like the monks training alongside her, she began to 'acquire the working knowledge of ritual procedures essential to their professional careers as priests' (Foulk 1988: 165) and was later installed as the head priest (*shinzan*) of her own village temple in Mie Prefecture, where she performed religious ceremonies for the local population 'just as if she were Japanese' (Rawlinson 1997: 365). Once she had become established in this role, she underwent the necessary ceremonies authorising her to be a teacher of Buddhism and an abbot of a monastery (*kessei*, or *ango*), and later received, from the *Sōtō* Administration Section, 'my teaching certificate ratifying Zenji Sama's True Transmission' (Kennett 1978: 251).[2] Kōho Chisan himself recognised Kennett as 'my direct disciple [...] one of my Dharma Heirs' (quoted in Kennett 1978: 36) and bestowed upon her the honorific title of *Rōshi* ('elder teacher').[3]

Kennett's training in Japan and the privileges afforded to her by Kōho Chisan must be understood against the backdrop of the post-Second World War status elevation movement of Japanese *Sōtō* nuns. By the time Kennett arrived in Japan in the early 1960s, the most fundamental issues had been resolved, but the nuns had not yet achieved their desired goal of perfect equality 'in which they would be regarded not as secondary or exceptional cases, but as being in the same category as monks' (Uchino 1983: 188). Kōho Chisan was an enthusiastic supporter of this ongoing campaign for equality, and his widely opposed decision to admit Kennett into *Sōjiji* and to promote her rise through the priestly ranks was an important statement in this respect.

Rawlinson correctly observes that the recognition of her inner attainment was just as, if not more, important to Kennett as the formal or external endorsements of her status within the *Sōtō* lineage. Much significance is attached to the ratification of her understanding by the Japanese master Kodo Sawaki (1880–1965), 'the greatest living saint of our school' (Kennett 1978: 87).[4] Furthermore, her spiritual kinship and unity with Kōho Chisan is persistently prioritised over the official stature stemming from the relationship. Although Kennett saw him only rarely, having to 'rely on others, some of whom were not well disposed towards her' (Rawlinson 1997: 364), she describes her relationship with Kōho Chisan in highly intimate terms, mobilising the central Zen symbol of the 'mind-to-mind transmission' to illustrate its deeply spiritual nature.

Another major theme of Kennett's diaries concerns her development of a small, but committed, group of Western disciples. Kōho Chisan had asked her to deal with the increasing numbers of Western visitors to *Sōjiji*, most of whom were tourists from American military bases. Amongst these, Kennett found a much-needed basis of friendship and support, and she developed a regular programme of teaching and meditation to nurture their growing interest in Zen. Whilst her endeavours in this direction were criticised and resisted by some sections of *Sōjiji*, Kennett's project of training westerners had the blessing and support of Kōho Chisan, who encouraged her to 'consolidate them so that I may turn them into a firm body that cannot be broken' (Kennett 1977a: 170) and who later gave her the official title of 'Foreign Guest Hall Master'.

During her final years in Japan, Kennett concentrated upon the development of the *Sōjiji* Foreign Section from her own village temple and made plans to return to the West. She united her American disciples here and shielded them from the hostile elements of the Tokyo temple by sending out newsletters and running meditation retreats. The fate of the Foreign Section was sealed when, in November 1967, Kōho Chisan died and Kennett 'lost the only real support she had in Sojiji and Japan' (Batchelor 1994: 132). From this time onwards, the development of the Foreign Section took place entirely outside the context of *Sōjiji*; westerners were now excluded from the Tokyo temple, Kennett's title of Foreign Guest Hall Master was deleted from the list of *Sōjiji* office appointments, and she made her final visit there towards the end of 1968. The Administration Section of the *Sōtō* sect also began to display a rather ambivalent attitude towards Kennett during these years. Whilst her progress through the ranks of the priesthood had received all the necessary formal endorsements, when she began to ordain and train Western disciples of her own it was reluctant to officially register them. Kennett nevertheless claims that she became, 'in spite of appearances', the official representative of the *Sōtō* sect when, just prior to leaving Japan for the West, she 'received a certificate asking me to become the official pioneer missionary of the *Sōtō* Sect in America' (Kennett 1978: 300).

Kennett's American disciples in Japan had informed her as early as 1965 that they would provide the necessary financial backing for her return westwards. When she finally left Japan in November 1969 to embark upon a lecture tour of the West, then, her first port of call was the west coast of America, where she could both consolidate and build upon this support. The perceived hostility and antagonism of the British Buddhist establishment was another factor influencing Kennett's decision to make America her missionary base. The personality conflicts that had emerged in London during the 1950s escalated considerably whilst Kennett was training in Japan. This development began in 1964 following a request made by Christmas Humphreys to Kōho Chisan for a Sōtō teacher to be sent to England. When Kōho Chisan offered Kennett, his nominated 'Bishop of London', Humphreys replied that she would not be accepted within the Buddhist Society as a Zen master and specifically requested a Japanese male Rōshi instead.[5] In the following year, Kennett was visited by Maurice and Ruth Walshe, also influential within the Buddhist Society. According to Maurice Walshe, their impressions 'were not wholly favourable: we thought there were signs of some imbalance'.[6] Consequently, they returned to England confirming the society's rejection of her. In contrast to the enthusiasm and commitment of her American followers, the deterioration of Kennett's Buddhist Society contacts led her to conclude that 'America presents a much cleaner atmosphere than does the present political scene in England', where 'certain selfish people [...] are anxious that the Truth should be what they believe and not what is necessarily True'.[7]

Shortly after her arrival in San Francisco, Kennett established the Zen Mission Society (ZMS). Committed to the project of transmitting Sōtō monasticism to the West, she set upon creating a disciplined communal environment, ordaining enthusiastic disciples into the priesthood whilst simultaneously building up a supportive network of lay practitioners. Owing to the speed at which the congregation grew, the temple was moved in 1970 to Mount Shasta, where Shasta Abbey was founded as the permanent monastic headquarters of the society. This final move was also motivated by the extent of the 'guru hopping' and 'constant jockeying for position of the religious groups'[8] in and around the Bay Area at that time. In this respect Kennett likened herself to Dōgen, the founder of the Sōtō school, who also, according to tradition, moved his community to the mountains to avoid becoming embroiled in sectarian and political shenanigans.

The increased stabilisation of the ZMS resulting from the creation of Shasta Abbey was enhanced by Kennett's innovative decision to introduce a postulancy programme. This aimed to 'weed out' those who, because they did not appreciate the seriousness and commitment that was required of those wishing to enter the monastic vocation, were liable to 'drop out' of their priestly training. The subsequent years saw the steady consolidation of the abbey and the institutional expansion of the ZMS through the founding of priories in England (Throssel Hole Priory, in 1972) and America (Berkeley and Eugene Priories, in 1973). These were established largely in response to the needs of the lay congregation, the growth of which was assisted by the publication, in 1972, of Kennett's first text on Zen Buddhism, *Selling Water by the River: A Manual of Zen Training*. Released by an independent publisher, this text reached a much wider audience than her later texts which, following the creation of Shasta Abbey Press in 1975, were distributed primarily *within* the ZMS.

The successful transplantation of Sōtō Zen Buddhism in Britain was made possible by the appearance, during the 1960s, of alternative sites of Zen activity outside of the Buddhist Society. In particular, Kennett's contacts with a small, non-sectarian meditation group in Mousehole, Penzance, provided an avenue through which she could organise her return visits to Britain and mobilise support. Mousehole Buddhist Group was the first Zen group to develop an interest in the Sōtō school. In 1967, the group's founder began corresponding with Kennett and helped her to organise, publicise and support her first return visit to Britain in the spring of 1970. During this visit, Kennett lectured and led a number of successful and well-attended *sesshins* (meditation retreats). Following one *sesshin* held at a Gloucestershire farmhouse, twelve people took vows of lay ordination and a further five decided to return with Kennett to pursue a monastic vocation at Shasta Abbey. Included amongst these early British followers were former disciples of the Friends of the Western Buddhist Order's founder Sangharakshita, as well as a few dissatisfied members of the Buddhist Society Zen Class.[9]

Kennett decided to return to Britain again in the spring of 1972, and she sent Daiji Strathern, one of the British monks at Shasta Abbey, ahead of her to make the practical arrangements and to find a suitable base for a permanent monastic training and lay retreat centre. Towards this end, and using funds of his own, he purchased Throssel Hole Farm near Hexham, Northumberland. Kennett arrived in England shortly afterwards and formed the 'British Zen Mission Society', leading the first *sesshins* at the farm which she renamed as Throssel Hole Priory. A monastic community at Throssel Hole was established with Strathern as its prior. The creation of Throssel Hole Priory was a significant development in the history of British Zen Buddhism. It represented the earliest institutional establishment of Sōtō Zen, was the first sign of organised Zen activity in the north of England and was home to the first British monastic community in the Zen tradition.

The visit that Kennett had planned for Britain in the summer of 1974 did not transpire for a number of reasons. Apart from the pressures of commitments in America, her continuing health problems and the financial cost of another trans-Atlantic trip, a situation of conflict had developed between her and Daiji Strathern. This had its roots in the fact that Throssel Hole Priory was not owned by the ZMS. Shortly after the priory was established, Kennett began to feel that Strathern's personal ownership of the property restricted the control she had over the course of its development. She was unhappy with its location and became increasingly critical of the way he was running it. Her decision in the summer of 1974 to open another priory in London thus had a dual function: whilst making Sōtō Zen available to people in the south of England, it enabled Kennett to reassert her authority within the British ZMS. Another factor behind the cancellation of her 1974 visit was Kennett's perception that the

London Buddhist Society was becoming increasingly hostile towards her. Although she gave lectures on *Sōtō* Zen at the Buddhist Society in 1972, she later became convinced that Humphreys had deliberately snubbed her. She thus began to expect an increasingly exclusive commitment from her disciples, encouraging them to adopt a policy of non-participation with respect to other Buddhist groups – especially the Buddhist Society – and severely chastising those who actively sought and nurtured such links. When Kennett's health suddenly deteriorated early in 1976, the stress caused by the 'disloyalty' of these British students was identified by Shasta Abbey as the primary cause.[10]

Kennett considered that the Buddhist Society's rejection of her placed 'a tremendous limitation' on her activities in England, and this was the most important factor behind her decision to settle permanently in America, where she felt 'wanted and loved'. She did not want to 'create political friction by being physically present', but nevertheless regarded the creation of the London Zen Priory as an important statement to Humphreys, 'the Pope of Eccleston Square', that 'we are not afraid to be in the metropolis'.[11] This rather confrontational view, coupled with her complaint that the main problem with Throssel Hole was 'the desire of its inmates to stay in the mountains and not go down to London because of the L.B.S.', represented an interesting reversal of her earlier praise and imitation of *Dōgen*'s retreat from Kyoto to the mountains.

The ideological development of the ZMS, 1962–76

An important theme underpinning the following discussion of the teachings of Kennett and the ZMS is that of the intimate relationship that has existed within this movement between text and context. This theme manifests itself in three ways, the first being Kennett's deliberate engagement with the assumptions, misconceptions and concerns of her Western disciples. As a Western practitioner herself, she was in an excellent position to address the concerns of her followers and was a skilful cultural negotiator. She was aware of the religious and cultural baggage westerners carry with them into their Buddhist practice and of the idealisations and misconceptions that can result, and she sought to meaningfully respond to these. Secondly, in the same way that Geshe Kelsang's exclusivism was hardened by his experience of Western disciples, Kennett's thought also developed in response to the internal dynamics of her religious movement. The dialectical relationship between her teachings and processes within her community is most markedly seen with respect to the innovations emerging from her third *kenshō* experience. Whilst the new ideas and practices emerging within the movement at this time were firmly rooted in her personal experiences, they could only be developed and integrated with the cooperation and participation of her close disciples. Consequently, some aspects of her teachings were not successfully taken up into the movement's general canopy of beliefs but became relatively minor ideas. The ZMS's structure of belief has largely developed, therefore, through subtle interactions between Kennett and her followers and through the degree of 'reinforcement' her ideas received. Thirdly, the relationship between text and context is manifested through the way in which literature functions within the movement. It is clear that Kennett's texts have played an important role, not only because they express – and occasionally revise – right doctrine and practice, but also because of their inspirational, exemplary and legitimative qualities. The journals also function dynamically within the movement. *The Journal of Throssel Hole Priory*, for example, has been central to its development in Britain, providing a medium through which practical and ideological developments are articulated, a public forum within which tensions and conflicts are expressed and resolved, and the means for a geographically dispersed congregation to maintain communication with the centre and express its collective identity.

Kennett's first text, *Selling Water by the River* (1972), was released when she was laying the foundations of the ZMS in the West, creating monastic communities both at Shasta Abbey and at Throssel Hole Priory, and expanding her basis of lay support on both sides of the Atlantic. It became available, then, at a highly fortuitous time, becoming the main textual resource for the teachings and practices of the ZMS during the early period. As well as providing an accessible introduction to *Sōtō* Zen (with an appeal to a wider audience that has not been matched by any of her subsequent books), the text also reflects Kennett's personal spiritual biography and her sensitivity towards a Western readership. Most of the ideas found in *Selling Water* have characterised her teachings down to the present; however, as will become evident, there have also been important shifts and revisions.

The opening chapters of *Selling Water* place Zen within the broader historical and doctrinal contexts of *Theravāda* and *Mahāyāna* Buddhism. The shifting understanding of the Buddha whereby he was regarded first as a historical and later as a 'cosmic' figure, and the development of a pantheon of heavenly Buddhas and *Bodhisattvas*, is examined. Kennett maintains that, unlike Christianity, the Zen way is essentially intuitive and meditative and thereby requires personal spiritual responsibility. Faith is nevertheless important because in order to have this direct, intuitive realisation of universal mind, the trainee must have 'a trust in the heart' (Kennett 1972: 18) or 'the heart of faith' (Kennett 1972: 12).

Her outline of Zen training proper begins with a discussion of the foundational *Sōtō* practice of *zazen*, or sitting meditation. Following the classical *Dōgenist* view that practice is enlightenment, she maintains that meditation is not limited to seated *zazen* but should be expressed in work, in ceremonial and in all of life's daily activities, which are all 'means of doing moving meditation' (Kennett 1972: 33). She also reflects upon the phenomenon of *makyō* in Zen training, hallucinations and visions that are caused by over-asceticism or incorrect posture and breathing. Far from being an indication of spiritual development or holiness, *makyō* experiences – which may include seeing Buddhas and holy beings or receiving penetrating insights – are 'abnormal' psychological states, 'figments of an overstrained mind and thus not truly religious' (Kennett 1972: 27). If one becomes attached to *makyō* experiences, they become a serious impediment to authentic spiritual progress and so they should simply be ignored.

In order to 'bring to fruition the seed of Buddhahood', one must realise great compassion, love and wisdom within one's whole being and exhibit these qualities in daily life (Kennett 1972: 19). The rediscovery of the 'original true self' requires meditation and 'the intuitive understanding which the teacher is always exhibiting to the pupil' (Kennett 1972: 45). Whilst the role of the teacher is crucial, the trainee always remains responsible for his own realisation (Kennett 1972: 45).

Kennett concludes *Selling Water* with a discussion of the meaning of priestly ranks and titles in *Sōtō* Zen. This outline, based upon her experience of *Sōjiji*, reflects the traditional, hierarchical system of *Sōtō* monasticism. Upon returning to the West, Kennett adopted the Japanese model, albeit with a few minor modifications, as the basic framework of ZMS monastic practice. Most of her time is devoted to an examination of the meaning of Dharma transmission, which is central to the identity and legitimation of Zen lineages. At the core of Zen's self-understanding and 'claim to centrality in the Buddhist world' (Reader 1983: 48) is the story of 'the raising of a flower and a smile' (*nengōmishō*), whereby *Mahākāśyapa* received the essence of the Buddha's teaching in a direct mind-to-mind transmission (*ishindenshin*). The *nengōmishō* image underpins the claim that this essence has been transmitted non-verbally to the present through unbroken lines of successive Patriarchs and the attendant characterisation of Zen as a 'teaching outside the scriptures' (*kyogebetsuden*). This belief that the essence of the Buddha's teaching can only be transmitted within the context of the teacher–disciple relationship underpins a complex ceremonial procedure within Zen schools known as 'Dharma transmission', a ritual and institutional requirement that preserves the continuity, integrity, and viability of the teachings and tradition. According to Zen myth and tradition, transmission is given when the disciple has displayed a sufficient degree of awakening, or spiritual realisation. During the ceremony, he is formally received into the lineage of Patriarchs and is accorded the authority to transmit the teachings to others, thus becoming a 'Dharma heir' of his master.

Although *Rinzai* and *Sōtō* Zen both stress the mythic, doctrinal and institutional significance of Dharma transmission, in certain respects their interpretations are very different. In *Rinzai*, the Zen master's 'seal of approval' (*inka shōmei*) is traditionally only granted once the disciple has 'finished the great matter' (*daiji ryohitsu*) of his *kōan* study, whereas in *Sōtō* the 'three regalia of transmission' (*sanmotsu*) 'are given routinely to all monks once they have finished a few years of monastic training and are ready to assume a post as temple abbot (*jushoku*)' (Sharf 1995d: 433).[12] The routine nature of transmission within the *Sōtō* sect can be traced, in part, to a formalistic attitude that became engrained following the seventeenth-century reforms of *Manzan*

Dōhaku, who claimed that Dharma transmission can occur whether or not a disciple is enlightened (*go migo shiho*).[13] Manzan's proposals were resisted by other *Sōtō* priests who represented 'a more individualistic tendency' (Faure 1996: 66) and who argued that 'realization constituted the prerequisite for any real Dharma succession' (Mohr 1994: 362). Sharf has maintained, contrary to this, that the transmission ceremony has never been more than 'the ritual investiture of a student in an institutionally certified genealogy' (Sharf 1995c: 273). Historical and ethnographical evidence, he argues, clearly indicates both the routine nature of Dharma transmission and the fact that it has had 'little if anything to do with verification of any specific "religious experience"' (Sharf 1995b: 42).

According to Kennett's presentation, Dharma transmission within *Sōtō* Zen is not a 'routine' institutional requirement. It represents, rather, the essentially *spiritual* event of joining the 'apostolic line', and it is dependent upon the disciple's spiritual realisation and maturity, which the ceremony serves to confirm and certify. Sharf would probably argue that her presentation reflects modernist images of Zen, confusing 'pious mythology' with 'institutional reality'. Such an assessment, however, would be unfair. The view that spiritual realisation is the essential prerequisite to transmission is, as we have seen, well attested to within *Sōtō* history, and it is not unfeasible that Kennett was awarded transmission upon this basis. Furthermore, she clearly situates Dharma transmission within its traditional monastic, institutional and ceremonial context, presenting it as just one of the steps towards becoming a Zen teacher. Her presentation thus brings the theoretical ideal and the institutional reality of Dharma transmission closer together.

Selling Water by the River is a sound exposition of the self-understanding of *Sōtō* Zen and of the core concepts, teachings and practices that characterise *Dōgen*'s approach to religious training. The intuitive realisation of Buddhahood requires an attitude of selflessness and faith in one's inherent enlightenment. Meditative awakening, or wisdom, forms only part of this realisation that must also manifest itself through acts of compassion and love. The master–disciple relationship, *zazen* meditation, preceptual adherence and ceremonial activity are the central religious forms through which faith and wisdom are developed. *Sōtō* Zen, however, is the path of non-attainment, practice and enlightenment are indivisible, and Buddhahood must be exhibited in the midst of daily life activities. In this text, Kennett thus provided a comprehensive manual of training and a practical context for understanding the translations of *Dōgen*, *Keizan*, and the ceremonial instructions that are included. Her introductory biographies of *Dōgen* and *Keizan* accurately reflect the classical perception of these figures within the *Sōtō* tradition. *Dōgen* was a 'puritanical father' who emphasised the 'hard way' of monastic purity (Kennett 1972: 71–72), whilst *Keizan* was the 'intuitive genius' who 'exploited the temper of the times' in order to expand *Sōtō* and make it available to a wider Japanese audience (161–164). Kennett observes that ceremonial innovation was one method

Keizan used to expand the base of the *Sōtō* school, and she includes ritual and ceremonial activity as a central component of her own presentation. As discussed earlier, Sharf (1995a, 1995b) believes that Zen Buddhism has been widely misunderstood in the West as an iconoclastic, anti-institutional form of spiritual gnosis. Although there are aspects of *Selling Water* that may support his critique, with respect to the formal, institutional and ceremonial dimensions of monastic practice, Kennett's presentation is largely in accord with traditional models of monastic training.

In contrast to *Selling Water*, Kennett's early articles were primarily distributed internally to members of the congregation.[14] As a consequence, they tended to be informal and often highly opinionated, and they generally lacked the technicality and structure that characterised her textual outline. Whilst reflecting the normative position articulated within *Selling Water*, they presented the contours of Zen training using a style and terminology that had a more intimate, personal and practical resonance.

Selling Water described the motivation for spiritual practice using classical terminology, explaining that Buddhism provides a path to the realisation of Buddhahood and the extinction of suffering caused by desire and delusion. In her articles, the discussion of 'why people turn to religion' was less technical and reflected Kennett's interpretation of the conversion process of Western Buddhists. The main motivation, she argued, emerges from a sense of deep dissatisfaction with oneself, the recognition that 'we have made a mess of ourselves'.[15] Kennett sometimes talked of this recognition in terms of an inner prompting of the Buddha within the heart, a 'little voice which says you could do better'. When explaining the nature of Zen Buddhist training, she commonly referred to it as 'doing something about oneself'.

A central theme was her democratising and laicising emphasis on personal responsibility and authority. This appeared in *Selling Water* in her exhortation to practitioners to 'do Zazen and get your own realisation' but was usually expressed in her articles in terms of 'grasping the will'. To 'do something about oneself' requires personal resolution, determination and action, and this is to 'take charge of the will'. This theme can also be detected in her emphasis on having faith 'in the Buddha within our own hearts' and the attendant view that practitioners must not accept her teachings 'on faith' but must test their validity through personal experience. Buddhism was thus depicted as 'a religion for spiritual adults';[16] there is no doctrinalising and each individual must accept the responsibility for the karmic consequences of his actions and for the process of 'cleaning up the mess'.

Faure has examined an important tension within the Zen tradition, contrasting the 'rhetoric of immediacy' of orthodox Zen discourse, wherein all mediations – such as scripture, ritual and moral codes – are theoretically disavowed, with the institutional reality of Zen monasticism that has, in practice, always relied upon these traditional religious forms. He also contrasts the doctrine of emptiness that 'seems to block the path to the imaginary' with the ideology of karmic retribution from which 'unfolds an *imaginaire* made up of rebirths and metamorphoses determined by karma' (Faure 1996: 11). Kennett's presentation of spiritual development was structured around this tension between the immediate realisation of Buddhahood and the need to overcome karmic obscurations gradually through a path of moral discipline and character development. She presented Buddhist training as a process of reorientation and cleansing, of effecting a return to the original and natural state of 'adequacy' by 'transcending the egocentric "I" into the real "I" which is the Buddha Nature'.[17] This entails the acceptance of and repentance (*sange*) for previous sin, the resolution not to perpetuate it any longer and the cleansing of karmic suffering inherited from past existences in order to 'become clean and pure and find the Buddha Nature within'. Whilst the trainee is purified and released from past sin (*matsuzai*) at the moment of repentance, Kennett stressed that grasping the will and taking the precepts at *Jūkai* is only the beginning of the cleansing process. The trainee remains subject to the karmic momentum of his former errors, delusive habits and opinions that must be continually uprooted or cleansed on a daily basis. In fact, it is only when one begins to earnestly train that one realises 'what a mess you're in and what you've really got to do about it'.[18]

Kennett's outline of the preceptual path relied heavily upon an important *Sōtō* text called the *Shushōgi*.[19] The *Shushōgi* was created during the nineteenth century to provide a standardised outline of the sect's beliefs and practices that was accessible to lay people. Believing that *zazen* was too difficult for lay Buddhists, its compilers made the practice unnecessary by developing the notion that preceptual adherence and *zazen* are equally efficacious gateways to *Sōtō*'s 'true transmission'. Reader's survey of modern *Sōtō* literature indicates that the focus of the modern sect remains that of encouraging its lay followers to adopt the precepts, not to practise *zazen*. He also found that the majority of the sect's ordained priests are not interested in *zazen* either; a situation which reflects both the hereditary nature of temple inheritance and the central function of priests within a Japanese socio-religious context as performers of ceremonies relating to the death process. There is thus a discrepancy between the sect's theoretical and constitutional emphasis on *zazen* and its institutional actuality (Reader 1983, 1986).

Kennett's teachings reflected the *Shushōgi*'s central principle that preceptual adherence, like *zazen*, is in itself a complete expression of enlightenment, commenting that the daily application of the precepts is itself 'the finding of *Nirvāṇa* within birth and death'.[20] Nevertheless, in certain important respects she diverged from the teachings of the *Shushōgi* and the contemporary Japanese *Sōtō* sect. Preceptual observance was not promoted, as in contemporary *Sōtō*, as an accessible *alternative* to *zazen*. For Kennett, adherence to the precepts and *zazen* meditation were the two complementary co-essentials of the religious path and must be practised in tandem on a daily basis by priests and laity alike. The emphasis on *zazen* within the ZMS reflects both the Japanese Zen modernist and the late twentieth-century Western perception of Buddhism as a meditative system that focuses on the soteriological goal of enlightenment. Against this backdrop, the primary function of ZMS priests in relation to the Western laity was never to perform ancestral or funerary rituals; rather, it was to provide religious teaching, spiritual guidance and inspiration.[21] Inevitably this also meant that the basis of the laity's financial support of the ZMS's monastic order was quite different to the ritual basis of economic support found in Japan. Bell (1991) found that British *Theravāda* lay practitioners support monks not on the traditional basis of earning merit for a better rebirth, as is widespread in Eastern contexts, but in their capacity as exemplars and teachers of meditation. A similar shift, also rooted in the preoccupation with meditation, has occurred in the transplantation of *Sōtō* Zen to the West. This shift has been observed by Asai and Williams (1999) who found that, unlike Euro-American Zen centres that focus upon meditation and derive their main revenue from programmes related to meditation and Zen study, Japanese American temples are relatively 'zazenless', deriving their income mainly from the performance of death rites and 'Japanese culture' activities.

Aspects of Kennett's Zen

Buddhism and Western culture

Earlier we observed that the relationship between Buddhism and British culture has been analysed by scholars on a number of different levels, ranging from the impact of Buddhism on British society, the appeal of Buddhism and the 'limits of dissent', and the impact of British culture on Buddhism. We also noticed that transformations of Buddhism are not explicable simply in terms of unconscious cultural processes. In addition to cultural interactions on a subtle level – which, scholars argue, lead to transformations that are either 'Protestant' in character or reveal continuities with modernity – Buddhist groups *consciously* develop policies of adaptation to facilitate their acceptance and transplantation. They also exhibit differing degrees of awareness with regard to their relationship with wider religio-cultural trends, some groups being more self-conscious and discriminating than others.

The question of the extent to which Kennett's interpretation and presentation of Zen was informed by unconscious Western religio-cultural values is of considerable theoretical interest. Before we speculate about the influence of unconscious cultural forces, however, it is important to examine Kennett's *self-conscious* relationship with her indigenous context, and the deliberate policies she developed for the purposeful adaptation of Zen for the West. A striking feature of her presentation was her awareness of the subtle levels on which Buddhism and Western culture interact. She believed that as a westerner herself, she had a grounded understanding of the Western psyche, and often reflected upon her own 'conversion' to Buddhism, presuming that her personal experiences had resonance for others. She also attempted to engage with the attitudes, assumptions and idealisations of her disciples which, in her opinion, obstructed their understanding of Zen. She was undoubtedly a skilful cultural negotiator, enabling her disciples to understand the 'cultural baggage' informing their practice and making her presentation effective by responding, in Bishop's terms, to 'the pathologies of the West' (1993: 19).

The spiritual biography of Kennett, whose 'conversion' to Buddhism was prompted by a growing disillusionment with the Anglican Church, reflects a wider pattern. She was aware of the wider 'reactionary' appeal of Buddhism, regularly elucidating key Buddhist concepts in terms of their fundamental – and favourable – differences to those of Christianity. Her articles in particular speak candidly about the reasons behind her embrace of Buddhism and make explicit references to Christianity, against which she airs her grievances without restraint. The 'spiritually autonomous' nature of Buddhist morality, for example, was contrasted explicitly with the heteronomous character of the Christian commandments.[22]

The term 'orientalism' has been coined by cultural critics like Said and Bishop to describe the manner in which the East has been organised, restructured and controlled by the Western imagination. It refers to the mechanism of defining and interpreting the East – and specifically Buddhism – through a 'conceptual filter' that incorporates and reflects the culture and self-understanding of the West. For Kennett, 'orientalism' referred to the tendency of westerners to idealise the religion and culture of Japan and uncritically accept the authority of Eastern teachers. She regarded the idealisation of Asian Buddhist forms as a major obstacle to the spiritual progress of Western students generally and to the acceptance of her teachings specifically. Adopting a thoroughly essentialistic perspective, she criticised the basic orientalist assumption that confuses Japanese culture with Zen, arguing that westerners should positively value their own customs and culture and should express Zen in a Western style. From a Zen point of view, orientalism is a hindrance to spiritual understanding, first because it is based on a misplaced dualism between East and West, and secondly because the aim of Zen is 'to become yourself', and 'if you become a Japanese you are not yourself'.[23]

Kennett's views on the problems of orientalism need to be seen against the context of her uneasy relationship with prominent members of the London Buddhist Society, particularly Christmas Humphreys. By the early 1970s, the conflict had become, at least from Kennett's perspective, an ideological dispute concerning the nature of Zen Buddhism and its transplantation to the West.[24] The energy of her rhetoric against the Buddhist Society indicates the effect on her, emotionally and psychologically, of her perceived rejection. In the first *Throssel Hole Priory Newsletter*, she described the British Buddhist landscape as spiritually sterile, consisting of monopolising 'debating societies' made up of insincere 'dilettantes' who 'talk about it and toy with it' but are 'absolutely terrified of genuinely learning Buddhism'. The British Buddhist establishment, she claimed, was scared by her emphasis on meditation and monasticism, and she interpreted its 'faddish' appropriation of oriental culture as a resistance to the existential project of self-transformation. In Kennett's view, the truth of Zen must be expressed within the idiom of one's own culture and cannot be penetrated by following 'spurious oriental teachers'. Whilst this critique was initially directed only at the London Buddhist Society, as Kennett's relationship with certain segments of her British congregation deteriorated, she extended it to include *all* British Buddhists.

Whilst Kennett's evaluation of Western culture was generally positive, one trait she identified as a major obstacle to Zen training was the Western tendency to over-intellectualise. The truth, she emphasised, cannot be realised theoretically but only through practice and experience; *Dōgen's* Zen is 'an intuitive method of spiritual training' (Kennett 1972: 72) not dependent upon words, scripture or theology. Her own presentation revealed a proclivity to avoid philosophical issues, and trainees were encouraged likewise to eschew erudition and cultivate the 'heart of faith' or 'intuition', the essential quality required to understand Zen (Kennett 1972: 63).

Buddhism and gender

The primary source of Kennett's discontent with Christianity was the sexual prejudice she encountered within Anglicanism. Although she was 'damaged' by the institutionalised inequality of the Church, 'out of it came something good' inasmuch as it 'sent me back to studying my own original religion, Buddhism', thus making possible 'the discovery that I was adequate; that I did have a soul in Christian terminology'.[25] Kennett's teachings on sexuality in Buddhism were usually set in contradistinction to her understanding of Christian institutions and teachings. In *Selling Water*, she compared the Christian Church with Sōtō Zen, wherein 'the ideal is complete sexual equality' and 'women and men can go up the ranks of the priesthood equally' (Kennett 1972: 58). She was far more detailed and direct, though, in her articles. The refusal of the Church to allow women into the priesthood now amounted to 'the gravest wrong done to women over the centuries' because it has denied the equality of the male and female soul, making it 'impossible for a woman to believe completely in herself'.[26] The struggle for equal rights in contemporary society, Kennett concluded, must therefore strike at the essentially *spiritual* roots of the problem.

Kennett maintained that the original teachings of the Buddha were, like those of Christ, sexually egalitarian and that discrimination was introduced into the Buddhist tradition only at a later date. Although she acknowledged that the historical and institutional reality of the Sōtō tradition has not always reflected Dōgen's ideals, Sōtō Zen was regarded as fundamentally egalitarian. Dōgen made it clear that 'both male and female are equally sharers of the Buddha Nature', and this, for Kennett, placed the female Zen practitioner 'in a totally different position from that of the Christian woman'.[27] With respect to the role of Buddhist women in the West, Kennett emphasised the importance of following the *essential* teachings of Śākyamuni Buddha and *Dōgen*, and of stripping away the layers of cultural prejudice in order to 'keep the teaching of Zen in its original purity' (Kennett 1972: 66). She herself made gender equality an institutional reality within the ZMS from its inception. Male and female priests were both called 'monks', and no distinctions were made in terms of priestly progression, hierarchy or daily life activities.

Kennett's attraction to Buddhism was rooted in her perception that it was, unlike the religion of her birth, doctrinally and practically egalitarian. In this respect her biography reflects the lives of a broader range of Western women Buddhist converts. The British women interviewed by Bell, for example, like Kennett,

> wished to take advantage of the fact that, at the 'theological' level, Buddhism is a religion with a soteriology that makes no distinction on account of gender.
>
> (Bell 1991: 285)

Her rejection of *Theravāda* Buddhism seems to have been informed by two principal considerations. First, she discovered that significant differences of opinion exist within the Buddhist world, and that the tradition of her choice, the *Theravāda*, was one of the most 'conservative', lacking a legitimate *bhikṣuni* order. By contrast, the lineage for the ordination of women has survived within Far Eastern *Mahāyāna* Buddhist traditions. Secondly, a major component of monastic training in Japan, both for monks and nuns, concerns the acquisition of ritual skills and procedures required for the priestly service of the laity. As we have seen, Kennett's 'deep calling' to ordain as an Anglican priest – as opposed to becoming a nun – was frustrated by the policy of the Church in the 1950s. *Sōtō* Zen seemed to offer her the opportunity to fully realise her vocation of priestly ordination and service, albeit within a different religious system.

Kennett's interpretation of the teachings of *Dōgen* and the historical position of women within *Sōtō* Zen is supported by the account of Uchino, who states that *Dōgen* 'was exceptionally understanding of women and [...] emphasized the equality of men and women in attaining Buddhahood' (Uchino 1983: 178). Textual and historical research, however, suggests that Kennett's and Uchino's accounts are incomplete. Faure rejects the idea that *Dōgen's* teachings are intrinsically egalitarian, maintaining that 'the Chan rhetoric of equality' derived more from the need for economic support from aristocratic noble women than from any doctrinal or theoretical premise such as the *Mahāyāna* principle of non-duality. *Keizan* was more willing to put into practice the theoretical equality of the sexes in *Ch'an* discourse, but even under his spiritual guidance 'nuns were still on the margins of the male monastic community' (Faure 1991: 245).

Kennett's discussion of women in *Sōtō* represented a 'feminist revalorization of Buddhism'. This term is used by Gross to describe the project of analysing, in light of feminist values, the history and conceptual system of Buddhism in order to 'repair' the tradition or bring it 'more into line with its own fundamental values and vision than was its patriarchal form' (Gross 1993: 3). In order to construct a 'usable past' for her modern movement, Kennett presented a highly selective reading of *Dōgen*'s doctrine and monastic practice, omitting unhelpful elements. Coupled with her critique of the degeneration of his ideals, and her claim to have re-established his original, or 'pure', standard in the West, her articles on women in *Sōtō* attempted to 'revalorise' the tradition inasmuch as they

> explore the contradiction between the egalitarian concepts of Buddhism and its patriarchal history, seeking both to explain that contradiction historically and to rectify that situation in a future manifestation and form of Buddhism.
>
> (Gross 1993: 4)

The self-conscious engagement displayed by Kennett with respect to the problems of gender bias within *Sōtō* is, according to Gross, untypical of the majority of Western Buddhists, most of whom are 'ignorant about the androcentric values prevalent through most Buddhist history and hostile to an articulate and self-conscious feminist Buddhist position' (Gross 1993: 25).

The adaptation of Zen for the West

Kennett was aware of the need to adapt the traditional forms of *Sōtō* Zen for a Western cultural context, and she consciously developed specific perspectives towards culture, tradition and authority. Her Zen presentation must not, therefore, be explained away as the product of cultural forces of which she was unaware; any assessment of this Buddhist teacher must acknowledge and examine the very *deliberate* nature of her engagement with Western culture. Kennett provided a succinct outline of her policy of adaptation in the opening passages of *Selling Water*, indicating that the project was integral to her presentation from the outset. She adopted a basically non-traditional, 'essentialist' position:

> From the moment I arrived in Japan [...] I was constantly told that I must concentrate on the basic Truth and not worry about customs and culture, as the West can only make use of this Truth to build its own form of Zen.
>
> (Kennett 1972: xxiv)

On the basis of this, she chastised the exoticism, or orientalism, of westerners, maintaining that the project of building a Western form of Zen would be executed most successfully by a Western teacher such as herself. She was even critical of *Dōgen* for 'attempting to transplant the Chinese form of Zen to Japan'

(Kennett 1972: xxiv). Rather than importing the traditional religious forms of Japan, Zen must thus be 'reborn in the West':

> First and foremost, we are ourselves British Buddhists; we are not studying Japanese Zen, we are studying British Zen; we are not wearing Japanese robes, we are wearing British robes [...] We are maintaining the spirit of Zen, at the same time expressing it in a British way.[28]

Kennett therefore adopted an approach towards Buddhism and the adaptation process, whereby adaptations are legitimated by direct reference to the essence of *Sōtō* Zen, which is similar to that of Sangharakshita, founder of the FWBO. Religious 'form' is valued positively only where it facilitates the interiorisation of its essential 'content'. This emphasis on the subjective experience of the individual, rather than on external forms, permeates *Selling Water* and was particularly evident in Kennett's interpretation of the *Sōtō* preceptual code, the 'outward form' of which is 'transcended' when the individual becomes its 'living embodiment' as a 'spiritually autonomous' moral agent (Kennett 1972: 54–55). This outlook also underpinned her translation of *Sōtō* texts and her interpretation of ceremonial. Rather than translating *Dōgen* literally, she attempted to capture his 'true feeling' and 'religious fervour', and *Keizan's* ceremonial was presented primarily as an aid for the inner development of the individual:

> Each ceremony was designed [...] to indicate the attitude of mind which leads beyond ceremonial as a form and turns it into meditation.
> (Kennett 1972: 163)

Adaptations and simplifications of *Sōtō* ceremonies were thus legitimated by the view that 'the exact copying of outward form is not nearly as essential as the understanding of the internal spirit' (Kennett 1972: 164).

Whilst Kennett's understanding of Zen and her adaptation policy had much in common with Sangharakshita, there were also a number of differences. The main difference concerned the structure of authority within the two movements. Within the FWBO, the 'essentials' of Buddhism and the form these should take are articulated by Sangharakshita and legitimated not primarily by an appeal to continuous tradition, but by his personal claim to possess charismatic authority. Kennett, by contrast, legitimated her essentialist approach by appealing to her continuity with the *Sōtō* tradition and the charisma she inherited by virtue of this association. She maintained, first, that the idea of focusing on the essentials to create a Western form of Zen was transmitted to her by Kōho Keidō Chisan (Kennett 1972: vi). By appealing to the authority of her transmission master, Kennett simultaneously evoked the powerful image of lineal continuity that provides an important basis to Zen claims of legitimacy. In addition to this, there are other traditional images that she appealed to for legitimation, such as *Keizan* who 'exploited the temper of the times' to make Zen accessible to a wider

Japanese population. Like *Keizan*, Kennett claimed to be maintaining 'the spirit of the tradition' without being bound by its outward form.

Her status as a Dharma-successor, a teacher with the authority to transmit the truth of Zen to others, also provided Kennett with the personal charismatic authority to identify and separate the essential principles of *Sōtō* Zen from their Japanese cultural forms. According to Zen belief, the true essence of the Buddha's message is transmitted not through verbal teaching or scripture, but *experientially* in the direct mind-to-mind contact of master and disciple. The concept of the 'face-to-face transmission' embodies a 'dual matrix' of legitimation that is both historical, through the image of Patriarchal descent, and transcendent, in that the same essence is transmitted and experienced in every encounter (Reader 1983: 51). Entry into the Patriarchal line via Dharma transmission imbued Kennett with authority that was simultaneously traditional, emphasising lineal continuity, and charismatic, bypassing tradition through the direct realisation of the Buddha Śākyamuni's 'true law'. There is therefore a synthesis of traditional and charismatic authority in Japanese *Sōtō* of the kind that is identified by Bell (1991) within the Thai forest monastic tradition.

In Kennett's view, the establishment of Zen in the West is partly a process of extracting and transplanting the fundamentals and leaving the culturally incidental behind 'so that the mind shall in no way be disturbed by unfamiliar or foreign externalities'.[29] This logic was applied to a number of adaptations, such as the abandonment of the *kyōsaku* (awakening stick) in the meditation hall and the wearing of civilian clothes by monks when outside the monastery grounds, as well as to minor details of daily life, such as the decision to eat with knives and forks instead of chopsticks.

Kennett's appraisal of Western culture was generally positive. Zen teaches 'how to become yourself', and since culture forms an integral part of personal identity, this realisation must be made through one's indigenous cultural idiom. She thus maintained that the truth or essence of Zen should be expressed in Western contexts through the skilful appropriation of Western cultural forms and customs. Whilst her authority to identify the essentials of *Sōtō* Zen was sanctioned by tradition and personal charisma, she claimed that it was her British identity that qualified her to marry this essence with suitable cultural forms.

Kennett considered the modern penetration of Japanese culture by Western egalitarianism as beneficial for *Sōtō* Zen, enabling more women to realise *Dōgen*'s ideal of sexual equality. Another value that dovetailed significantly with her understanding of Zen was that of individualism. She presented her teachings on personal responsibility and authority within Zen as in line with 'the Western system of orientation which trains people to become autonomous in individuation'.[30] At the same time, however, she recognised how excessive individualism might pose an obstacle to the successful establishment of Zen monasticism in the West. She attempted to mitigate against this potential obstacle by maintaining that whilst one can rediscover one's Buddha-nature 'without any outside help' (Kennett 1972: 64) from a priesthood or even from a

Zen master, the proper context of Zen training is that of temple monasticism. She also simultaneously affirmed the values of individualism and monasticism by referring to the monastery as a place where one can 'do something about oneself'. There are some similarities here with the FWBO's concept of '*Sangha*' as a 'community of individuals' intent on personal development.

Although disenchanted with Christianity, Kennett nevertheless retained a real affection for her former religion. Her reflections on the position of women in Christianity, where she stated that her objection was not with the teachings of Christ per se but with later institutional structures, were highly suggestive in this respect. The main strategy she used to adapt Zen Buddhism for a Western cultural context was the appropriation of Christian religious forms, an approach that can be identified in the organisational, ritual and doctrinal dimensions of the early ZMS.

Upon her arrival in America, Kennett began to self-consciously style her Buddhist monastic movement in a Christian form. She named it the 'Zen *Mission* Society' and favoured the terms 'abbey' and 'cloister' as opposed to 'meditation centre'. The subsequent institutional growth of the ZMS entailed the creation of 'priories' led by senior disciples who acted as 'priors' under her leadership as 'abbess'. Traditional Christian monastic titles were used to describe the various departments of the monastery, and the responsibilities allocated to individual monks included those of 'sacristan' and 'infirmarian'. Monastic attire was also adapted in a Christian style, the traditional Japanese *kimono* being replaced by the cassock, clerical shirt and dog collar of the Anglican or Catholic priest. Through these adaptations, Kennett maintained, the extraneous culture of Japan was stripped away, enabling the 'essence' of Zen to be transmitted to the West in a more suitable form.

Kennett also adapted *Sōtō* ceremonial and liturgical practices using Christian ritual forms. In *Selling Water*, she outlined a selection of ceremonies included within the annual calendar of Shasta Abbey based upon the yearly ceremonial programme of *Sōjiji*. She considered that certain Buddhist ceremonies and festivals had a Christian parallel, and so restructured the traditional ritual calendar accordingly. For example, instead of performing the ceremonial 'Feeding of the Hungry Ghosts' (*Segaki*) in July as is customary in Japan, this ceremony was performed at Shasta Abbey in October on the occasion of Halloween. Similarly, the festival of the birth of the Buddha (*Hanamatsuri*), which in Japan takes place during April, was celebrated by the ZMS on Christmas Day 'following the old Buddhist custom of adapting religious celebrations to the indigenous holidays of the country' (Kennett 1976: 391).[31] In this way, the cultural sensitivities of her Western disciples to Christian ritual observances were mobilised, effecting a redefinition of religious sentiment from within. The same logic was applied to the utilisation of medieval Christian musical forms for daily scripture recitation. Prioritising meaning and understanding above sound and repetition, Kennett translated the scriptures into English and, drawing upon her specialised knowledge of early medieval music, set them to Catholic plainsong. Christian chants were thus used as 'a wonderful bridge', just as Buddhism in the Far East had also, many centuries earlier, 'picked up the old chants of the previous religions' (Kennett, quoted in Boucher 1985: 140). The chanting of scriptures during morning and evening services, known within the ZMS as 'matins' and 'vespers' respectively, was also supplemented by the singing of Buddhist 'hymns' with traditionally Christian melodies to the accompaniment of organ music.

Kennett was not the first to utilise Western religious, and in particular musical, forms in this way. Significant figures in the development of American Buddhism, such as Paul Carus and Phillip Kapleau, preceded her in this enterprise, and Japanese-American Pure Land Buddhism has also adapted in similar ways. Important precedents for these developments, it should also be noted, had already emerged upon the Japanese religious landscape, as Buddhism adapted and modernised itself in line with the pro-Western ideology of the Meiji authorities.[32] Although Kennett never referred to these Japanese precedents, they may have provided her with additional legitimation to adapt Zen along Christian lines, thus underlining the role of trans-cultural processes in the transplantation of Zen in the West.

Finally, Christian religious terms were also appropriated to facilitate her presentation of certain Zen Buddhist concepts. She explained the meaning of *nirvāṇa* by quoting the Christian mystic Meister Eckhart (Kennett 1972: 48), referred to the concept of 'transmission' as a Zen form of 'Apostolic Succession', and found parallels between the Eastern Orthodox Church and Zen on the subject of *kenshō* experiences. She also used Christian concepts to explain the doctrine of the Buddha-nature. Although she was careful not to affirm the existence of a permanently existent self, she linked this doctrine to the Christian concept of the 'soul'. In another context, Buddha-nature was equated with the 'Holy Spirit'.[33] Following this interpretation, the breaking of the moral precepts became analogous to sinning against the Holy Ghost. The employment of quasi-theistic terminology was also expressed through Kennett's occasional references to the 'Cosmic Buddha', an image representing the personalisation of the impersonal absolute. Although she usually described Buddhahood in an impersonal way, it is important to acknowledge that this image, a key element of her teaching in later years, was present during the early stages of her thought.

A Protestant form of Zen?

Certain aspects of Kennett's thought could easily be interpreted in support of the Protestant Buddhism thesis. She herself acknowledged that Western religio-cultural forces of which she was not always aware influenced her teachings:

> That is what comes of being Western; coming out of a Western background. I still tend to be conditioned by that which is my own past.
> (Kennett 1977a: 122)

In particular, a strong strand of individualism underpinned her presentation, as was evident in the importance she attached to self-reliance, individual responsibility and personal experience. Her essentialistic and personalistic attitude towards adaptation and religious form was also suggestive of a Protestant outlook. Outward forms, such as the precepts and ceremonies, were deemed of value primarily because they facilitate appropriate psychological attitudes in individual practitioners, and once these mental states are realised, the external religious forms are 'transcended'. Finally, her critique of Christianity reflected elements of the Protestant critique of Catholicism. She described Sōtō Zen, for example, as a non-doctrinal, intuitive spirituality in direct contrast to Christianity, which she characterised as doctrinaire, judgmental and excessively authoritarian.

According to Mellor, the discourse of the FWBO is 'firmly in line with Western culture' and consequently is 'not a wholly legitimate discourse' (Mellor 1989: 340). The discourse of the British Forest Sangha, by contrast, is regarded as more legitimate because it has a self-conscious and discriminating relationship with Protestantism, creating a form of Buddhism 'that is traditional yet sensitive to its local context' (Mellor 1989: 352). Whilst Kennett's thought revealed a number of significant continuities with Protestant values, it would be wrong to regard her teachings as 'illegitimate', because, like the Theravāda teachers of Mellor's study, she was also a reflective and discriminating cultural mediator. She was aware of the values her disciples carried with them into their practice and tailored her presentation accordingly through a process of assimilation (of egalitarianism, individualism and elements of Christianity she valued positively) and rejection (of orientalism, intellectualism and aspects of Christianity she viewed negatively).

A number of other factors should make us cautious about using the 'Protestant' designation with respect to Kennett. The democratised and individualistic emphasis of her teachings was always counterbalanced by her commitment to the establishment of a Western monastic order, organised along traditional lines with a clear hierarchical structure. Whilst the laity was given high priority by Kennett, teaching was to remain the preserve of ordained monks and the ritual protocol of lay-monastic relations was to reflect traditional hierarchies. The importance attached to the laity is, in any case, not necessarily suggestive of Protestant influences. As well as having the explicit textual sanction of Dōgen,[34] lay religiosity has come to the fore within the modern Japanese Sōtō sect, which has involved lay figures both in policy making and in doctrinal formulation.

Similarly, religious form may have been interpreted in a personalistic way but this did not undermine its importance to the monastic life of the ZMS, every aspect of which, on a daily or annual basis, was ritually structured and routinised. It would be quite misleading, in fact, to assume that Kennett's 'utilitarian' understanding of religious form can be explained solely in terms of the influence of Western Protestant values. The view that form is ultimately empty and therefore dispensable is a *Mahāyāna* Buddhist perspective that has a long pedigree and which is reflected clearly within the Zen school, which defines itself as 'a transmission outside the scriptures'. Both Faure (1991) and Sharf (1995c, 1995d) have demonstrated how, in spite of its 'rhetoric of immediacy', Zen is historically a highly institutionalised and hierarchical tradition that is rich in religious ritual. Kennett's teaching on the emptiness of ritual form and the apparent contradiction of the institutional and ceremonial reality of the ZMS thus reflected an ambiguity inherent within the Zen tradition.

Sharf might reply that Kennett's interpretation of ritual action in terms of its ability to bring about a transformative shift in the individual subject's consciousness indicated a Protestant form of individualism that is absent from more traditional monastic contexts. Indeed, few scholars would question the point that the approach of westerners to Buddhist meditation and ritual is often more soteriological than that of their Eastern counterparts. Kennett, however, was careful to ground her experiential reading of ritual within the traditional rhetoric of Japanese Zen. The traditional position states that ritual manifests the inherent enlightenment of all things. From this, Kennett extrapolated the view that ritual action can thereby prompt the subjective realisation of enlightenment that will ultimately transcend ritual form.

Nor was the essentialism characterising her thought necessarily suggestive of Protestant influences either. Pye has shown that the application of an abstracted concept of the 'essence' of Buddhism is not just a feature of Western scholarship and practice but is a hermeneutical device rooted in the ancient self-understandings of Buddhist traditions themselves. It is therefore possible to talk of the 'essence of Buddhism as an Asian question' (Pye 1973: 38). Kennett certainly regarded essentialism as a traditional and authentic perspective with a sound doctrinal basis rooted in Zen Buddhism's self-understanding as a 'mind-to-mind' transmission of the truth. Furthermore, she did not reject traditional authority but, rather, appealed to tradition for legitimation. Her outlook was thus quite different from that of figures like Sangharakshita and D. T. Suzuki who, scholars argue, have promoted a non-traditional, Protestant-informed essentialism.

A final cautionary note concerning the applicability of the Protestant Buddhism thesis to Kennett concerns the nature of her critique of Christianity. First, whilst Buddhism was regarded favourably as compared to Christianity, this in no way entailed an idealisation of the former and demonisation of the latter. Kennett viewed elements of Christianity positively, and criticised Buddhist history and practice whenever it deviated from her view of the essentials. Such criticisms of Buddhism could also be viewed, of course, as evidence of Protestant influences. However, her adaptations that drew on Christianity were more suggestive of High Church Anglican or Catholic influences rather than Low Church or liberal Protestant traditions. Her modifications of Zen monasticism and ceremonial in particular indicated the influence of her Anglican background. The view that British Buddhists, when criticising Christianity, are really aiming to differentiate themselves from non-Protestant traditions is therefore not borne out in the case of Kennett and the ZMS.

Religious innovation and charisma

A popular explanation for innovative processes in religion is the 'crisis explanation':

> Religious individuals and communities experience a crisis with which the existing religious tradition does not allow them to cope, and so they innovate.
>
> (Williams *et al.* 1992: 7)

Whilst social disruption and personal anxiety are 'ever valid components in the explanation of religious innovation', Williams *et al.* consider that 'crisis has been much over-used as an explanation' (Williams *et al.* 1992: 8). Finney's 'culture diffusion model' of the transplantation of Zen in America supports this assessment by incorporating important historical and cross-cultural data alongside sociological and social-psychological explanations. He also emphasizes that the strategies adopted by the individual teachers and institutions implanting the new cultural form 'have a profound impact on whether it takes root' (Finney 1991: 394). His account thus acknowledges the importance of individual religious genius to the successful growth of specific organisational forms. Williams *et al.* also underline the crucial role of religious genius, or, in Weberian terms, 'charisma', in explaining religious innovation:

> it seems impossible to deny the extraordinary talent possessed by certain individuals for creating and communicating new religious symbols, ideas or forms.
>
> (Williams *et al.* 1992: 9)

Earhart's (1989) explanation of the rise of the Japanese new religions also focuses on the role of personal charisma. He argues that alongside social and personal crisis, the prior historical development of religious traditions and the personal contribution of innovating individuals must also be taken into account.

What emerges very clearly from the previous discussion of the history and world-view of the ZMS during its early period of development is the role played by the religious genius of Kennett. Whilst crisis explanations may help to account for the receptive attitude of Anglo-American culture towards the ZMS, and whilst the cross-cultural diffusion model incorporates the historical and institutional roots of the organisation in Japan, in order to understand the specific nature and success of the ZMS we must also focus upon the personality and charisma of its founder. Kennett possessed in ample measure the 'creativity needed to generate new culture' (Stark 1992: 23), the characteristic talents that, according to Waldman and Baum, are required by successful 'prophets'. Whilst their ability to attract a following depends on 'many things other than perception of extraordinary personal qualities', they must nevertheless

> be both recognizable through familiar paradigms and also different enough to rework, recombine, and transcend them [...] sensitive, flexible, adaptive, and insightful into their own cultures [and must exhibit] unusual synthesizing abilities, managing to align a number of potentially disjunctive elements.
>
> (Waldman and Baum 1992: 263–274)

6

THE LOTUS BLOSSOM PERIOD, 1976–83

Introduction

The next stage of the history of the Zen Mission Society (ZMS) was dominated by developments rooted in a prolonged religious experience that happened to Kennett over a period of around eight months, between June 1976 and January 1977. From the viewpoint of the British congregation, this period of change and instability ended in 1982 when Kennett's British monks, having trained at Shasta Abbey for five years, returned to resume their training at Throssel Hole. Described as her 'third *kenshō*', Kennett's experience was recorded and published as *How to Grow a Lotus Blossom or How a Zen Buddhist Prepares for Death* (1977b). Comparatively speaking, it was a highly unusual experience and it led to a series of doctrinal and practical shifts that were not always accepted uncritically by her disciples. In this chapter, I place Kennett's *kenshō* in a comparative and historical perspective, outline the nature and meaning of her experiences, and comment upon the various developments and innovations resulting from them. Following an examination of the manner in which these innovations were received by her disciples – assimilation or rejection – I outline and comment upon the effectiveness of the various strategies she used for resolving conflict and resistance within her movement.

Zen Buddhism and meditative experience

According to Sharf, the popular view of Zen as an essentially meditative and mystical tradition is a distorted reconstruction that reflects the impact of modernising, Westernising and nationalistic forces on Japanese Buddhist intellectuals during the Meiji period. The weight of historical and ethnographic evidence, he argues, reveals that Zen monasticism is primarily concerned not with private ineffable experiences, but with public enactments of awakening, or 'ceremonial affirmations of the reality of *nirvāṇa*' (Sharf 1995c: 270). A consequence of approaching Zen through a 'hermeneutic of experience' is that technical terms and categories relating to monastic practice 'are frequently presumed to be grounded in a non-conceptual mode (or modes) of cognition' (Sharf 1995c: 230). In particular, the terms *kenshō* (seeing one's nature), *satori* (understanding) and even *makyō* (realm of illusion) 'are assumed to designate discrete "states of consciousness" experienced by Buddhist practitioners in the midst of their meditative practice' (Sharf 1995c: 231). Such interpretations, Sharf argues, cannot be attested in the pre-modern period. Traditionally, these terms denote a monk's understanding and appreciation of key Buddhist doctrines such as 'emptiness' or 'Buddhahood', and there are 'simply no a priori grounds to conceive of such moments of insight in phenomenological terms' (Sharf 1995a: 125).

As noted earlier, the modernist, experiential view of Zen gained currency in the West through apologists like D. T. Suzuki who placed the mystical experience of *kenshō* at the centre of his Zen exegesis. This view of Zen is promoted in Japan today through lay-orientated organisations such as the *Sanbōkyōdan* ('Three Treasures Association'). This organisation has, in spite of its sociologically marginal status in Japan, been very influential in the development of Western Zen because a number of key figures in the Western transmission are, or have been, affiliated with it.[1] These figures continue to present the essence of Zen 'as rooted in an experience of oneness with all things' (Sharf 1995a: 142).

Sharf's critique of the modern rendering of Zen Buddhism in Japan and in the West has widespread support,[2] but I will only focus here on the work of Faure. Faure reiterates that mainstream Zen monasticism is 'a far cry' from the mystical, antinomian and anti-ritual teaching presented by Suzuki for Western consumption. Furthermore, he argues that this 'deep bias against ritualism' also constitutes 'a basic methodological problem' of Western scholarship which, informed by rationalist and Protestant values, has tended to focus on Zen doctrine and philosophy at the expense of its ritual components (Faure 1991: 284–285). Within a traditional Zen monastic context, *zazen* meditation should be understood 'not as a form of knowledge (*jñāna*) but rather as a form of ritual activity' (Faure 1991: 295), whilst awakening itself 'is a ritual reenactment of (or identification with) the Buddha's wakening' (Faure 1991: 299). Similarly, *Ch'an*/Zen masters are not so defined because of their experiential realisation of the truth, but because 'having been socially defined as Chan masters, what they teach has the performative power of being the truth' (Faure 1991: 22).

Unlike Sharf, however, Faure does not explain the anti-ritual bias characterising modern accounts of the Zen tradition solely in terms of the influence or projection of Western religio-cultural values. He also considers it as an expression of a fundamental ambivalence at the heart of the tradition itself. In theory, the Zen tradition 'distinguishes itself from other religious trends by its insistence on immediacy and its denial of all traditional mediations' (Faure 1991: 305), but in practice it accepts and maintains a complex structure of symbolic mediations, including the worship of relics, reliance upon dreams and ritual observance. Faure argues that 'classical' Zen discourse reveals a demythologising tendency – rooted in the *Mahāyāna* philosophy of emptiness and later reinforced by the importation of Western rationalism – which has constantly striven to undermine (or 'empty') traditional mediating practices. Given the 'irrepressible multivocality' of the tradition, he suggests that the demytholo-gising interpretations of modern Zen scholarship 'are deeply indebted to the tradition itself', and that Suzuki's anti-ritualism is in certain respects 'faithful to the tradition' (Faure 1991: 285–287) and not simply a modern reconstruction.

Kennett's religious experience: preliminary considerations

A phenomenological description of Kennett's religious experience is presented below, following the guidelines of Yandell who defines such an account as 'one that describes the experience "from within" or in terms of how things appear to the subject of the experience as she has the experience' (Yandell 1993: 17). An accurate phenomenological description of a religious experience is one that 'expresses its content and reflects its structure' (Yandall 1993: 24). With regard to the type of experience, one important structural difference identified by Yandell is that between the 'subject/consciousness/object structure' experience on the one hand, and the 'subject/aspect structure' experience on the other. The former are 'perceptual' experiences inasmuch as 'the subject seems to expe-rience something external to themselves – something they are in danger of identifying with themselves' (Yandall 1993: 30). Yandell equates these, typically monotheistic, experiences with Rudolf Otto's notion of the 'numinous', wherein the subject seems to experience an awesome, holy, mind-independent being 'to whom reverence, awe, recognition of one's guilt, humility, gratitude and worship are appropriate responses' (Yandall 1993: 262). Another experiential modality is that 'having numinous experience involves having imagery (visual and auditory)' which 'mediates numinous content' (Yandall 1993: 263). By contrast, the latter, typically non-monotheistic, type of experience 'concerns aspects rather than objects' and is introspective inasmuch as the subject 'recog-nizes certain things about herself' (Yandall 1993: 43). Some traditions combine both types of experience. Within *Advaita Vedānta*, for example, the experience of *mokṣa* 'either is numinous or involves an awareness of the identity of oneself with qualityless Brahman' (Yandall 1993: 22).

This structural distinction is reiterated by Smart who contrasts the 'numi-nous' with a kind of experience he describes as 'mystical' (Smart 1995: 58–73). He associates the former most closely with the monotheistic belief systems of the Semitic traditions, and the latter with the non-theistic meditative systems originating in India, particularly Buddhism. Unlike the dynamic and shat-tering, dualistic and image-rich experience of the numinous, the mystical experience is often quiet, non-dual and empty of images. Furthermore, the mystical perspective encourages self-reliance and meditative realisation of the ultimate truth that lies within, as opposed to worship, prayer and reverential 'dependence on the Other'. Smart also discusses branches of religious tradi-tions 'within which the two strands of religious experience are woven together', but he recognises that the *accent* of the experience often remains on either the numinous or the mystical.

As it is described by D. T. Suzuki, the non-dual and unmediated inner event of *kenshō* or *satori* reflects the main features of Smart's 'mystical' category of religious experience. Along with many other significant figures in the Western transmission of Zen, Kennett's understanding of Zen was informed, at least in part, by Suzuki's modernist writings, and she described her 'great experience' as a *kenshō*. Whilst she inherited the emphasis on *kenshō*, however, her experience and interpretation of it was significantly different from the 'mystical' events described by others. Unlike the accounts of Suzuki *et al.* – which, we should not forget, present a species of experience that may itself be unusual within the historical context of Zen monasticism – Kennett's *kenshō* took the form of a prolonged series of 'complete visual and sensory experiences' or 'waking visions' (Kennett 1977b: ix), each loaded with imagery and symbolism. Many of the visionary episodes provided her with an experience of, or an insight into, her past lives and in this respect can be regarded as examples of Yandell's category of introspective, 'subject/aspect' experiences. Other visions gave her a deeper understanding of the teachings and her role and purpose as a Zen teacher. Each successive vision – of such things as giant lotus blossoms, towers, columns of light, fountains, heavenly Buddha Lands, Buddhas and lineage-Patriarchs – superimposed itself onto her immediate physical surroundings. She observed, moved, acted and interacted within the context of each unfolding vision – by climbing glass mountains, for example, or by travelling to different realms and conversing with celestial beings – but she remained awake and alert throughout, constantly 'aware of things going on around me' (Kennett 1977b: 263). These experiences have more in common with the 'numinous' category inasmuch as their religious content was mediated through symbolic imagery and they involved encounters between Kennett and various, seemingly mind-independent, celestial places and beings. In particular, she experienced an awesome and holy being whom she variously described as 'the Cosmic Buddha', 'the Lord of the House' or simply 'the Lord', and to whom she related in a deeply reverential, penitential, humble, obedient and prayerful way. At other times, however, her presentation was ambivalent about the ontological status of the places and beings in her visions that, she explained, were themselves 'empty' or merely symbolic expressions of Buddhahood. This ambivalence is observed by both Rawlinson and Batchelor who describe Kennett's Zen as 'theistic' or 'quasi-theistic' whilst acknowledging that she upholds 'basic Buddhist teachings' (Rawlinson 1997: 368) – like *anatta* (no-self) and *śūnyatā* (emptiness) – and that the Christian associations are therefore 'more apparent than real' (Batchelor 1994: 136). Kennett's experience, then, may best be understood as a combination of the numinous and the mystical.

In the years following her *kenshō*, Kennett herself drew a distinction between 'imaginative visions' and 'intellectual visions',[3] and this helps us to understand

148

where, in Smart's terms, the 'accent' of her experience lies. Whilst the former 'may include sight, hearing, smell, touch, feeling, certainty, knowledge', the latter are inner experiences and completely absent of imagery. There are some obvious structural similarities between the types of vision identified here and the categories of experience identified by Yandell and Smart. According to Kennett's typology, however, both imaginative *and* intellectual visions are understood as numinous experiences. Thus, even in an intellectual vision

> a person knows for certain that there is something greater than himself with him (or her). I have often had monks say to me: 'I can feel the Lord of the House here. I know He is sitting with me. I haven't seen Him – I just *know*'.

Batchelor suggests that Kennett's visionary episodes 'are more reminiscent of the experiences of Christian saints than Zen Masters' (Batchelor 1994: 135–136). When we examine them against her biographical and religio-cultural context – that is, non-phenomenologically – it will become clear that her experiences do indeed display undeniable Christian parallels. However, it is important to note at this stage that, contrary to popular representations of 'Zen mysticism', Kennett's visionary experiences – and also her ambivalence about the status of their content – are *not* unprecedented within the Zen tradition. Significant in this respect is the research of Faure (1991) on the ontological status and soteriological value of dreams in traditional Zen contexts.[4] Within Asian cultures, dreams are widely regarded in a visionary sense as 'channels of communication with the invisible world' (Faure 1991: 213). Faure discovered that although the Zen tradition has in theory rejected dreams as illusory, in practice 'the intermediary world of dreams' has provided an important aspect of its metaphysics of presence and has often 'played a significant role in the life of Chan/Zen communities' (1991: 209). He outlines examples of masters experiencing 'all kinds of dreams or visions' during sleep and meditation, including premonitory and revelatory dreams, 'dreams of ascent' to celestial places, and visions of *Arhats*, *Bodhisattvas* and various deities. It is also important to recognise that dreams played a crucial role in the specific development of *Sōtō* Zen, the tradition within which Kennett received her training. Whilst *Dōgen's* ambivalent attitude towards dreams erred upon the side of orthodoxy, *Keizan* 'lived his dreams' or 'dreamt his life':

> Although upholding the *Mahāyāna* tenet of emptiness (*śūnyatā*), Keizan lived in a world impregnated with very real dreams.
> (Faure 1991: 221)

His recorded dreams detail encounters with *Arhats* and *Bodhisattvas* such as *Kannon*, and according to Faure, 'one of their functions is obviously to legitimate him and his teaching' (1991: 225). Of particular relevance to our examination of Kennett's religious experiences are the various visions that *Keizan* had of his past lives.

The phenomenology of Kennett's experience

Kennett's religious experience occurred during a lengthy period of intensive meditation that began in earnest in the spring of 1976. According to Daizui MacPhillamy – a senior disciple who acted as her nurse and personal assistant throughout – she embarked upon her retreat in response to a crisis precipitated by three events: first, she fell very ill and was informed by her doctor that she might only have a short time left to live; secondly, the disciple whom she regarded as her chief descendent and future successor wavered in his commitment to her; and thirdly, a 'practitioner of an esoteric Oriental healing art' (Kennett 1977b: viii) pronounced that the cause of her illness was her own faulty teachings and lifestyle. Kennett herself explained her retreat as a time of spiritual preparation for her imminent death (Kennett 1977b: 7–8); her critics, by contrast, have described it as a period of emotional and psychological breakdown and fragmentation.

In a state of physical weakness and mental turmoil, she retired from her duties as abbess of Shasta Abbey and, having appointed a board of directors to oversee the running of the ZMS, she began her meditation retreat, undertaking the first part of the retreat at Berkeley Buddhist Priory and the latter part at Shasta Abbey. This was a largely isolated retreat, Kennett permitting visits only from her closest monastic disciples. She even refused, apparently, to see a doctor, 'relying solely upon her meditation and a few simple foods and herbs' (Kennett 1977b: viii). However, she did receive an oriental masseur twice weekly. Massage formed an integral part of Kennett's retreat because it prepared her, physically and mentally, for her visionary episodes. The manipulation of energy points on the body also became an important aspect of her teachings during this period.

The opening visions described in *How to Grow a Lotus Blossom* are of an immense mountain range. This represents religious training which, though daunting, is seen as the only meaningful option for Kennett. The task of training is described here in terms of karmic cleansing:

> I tear into my past and drag it naked and trembling into the light. I cleanse my karma of body, mouth and will [...] for that which has not been taken care of since my first *kenshō*.
>
> (Kennett 1977b: 26)

Kennett is 'given the chance to see my past [...] and to deal with what I had done', and she purifies her past wrongdoing with 'tears of repentance'.

Her next visions teach her about the meaning of true monkhood, which she realises concerns 'the harmony of body and mind'. At this point Kennett petitions 'the Lord of the House' or 'That Which Is' for instruction and learns the importance of cleansing karma from this and previous lives and of obeying 'the will of the Lord'. Whilst on one level a *kenshō* experience 'wipes the slate clean', and preceptual training keeps it clean, the wheel of karma can only be arrested completely by 'cutting the roots of karma':

> It is not enough to have a *kenshō*; I must go back to the source of the karmic stream; I must return to that source to find out what set it going.
>
> (Kennett 1977b: 46)

Kennett next experiences a number of her past lives (see Figure 6.1) so that she can 'clean the impregnations that the karma of my past lives has left upon my skhandas [*sic*]'. Cleaning or 'converting' inherited karmic propensities is a prerequisite to becoming 'one with the Eternal Lord'. The past-life images that flash before her here are also seen by her assistant disciple:

> He looks at me and for a fleeting moment sees a very old European Christian monk; he is very happy, he has left behind no unclean impregnations [...] Further and further back I go [...] Down the centuries I have been a monk so many times; fifteen times Christian, fourteen Buddhist, sometimes male, sometimes female.
>
> (Kennett 1977b: 51–53)

Once her karma on the human plane of existence is dealt with, she goes on to purify 'the karma from lives in the formless realms and from animal lives'. At this point she undergoes a key past-life experience, that of 'a white tiger, captured whilst eating a heron, by a tribe of Indians whose religious cult was one of tiger worship' (Kennett 1977b: 66). The tiger's despair, pain and longing for freedom 'echoes through every fibre of me as clearly as it did three thousand years ago'; the emotional and physical difficulties Kennett experienced at *Sōjiji* are now understood, for example, as karmic memories. She cleanses this fundamental karmic stream of 'anything that is not of the Eternal Lord' by encouraging the tiger to forgive its captors.

Having cleansed the karma of her past lives, Kennett finds herself in 'the Buddha Land' where she is 'seated in a lotus blossom' within an immense sea '*full* of lotus blossoms just like mine', each representing the 'flowering' of Buddhist training. In a particularly striking vision, she witnesses *Śākyamuni* Buddha

> become absorbed into the great, golden Cosmic Buddha that I now see in the sky. He is taken into the Cosmic Buddha and yet is separate from Him. He is not the Cosmic Buddha but there is nothing in him that is not of the Cosmic Buddha; the two are inseparable and different.
>
> (Kennett 1977b: 93–94)

151

Figure 6.1 Plate from *How to Grow a Lotus Blossom* showing Jiyu-Kennett's past-life
   experiences

Source: Reprinted with permission from Shasta Abbey.

Later she ascends beyond the Buddha Land itself to 'a place where there are
golden beings [...] whom I know to be the past Buddhas'. She becomes 'a *real*
monk' by undergoing a cosmic ordination into the 'Monastery of the Lord of
the House' and now realises that her duty 'as a new monk in the temple of the
Lord' is not to abide in the heavenly place but to fulfil the *Bodhisattva* vow by
leading others there. Individuals who 'grow their stems' of training so that they
reach the Buddha Land must take their knowledge and certainty of the Cosmic
Buddha 'back down their stems to this world for the good of all beings' (Kennett
1977b: 104–109).

The remaining visionary episodes serve to deepen Kennett's understanding of
monkhood and clarify her specific mission. They revolve around the sudden
appearance of five golden columns of light coming out of her body, each representing different aspects of monkhood (see Figure 6.2). Kennett understands

that her mission 'in the monastery of the Lord' (Kennett 1977b: 120) is to manifest the five aspects of monkhood so that her disciples may strengthen the 'stems' of their training until, like her, they 'blossom'. In the first column, Kennett learns of 'how earth penetrates heaven' (Kennett 1977b: 111), that the Buddha appears in all things 'if we have the willingness to look through eternal meditation' (Kennett 1977b: 136). As she entered the next columns, she was facing another crisis in her organisation, one that had been precipitated by the *kenshō* itself:

> There have been those, in the last few weeks, who have been horrified by what I have told them; there have been those who have sworn that I am ruining the teaching, those who have gone away; how sad I am for them.
>
> (Kennett 1977b: 139)

The visions of the second, third and fourth columns responded directly to this problem of dissension, teaching her of the loving and accepting nature of the Lord (symbolised here as 'the cleansing water of the spirit') and showing her that she could only help her lost disciples 'by staying in meditation so that they may have the opportunity to see the light for themselves' (Kennett 1977b: 143). In the fifth column of light, Kennett learns that the physical body is the 'means by which man may know the Lord'. Here she identifies a series of correspondences between the columns of light and the organs of the human body, explaining that physical illness and disease are always products of some spiritual deficiency or imbalance. According to Kennett, union with the Lord harmonises heaven and earth and body and mind; hence, she believed that her *kenshō* resulted in her own complete physical recovery from illness. Practical guidelines are also provided on how to attain and maintain this harmony. In addition to meditation, these include celibacy, vegetarianism and the avoidance of sensory indulgences that are likely to cause tensions within the mind and body.

In light of her experiences, Kennett devised a typology for understanding *kenshōs* (Kennett 1977b: 1–8). There are, she maintains, three basic types characterised by differing degrees of depth and intensity and experienced sequentially by sincere practitioners as their training matures. The first type of *kenshō* is the 'Kanzeon' or 'Penetration of Heaven'. Characterised by a 'great flash of deep understanding', this experience most closely approximates the popular descriptions of *kenshō* that can be found elsewhere. It was her own experience of this *kenshō* in 1962, she claims, that qualified her as a Zen teacher in the eyes of Kōhō Chisan.

Kennett emphasises that whilst documentation of them is 'extraordinarily scant', there are other types of *kenshō* that can occur. The second type is described as the 'On-Going Fugen *kenshō*', which is 'not associated in the mind with any *one* moment' but consists of 'little flashes' of understanding that occur

Figure 6.2 Plate from *How to Grow a Lotus Blossom* showing Jiyu-Kennett's vision of the
five aspects of monkhood

Source: Reprinted with permission from Shasta Abbey.

between the great first and third *kenshōs*. *How to Grow a Lotus Blossom* presents
a detailed account of Kennett's experience of the third great type of *kenshō*, the
'Harmonisation of Body and Mind' (Kennett 1977b: 170). This experience
occurs to people naturally 'shortly before their death', but it is possible and
desirable to experience it within the context of spiritual training. The sudden or
instantaneous first *kenshō*, described as 'a swift comprehension of grace', is
contrasted with the gradual and conscientious third, which 'takes place slowly
and deliberately with plenty of time to comprehend each step of the way'. The
third *kenshō* both reflects and facilitates advanced spiritual development, since
the experience of past lives enables the trainee to 'clean up the impregnations
[...] left upon his skhandas [*sic*] both in this life and in his previous ones'. It is
not, therefore, 'the end of training' but should be regarded as a new beginning,
for it reveals in greater depth what a trainee must 'do about himself'. Reliving
past lives – visually, emotionally or both – is presented as a key feature of the

experience, although such episodes will evidently reflect the unique karmic continuums of individual trainees.

A contextual explanation

Having presented a phenomenological account of Kennett's *kenshō*, we are now in a position to examine it from a more critical and contextual perspective. In doing so, however, we must avoid the temptation to explain it away simply as a product of her religious, social and intellectual environment. Yandell traces the reductionist impulse to a 'vaguely conceived but widely influential assumption' that the subject of the experience 'is active in *producing* experience as much as *undergoing* it' (Yandall 1993: 194). Whilst accepting that 'other things besides experience may affect the content of the description of an experience by its subject', he maintains that religious experiences are not necessarily imprisoned by religious concepts and beliefs but can and do occur independently and spontaneously. In his attempt to construct a 'rational theory of revelations', Stark also rejects reductionist models, arguing that it is important 'to acknowledge the possibility that revelations actually occur' (Stark 1992: 21). In light of these comments, we may, without posing a challenge to the integrity of Kennett's experience itself, examine the religio-cultural and doctrinal factors which shaped her account of it.

Batchelor is right to suggest that Kennett's experiences should be situated within the context of the Christian mystical tradition. Her familiarity with the mystical writings of Western monasticism is indicated both by her references to Meister Eckhart in *Selling Water by the River* (Kennett 1972) and by journal articles in which she compared and contrasted the stages of the Christian mystical path, as recorded by figures such as St Teresa of Avila (1515–82) and St John of the Cross (1542–91), with her unique understanding of the series of *kenshōs* experienced by advanced Zen practitioners. One way in which her presentation reflects the accounts of Christian mystics is in terms of structure. Catholic mystical theology typically divides the spiritual life into three stages: the Purgative Life, the Illuminative Life and the Unitive Life.[5] Whilst the literature is full of 'oscillations between stages' (Cox 1986: 28), the path is ideally one of movement and progression, from a state of worldly, sinful alienation through a process of purification and contemplation towards increasing holiness and eventual union with the Godhead. Kennett frames her *kenshō* in similar terms, conveying a distinct sense of progression through a number of identifiable stages towards union with 'the Lord'. The early sequence of her visions bears a resemblance to the purgative stage, inasmuch as the purification of past karma is described as a process of stripping away 'anything that is not of the Eternal Lord' (Kennett 1977b: 71). In the Christian mystical tradition, purification 'results in the generation of a specific and pervading realization of the Absolute', a stage paralleled by Kennett's visions of ascending to the Buddha Land. Whilst union with God is the 'ultimate attainment of the Mystic Way', the crowning moment of Kennett's *kenshō* is her cosmic ordination, which occurs after her ascent to the highest level of the heavenly realms. In Christian mysticism, this unitive stage 'always maintains the "otherness" of God and the uniqueness of the creature' (Cox 1986: 30–32). Similarly, the 'accent' of Kennett's experience is often on the numinous, as is indicated by statements such as 'I am not the Lord [...] but there is nothing in me that is not of the Lord' (Kennett 1977b: 164).

The images Kennett uses to describe her *kenshō* are also reminiscent of the symbolism found in Christian mystical writings. The opening image of the glass mountain and her references to towers are prefigured by St John of the Cross in *The Ascent of Mount Carmel* and St Teresa of Avila's *The Interior Castle*. Her use of water symbolism also has parallels in St Teresa – water was 'her favorite element' (Graef 1966: 239) – and St John's *The Dark Night of the Soul*, which refers to God's grace as 'the fountain of the sweet spiritual water'. These figures also refer to the final stage of the mystical path as a 'spiritual Marriage', an image Kennett evokes when describing the fourth column of light (Kennett 1977b: 113). The image of ascending to the clouds, beyond which lies a reality that 'must not be seen with mortal eyes' (Kennett 1977: 105), is also suggestive of the fourteenth-century English mystical treatise *The Cloud of Unknowing*.

Another context within which Kennett's experience should be situated is doctrinal. Yandell observes that a religious tradition will typically 'supply forms for its adherents to use in reporting their religious experiences' (Yandall 1993: 193), with the result that 'what counts as a religiously genuine experience in part is decided by whether it is an experience in which the correct doctrine is "seen to be so"' (Yandall 1993: 293). Stark also argues that religious experiences, even of a revelatory kind, will 'usually be interpreted *in support* of the prevailing religious culture' (Stark 1992: 23). This reflects both the effectiveness of institutional mechanisms in dealing with 'the risks involved in uncontrolled mystical activity' and the fact that most people who communicate with the supernatural 'are deeply committed to the prevailing orthodoxy and few are possessed of the creativity needed to generate new culture' (Stark 1992: 23). As the founder of the ZMS, the prevailing religious culture within which Kennett was operating at the time of her *kenshō* was largely self-generated, consisting of her own unique interpretation of *Sōtō* Zen. Her experience was in many ways an 'orthodox revelation', reflecting and confirming the 'conventional faith' of her organisation. This was, as we have seen, largely in line with the Japanese tradition, but it was also highly idiosyncratic; significant adaptations had been instigated, many of which revealed her increasing proclivity to 'Christianise' the teachings. The traditional themes of her early presentation – such as the cleansing of karma, acceptance, repentance, faith, meditation, preceptual obedience and ceremonial activity – and the non-traditional, predominantly Christian, adaptations were expressed, reaffirmed and 'seen to be so' in her visionary accounts.

The conventional orthodoxy of the ZMS, however, was not simply restated in an unmodified way. Kennett's *kenshō* was a 'novel revelation' inasmuch as it prompted a number of significant doctrinal and practical transformations and innovations. It is important to acknowledge once again that this scenario has traditional precedents. According to Faure, the recorded visions and dreams of Zen masters 'are not mere doctrinal illustrations' but are 'essentially transformative', prompting doctrinal shifts and modifying social structures:

> Some of the most important changes in the history of East Asian Buddhism were the result of dreams.
>
> (Faure 1991: 227–228)

According to Stark, the number of people who receive novel revelations and the number willing to accept them as authentic is maximised during periods of social crisis and unrest (Stark 1992: 27). Personal and institutional crisis was certainly an important factor behind Kennett's meditation retreat and *kenshō* experience. Another particularly salient aspect of Stark's model for understanding Kennett's *kenshō* concerns the extent to which rejection or reinforcement influences revelations. The greater the reinforcement received, 'the more likely a person is to have further revelations'. Revelations also tend 'to become more novel (heretical) over time':

> the interaction between a successful founder and his or her followers tends to amplify heresy [...] the initial revelations will tend not to be too heretical because there is a selection process by which the initial credibility of founders is established. But, once a credible relationship exists between a founder and a set of followers, the stage is set for more daring innovations.
>
> (Stark 1992: 29)

The importance of 'follower reinforcement' to the unfolding of Kennett's *kenshō* was made clear in *How to Grow a Lotus Blossom*. Whilst some of her closest followers at Shasta Abbey were unwilling to accept the legitimacy of her experiences, she received enough reinforcement to be convinced of the validity of her visions and was encouraged to have more. According to her account, a number of the visions were shared by her followers; they witnessed her past lives, for example, as well as her ascension to the Buddha Land and cosmic ordination. In particular, the monk who served as her personal assistant throughout accompanied Kennett on her spiritual journeys, helped her to interpret what she saw, and, at certain points, even mediated between her and the Cosmic Buddha.

We will return to the question of the importance of reinforcement when we examine the manner in which Kennett's visionary experiences and doctrinal innovations were received by her wider organisation. Before we do this, though, it will be useful to examine how she 'routinised' the new teachings and practices inspired by her visions in *The Book of Life* (Kennett and MacPhillamy 1979), and to reflect upon the nature of the developments and innovations.

The Book of Life presents Kennett's insights into the cleansing of karma, the harmonisation of body and mind, and the attainment of union with the Lord, in a structured and systematic form. In the first part of the book, she explains that each person's karmic continuum can be traced back to a 'slightly dirtied, or saddened, love' (Kennett and MacPhillamy 1979: 49), a term she uses to describe the first arising of the egoistical self. The 'so-called individual soul or spirit' of an individual 'returns to the Source' in its entirety '*only* if *all* past karma, both of the life-existence just ended, and those life-existences prior to it, has been purified' (Kennett and MacPhillamy 1979: 4). The aim of *The Book of Life* is therefore 'to show people how to bring body and spirit back into harmony from within and bring up future generations without this split ever taking place' (Kennett and MacPhillamy 1979: 8). Subsequent sections examine how the disharmony of body and mind can be prevented or overcome through childrearing and the responsible handling of the death process. Kennett encourages parents to meditate with their children and help them discover and cleanse the karmic causes of disharmonising character traits. Raising a child in this way enables both parents and child to enjoy a healthy life at the end of which they are 'united with the Lord wholly and with all karmic debts cleansed' (Kennett and MacPhillamy 1979: 31–35). People who are sick and dying should also be taught about meditation and the need to cleanse karma (Kennett and MacPhillamy 1979: 36). A series of eight exhortations, to be read to dying people both before and after clinical death, are provided. Kennett's teachings on how to deal with death are largely drawn from traditional Zen sources, but she also draws on the *Tibetan Book of the Dead*. This is unsurprising as, in Bishop's terms, it is 'one of the most important Eastern sacred texts to have reached the West in the twentieth century' (Bishop 1993: 53), exerting a tremendous hold on the Western imagination. The final ingredient of her description of the intermediary realm and guidance for the dead is the quasi-theistic personalism characterising her teachings at this time. Thus, the 'individual' is not only encouraged to recognise the emptiness of self, but is also urged to accept and embrace 'the Lord' (Kennett and MacPhillamy 1979: 39–40).

Kennett also discusses how physical and mental illness can result from the disharmony of body and mind caused by inherited karmic debts. She provides tables which link specific illnesses (e.g. spinal deformity) and weaknesses (e.g. bladder weakness) with types of violent death (e.g. hanging) and uncleansed character traits (e.g. failure to deal with fear). Using them as a 'key as to where to look in one's character for the *cause* of the disharmony of one's body and mind', trainees should clear away their inherited karmic debts and cure themselves 'of the *potential* for illness' (Kennett and MacPhillamy 1979: 22). The second part of *The Book of Life*, composed by Kennett's disciple Daizui MacPhillamy, develops these ideas, outlining a method for discovering the spiritual cause and cure of physical and mental illness that uses massage to affect energy flows in the body. Kennett used this practice in preparation for the visionary episodes of her third *kenshō* and encouraged its use amongst the monks of Shasta Abbey to facilitate their own past-life experiences. The bulk of this section presents diagrams indicating the location of energy points on the body and the meridians affected by them, lists of factors (behavioural, emotional and dietary) that are beneficial and harmful to the meridians, and explanations of various sequences of massage, described as 'mudras of harmonisation'. Each *mudrā* – there are forty-three altogether – involves the activation of a sequence of 'mudra points' and is directed towards the restoration of energy-flow through the meridians and the alleviation of particular physical, mental and karmic tensions.[6] The rest of the text provides practical guidelines for choosing and using specific *mudrās* and explains the religio-philosophical foundations of the practice. *Mudrās* should be used when one 'becomes aware of a persistent tension or other sign of some disharmony of body and mind' (Kennett and MacPhillamy 1979: 67) and wishes to find out its causes and cure. Minor physical and mental tensions are immediately relaxed by *mudrās*, whilst the causes of major tensions – e.g. the persistent breakage of precepts or repressed emotions – are brought into consciousness, facilitating greater self-understanding and the ability to overcome disharmonising habits and thoughts. Much of the text is devoted to explaining how *mudrās* can help trainees to ease meridian disturbances 'which have their origin in, or are manifested as, karmic memories from earlier in this lifetime or from times prior to this lifetime' (Kennett and MacPhillamy 1979: 70). Each trainee must rely upon his own religious intuition in deciding when the crucial events of past lives are 'ripe' for being explored and accepted. Diagrams and tables are provided to help in deciding which *mudrās* of harmonisation to use and in locating specific *mudrā* points, but much of the practice should come intuitively if one regards one's hands 'as literally the Hands of God' (Kennett and MacPhillamy 1979: 80).

Developments and innovations

How to Grow a Lotus Blossom includes, as an appendix, a transcribed exchange in which Kennett is questioned by a group of disciples about the nature and significance of her *kenshō* (Kennett 1977b: 251–267). At one point, she was asked whether the practice of *zazen* is enough or whether she was advocating new practices. She responded by affirming the conventional orthodoxy of the early period and denying that anything had changed:

> How do you think this happened to me? I did Zazen; I studied the Scriptures in detail; I followed the Precepts.

Kennett later explained the apparent discontinuities in her teaching between this and the early period as an instance of 'skilful means':

> If I had told the British community when I first went over there that Zen led to the equivalent of the spiritual marriage and the realisation

of the Cosmic Buddha, half of them would have gone away and said, 'We might as well stay Christian'.[7]

Such statements have to be understood in context. They were largely a situational and strategic response to the negative reactions of a number of disciples towards Kennett's *kenshō*, which threatened to undermine her authority and destabilise her organisation. In reality, it is clear that her experiences resulted in a number of substantial developments, a fact that later statements and publications emerging from within the organisation freely acknowledge.[8] Kennett's experience, then, was both an 'orthodox revelation', reflecting the ZMS's early religious culture, and a 'novel revelation', adapting the existing world-view and inspiring innovations. Before examining the reactions of her disciples in more detail, and the strategies she employed to negotiate conflict and dissension, it will be useful to examine how her experience transformed – and not simply restated – the early teachings.

Kennett's early depiction of the religious path as a 'cleansing process' through which one 'does something about oneself' underwent significant modification. Trainees were previously taught that they would, through *zazen* and preceptual adherence, become aware of and transform the delusive opinions and habits obscuring innate enlightenment. It was now insufficient, however, to simply understand the nature of delusive tendencies in the present; to fully cleanse and transform them, one must trace karmic obscurations back to their source. Towards this end, trainees were now encouraged 'to concentrate in a slightly different way from that used in pure Zazen', *consciously* entering into thoughts, images, emotions and sensations that they regarded as 'intuitively important to follow' (Kennett and MacPhillamy 1979: 79). Furthermore, the cleansing process now involved the vivid re-experience of events from one's present and past lives.

A second major development of the existing world-view was the intensified employment of positive and personalistic images to describe Buddhahood. It is important to acknowledge that such expressions of Buddhahood are commonplace within traditional contexts. Images of cosmic or heavenly Buddhas and *Bodhisattvas*, presiding over Buddha Lands (*Buddhakṣetra*), abound within the cosmology of *Mahāyāna* Buddhism. In popular practice these beings 'are treated as wholly real', rebirth in their Pure Lands 'is ardently sought through faith', and they are believed to help, protect and teach suffering beings 'in dreams and meditative visions' (Harvey 1991: 128–133).[9] Kennett's visions, then, were not unprecedented. Furthermore, she justified her approach in Buddhistic terms: since Buddhahood is beyond all dualisms, personalistic images are as legitimate – or illegitimate – as any other kind to describe it.

The personalistic imagery Kennett evoked to describe Buddhahood must also be understood, however, as an expression of her commitment to Christianity as a suitable form to translate Buddhism in the West. She continued to use traditional terms – *Dharmakāya*, Buddha-nature, etc. – but her preferred manner of referring to ultimate truth was now highly suggestive of a monotheistic, and explicitly Christian, cosmology, including expressions like 'Lord of the House', 'the Lord', 'the Holy Spirit' and even 'God'. She rejected the idea 'that Buddhism is a God-less religion'[10] and maintained that 'in the very deep levels we can see that God and the Cosmic Buddha are identical'.[11] Kennett was not the only, or even the first, Zen master in the West to employ such 'God-language'. Phillip Kapleau used this strategy, as did Taisen Deshimaru, founder of the International Zen Association. It is important, though, to consider the broader institutional context within which these ideas were conveyed. Wider Buddhist precedents notwithstanding, the 'Christianisation' of the ZMS during the early period ensured that Kennett's increased personalisation of ultimate truth would be loaded with Christian associations. This was enhanced, as we have seen, by her intensified employment, during the Lotus Blossom period, of Christian terminology, imagery and symbolism.[12] Indeed, by finding Christian equivalents for such things as *kenshō* and past-life experiences, the *Trikāya* doctrine, and *zazen* meditation, Kennett was no longer simply *borrowing* from one religious system to make another more acceptable; she appeared, rather, to be asserting the deep and essential *identity* of the two traditions.

Since sacred canopies are 'woven out of a vast complex of interdependent parts' (Kurtz 1995: 152), the transformation of one aspect necessarily prompts changes elsewhere in the system. Kennett's increasing tendency to conceptualise ultimate truth in personalistic terms led to further reinterpretations of the ZMS's conventional orthodoxy. Central amongst these were the concepts of willingness and faith. During the early period, willingness referred to the ongoing resolution of the trainee to continually accept the personal responsibility of training. This was given a new emphasis in the Lotus Blossom period, and now referred to the determination to accept and obey 'the will of the Lord'. Similarly, whilst Kennett previously emphasised the importance of having faith 'in the Buddha within', she now talked of having unswerving faith 'in the Cosmic Buddha'. The function of ceremonial was also reinterpreted as an activity 'to show a person how to be correct in his daily life in order to find the Cosmic Buddha'; the *gasshō* (a gesture of respect which involves holding the hands up with palms together), for example, now represented and expressed 'the Mind of the Cosmic Buddha'.[13]

During the Lotus Blossom period, Kennett also introduced new ideas and practices that were without precedent in the early phase. Primary amongst these were her views on the nature and importance of the *kenshō* experience. Kennett referred to *kenshō* only rarely during the early period, and her understanding of it – that is, as the meditative 'flash of understanding' – reflected the popular modernist view promoted in the West by D. T. Suzuki. Her teachings changed radically in the Lotus Blossom period, *kenshō* no longer being described in nature as a purely private, mental and immediate experience of reality. Furthermore, we were now informed that there are different types of *kenshō* relating to differing stages of spiritual progress. Other writers acknowledge that *kenshō* experiences can be of different depths,[14] but the creation of a threefold structure and typology was unusual. Her early accounts of the experience now corresponded only to the first level of insight obtained via the 'Penetration of Heaven' *kenshō*. By contrast, later experiences, particularly the third *kenshō*, can be of a very different nature. Kennett's paradigmatic *kenshō* was thus a sensory, emotional and visual experience; it was mediated through imagery and symbolism; and it was public inasmuch as her closest disciples, in some sense, both witnessed and participated in it. During the early period, *all* such visual images experienced during meditation were dismissed as *makyō*, or 'figments of an overstrained mind'. Her reformulated understanding of *kenshō* now demanded that this teaching was revised to distinguish psychologically abnormal and harmful experiences from spiritually authentic and beneficial ones.

A second innovation was the teaching that the harmonisation of body and mind via the third *kenshō*, and ultimately full enlightenment, requires total sexual abstinence. During the early period, celibacy was not required of trainee priests, and married couples were accepted for monastic ordination. This relaxed attitude was now reversed, Kennett's *kenshō* proving to her that sexuality was one of the greatest obstacles to advanced spirituality, a 'desecration of the Lord' and a 'wasting of the Lord's gifts' (Kennett 1977b: 169–170). The monastic policy of the ZMS was thus gradually revised during subsequent years. A formal vow of celibacy was introduced for trainee priests, whilst married couples were no longer eligible as monastic candidates. Kennett later decided to ban marriage within the priesthood altogether and asked her ordained disciples to commit themselves to their monastic vocation or to their marital and familial lives. She would later maintain that a role of the Zen master is to deprogramme her disciples of their sexuality 'so that what they're looking for is the Eternal rather than a mate' (Kennett, quoted in Friedman 1987: 187).

Kennett's rather idiosyncratic teachings on karma, and particularly her emphasis on past-life experiences, constituted another major innovation of this period. Although she insisted that her account was verified by traditional Buddhist sources, containing 'nothing invented or imagined', she nevertheless admitted that it 'revolutionizes karmic theory as it is usually taught' (Kennett and MacPhillamy 1979: 2). Her interpretation of karma was unconventional in a number of ways. For instance, the idea that beings are born for the purpose of purifying uncleansed karma gave the Buddhist concept of *saṃsāra* an unusually teleological slant. This stemmed directly from her quasi-theistic vision of ultimate truth that casts 'the Lord' as the controlling force behind the rebirth process. The result was a curious synthesis in which she seemed to combine her favoured elements of Christian theism with the Buddhist theory of karmic causality.

Kennett's emphasis on re-experiencing past lives remained the most central and innovative aspect of her teachings on karma. The notion that one can see or experience past lives during meditation has, she rightly observed, a long

Buddhist pedigree. The memory of previous lives was the first of the 'three knowledges' that the Buddha (according to the traditional biography) experienced prior to attaining enlightenment, and it subsequently appears amongst lists of supernatural powers or knowledges that highly realised meditators and *Bodhisattvas* are believed to possess. Historically, the attitude of the Buddhist tradition towards supernatural powers has been ambivalent. In the *Sōtō* tradition, this ambivalence manifests itself through the generally negative attitude of *Dōgen* towards thaumaturges on the one hand, and the more positive appraisals of occult powers emerging from within the lineage of *Keizan* on the other. In valuing past-life experiences positively, Kennett's teachings thus reflected one side of a traditional divide, and specifically represented the lineage of *Keizan*. Her outlook remained unconventional, however, in a number of ways. First, she regarded the reliving of past lives not simply as a sign or byproduct of advanced meditation, but as a desirable, integral and creative aspect of the cleansing process of individuation. Secondly, and as a consequence of this, the experience of past lives within her movement became commonplace. This, as Harvey observes, is in marked contrast to the Buddhist mainstream (Harvey 1991: 44). Thirdly, this teaching was again overlaid with a quasi-theistic import; past-life experiences should be regarded as a 'teaching from the Lord', an opportunity to deepen training that must be willingly accepted.

A fourth major area of innovation was Kennett's teaching on the harmonisation of body and mind, and the use of *mudrās* to ease disturbances of a physical, mental and karmic nature.[15] The oriental healing arts are widely known and applied within Eastern Zen temples,[16] and Kennett was thus able to observe her fellow monks at *Sōjiji* practising moxibustion and 'holding various places on their bodies' (Kennett and MacPhillamy 1979: 54) to ease physical and mental tensions. The practice encouraged in *The Book of Life* takes as axiomatic certain ideas that are fundamental to all of these practices, such as the flowing of energy (*ki*) through meridians, but it borrows primarily from a massage technique known as '*amma*'. It was a somewhat eclectic spiritual exercise, though, drawing upon and synthesising a variety of sources including traditional Buddhist iconography, the practices witnessed by Kennett in *Sōjiji* 'and our own meditation' (Kennett and MacPhillamy 1979: 57). These were coupled with Kennett's view that the healing process essentially concerns the harmonisation of oneself with 'the Lord', often via the vivid experience of past lives. Many East Asian Buddhists, of course, believe that karma, alongside other factors, plays 'a profound role in the origin and course of a disease' (Lock 1980: 225). Kennett attached much greater significance to such causes, however, and brought her own idiosyncratic interpretation of karma to bear on the subject. Her magico-ritual interpretation of certain *mudrās*,[17] and her view that *mudrās* facilitate union with Cosmic Buddhahood, were also suggestive of Esoteric Buddhist or Shingon influences. The resulting practice of harmonising *mudrās*, then, was in many ways a new invention, reconfiguring traditional elements and adding new features in a syncretic mix.

Assimilation and rejection

During the early period, the process of assimilation within the ZMS was smooth and successful as Kennett's teachings filtered down to the level of community belief and practice without any sign of resistance. The years following her religious experiences were, by contrast, the most turbulent and unstable in the development of the organisation. During this period, the wider monastic and lay community gradually became aware of the nature of Kennett's 'third *kenshō*' and the doctrinal and practical innovations stemming from it. This initially took the form of leakages and rumours resulting from the controversial disrobing and denunciation of Kennett by a number of her closest and most senior disciples. Kennett also began to induct the wider community into her experiences and innovations herself, though, through her publications and journal articles.[18] Practitioners within the wider organisation responded to this information in a number of ways, ranging from wholesale acceptance and assimilation to outright rejection. The responses of Kennett's disciples, and the decision-making processes through which they assessed the reliability and authenticity of her experiences and innovations, will now be examined using the work of Waterhouse on authority in British Buddhism as a framework.

Waterhouse identifies four main categories of authority sources recognised with differing focuses by British Buddhist groups: the authority of teachers as exemplary figures; the Buddha's word as represented in texts; lineage-tradition; and personal experience. Changes and adaptations must be legitimated, she argues, through recourse to the contrasting authorities that different Buddhist schools call upon to authenticate their religious practices. The appeal to contrasting authorities to authenticate practice and legitimate adaptation can be observed both at the public or organisational level and also at the personal level as practitioners 'reach compromise positions on the traditional authority structures which are offered, including the authority of experience' (Waterhouse 1997: 39). It is probable, Waterhouse maintains, that members of all Buddhist groups reach different compromise positions on authority, 'but without the challenge of splits and disputes these positions are not tested' (1997: 213). Rawlinson's distinction between legitimacy and authenticity is proposed as another useful model for understanding 'the tensions which exist for practitioners when they accept the validity of a particular Buddhist path' (Waterhouse 1999: 26). Whilst legitimate authority is *external* and stems from 'the formal procedures by which representatives of traditions are appointed or recognised', authentic authority is *internal* and stems from 'the states of realisation these representatives have attained and which justify their interpretations of tradition' (Rawlinson, quoted in Waterhouse 1999: 27). Both the representatives of Buddhist schools, when presenting their teachings as reliable, and individual practitioners, when making decisions about the path, rely on a balance of legitimacy and authenticity. Whilst the legitimacy of tradition remains an important test of reliability, Waterhouse suggests that Western

Buddhists, living within a post-traditional order characterised by individual authority and reflexivity, usually give precedence to authenticity.

The successful transplantation and growth of the ZMS in the West can be understood in terms of Waterhouse's work on authority. Kennett legitimated her teachings and adaptations during the early period by appealing, first, to the authority of her transmission master Kōhō Chisan; secondly, to her legitimate position within the Sōtō Zen lineage-tradition; and thirdly, to her personal charismatic authority stemming from her direct experience of the truth. American and British practitioners supported the ZMS because, through recourse to a variety of authority sources including that of personal experience, they found Kennett and her adapted form of Sōtō Zen to be both attractive and reliable. Different practitioners may have attached primary significance to different authorities but this is difficult to detect because they were not tested or challenged in any significant way during this time. The radical developments of the Lotus Blossom period, however, disturbed this relative equilibrium. Kennett's 'third kenshō' put pressure upon the authority sources recognised by practitioners who now had to reassess the reliability of the teachings and make important decisions of commitment and discipleship. With reference to a variety of authorities, most disciples assimilated the innovations whilst a substantial minority rejected them. To defend her reputation and mitigate against destabilising forces, Kennett developed a number of action strategies, reasserting and reconfiguring the authority sources called upon during the early period whilst calling upon extra, previously unrecognised or latent, authorities. During this period, then, 'authority' was subjected to dispute and contention within the ZMS.

Kennett's closest American disciples at Shasta Abbey were witnesses of and participants in her visions and past-life experiences, their receptivity providing her with the sanction and space to have further experiences of a more complex and daring nature. These followers 'began to have similar experiences' of their own, thereby discovering that 'there are many more planes of existence than just the human one'.[19] The reliving of atrocities committed and suffered within Nazi concentration camps appears to have been a particularly common past-life experience, although even more dramatic and significant episodes were allegedly experienced by the abbey's monks. Furthermore, Kennett participated in her disciples' experiences in the same way that they had participated in her's. The fact that they were 'players' in each other's experiences, and the subsequent joint authorship of The Book of Life, suggests that her innovative new teachings were not only assimilated as they were being formulated, but were actually developed and articulated in close dialogue with a core of trusted followers.

The first signs of assimilation within the wider community can, predictably, be detected in articles composed by monks. The British monastic community was invited to train alongside Kennett at Shasta Abbey in 1977 and so enjoyed a closer proximity to the source of the teachings. Furthermore, they were expected to play an important mediating role between her and the British laity.

Articles by lay practitioners reflecting the new ideas came later, and their initially sporadic appearance suggests that the lay congregation assimilated the teachings in a more gradual and cautious way. The earliest article of Kennett's which reflected her new teachings appeared in *The Journal of Throssel Hole Priory* in the spring of 1977. This article taught the importance of being obedient and humble before 'the Lord of the House' and of cleansing oneself by finding 'the source of the karmic stream'.[20] From around this time, articles by British monks and lay practitioners reflecting this new manner of conceptualising Buddhahood and spiritual training also began to appear. Earlier and more traditional ways of describing ultimate reality such as 'Buddha-nature' or 'Buddha-heart' were now increasingly replaced by Kennett's quasi-theistic language of 'Lord', 'Cosmic Buddha' and 'God'. Articles now taught that experiential confirmation of the existence of God could be received in meditation, and there were reports of visionary encounters with the Cosmic Buddha by both monastic and lay practitioners. The twin ideas of having 'faith in the Lord' and the willingness to seek and be obedient to His will as revealed in meditation or prayer became popular themes during this period, and one monk aptly characterised the religious path as one of 'seeking first the Kingdom of God'.[21] Alongside these ideas, Kennett's new teachings on karmic cleansing and past lives also began to appear. Problems encountered in training were now understood as loving teachings from the Cosmic Buddha which revealed layers of self to be cleansed or 'offered up' to the Lord. Past life experiences were to be regarded in the same way and whilst there was a reluctance to describe specific experiences in detail, they were nevertheless discussed as an important aspect of training. Discussion by monks of the practice of harmonising *mudrās* was, in contrast to the other new themes, infrequent. In fact, there appeared to be a degree of caution in some monastic quarters towards this practice:

> In recent years monks at Shasta Abbey have investigated aspects of various healing arts, both eastern and Western [...] The essential point is that these things are an aspect of training, not a substitute for it [...] The monastery which [...] practices physical healing must not drift into becoming a health farm.[22]

The basic principles underlying the practice, however, seem to have been assimilated more easily. The characterisation of religious training as a process of harmonising body and mind, and the idea that physical illness has a spiritual basis, for example, were widely accepted even though the use of *mudrās* was not.

Those who assimilated Kennett's new teachings and practices assessed, and became convinced of, their reliability by appealing to the authority sources identified earlier. The authorities of lineage-tradition and scripture, however, were invoked with less frequency than those of the teacher and personal experience, suggesting that these trainees, like the Buddhists of Waterhouse's study, valued authenticity above legitimacy. A number of reasons were given to justify their continuing faith in Kennett. The quality of her teachings during the early period and her skilful adaptations for the West were invoked. According to one former monk, the community at Throssel Hole Priory survived the turbulent period immediately following Kennett's religious experiences 'by hanging on to what we had learnt in the past and refusing to listen to hearsay'. Appeal was also made to her personal qualities and experience and the model she offered as a living embodiment of the teachings. Faith in the teacher was balanced with the authority of personal experience of the teachings, as can be seen in articles recording confirmatory experiences of the Cosmic Buddha. Appeal was also made to the experience of others within the ZMS; the British monks travelled to Shasta Abbey to train alongside those with more experience, whilst articles by the British laity emphasised the importance of taking refuge in the monastic *Sangha*.

In *How to Grow a Lotus Blossom*, Kennett alludes to a number of followers who had rejected her 'third *kenshō*' and renounced their discipleship. Although there are no means of accurately quantifying the numbers of her dissenters and critics from this period, the fact that they organised themselves into support groups and independent centres indicates that we are dealing here with a significant minority. The first of these, a support group called 'Sorting It Out', was created in the late 1970s by a former American monk to help disaffected members of the ZMS and other religious groups make the transition back to ordinary life. According to its founder, over thirty ex-disciples of Kennett and over three hundred practitioners from other religious groups came to it for help. The crisis that occurred in Britain, however, was, for a variety of reasons, even more disruptive than that in America. Although the American dissenters were numerically greater, the well-established Californian monastic and lay congregation was not severely depleted by their departure. Furthermore, the leadership of the American community, with Kennett at the helm supported by a senior group of dedicated monks, remained largely intact and 'in touch' with the wider community. The British congregation, by contrast, was relatively rootless and small, and it was distant – literally *and* figuratively – from Kennett's leadership. It was thus ill-equipped to cope with conflict and fragmentation on anything but a small scale. Reactions to Kennett's *kenshō* in Britain, though, were not small scale. A number of key figures behind the growth, development and leadership of the British ZMS renounced their discipleship at this time, creating a sense of uncertainty and crisis within the community.

In Britain, this period of turbulence began following the return of Daiji Strathern, late in 1976, from a three-month stay in America. Whilst in the throes of her *kenshō*, Kennett had summoned him to Shasta Abbey 'so that he might see for himself what took place and perhaps experience one himself'.[23] Having inducted him into her new ideas, she expected him to return to Britain and introduce them to others. Strathern, however, did not react to the things he witnessed and read about at Shasta Abbey in the way she had hoped. Rather than providing additional reinforcement to her experiences and innovations, he rejected their authenticity and legitimacy and renounced his discipleship. Since he was a popular figure under whose leadership the British community had grown during the early period, his decision to disrobe naturally aroused great curiosity and confusion. According to one former monk, Strathern's departure 'shocked the UK community to the foundations' and, since the primary loyalties were with him rather than with Kennett – whom many had never even seen or met – support for the priory 'melted away'.

Strathern was not the only influential and high-profile figure to renounce Kennett in Britain. The meditation group in Mousehole, originally so important to the successful transplantation of the ZMS, also withdrew its support, and there were further secessions from within the monastic community. Most importantly, the prior of the London Zen Priory disrobed and, taking the priory with him, disaffiliated from the ZMS, renaming it as the 'Dharma House Trust'. In 1978, the Trust moved to Penzance where it merged with the Mousehole Group. Kennett publicly denounced these developments, condemning the creation of the Dharma House Trust as a 'take-over bid'.[24] Disaffected British disciples did not flock to join the Trust, however, which remained a small and isolated meditation group, focusing on *Sōtō* Zen but without affiliating with a specific teacher or lineage.[25]

The initial obstacle faced by many disciples was the nature of Kennett's *kenshō*. Trainees clearly defined the *kenshō* experience in terms of the mystical 'flash of insight' popularised by Suzuki and others, including Kennett herself in her early publications. In light of this normative understanding, her 'third *kenshō*' was deemed for a number of reasons to be an inauthentic expression of Zen. The status and significance that Kennett attributed to her visual and sensory encounters was challenged. Many interpreted these as *makyō* and they questioned the motives behind her attachment to them. Others, unwilling to accept the spiritual pedigree of her experiences, brought a psychological interpretation to bear and argued that her visions were actually highly symbolic expressions of unresolved personality issues buried deep within her unconscious.

Kennett's claim to have experienced past lives, and the importance she attached to such experiences, posed another major stumbling block. Many criticised her for emphasising as essential an experience that, from a traditional perspective, is neither common nor particularly important spiritually. Others acknowledged that past-life experiences could be useful – for example, in understanding the deeper layers of self – but objected to the emphasis placed upon them. There was, more importantly, a widespread scepticism about the authenticity of the experiences that Kennett and her disciples claimed to be undergoing. The manner in which they became 'players' in each other's past-life dramas was challenged from a Buddhistic point of view, and the use of oriental massage to facilitate past-life experiences made Kennett vulnerable to the accusation that she was inducing these experiences artificially. Former disciples from this period do not substantiate this accusation but do maintain that the experiences were expressed within a highly charged atmosphere of intense collective reinforcement. One referred to Kennett as the 'over-consciousness of the group' and described how the monks of Shasta Abbey 'tuned into' this and participated in a kind of 'collective dream'.[26] The former prior of Throssel Hole also described how, through this powerful dynamic of reinforcement, increasingly elaborate past-life episodes were constructed in which the monks experienced themselves as important figures like *Bodhidharma*, St John of the Cross and Jesus.

Another problematic area was Kennett's increasing reliance on Christian forms and, in particular, her use of quasi-theistic imagery and terminology. One former monk recalled that the doctrine 'became more theistic, more magical and more mysterious'. As the new teachings filtered out into the wider community they also met resistance from lay trainees who questioned the synonymous usage of 'Cosmic Buddha' and 'God' and the Christian resonance behind references to 'the Lord'. Not all of the disciples who broke their affiliation with Kennett during these testing times found such terminology problematic, however. Whilst rejecting other elements of her teachings, such as her emphasis on past lives, some were untroubled by her increasing use of personalised and theistic imagery. One former trainee defended her use of 'Cosmic Buddha' Buddhistically, equating it with traditional images of the Buddha *Vairocana*. To understand why Kennett's theistic language provoked such strong reactions it is important to remember the wider, significantly Christianised, context within which it was being used. According to a former British monk, it was not the *fact* that Kennett used Christian forms but the 'particularly consistent' way in which she used them that many found unacceptable.

Finally, a number of disciples were disgruntled with Kennett's revised perspective on celibacy and the increasingly authoritarian tone of her teachings. Part of the attraction of the ZMS in the early period was its married priesthood, which allowed individuals to commit themselves to both a married and a monastic lifestyle. The mandatory celibacy ruling of 1976, and the later edict banning marriage in the priesthood, were met with 'violently mixed feelings'.[27] They put pressure on marriages and ultimately led many individuals to opt out of the organisation, some with and some without their partners. Former disciples also recall how Kennett became increasingly exclusive and authoritarian during this period. Alongside her emphasis on having faith in the Cosmic Buddha, she now stressed that faithful acceptance of the teacher's authority was 'the essence of the teaching'.[28] One former monk found 'the single-minded devotion' Kennett demanded 'exhausting';[29] another reflected that despite having 'those first intimations which would become the foundation of my interior life under her guidance', he 'learned much about capricious leadership and the excesses of power that a *rōshi* can exercise'.[30] In the early 1980s, the related concerns of celibacy and authoritarianism led another of Kennett's priories – the Oregon Zen Priory – to sever its formal connections with Shasta Abbey. The Dharma Rain Zen Centre in Oregon was subsequently established as an independent temple by a number of disaffected married priests and lay practitioners.

Those who rejected the validity of Kennett's teachings also appealed to the main authority sources identified by Waterhouse. The reflexivity of this process was also evident, individual practitioners attaching primary value to different authorities. It is noticeable, however, that dissenters and critics generally attached greater value to the legitimate authorities of lineage-tradition and scripture. Waterhouse states that

> Legitimacy in terms of Buddhist traditions and the consultation of the wise people who represent traditions must be important if a practitioner wants to regard herself as situated within Buddhism.
>
> (Waterhouse 1999: 30)

Since these practitioners were, unlike Kennett's assimilating followers, seriously worried that her experiences and teachings had taken her beyond the Buddhist pale, their demand for legitimate authority and guidance had been heightened.

A number of practitioners deemed Kennett's experiences and teachings to be invalid by appealing to the authority of the *Sōtō* Zen lineage-tradition. Some consulted or aligned themselves with alternative teachers whose legitimacy within the *Sōtō* lineage was considered unquestioned. One British trainee initially sought guidance from Taizan Maezumi *Rōshi* before, shocked and disillusioned by his alcoholism, he travelled to Japan and found a temple 'where the practice is pure, traditional and wholly good'. The most common way in which traditional authority was invoked, though, was through an appeal to Zen doctrine as popularly understood. Although Kennett's experiences were not unprecedented in *Sōtō* Zen, they could not function for her, as they did for *Keizan*, as a source of legitimation. Dreams and visions do not command the same status and authority in the modern West as they did in medieval Japan, and, more importantly, her critics were unaware of the traditional visionary precedents and so argued that they 'didn't make sense according to traditional Zen'.[31] One former disciple, referring to *How to Grow a Lotus Blossom*, stated that 'any rational person versed in Buddhism couldn't really accept it at all'. Kennett's early teachings, described as 'straightforward *Sōtō*' and 'meaningful and good', were now regarded favourably as compared to her later thought, described by one former trainee as 'madness'.

Critics also invoked the legitimate authority of sacred texts. Waterhouse argues that the idea of scriptural orthodoxy is more important than the actual study of canonical material for most British Buddhists who are 'happy to hear the word of the Buddha indirectly, through the interpretation of others' (Waterhouse 1999: 31–32). This accurately describes the situation of Kennett's disciples, most of whom accessed the Zen scriptural tradition via popular English-language translations and interpretations, including those of Kennett herself. A small number of British trainees did make a more direct appeal, though, to the authoritative texts of the Zen tradition:

Well, how do you equate Kennett's *How to Grow a Lotus Blossom* with, say, the Diamond *Sūtra*, with its talk about the void and the non-concepts and all this sort of thing [...] We'd look over the various *sūtras* and say, 'Well, can we accept this? Is this really Buddhism? What is this about?'

Whilst lineage-tradition and scripture were important referents of legitimate authority, personal experience remained central to the decision-making process. A letter written by a British trainee to advise an American meditation group experiencing collective doubts about Kennett's new teachings emphasised that 'in Buddhism there is no authority, no ultimate authority, except the intuition of the individual'.[32] According to a former American disciple, in making his decision to renounce Kennett the perceived discrepancy between her teachings and traditional Zen doctrine was a secondary concern: 'the crucial thing' was that the practice 'didn't feel good'.[33] Others have also described how they 'found the master inside myself again' and listened to their own 'inner voice'.[34] Their experiences generated various responses to *guru*-based forms of Buddhism, ranging from complete cynicism to healthy scepticism. As well as relying on the authority of their own personal experience of the teachings, critics also appealed to the experiences of others. Some argued that Kennett herself was 'beyond her own experience'[35] and that she needed to seek the guidance of a teacher, someone who could 'call her on her own shit'.[36] The Lotus Blossom period was so turbulent in Britain because the experiences of high-profile dissenters were regarded as authoritative to the wider community. Former British and American trainees sought guidance from other spiritual teachers and groups and, as we have seen, formed their own support networks and alternative practice centres.

Strategies and arguments

Dissension within the ZMS on both sides of the Atlantic necessitated a response from the movement's leadership. Kennett and her senior disciples devised a number of strategies to defend her reputation and provide assurances of the continuing authenticity and legitimacy of her teachings. A variety of action strategies and arguments were mobilised in an attempt to restore stability to an organisation rocked by conflict and dispute. Some were aimed at the movement as a whole, whilst others were directed specifically at the British community. Kennett's first strategy was to respond directly to the criticisms levelled against her, privately through personal letters and publicly through ZMS publications and journals. Particularly salient in this respect was an appendix to *How to Grow a Lotus Blossom* in which she answered questions about her religious experiences (Kennett 1977b: 251–267). This exchange anticipated and responded to the major areas of concern and criticism that were being raised throughout the organisation. The appendix was naturally omitted from the second edition of the text, published in 1993 when the authenticity and validity of her 'third *kenshō*' was no longer disputed within the organisation. Journal articles during the Lotus Blossom period were also tailored to respond to the challenge posed to Kennett's authority, experiences and teachings. This period witnessed a spate of articles, for example, that asserted the importance of having faith in and commitment to the Zen master.

Kennett's religious movement also underwent a number of name changes during the Lotus Blossom period, beginning in 1976 when the ZMS also became known as the 'Reformed *Sōtō* Zen Church'. An important reason for this name change was clearly the reformulation of Kennett's thought following her religious experiences, and her wish 'to make a firm bond' between the temples and priories under her direction. The movement's name changed again in 1978 to the 'Order of Buddhist Contemplatives of the *Sōtō* Zen Church' (the OBC), a designation that was firmly in line with Kennett's intensified use of Christian imagery during this period.[37] This name change should also be interpreted strategically as an instance of 'social amnesia' or forgetfulness. Coney observes that it is

> characteristic of a number of NRMs [new religious movements] that the name of either the leader or the group changes to suit the new mood of the times. Memories associated with the previous designation tend to recede with its disappearance from usage, and new memories are produced in their stead.
>
> (Coney 1997)

The conflict and disunity experienced by Kennett's movement was at its most intense during the latter stages of, and immediately following, her *kenshō*. By changing its name she may have been attempting, consciously or unconsciously, to erase 'unwelcome memories' of discord, promoting a more stable narrative upon which its future growth could be predicated.

Another strategy aimed at restoring stability within the organisation as a whole was that of institutional innovation. The crisis of this period was exacerbated by a lack of communication between the monastic centre and the wider laity, and assessments of the teachings were often made on an insufficient basis of rumours and leakages from disaffected monks. Kennett recognised this unsatisfactory situation and responded to it effectively by reopening the channels of communication between herself and the laity. Significant in this respect was her creation in 1979 of a new category of lay trainee, the Lay Minister, who had the authority to assume minor roles of spiritual instruction and encouragement, and the responsibility to liaise closely with the abbey. The Lay Ministry was intended to provide an important bridge and point of contact between the monastic and lay communities, and as such it has been central to the stability, growth and development of the OBC. The creation of this programme was therefore a timely innovation that lends support to the crisis explanations of religious innovation discussed earlier. In addition to this institutional measure, Kennett also began to temper the excesses of mystical activity at Shasta Abbey. Particularly in response to the disrobing of Daiji Strathern, she began to discourage the more unusual kinds of past-life experience. The controlling of religious experience by the OBC's leadership reached its fullest expression during the later period of routinisation and consolidation, discussed in the next chapter.

The critical and disparaging view of British Buddhists held by Kennett during the early period was reinforced during the Lotus Blossom period and, owing to her belief that British trainees had particular difficulties in assimilating the teachings and somehow posed a unique challenge to her authority, a number of strategies were devised specifically for them. An early approach was to distance herself from the British congregation, or, in the words of one of her assistants, to 'wash her hands completely of England until there is some demonstration of a willingness to trust her'.[38] She was initially unwilling to send any of her senior American monks over to England to take charge of Throssel Hole Priory and also considered restricting the distribution of How to Grow a Lotus Blossom to her American disciples. The decision to withdraw her support and involvement was not really implemented beyond an attitude of 'coolness' towards British affairs, however, and it seems to have functioned more as a warning than as a policy of action. In reality, there was throughout this period a steady stream of letters passing between Shasta Abbey and British trainees through which an attempt was made to discuss and resolve areas of dispute and contention. Kennett even addressed the British congregation as a whole via letters distributed in 1977.[39] The first of these reassured her disciples that she was teaching nothing 'that is not a part of genuine Zen practice', and encouraged them to 'behave like spiritual adults' by redoubling their efforts in meditation and by ignoring damaging rumours. In the second, she blamed the rejection of her kenshō on the 'authoritarian' and 'witch-hunting' attitude of British Buddhism.

Another strategy was that of nurturing the British contingent through this turbulent phase. Kennett blamed the disaffection of her senior British monks on their own indiscipline and spiritual immaturity and decided to transfer the remaining faithful to Shasta Abbey to train under her direct supervision alongside the American monastic elite. A small number of lay trainees were also invited to participate in the Lay Ministry programme to provide a sound basis for its introduction in Britain. The British laity responded positively to Kennett's call for increased trust and commitment, and so, in place of the absent British monks, she commissioned a rotating system of senior American monks as priors of Throssel Hole. These nurtured the British laity by maintaining the journal and leading retreats and their leadership had a stabilising effect on the community, facilitating the assimilation of new teachings and encouraging further growth. Her confidence in British Buddhists restored, Kennett also promised from this time 'to take a much more active part in what happens in Britain'.[40]

Once the initial crisis had subsided and a state of relative equilibrium had been restored, a culture of acceptance was promoted within the British laity through the inclusion, within the journal, of articles and letters reflecting the successful assimilation of Kennett's new teachings by British trainees. During this period, then, the journal served two important purposes. As well as providing a forum for practitioners to share their understanding of the teachings as applied within the context of their lives, it also functioned as a mirror in which the assimilation of the teachings by individual practitioners was reflected back to the community. The inclusion of regular bulletins providing news of the British monks deepening their training at Shasta Abbey also facilitated the process of acculturation.

Underpinning the strategies of action, a wide variety of arguments were articulated to defend the authenticity of Kennett's experiences and continuing reliability of her teachings. A particularly noteworthy feature of Kennett's reaction to the conflict and dissension of this period was her increased dependence upon the legitimate authorities of lineage-tradition and scripture. This was largely a reaction to the claims of her critics that what she was teaching could no longer be legitimately regarded as 'Buddhism'. There was also a marked increase, compared to the early period, in the appearance of teachings stressing the role of 'faith' in spiritual practice. An appeal to the authority of personal experience, however, remained at the forefront of her presentation and was the bulwark of her defence. Kennett appealed to the personal experience of her followers by encouraging them to 'practice the form of Zen meditation suggested herein wholeheartedly and then see if the results are good' (Kennett 1977b: xiii). She nevertheless asked her British students to rely upon, or have faith in, the experiences of her American disciples until they could experience for themselves how her teaching 'makes Zen warm and alive'.[41] Appeal to her disciples' experience was secondary, though, to her emphasis on the authentic authority of her own personal experience of the truth. Responding to the queries of a British trainee, an American monk stated that Kennett 'only speaks from what she herself personally knows to be true'.[42] Kennett claimed that, through experience, she knew the reality and love of the Cosmic Buddha. She also argued that any Zen master who undergoes this profound experience must make it the basis of all their subsequent teaching. With respect to the perceived clash between her experiences and Buddhist doctrine, one position she adopted was that since doctrine is based on the experiences of meditation masters, it is necessarily fluid and changeable. This argument, when taken to its extreme, rendered all external formulations superfluous and asserted a form of perennial philosophy:

> the Christian and the Buddhist and the Muslim and the Jew, once they *know* the Ultimate, are beyond such things as theologies, doctrinal disputes and 'isms'.[43]

During the early period, ZMS teachings focused mainly on the 'internal' aspect of faith, that is faith in one's inherent enlightenment. This was given a different emphasis with the appearance of *How to Grow a Lotus Blossom*, which encouraged students to have faith in 'the Lord'. The rejection of this text by a number of disciples prompted a further shift in Kennett's thought and she now began to prioritise the 'external' aspect of having faith in the teacher. Articles from this period stressed the importance of having 'faith in both the teaching and the Teacher especially when they don't conform to our ideas and opinions'.[44] Within the context of training, faith entails accepting the teachings as 'working hypotheses'[45] until they are confirmed through personal experience. Personal experience of the truth of the teachings will, in turn, lead to a deepening of faith. Although these teachings were largely a situational response to a challenge to Kennett's authority, the model presented here is in tune with traditional Buddhist beliefs about faith (*saddhā*).

The appeal to legitimate forms of authority became a significant aspect of Kennett's presentation during this period, as she attempted to stabilise an organisation which had seen her legitimacy as a Buddhist teacher challenged and disputed. Her invocation of the authority of the lineage-tradition took a number of forms. First, she denied that her experiences and teachings deviated from or changed the traditional beliefs and practices of *Sōtō* Zen in any way, claiming, to the contrary, that they '*proved* Buddhist doctrine' (Kennett 1977b: 267) and were entirely in keeping with tradition. Defending the legitimacy of her visions, she argued that 'historically some Zen masters have reported experiences such as this, others have not' (Kennett 1977b: xii), whilst experiences of past lives 'are very common in Zen temples in the east'.[46] In a letter to the British congregation, she made the rather astonishing claim that

> The experiences of hearing the voice of the Cosmic Buddha and seeing one's past lives, as well as the temptations of Mara, are part of the history not only of Shakyamuni Buddha's own enlightenment experiences [...] but also of the kenshō experience, in varying degrees, of every true Zen Master that there has ever been.[47]

Various Buddhistic defences of Kennett's personified expressions of ultimate truth, referring to the traditional precedents of *Vairocana* Buddha and a host of *Bodhisattvas*, were also presented. The perennial philosophy advanced by Kennett also enabled her to draw on resources from outside the Zen tradition to provide extra legitimation for her experiences and teachings. Her visions were compared with similar experiences recorded in the hagiography of the Thai *Theravāda* meditation master Phra Acharn Mun, and parallels to her *kenshō* were perceived in a variety of religious traditions, including Judaism and Christianity.

Kennett's experiences and teachings were also legitimated through recourse to the authority of her position within the *Sōtō* Zen lineage, derived from her relationship with Kōhō Keidō Chisan. The importance of this relationship was reinforced during this period by the inclusion of articles by, and photographs of, Kōhō Chisan within OBC journals and publications. In particular, Kennett claimed that she had received the teachings on the nature and grades of *kenshō* via an esoteric oral transmission within the *Sōtō* school. This claim provided a convenient response to her critics since it was argued that this secret transmission 'has given rise to the situation where students can criticize teachers for not being "traditional" because the student does not know what the real teaching is'.[48] This process, whereby the adoption of something different and new is presented as 'a *recovery* of something prior but abandoned', is a common feature of prophethood referred to by Waldman and Baum as 'innovation through renovation' (1992: 262).

Great emphasis was also given by Kennett to the fact that her particular line of descent within the *Sōtō* school included a number of prominent puritanical reformers such as *Manzan Dōhaku* (1636–1715). Kōhō Chisan was also cast as a purist who strove to combat laxity and degeneracy within the modern *Sōtō* sect. This pure/degenerate polarity was most fully explored in her two-volume record of training in Japan, *The Wild, White Goose* (discussed in more detail below). By aligning herself with a purist or traditionalist strand of *Sōtō* Zen, Kennett invoked a particularly potent form of lineal authority to legitimate her teachings. The appeal to a pure lineage was particularly important for legitimating the reforms Kennett had implemented within the monastic order. The new rulings regarding celibacy and marriage were justified with the claim that she was 'purifying' the practice, re-establishing a pristine model and creating the optimum conditions for successful spirituality.

During the early period of the ZMS's development, Kennett's historical background within the Japanese *Sōtō* sect naturally provided an important referent of legitimation. In light of the critical stance adopted towards mainstream *Sōtō* during the Lotus Blossom period, we may have expected Kennett to distance herself from the Japanese sect, but this was not the case. By contrast, links and associations were actively maintained, sought after and publicised. In fact, the appeal to an institutional form of traditional authority intensified during this period as she attempted to reassert her credibility as a teacher of Zen by invoking the official arbiters of *Sōtō* orthodoxy. Kennett invoked the authority of Japanese *Sōtō* initially by claiming that *How to Grow a Lotus Blossom* had received an 'imprimatur' from the chief abbot of *Sōjiji*.[49] Visits by Japanese representatives of the *Sōtō* sect to Shasta Abbey were subsequently presented as an endorsement of her status as a teacher and occasions of spiritual bonding. The emphasis during this period, then, was very much upon unity and connection rather than difference and separation:

> Throssel Hole Priory is a daughter monastery of Shasta Abbey, Mt. Shasta, California, which is a daughter monastery of Dai Hon Zan Sōjiji, Yokohama, and, although we are politically autonomous, both are part of the Sōtō Zen Church of Japan.[50]

The authority of scripture also became an important referent during this period. The *Avataṃsaka Sūtra* was cited by an assistant of Kennett's as one example of many scriptural accounts that describe 'similar and in many cases identical experiences to Rōshi's, including the various sights such as lotuses, towers, etc.'. The same assistant also claimed that 'nearly every Buddhist sūtra I have ever read, and most of the Zen texts, speak clearly of past lives [and] the benefit gained from remembering them'.[51] Kennett herself appealed extensively to the Shōbōgenzō, the prime scriptural authority of Sōtō Zen, to legitimate her new teachings. In a series of commentarial articles, she presented her ideas on karmic cleansing, past-life experiences and union with the Cosmic Buddha as integral aspects of Dōgen's encyclopeadic work, a project that required a substantial degree of contrivance and creativity of interpretation. Although Kennett made extensive appeal to Buddhist scripture as a legitimate form of authority, she retained the primacy of experience, claiming that the scriptures are 'direct accounts of what happened to real people like us' (Kennett 1977b: 266). The view that scriptures are authoritative because they are 'outpourings of those who have seen'[52] sanctioned Kennett to adapt the teachings and legitimated the inclusion, in the eyes of her disciples, of her own texts under the rubric of 'Buddhist scripture'.

The foregoing discussion of the responses Kennett's visionary experiences elicited and the various strategies she devised in reply reveals much about the internal dynamics of religious movements. Stark's comments concerning the influence of follower reinforcement and rejection on the innovative experiences of religious founders are strongly borne out by the processes at work within the OBC. Kennett experienced the visions recorded in How to Grow a Lotus Blossom, and articulated the doctrinal and practical innovations stemming from them, in consultation with her closest disciples who provided her with the reinforcement and reification needed to continue. By contrast, the rejection of her by another section of the community prompted her to curtail the excesses of experience and to respond reflexively to the concerns and demands of her disciples. The action strategies and arguments she employed thus revealed how the institutional and ideological development of the OBC was a dialogical process involving both the leadership and the wider community in equal measure. An examination of this organisation during a period of crisis also underlines Waterhouse's argument that an understanding of authority structures is essential to understanding the development and adaptation of Buddhism in Britain. This period of the OBC's development was one in which 'authority' was challenged, problematised and contested. A synopsis of the arguments invoked by both Kennett's assimilating and dissenting disciples, and by Kennett herself in reaction to her critics, has revealed how opposing positions were adopted, defended and contested through recourse to the same authority sources differently interpreted.

Text and context in the OBC: The Wild, White Goose

The two-volume text The Wild, White Goose (1977a and 1978) purports to be an edited transcript of the diaries maintained by Kennett whilst training in

Japan between 1962 and 1969. Although it did not go to press until the late 1970s, it had been written and prepared for publication by the early part of 1974. The bulk of the text thus belongs to the early period of Kennett's thought, reflecting and reiterating the teachings found in *Selling Water*. The period between 1974 and 1977, as we have seen, was one of radical development, change and instability. Given the pace of change and the ensuing turbulence of this period, it is unsurprising that the publication of *The Wild, White Goose* was delayed for so long. Furthermore, before going to press, the text underwent further revision and modification in light of shifts in Kennett's thought. It must thus be seen as a text-in-transition, straddling and reflecting two distinct phases in the development of a movement in which history and identity were being constructed and reconfigured.

As we have seen, revision and reconfiguration of the past is commonplace within religious movements which are more concerned with issues of identity and ideology than with notions of historical veracity. The construction of personal history through autobiography similarly involves the selective reconfiguration of memory and forgetfulness. Far from being a historian, objectively recollecting and recording an accurate picture of life as it was lived, the autobiographer 'adds to experience itself consciousness of it' (Gusdorf 1980: 38), retrospectively conferring meaning and purpose onto the past. The autobiographer distances himself from his life 'in order to reconstitute himself in the focus of his special unity and identity across time' (Gusdorf 1980: 35). The social context is also central to the autobiographical enterprise since 'the truth of literature is created as much by the reader as by the author' (Mandel 1980: 56). It is the 'borderland of experience', where the assumptions and values of the author overlap with those of the reader, that imbues autobiographical statements with power.

It seems reasonable to consider, in light of these observations, that autobiography may furnish religious movements with a particularly effective vehicle for constructing, mediating and preserving group history and identity. A closer examination of the nature and function of *The Wild, White Goose* reveals that this is indeed the case within the OBC. On the surface, the text claims to represent Kennett's personal diary of religious training in Japan. We cannot, however, uncritically accept it as such. According to Gusdorf, the author of a private journal or diary, 'noting his impressions and mental states from day to day, fixes the portrait of his daily reality without any concern for continuity' (Gusdorf 1980: 35). This may accurately characterise Kennett's original enterprise, but it does not capture the creative process of transforming her diaries into a meaningful narrative for public consumption. *The Wild, White Goose* is neither a faithful record of daily reality nor unconcerned with continuity; rather, it represents a retrospective and purposeful reordering of experience. Kennett herself acknowledges that she has given herself 'a certain amount of poetic license' in order to give the events of her training 'a better flow', changing names and dates, inventing characters and conversations, and

178

including 'teachings discovered *later* in conversation form *here* for the sake of making a complete book'. She concedes that, whilst it is rooted in historical fact, the book is largely 'a work of fiction' (Kennett 1977a: xi). *The Wild, White Goose* is thus more properly regarded as an autobiographical text.

Kennett's initial aims in publishing *The Wild, White Goose* were to exemplify the early doctrine and practice of the ZMS and to provide both herself and her movement with legitimation. Her early teachings, as outlined in *Selling Water*, were delineated and expanded within *The Wild, White Goose*. They were also imbued with a powerful normative value since they were presented within the exemplary context of Kennett's religious training, the 'borderland of experience' that was shared by her disciples. The authority of the text was further enhanced by her refusal to idealise the past; annotations that retrospectively reflected upon the mistakes and difficulties she encountered in Japan invested the account with additional realism and authenticity.

The autobiography is, above all, a work of personal legitimation whereby the demands of historical fidelity are subordinated to the author's higher purpose of revealing a sense of unity, progress and even destiny in her life. In *The Wild, White Goose*, Kennett traced the progress of her spiritual career within the Japanese *Sōtō* system, from being the 'untamed goose' of a newly ordained priest to being the 'goose at rest' of a Zen master. Her selection of diary entries, careful structuring of the text and inclusion of retrospective annotations all created a sense of progress and continuity that was not apparent at the time of the events themselves. Her identity as a Zen master with a special role in the development of Western Buddhism was also portrayed as the fulfilment of destiny. The claim that as a child she longed to cross the sea and meet 'someone with a smile in his heart that will match the smile in mine' (Kennett 1977a: 66) evoked the image of her transmission master. Similarly, the restless urgency of 'beating wings' was frequently alluded to during her remaining months in Japan until she finally flew to America, 'no longer an eaglet but an eagle' (Kennett 1978: 282).

Besides being a work of personal legitimation, *The Wild, White Goose* also provided the OBC with a broader, legitimating context. Kennett was concerned to display the 'deeply historical roots' of her organisation, distinguishing it from other religious innovations through an appeal to a 'cultural diffusion' model of transplantation (Finney 1991). She described Shasta Abbey as the fulfilment, in the West, of an embryonic movement originating in Japan in the form of *Sōjiji's* 'Foreign Section'. More importantly, she portrayed her Japanese teacher, Kōhō Keidō Chisan, as the founder and inspiration of the movement, and herself as his 'favourite disciple' (Kennett 1978: 105).

As a work of personal and institutional justification, *The Wild, White Goose* attached great value to the legitimate authority of Kennett's historical and official background within the Japanese *Sōtō* sect. The text described her acceptance as a trainee by Kōhō Chisan, before charting her monastic career and subsequent tenure as priest of a Japanese temple. However, Kennett consistently prioritised connections of a more spiritual or transcendent nature above such historical and official markers. This was most evident in her use of the symbol of the 'mind-to-mind transmission', the main basis of her claim to legitimacy. She described the ceremony in which she received the transmission from her master as a deeply *spiritual* event, involving 'none of those external trappings which ruin religion; just the intense beauty of being together, our hearts One Heart within the Buddha Nature' (Kennett 1977a: 124). Similarly, the official stature stemming from her relationship with Kōhō Chisan was secondary to the highly personal and intimate terms in which it was couched, including a sprinkling of moments where master and disciple communicate telepathically or 'mind-to-mind'. The 'beating wings' Kennett felt urging her to return westwards were also seen as a message from her master, whilst the assistance she received from supportive westerners was portrayed as the providential working of the Buddhas and Patriarchs. Consequently, the main referent of authority appealed to was the authenticity of spiritual experience. This could be interpreted in various ways: as a type of 'Protestant' discourse, for example, or as a consequence of the modern emphasis on personal authority. A more mundane explanation might lie in the discrimination and prejudice Kennett received from certain sections of the *Sōjiji* hierarchy during her time in Japan, which clearly problematised notions of institutional support and legitimacy.

This conflict and discord influenced Kennett's assessment of mainstream institutional *Sōtō* as corrupt and degenerate. Japanese *Sōtō* was presented by Kennett in a dualistic way: corruption was heavily criticised whilst a small number of exemplary figures or 'saints', who continue to embody *Dōgen's* pure and anti-institutional ideals, were acknowledged. She sought to simultaneously dissociate herself from the corruption and politics of institutional *Sōtō* whilst identifying herself with its exceptional individuals, foremost amongst whom, of course, was Kōhō Chisan. She thus vowed to maintain their high standards and establish an uncorrupted, non-bureaucratic form of *Sōtō* in the West.

The 'reformist' outlook underpinning Kennett's presentation is, according to Finney, a characteristic feature of the transplantation of Zen in the West, which 'has involved one of those revitalizations or "reformations" of religious practice that have been common in the history of both Eastern and Western religions' (Finney 1991: 392). His main evidence of the decline of Zen in Japan and its reformation in America is the difference in daily practice; that is, the central importance attached to meditation and experience in America compared to the ritualism, formalism and relative absence of *zazen* practice in Japan. Whilst Finney acknowledges that the reformist impulse has many traditional Japanese precedents, his own assessment of the state of modern *Sōtō* is a clear example of what Sharf identified as 'Protestant Zen' discourse.[53] This kind of approach to Japanese *Sōtō* has been criticised by Reader:

> by idealising Zen as a thought/practice system that focuses on enlightenment, we are disregarding the whole socio-historical context in

which it has grown and developed in Japan and are neglecting the general role and function of institutional Buddhism in Japan.

(Reader 1986: 7–8)

Whilst Kennett's critique of Japanese *Sōtō*, and her claim to be purifying it in the West, may have 'Protestant' overtones, we must once again exercise caution with this label. Having been part of the *Sōtō* monastic and parish-temple system for several years, she was well aware of the socio-historical context and function of institutional Buddhism in Japan. Her main criticisms of the sect, in contrast to Finney, do not revolve around the absence of *zazen* and meditational experience and 'the preoccupation with ritual prayer-offering' (Finney 1991: 387). She is far more concerned, rather, with avoiding the institutional excesses and abuses of power that she witnessed and experienced within *Sōjiji*, and with establishing *Dōgen's* ideal of sexual egalitarianism. There have been well-established movements, historically and in contemporary times, for institutional reform in these areas of *Sōtō* policy and practice.

Before it went to press, *The Wild, White Goose* was revised in light of the doctrinal developments and institutional instabilities of the Lotus Blossom period. Part of Kennett's revisionist impulse involved an attempt to bring her earlier teachings into line with the current ideology of the OBC. Recognising that religious movements are, in Stark's terms, 'served best by a completed faith' (Stark 1992: 29), she projected 'teachings discovered later' (Kennett 1977a: xi) – such as her ideas about 'the Lord', the importance of past-life experiences and the various grades of *kenshō* – onto the past by carefully knitting them into the autobiographical narrative. Various experiences that she had in Japan were thus retrospectively interpreted in terms of a *kenshō* typology that was devised much later. Reflective annotations also provided commentary and reinterpretation of significant events and teachings, and the reader is referred to *How to Grow a Lotus Blossom* for further illumination. Indeed, Kennett claimed that *The Wild, White Goose* and *How to Grow a Lotus Blossom* form a unity and should be studied in conjunction with each other. She imbued her ideological revisions with authority by accrediting them to exemplary figures like her master. At one point, for example, Kōhō Chisan is identified as the source of her experiential and quasi-theistic view of Zen (Kennett 1978: 71).

Besides incorporating changes in OBC ideology, Kennett used *The Wild, White Goose* in a strategic way to promote institutional stability. The text included lengthy passages, for example, which explored the meaning and importance of being faithful and obedient to one's master. Her increased emphasis on an institutional form of legitimate authority during this period was also expressed through the text. Her critique of the Japanese *Sōtō* sect in the main body of the text was thus qualified and softened by later annotations. It was only in later years, when the legitimation provided by such trans-Pacific ties and connections was no longer depended upon, that Kennett challenged Japanese degeneracy openly, without softening her critique.

The storm weathered

By the early 1980s, the storm of the Lotus Blossom period had been successfully weathered and the OBC entered a new period of growth, relative stability and routinisation. New priories were established in America, and Shasta Abbey certified the Order's first Lay Ministers. Under the leadership of the rotating American abbacy, the British community stabilised and matured. Funds were raised to purchase the priory buildings and grounds, and, in 1977, Throssel Hole Priory was registered as a charitable trust. Encouraged and sustained by the growth of the British monastic community training at Shasta Abbey, the lay congregation steadily grew, and by 1981 there were ten meditation groups affiliated to the priory. In 1982, following their completion of a five-year training programme at Shasta Abbey and certification as 'Teachers' within the OBC, five of the British monks returned to Throssel Hole. Daishin Morgan, a British monk who had been certified by Kennett as a *Rōshi*, or 'Master', in 1981, was installed as its abbot 'and a new period of development began' (Morgan 1994: 141). The presence of qualified British Zen teachers and masters, with the authority to guide, ordain and transmit disciples, marked the beginnings of Throssel Hole Priory's autonomous, and largely self-regulating, development. The growth of the monastic training programme enabled the priory to accept more invitations from congregation members to lead outside retreats, and this, along with the introduction of the Lay Ministry programme in 1983, injected a new-found enthusiasm, dynamism and vitality into the laity. According to Daishin Morgan, the OBC in Britain was entering 'an exciting time of growth' in which there were 'tremendous opportunities for the Sangha as a whole'.[54] Our examination of the later development of the OBC in the next chapter will show that this optimism about the Order's growth was well founded.

7

THE LATER PERIOD
Routinisation and consolidation

The routinising impulse

Religious movements founded through charisma or revelations 'cannot long sustain constant doctrinal revision', nor can they allow unrestricted revelation, and so, in Weberian terms, they become 'routinised':

> as movements grow and develop more ramified organizational structures, pressures build up against further revelations, for organizations are served best by a completed faith.
>
> (Stark 1992: 29–30)

This accurately describes the historical and ideological development of Kennett's movement towards the end of the Lotus Blossom period and during the later period, which was mainly a time of consolidation, stabilisation and routinisation. In 1983, the OBC was established as a separate legal corporation from Shasta Abbey. Clear structures of authority, organisation, doctrine and practice were defined and incorporated through the *Bylaws of the OBC* and the *Rules of the OBC*, formulated by Kennett and her senior disciples 'to govern and bind together in one Sangha [...] the monasteries, priories and meditation groups affiliated with the OBC'.[1] Kennett's later publications also shifted away from innovation towards systematisation. The organisational structure of the OBC was elucidated and reaffirmed, and she also treated OBC doctrine and practice in a more methodical and codified manner. In one article, she attempted 'to lay out clearly what are and are not our teachings',[2] summarising the main features of practice for the laity and the priesthood. A thread of articles entitled '...And to the source kept true', which appeared in the Order's journals between 1989 and 1991, had a similar resonance to this inasmuch as they clarified and defended the OBC's perspectives on specific aspects of belief and practice.

This chapter examines the structural, organisational and ideological routinisation of the OBC by summarising the contents of the *Bylaws* and *Rules* and by surveying the writings of Kennett. Although she was striving to create a 'completed faith', restating and systematising earlier teachings whilst intro-

183

ducing measures to curtail the excesses of religious experience, she nevertheless continued to be a revisionist and religious visionary; thus, an awareness and sensitivity to the ongoing development of her thought is required. The success of the routinising project is measured and assessed and the assimilation of her teachings within the Order during this period is examined. I end with a discussion of the growth, consolidation and positioning of the OBC upon the British Buddhist landscape during the 1980s and 1990s.

The structure and identity of the OBC

In the *Bylaws of the OBC*, the organisational structure of the Order is delineated, its identity is defined, and its main doctrines and practices are summarised. Final and supreme authority within the OBC, both spiritual and temporal, rests with the Head of the Order. The first holder of this position, which is held for life, was naturally the Order's founder figure, although subsequent Heads were to be democratically elected by, and from within, the Order's pool of certified masters. Since the investment of so much power and authority in one figure carries with it the danger of abuse, corruption and loss of distinctive identity, a mechanism for the removal of the Head was established, to which the membership has recourse in exceptional circumstances. Kennett also safeguarded the integrity and continuity of her movement by establishing a rule that allows OBC members to resign from, reunite and re-establish the Order in the unlikely event that 'after the death of its Founder [...] the Order becomes corrupt'.[3]

The Order embraces three levels of institutional affiliation: training monasteries, regional priories (or 'parish churches') and local meditation groups. The emphasis of the monastery, of course, is upon monastic training, which is overseen by an abbot, the '"father" of all monks in the community'.[4] Within the specific micro-context of a monastery community, the abbot fulfils a similar function to that of the Head of the Order; for example, he formulates, modifies and enforces a set of monastery rules to cover issues specific to that community. Regional priories are created mainly for the benefit of the lay congregation. Priests who are appointed as OBC 'priors' are expected to fulfil a number of priestly functions, leading services and retreats and offering spiritual guidance. Clustered around the priories at a local level are the Order's affiliated meditation groups, the organisation and running of which is one of the prime functions of the Lay Ministry. Lay Ministers are authorised to give meditation instruction and Dharma talks and to 'encourage other trainees to practice meditation, keep the Precepts, and deepen their Buddhist training'.[5]

The pattern of institutional expansion within the Order has not been identical in Britain and America. Despite its well-established and widespread meditation group structure, the OBC in Britain did not expand beyond Throssel Hole institutionally until the 1990s, with the creation of priories in Reading and Telford (founded in 1990 and 1997 respectively). By contrast, two new priories in America were established within three years of the founding of Shasta Abbey, with a further three being established since then. This difference has been explained by OBC members largely in geographic and demographic terms. The inaccessibility of Shasta Abbey to most of the American congregation created a demand for regional priories to be established elsewhere; the relative accessibility of Throssel Hole to the British laity, by contrast, did not create a similar demand. Instead of establishing and supporting many regional priories, then, the British laity developed a close and active relationship with Throssel Hole alone. These differing patterns of institutional growth have, in turn, shaped the character of the OBC's main sites of monastic activity. Shasta Abbey has been more strictly monk-orientated than Throssel Hole, which has seen a much higher level of lay activity. There has recently, though, in imitation of the American model of development, been a push from within the British congregation for more regional priories to meet the need for regular monastic guidance. If the proposed institutional expansion of the OBC around Britain is successful, it is likely that Throssel Hole will, like Shasta Abbey, develop a more rigorous and strictly monastic focus whilst its affiliated priories actively serve the lay congregation. Nevertheless, it is unlikely to relinquish altogether its role as a vital centre of lay activity; indeed, it is felt that Shasta Abbey can learn much from Throssel Hole on the subject of developing healthy monastic-lay relations.

Although the Order is an independent and self-regulating organisation, the definition of its religious identity is based upon the constitution of the Japanese Sōtō sect.[6] Kennett defines the 'serene Reflection Meditation Church' – her preferred translation of 'Sōtō Zen' during the later period – as 'the transmission of the Right Law of Shakyamuni Buddha, which has been handed down by successive Ancestors, from master to disciples, through direct communication from one heart to another'. The fundamental teachings of the OBC 'are serene reflection meditation (shikantaza), the principle "All beings are at heart Buddha" (sōkushinzebutsu) and gratitude', and its main objects of veneration are 'primarily Shakyamuni Buddha and, as its two Founders, Koso Joyo Daishi (Great Master Eihei Dōgen) and Taiso Josai Daishi (Great Master Keizan Jōkin)'. It is also emphasised that, in accordance with the teachings of the Shushōgi, to train within this school 'means to practice serene reflection meditation and keep the Precepts, since their practice embodies enlightenment itself (shushōfuni)'.[7] The Bylaws also outline the main scriptures and ceremonies used within the Order. Here again, notwithstanding Kennett's modifications and adaptations of the traditional forms, there is much continuity with the practice of Sōtō monasteries and temples in Japan. The scriptures of the OBC include important Mahāyāna texts such as the Lotus, Avataṃsaka and Vimalakīrti-nirdesa Sūtras, alongside the specifically Sōtō works of Dōgen and Keizan, as well as selected sayings of other Zen patriarchs, such as the Hokyozanmai of Tōzan (807–69) and the Shōdōka of Yōka Genkaku (665–713). The year-round schedule of 'standard ceremonies' in the Order includes memorial days for important patriarchal figures (e.g. *Bodhidharma* and *Dōgen*), celebrations of the three major events in the life of *Śākyamuni* Buddha (his birth, enlightenment and *parinirvāṇa*), and other observances such as the festival of 'Feeding of the Hungry Ghosts' (*O-Bon*). More irregular are the 'special ceremonies' that are performed whenever a cause for congratulation or condolence occurs in either the nation (e.g. Remembrance Day and Thanksgiving) or in the Order (e.g. lay and monastic ordinations, abbot installations, marriages and so on). In addition are the daily scripture-chanting services performed in OBC monasteries and priories, as in traditional Japanese contexts, three times daily.

Whilst the *Bylaws* outline the organisational and doctrinal structures of the Order, the *Rules of the OBC* concentrate on the roles, behaviour and conduct of its individual members, both monastic and lay. In formulating them, Kennett and her senior monastic disciples drew upon a variety of sources, including the guidelines of practice used within the modern Japanese *Sōtō* sect and the monastic rules of *Dōgen* and *Keizan*. Added to these were 'precedents from other widely accepted Buddhist sources, both *Mahāyāna* and *Theravāda*'.[8] The rules are not understood as fixed and final edicts, but as flexible and provisional guidelines that can be changed, adapted or expanded to suit the shifting circumstances of the Order. A supplement added in 1996 outlining the Order's policies and procedures regarding the misuse of power, authority and trust (with specific reference to sexual abuses) provides a good illustration of the adaptability of the rules. This was formulated in response to a number of scandals in America between Buddhist teachers and students[9] in order to safeguard practitioners and protect the OBC from potentially devastating allegations, litigations and controversy.

The basic trajectory of the monastic career as it was presented during the early period – whereby the trainee progresses through a sequence of grades, from postulant to teacher, within a regulated time structure – has remained intact throughout the Order's development and is still in place today. Through the *Rules*, Kennett reinforced this early schema, as well as systematising and routinising the modifications made to it during the turbulent Lotus Blossom period – adaptations which included the use of licences or identification cards, changes to monastic titles that more clearly reflect priestly rank, and the adoption of the rule of celibacy. The *Rules* recognise seven ranks of the priesthood, beginning with the postulancy which usually lasts for six months to a year. Priestly training proper begins when the aspirant is ordained, receives a new religious name[10] and is welcomed into the community by formally entering the monk's meditation hall (*sōdō*). After a period of approximately one year, the junior or novice priest undergoes a short term as Head Novice or Chief Junior, during which he has a responsibility 'to lead all trainees and to find wise and compassionate ways of helping others train to the best of their ability'.[11] When the trainee has 'demonstrated in his daily life that he knows how to train as a priest'[12] he undergoes the ceremony of Dharma transmission, which involves having 'one's spiritual maturity and sincerity of purpose acknowledged by one's master'.[13]

Following his completion of three years of monastic training, the transmitted monk is certified as a parish priest qualified to run temples, conduct public ceremonies, give pastoral counselling and lead retreats. He now swaps the black robes of a junior monk for the brown formal robe of the parish priest and uses the initials 'OBC' after his name. Having completed the priesthood training programme, the trainee now enters the teacher training programme, certification for which may follow after another two years. Teachers in the Order use the initials 'FOBC' ('Fellow of the OBC') and their rank is indicated by the adoption of a purple *rakhusu* (a symbol of the monastic robes worn around the neck). The final priestly rank of 'Master' is granted when Dharma transmission 'in its deeper meaning' occurs; that is,

> when a monk has completed the five year seminary program and has experienced the first or 'Penetration of Heaven' *kenshō* – the moment in training when a person knows absolutely his or her complete oneness with the Lord of the House.[14]

Masters use the initials 'MOBC' ('Master of the OBC') and are qualified 'to ordain, train, and Transmit others as a fully independent Zen Master'.[15] Only two (out of approximately twenty) OBC masters, however, have given Dharma transmission to their own pupils, a statistic that reflects the nature of the institutional growth of the Order, which, to date, has only two centres of monastic training.

Whilst acknowledging that the hierarchical nature of Japanese Zen monasticism 'may be disconcerting seen from Western views of egalitarianism', Leighton and Okumura nevertheless defend *Dōgen's* instructions on cultivating deference to seniority 'as guidance for newcomers in the respectful attitude most conducive to harmonious entry into the community' (1996: 11). Kennett also viewed such hierarchical attitudes positively, styling the monastic practice of her Order upon the traditional model. Seniority within the OBC is indicated by differences in priestly titles, vestments and functions, and also in the rules governing the relationships between junior and senior monks. These rules are based upon the spirit of *Dōgen's* essays, 'Regulations for the study hall' (*Shuryō Shingi*) and 'The Dharma when meeting senior instructors' (*Taitaiko Gogejarihō*), which provide 'injunctions for the appropriate etiquette when in the presence of senior instructors' (Leighton and Okumara 1996: 11). Translations of *Dōgen's* essays on priestly conduct, as found in Kennett's *Zen is Eternal Life* (1976), are also standard reading material for OBC monks.

The *Rules of the OBC* also provide guidelines for lay practitioners, particularly those belonging to the Lay Ministry. Lay Ministers are licensed by the OBC to fulfil a number of important roles, such as organising meditation groups and other congregation activities; giving meditation instruction and rudimentary talks on Buddhism; setting a good example and encouraging others in spiritual training; and performing public ceremonies (e.g. weddings and funerals) when ordained priests are unavailable. Lay Ministers are also autho-rised to represent the Order in the public domain; for example, by giving talks at schools or by attending interfaith conferences. In their ministerial and public capacities, Lay Ministers have been central to the development of the OBC. The primary emphasis of the Lay Ministry programme, though, has always been upon the deepening of the individual's practice. One long-standing British trainee described the Lay Ministry as 'more than anything else, an acknowledg-ment of one's own training and commitment to one's practice'. Another recalled her decision to enter the Lay Ministry as 'just one more step in training'. This emphasis on the individual's spiritual development is reflected in the procedure of becoming a Lay Minister. When it was initially introduced, anyone who had formally received lay ordination could apply to join the programme. In 1987, the programme was reorganised and made available by invitation only; that is, when the abbot became convinced of a trainee's sincerity in practice and selfless service to others. The training programme itself, which now lasts for approximately two years, involves the regular atten-dance of retreats, instruction in ceremonial procedures, and the personal study of OBC textual and commentarial matter. During this time, any doubts or confusions the individual may have about the Order's teachings are ironed out 'so that they can represent it as accurately as possible to others'.[16] The main emphasis, though, is upon meditation, preceptual adherence and 'the deepening of each individual's level of training'.[17] Consequently, there is 'no abstract stan-dard to be reached to "qualify" as a licensed lay minister': the trainee must simply 'be working on their own training in such a way that they are beginning to fulfil their own potential'.[18] This contrasts sharply with the structured training programmes in the NKT which involve regular collective study, the memorization of textual outlines and the sitting of written examinations in which the practitioner's understanding is formally tested and assessed.

Kennett's later teachings

Whilst I am chiefly concerned here with tracing the evolution and develop-ment of Kennett's thought, it is important to acknowledge that there was also much continuity and consistency underpinning her thirty-year career as a teacher of Zen. Her later writings embraced a host of familiar themes and endeavoured to reiterate the same basic message that characterised her earlier presentation. The areas most commonly dealt with, predictably, remained the practice of meditation, adherence to the moral precepts, and the cultivation of love, compassion and wisdom; in other words, the basic elements of her original text, *Selling Water by the River* (1972). The centrality of ceremonial activity and scriptural study was also given high priority, as was indicated by the publication during this period of a number of liturgical handbooks and compilations of Buddhist scriptures.[19] Kennett's enduring concern with gender issues, her ambivalence towards the Christian tradition and her sensitivity to the cultural baggage of Western converts to Buddhism also continued to characterise her later presentation. Discussion of harmonising *mudrās*, however, was sufficiently scant during the later period for this aspect of Kennett's teachings to constitute an instance of 'conscious forgetfulness'. She was also reticent, during the later period, to discuss the experience of *kenshō* 'because of the amount of misunderstandings this [term] has brought about'.[20] Forgetfulness with respect to this formerly central element of her teachings also stemmed from a general shift in Kennett's perspective concerning the role and regulation of religious experience in Buddhist training.

The major themes dominating Kennett's later teachings reflected and continued the impulse towards routinisation, systematisation and stability that characterised her presentation following the conflict and instability of the innovative early Lotus Blossom period. One way in which Kennett responded to the conflict and instability of this period was to elevate the role of faith – in the credentials and experience of the Zen master – above the role of personal confirmatory experience of the teachings. During the later period, this shift hardened and the early emphasis on individual authority was almost completely eclipsed by teachings stressing faithful obedience and measures aimed at regulating religious experience within the Order:

> Buddhism is a religion – and a religion requires faith and trust, not destructive discussion – it requires faith in the Eternal, faith in the Teaching, faith in its priesthood and trust in one's master. If there is not absolute faith and trust in these, spiritual growth is an impossibility.[21]

Kennett's early characterisation of Zen as 'a religion for spiritual adults' was thus reformulated; instead of signifying the priority of personal authority, 'spiritual adulthood' now described those who 'understand the position from which the master, as head of the Order, speaks in relation to the horizontal Transmission'.[22]

Although Kennett still described *kenshō* as a desirable byproduct of training, and whilst she continued to offer spirited defences of visionary experiences in Zen, she now adopted a more cautious approach that emphasised institutional stability. Only senior monks now had the maturity to pay attention to and learn from visions, and, furthermore, this had to take place within clearly demarcated institutional guidelines:

> When a True Buddhist believes he has certain knowledge of a communication from That Which Is, a Patriarch or Buddhist Saint he immediately takes refuge in the Sangha which means that he submits the matter to his seniors or fellows who, after deep meditation thereon, assist him by either confirming or denying the authenticity of the communication or advising more meditation on the subject.[23]

These shifts in emphasis were reflected clearly in *Zen is Eternal Life*, the renamed and revised edition of *Selling Water by the River*. When it was initially reissued, at the beginning of the Lotus Blossom period in 1976, only a number of minor revisions to the beginning and end matter of the text (reflecting Kennett's evolving understanding of ultimate truth) were included.[24] By the time of the third edition in 1987, more significant revisions to the body of the text, focusing upon faith and religious experience, became apparent. The original emphasis on the internal aspect of faith was now omitted, for example, whilst the view that the truth can be realised without a master was qualified by a greater emphasis on belief, obedience and formal validation. The original discussion of *makyō*, whereby all sensory and visual episodes experienced in meditation were described as 'figments of an overstrained mind and thus not truly religious', was also completely reformulated in the third edition. Explaining her earlier presentation of this as an instance of 'skilful means', Kennett now drew a distinction between the hallucinations that appear to beginners (*makyō*) and the genuine religious visions that appear to more advanced practitioners. The emphasis, however, was still very much upon the regulation of religious experience and of having visions 'checked out by a master' (Kennett 1987a: 30–31).

Following the original publication of her 'third *kenshō*' in 1977, Kennett herself continued to experience many past-life and visionary episodes. She chose not to publicise these 'deeper Truths' (Kennett 1993a: 260) immediately, due to the responses her earlier experiences had provoked, but they eventually appeared in the second edition of *How to Grow a Lotus Blossom* in 1993. The more cautious approach towards mystical activity encouraged during the later period was restated in this text; indeed, we were now informed that even Kennett's experiences cannot simply be accepted but require careful validation through recourse to alternative authorities:

> Always she has stressed the need to take refuge in Buddha, Dharma and Sangha when making decisions, and even at those times when a vision seemed relevant to an ongoing situation, we recognized that our limited understanding of its teaching could be flawed or incomplete and also that it is but one source of information.

(Daizui MacPhillamy, quoted in Kennett 1993a: 178)

The focus of Kennett's later visions was not simply upon her own training and self-transformation but upon the provision of inspiration and guidance for others. Towards this end, the visions functioned in three distinct, but interrelated, ways. First, they provided Kennett and her disciples with guidance on specific aspects of Buddhist training, such as dealing with past karma, the use of the will and the importance of obeying the master. Secondly, some visions functioned prophetically, giving Kennett 'warnings of what may occur if existing tendencies are allowed to go on unchanged' (Kennett 1993a: 177) and enabling her 'to take appropriate action to possibly prevent them from happening' (Kennett 1993a: 193). A vision in which she was encouraged to pass through a door leading to 'a black emptiness', for example, was interpreted as a warning against forging hasty institutional affiliations (Kennett 1993a: 228–229). Thirdly, some of the visions functioned specifically as visions of spiritual legiti-mation whereby Kennett's spiritual realisation was 'recognised by churches and religions different to my own' (Kennett 1993a: 243). These visions restated her belief that all religions point towards the same essential truth, described here as 'Eternal Life' (Kennett 1993a: 187). The most interesting and revealing was her vision of confirmation within Christianity in which, dressed as a bride, she dissolves into an image of Christ (Kennett 1993a: 189). This vision presented another vivid illustration of Kennett's continuing affection for the religion of her roots, whilst her interpretation of it returned once again to the main source of her disaffection:

> I understand the young bride in this vision to be myself [...] being refused my religious rights because of being female. The Eternal welcomed and embraced me [...] since I had kept myself a virgin and true to my life-long wish to be One with Him.
>
> (Kennett 1993a: 189–191)

Kennett's later work often returned to the project of adaptation, providing definitive statements of her policy and justifications for the main changes imple-mented within the OBC. Her early policy towards the adaptation of Zen, an essentialism combining traditional and charismatic elements, remained unchanged in the later period. Kennett's strategies of adaptation, and the main elements of Buddhist doctrine/practice that concerned her, also remained unchanged. The project of extracting the essential principles from their Japanese matrix, in order to transplant them in a more appropriate 'Western' – and specif-ically 'Christian' – idiom, continued to revolve around monastic discipline, sexual egalitarianism, ritual and ceremonial form, and the translation of Japanese and Buddhist terms and concepts. During the later period, she was most preoccu-pied with outlining and defending the language she used when referring to ultimate truth. As we have seen, during the Lotus Blossom period her preferred way of describing this was through terms that carried a quasi-theistic resonance, such as 'Cosmic Buddha', 'the Lord' and even 'God'. In the face of criticism and dissent, she had defended her use of such personalistic terms Buddhistically and maintained that she was 'not postulating a personal deity or creator-god'.[25] In response to the criticism these words had provoked, however, she began to temper her use of personalistic images and, by the mid-1980s, was preferring to use terms like 'the Eternal', 'the Unborn', 'That Which Is', 'the Immaculacy of Emptiness' and 'Purity'. Despite being more neutral and not so explicitly theistic, these terms continued to illicit criticism: first, because they appeared to contradict the traditional view that *nirvāṇa* cannot be understood or described in positive terms; and secondly, because Kennett never completely abandoned her personalistic interpretation of ultimate truth (continuing, for example, to refer to 'the Eternal' as 'He'). During the later period, then, she once again had to defend herself from the charge that she was promoting 'the personalist heresy'.[26]

Whilst Kennett's main strategy of adaptation remained the appropriation and use of Christian religious forms, during the Lotus Blossom and later periods she decided that certain adaptations initiated during the early period had strayed away from 'the source' and she thus took a number of backward steps. She abandoned, for example, the Anglican dog collar and clerical shirt and reverted back to using more traditional, Japanese-style robes. Adaptations made to the ceremonial calendar were also rethought. O-Bon continued to be celebrated at the time of Halloween, but *Hanamatsuri* (the festival of the Buddha's birth), which had been celebrated on Christmas Day within the OBC, was moved back to its traditional date in April. Instead, the Order decided (perhaps as a compromise adaptation) to celebrate the festival of the Buddha's enlightenment on Christmas Day 'in addition to the ceremony on December 8, the more traditional date'.[27] Kennett considered that her most significant 'departure from the fundamentals' had been her attempt at establishing a married priesthood, a mistake she rectified following her 'third *kenshō*':

> I am trying to keep true to the source as handed down to me by my master and, if someone wishes to be my disciple, I expect that person to keep true to the source in the same way as I have done [...] I accidentally strayed when I thought a married priesthood was possible. When I realised this, I opted for a celibate one.[28]

Another interesting development in Kennett's thought during the later period was her increasing tendency, when discussing adaptation, to make exclusive claims and sectarian statements. The basis of these statements, the bulk of which were directed towards Japanese *Sōtō*, was formed by the direct association she made between the 'source' or 'essential' principles of Zen and 'pure' Zen. She criticised Japanese *Sōtō* for degenerating, or 'pulling the teachings out of shape',[29] with respect to the practice of marriage within the priesthood, the subordination of women, the widespread concern for ambition and power in its temples, and the lack of practising vegetarians. She also criticised American Zen for its 'terrible deviations from the source' concerning sexual relationships between masters and disciples, and for generally 'degenerating into little more than parlour games'.[30] By contrast, Kennett believed that she and her Order were 'keeping true to the source', following the essential teachings or practising a 'pure' form of *Sōtō* Zen. She continued to compare herself with *Dōgen* and to stress that her master, who himself had stayed true to the source when surrounded by corruption in Japan, had instructed her to instigate important reforms and establish a 'pure' form of *Sōtō* in the West.

A new emphasis during the later period was the importance attached by Kennett to linkages and associations with her Chinese *Rinzai* lineage. Although ever since the early period of her settlement in America she had kept in contact with the Malaysian temple where she was originally ordained in 1962, these connections did not form an important part of the OBC's public identity until the mid-1980s. During this period, any communications which took place between Kennett and her Malaysian 'uncles in the Dharma', such as the reception of a portion of her ordination master Seck Kim Seng's ashes for enshrinement at Shasta Abbey, were well publicised in OBC journals. It is significant that Kennett's attempts to strengthen, and demonstrate, the OBC's ties with the Chinese *Ch'an* tradition coincided with the intensification of her critique of Japanese *Sōtō*. Perhaps she felt, in light of the challenges that she herself was posing to the authority of Japanese *Sōtō*, that another source of legitimate authority was now required to validate the teachings and practices of the OBC. This view is supported by the fact that she appealed to the 'purity' of her Chinese lineage, alongside the example of her 'exceptional' Japanese master, to bolster her critique of Japanese *Sōtō*.[31] A critique of the Japanese system may have become increasingly important to the identity of the OBC during the later period but this did not stop Kennett from periodically appealing to the legitimate authority of the Japanese *Sōtō* sect. A visit of a couple of OBC monks to *Sōjiji* in 1984, for example, which resulted in the reception of a portion of Kōhō Chisan's ashes for enshrinement at Shasta Abbey, was well publicised in the Order's journals and was illustrated with photographs and a copy of the accompanying certificate of authenticity. Kennett's translations of Buddhist scriptures were also, she claimed, sanctioned by the Japanese sect.

Assimilation and stability in the later period

Kennett's desire to make the later period of the OBC's development a phase of consolidation and routinisation was, in the main, realised. Articles by her monastic and lay disciples displayed a great deal of coherence and consistency in their elucidation of the contours of Zen training, a presentation that both reiterated the main themes from the early and Lotus Blossom periods whilst reflecting the new emphases of Kennett's later thought. Her movement away from explicitly theistic and personalistic terminology in the later period, for example, was assimilated; thus, the purpose of religious training – usually referred to during the Lotus Blossom period as 'uniting with the Lord' – was now more commonly described as uniting with, following the will of and experiencing in one's life 'the Eternal' or 'the Unborn'. Buddhist training was still described as a process of continually trying 'to do something about yourself' through cleansing the karmic inheritance that 'obscures the face of the Unborn'.[32] The main practices for realising these goals remained those of *zazen*, or serene reflection meditation, and preceptual adherence, and a good deal of attention continued to be given to the significance of ceremonial activity in both monastic and lay contexts. Kennett's ideas concerning the harmonisation of body and mind and the karmic origins of physical disease and mental illness were also reiterated, although this theme continued to be divorced from the unpopular practice of harmonising *mudrās*. One British Lay Minister reflected that whilst the use of *mudrās* to manipulate energy flows was popular with some when first introduced, and whilst monks may occasionally still use *mudrās* 'to keep fit', *The Book of Life* no longer had this practical application:

> At first we tended to think, 'Oh, I'm getting a bit stiff in the shoulders, so I'll go and do a mudra to deal with that'. But there's not much of that done now. In fact, I can't remember when I last actually did a mudra to deal with a spiritual block. So, in a sense, that particular side of the book has fallen out of use, but the information nonetheless is very useful.

Whilst discussion about past-life experiences was also infrequent it nevertheless remained a significant theme, and the appearance of personal accounts of these experiences within the OBC's journals indicated the increased stability enjoyed by the movement during the later period. One monk's discussion of what he described as 'the concentration camp experience',[33] for example, could not have been printed during the early Lotus Blossom period due to uncertainty and disagreement within the wider congregation at that time about the role and significance of past-life experiences in Zen.

Routinisation of the OBC world-view during the later period fostered the growth of a stable identity and strong sense of community within the wider congregation, as was illustrated by the emergence of a 'national *Sangha*' consciousness in Britain during the mid-1980s. Whilst differences in opinion continued to exist over elements of OBC doctrine and practice – such as Kennett's emphasis on ceremonial and her use of personalistic imagery – individual practitioners, in most cases, managed to successfully work through their concerns or negotiate compromise positions whilst remaining active and committed members of the Order. In contrast to the conflict and fragmentation characterising the Lotus Blossom period, then, the later period witnessed the OBC's increasing unification, stability and maturation.

The importance of faith and experience in Buddhist training, and the relationship between them, was as dominant a concern for her disciples during the later period as it was for Kennett herself. The Buddhist path was described as 'the life of faith'[34] and there was widespread agreement that faith, in both its 'internal' and its 'external' aspects, forms the basis of religious training and spiritual growth. Much significance also continued to be attached by trainees to their personal experience of the teachings. The emphasis here, amongst monks and laity alike, was mostly upon the 'gradual process' of making the Eternal the focus of life, the progressive cleansing of karma and the daily reorientation of life in accordance with 'the still, small voice' of meditation. This approach was in line with the *Rules of the OBC*, which encouraged trainees 'to discuss their experiences in training so that these experiences will help others' whilst discouraging discussion of 'the particular details of *kenshō*'.[35] The denial of the higher *kenshōs* to lay trainees does not, as a consequence, act as a disincentive to train within the OBC. One trainee, a Lay Minister in the Order, explained the goal of her practice in the following way:

> I don't meditate for experiences, for flashing lights or voices from the heavens. I believe that everybody does have the Buddha Nature, always has had, and always was enlightened. But from birth onwards, I have found so much rubbish on top of rubbish throughout my life that what I've done is bury the Buddha Nature. So what I'm doing when I meditate, hopefully, however slowly, is shovelling the shit, uncovering, until that which is within is also without.

Confirmatory experiences of a more irregular and profound nature, however, such as visions, past-life experiences, sudden flashes of understanding and *kenshō*, also remain significant. Trainees nevertheless understand that such experiences, though important, are not the goal of practice; rather, they are regarded as side effects of training or 'gifts from the Eternal'[36] which 'arise naturally if there is something we need to learn from them'.[37] Due to the Order's cautious policy towards religious experiences, practitioners are reluctant to discuss them in any detail, and whilst personal accounts can be found within the pages of the journals, they are rare. The following account of a British lay trainee's past-life experiences, and his reflections upon their significance, is thus worth quoting at length:

> Quite some time ago I was watching a film about the holocaust, and it was where a man in a Nazi uniform was beating up a Jewish boy. It struck a chord with me because I felt as though I was part of that. Something told me I was one of those; whether I was the Jew or the Nazi I'm not entirely sure. I often wonder whether this was a past-life experience, because the time of it would have been about 1938, and I wasn't born until 1940 [...] Another one. Until about three years ago I was a member of a battle re-enactment society. I was playing the role of a Benedictine monk but there was something far deeper going on as well. Something told me, 'I've been here and seen this before'. I've probably been some kind of religious in the past [...] I love organ music and when I've been sat there listening to the music my mind has gone back to about the Fifteenth century, the time of the Reformation, and there is a strong thread running that I have been there, in some position where I was able to influence what was going on at the time [...] I've tended to think, if I've been a religious in a former life, why have I

ended up living a perfectly normal, mundane life here? Had there been some evil karma built up? I've wondered whether I had been a church man in medieval times and abused my position. Certainly being in the Inquisition was an abusive position. It would also make sense if I was a Jew being persecuted, that could well have been a karmic consequence of the other [...] I use them [i.e. past-life experiences] as reference points as I go along. Rather like reading a text about something, and thinking, 'Didn't I hear about this somewhere else?', fishing out the reference and then carrying on with the text. You've picked up a bit of knowledge in your research that confirms what's in your textbook. Rather like a footnote to your training.

Whilst OBC trainees value personal experiences such as these very highly, the emphasis, following Kennett's lead, is upon having faith 'even when we are unable to believe'.[38] During the later period, depictions of the Buddha as a 'pragmatic empiricist' who dismisses faith were criticised, as was a perceived overemphasis in the West on the value of 'doubt'.[39] Within the OBC, faith in oneself, in the Eternal and in the master and her teachings was prioritised above personal, confirmatory experiences. Indeed, the mind of faith itself was understood to be 'essential before any real experience of the Truth can be known'.[40]

Another major preoccupation of OBC trainees during the later period concerned the nature and importance of monastic and lay training. Accounts of lay trainees getting to grips with their 'individual kōans' amidst the realities of daily life were abundant, as were personal reflections by monks about the contemplative vocation. Discussion often focused upon the relative values of monastic and lay training, although it was consistently stressed that monastic and lay forms of training are equally valid and valuable because the 'spirit of having left behind worldly concerns'[41] that should underpin both is much more important than the external forms themselves. The growth and consolidation of the British lay congregation during the later period led to an increase in articles by lay practitioners focusing upon 'training in the world'. Much attention was given, in particular, to the importance of Buddhist parenting and to the place of sexuality in religious training, especially in terms of its capacity to damage relationships within the Sangha. The most common theme, however, concerned the difficult project of training in the absence of the structures, schedules and ceremonial forms that most lay trainees found invaluable whilst on retreat at the monastery. The focus here was upon the ways in which monastic forms – such as bowing, altars and incense offerings, the recitation of verses and scriptures, meditation schedules, formal meals, etc. – can be skilfully used to support lay training or otherwise adapted to the demands of lay life. These articles also reflected the OBC's utilitarian approach towards religious form, emphasising fluidity and flexibility and warning against the dangers of attempting to replicate the monastic lifestyle in a worldly context. The most important thing is to 'live in the monastery of our own hearts',[42] turning 'everything we do into an offering to the Lord of the House',[43] whilst skilfully tailoring or adapting selected monastic forms to one's specific needs and circumstances.

This essentialist perspective on the utilitarian nature and ultimate 'emptiness' of religious form was also the context in which discussions of adaptation within the Order took place:

> The ultimate authority in the Zen tradition does not lie in the words of the Scriptures but in their essence [...] This essential nature, or Buddha Nature, is the final authority [...] Whenever the final authority lies outside a structure, the structure may at times be turned on its head.[44]

To facilitate their presentation of Buddhist themes, Kennett's disciples continued to borrow extensively from the imagery, expressions and textual sources of Christianity, particularly its mystical tradition. Opinions continued to be divided, however, about the value and legitimacy of the Order's use of positive imagery to describe ultimate truth. Whilst a minority continued to use explicitly theistic terminology, most trainees adopted Kennett's more neutral language of 'the Eternal' or 'the Unborn', and others still considered that even these terms were overly suggestive of theism, opting instead for more traditional designations ('Buddha', 'Buddha Nature', etc.). Further defences of the use of positive terminology were thus presented during this period. These rejected the theistic critique, maintaining that by using terms like 'Cosmic Buddha', 'the Eternal' and 'Him' to describe ultimate truth, 'we are not saying that it exists in some sense that is graspable, containable or measurable'.[45] The limitation of language per se in the depiction of 'what is essentially ineffable and unknowable by the power of human reason'[46] was emphasised, and the Order's positive terms were defended as flawed, but nonetheless preferable, alternatives to negative terms like 'void' and 'emptiness', which tend to engender despair.[47]

Growth and consolidation in Britain

During the later period, the development of the Order in Britain was characterised by consolidation, stability and growth. In this respect, it reflected and benefited from Kennett's emphasis upon institutional and ideological routinisation and systematisation. The return of the British monks from Shasta Abbey marked the beginning of this new and vital period. Their presence stimulated and invigorated the lay congregation, which, from a spattering of small and isolated groupings of local activity, soon developed into a thriving, active and unified community operating at a local, regional and national level. This lay growth, in turn, provided the monastic community with both an enthusiastic recruitment base and a healthy source of financial support. In this way, the traditional, symbiotic interdependence of monks and laity was enlivened and rejuvenated. Central to this period of growth and consolidation was the Lay

Ministry, an initiative that had been introduced with the return of the British monks. When outlining the later development of the OBC in Britain, we must be particularly attentive to the role of Lay Ministers as mediators, facilitators and organisers.

Following their return from America, the small British monastic community (at that time around eight strong) grew steadily under the leadership of Rev. Master Daishin Morgan, the abbot of Throssel Hole Priory. There are currently approximately forty monks and postulants in residence, around the same number of trainees as are training at Shasta Abbey. Many of these have now celebrated their tenth and twentieth 'ordination birthdays' and have risen through the priestly ranks to become teachers and masters of the Order. In 1997, the OBC's total membership of eighty-four monks and postulants included thirty-two teachers, of whom sixteen were British, and twenty masters, of whom five were British. In terms of monastic training, then, Throssel Hole Priory has gradually acquired a similar profile and significance to that of Shasta Abbey. Interestingly, this situation reflects the structure of Japanese *Sōtō*, which also, in the form of *Eiheiji* and *Sōjiji*, has two Head Temples.

Under the guidance of the abbot and other senior priests, the monks at Throssel Hole Priory lead a disciplined and structured communal life of meditation, manual labour, study, lectures and ceremonial observance. Following the traditional *Sōtō* view that 'spiritual cultivation should not be restricted to conventionally "religious" forms but [be] pursued in the midst of everyday activities as well' (Foulk 1988: 167), even seemingly ordinary activities are carried out in a spirit of mindfulness and ritual procedure. Verses are chanted, for example, before washing, teeth-brushing and listening to lectures, and mealtimes in particular are carefully choreographed affairs involving the chanting of prayers, gestures of respectful offering and strict prescriptions for handling one's bowl and utensils. The typical daily schedule includes three or four forty-minute periods of meditation; the chanting of scriptures during morning, midday and evening services; periods of manual labour, or 'working meditation'; mealtimes (which are taken in a separate dining area rather than in the monk's meditation hall, as is traditional in Japanese *Sōtō* monasteries); and times set aside for spiritual reading, lectures, communal tea, reflection and relaxation. In addition to this, the priory observes a wide array of daily and monthly ceremonies and a full calendar of annual festival celebrations. Sunday afternoons and Mondays are designated as 'renewal days', when the rigorous daily schedule is relaxed, rising time is later (7.45 a.m. rather than 6.00 a.m.), there are fewer formal meditation and work periods, and the monks rest, relax and engage in personal activities like writing letters. There are also times, however, when monastic practice becomes more intensive – during the twice-yearly monastic *sesshins*, for instance, when the monastery is closed to visitors and an emphasis is placed on meditation.

Offering teaching, spiritual counselling (*sanzen*) and other priestly services (e.g. weddings, funerals and memorial services) to the laity is another important activity of the monastic community. This has taken place mainly at the monastery itself, particularly through its retreat and residential lay training programmes, although it also takes place away from the priory. Following their return from Shasta Abbey, the British monks started to visit, on a monthly basis, the priory's affiliated meditation groups to give spiritual guidance and meditation instruction. As the number of groups increased, this activity was extended through the travelling priest programme. This programme, which involved monks making regional tours of meditation groups, was started as a means of assessing the potential for institutional expansion in Britain. In addition to this, monks have always travelled out from the priory to lead day and weekend retreats, give public talks, and perform priestly functions in lay trainees' homes (e.g. the house blessing ceremony). This activity has also extended beyond Britain; monks from the priory have led retreats in the Netherlands and Germany since the late 1970s.

Within the OBC, 'the traditional interdependence of monastic and lay communities'[48] is promoted and implemented. Throssel Hole Priory is thus funded entirely by donations made by its congregation in Britain and Europe, and it enjoys the financial advantages stemming from its status as a charitable trust. As we observed earlier, though, the primary basis of the laity's financial support has never been that of merit-making or priestly ritual performance as is common in Eastern contexts. The priory, like that of other Buddhist centres catering to Western practitioners, receives its main income from providing lay trainees with religious teaching, meditation instruction, spiritual guidance and encouragement. During the early period, the funds from the embryonic lay congregation were insufficient to support the priory's growing number of monks who, unless they had personal savings or alternative means of support, had to find work in neighbouring villages and towns. In contrast to their monastic counterparts in the NKT, the 'skilful' use of the state benefits system was never an option for Zen Mission Society (ZMS)/OBC monks:

> No person may represent himself or herself as a priest of the Zen Mission Society, Shasta Abbey, whilst living on welfare or dole or any other municipal fund other than a legally obtained scholarship for the purposes of study.[49]

During the critical Lotus Blossom period, largely in response to ultimatums issued by Kennett to her British followers, the financial situation of the priory improved. The British monks continued to be well supported following their return, enabling the priory to maintain an 'open-door' policy of allowing anyone who demonstrates a sincere desire to pursue a monastic vocation to enter the postulancy. The expansion of the monastic *Sangha* fostered the growth of the laity, which, in turn, provided further financial security, with individual donations and covenants now being boosted by collective fund-raising drives.

Besides teaching the lay congregation, Throssel Hole Priory has also endeavoured to establish close and friendly links with its neighbouring community. In

1984, Rev. Master Daishin Morgan gave a well-attended talk in nearby Hexham about the Order's beliefs and practices. This hoped to foster 'mutual understanding and respect' between the priory and the local community so that they could 'live together in harmony, and without suspicion'.[50] Members of the surrounding community have subsequently been invited to visit the monastery and talk informally with its resident monks. This sensitivity to social context is reminiscent of the British Forest Sangha, a group which is also 'critically aware of the manner of their insertion into British society' (Bell 1991: 164). Both groups share a low-key style of proselytisation that has enabled them to distance themselves 'from current preconceived ideas about NRMs [new religious movements] and public unease about their recruitment techniques' whilst presenting themselves as 'mainstream representatives of an established world religion, as opposed to the idea of a newly invented, faddish, unstable and exotic cult so feared by a large section of the British public' (Bell 1991: 168–169). Like the British Forest Sangha, the OBC has 'no clearly defined organised evangelical strategy' (Bell 1991: 158), adopting instead a more passive and exemplary policy towards proselytisation that similarly draws upon traditional *Theravāda* injunctions against teaching without prior invitation (Morgan 1994: 146). On the subject of missionary activity, then, the OBC and NKT are markedly different. The NKT is more akin to the Friends of the Western Buddhist Order (FWBO) of Bell's study, a group for which proselytisation 'is a major preoccupation' and which similarly adopts a more 'obtrusive' style of promotional activity.

The expansion of the OBC, both in America and in Britain, has thus been gradual rather than explosive, the maturation and spiritual deepening of the Order being considered more important than its outward physical and numerical growth:

> groups are not created to try to sell something; the aim is to give maximum benefit to those who genuinely wish to train rather than to obtain large numbers in membership.[51]

The number of meditation groups affiliated to Throssel Hole Priory has risen steadily, from three in 1973 to the current total of twenty-seven (including three in the Netherlands and one in Germany). The creation of new groups has never been the result of any kind of organised missionary activity. They are usually created by isolated or small groups of individuals who have developed an interest in the OBC's style of practice, often after an introductory retreat at the priory. A characteristically low level of promotional activity, combined with a rigorously contemplative emphasis of practice not immediately accessible to newcomers, ensures that few meditation groups attract more than ten regular attenders, and most average even less. As is typical of other Buddhist organisations, the development of the OBC in Britain has been characterised by considerable fluctuation at a local group level. The return of the British monastic community nevertheless introduced a greater degree of stability by enabling stronger links to be forged between local groups and the monastic centre.

Following the highly experimental, and short-lived, attempt to establish a priory in London during the 1970s, the institutional expansion of the OBC beyond Throssel Hole did not occur until 1990 when Reading Buddhist Priory was opened. Institutional expansion has been largely understood as a lay initiative, with new priories being established only when meditation groups in a particular area are ready to give the support required. In terms of its institutional growth, the OBC in Britain is currently at an important stage of development. Throughout 1995 and 1996, clusters of meditation groups based in Scotland, East Anglia, the West Midlands and the North West each launched separate appeals for funds towards establishing new priories. Priories were subsequently founded in Telford early in 1997, and in Edinburgh a year later, bringing the total number of permanent OBC centres in Britain to four. As noted earlier, this push for regional priories has brought the OBC in Britain closer to the American model of institutional development, and this may have important consequences for the future style of practice at Throssel Hole. The creation of new priories has taken place with the full endorsement and support of Kennett. Concern has recently been expressed, however, that in their eagerness to establish and support regional priories, local groups may be putting themselves and their practice under unnecessary pressure.

The OBC's claim that the higher levels of religious experience are unattainable outside the monastic path diverges from the radical laicisation and 'democratisation of enlightenment' evident in other Western Zen movements. However, this does not act as a disincentive to lay trainees because the Order's main emphasis is upon the daily actualisation of inherent enlightenment, and because there are types of experience other than the higher *kenshōs* that are open to lay trainees (e.g. past-life experiences). Furthermore, in all other respects, and in common with Western Buddhism generally, the validity and importance of lay practice has always been affirmed by the OBC. The teaching has been made available to the lay congregation in Britain in a number of ways. Upon being established, Throssel Hole Priory began to offer weekend and week retreats, as well as the Keeping of the Ten Precepts Retreat (*Jūkai*), to the laity. Following the return of the British monks in 1982, this programme was expanded. An Introductory Retreat was introduced, and day retreats, organised by meditation groups and led by monks away from the priory grounds, became a more regular occurrence. Some retreats are designed to coincide with traditional Buddhist festivals, whilst others focus on specific areas of teaching – such as the life of the Buddha or the texts of *Dōgen* – and give greater emphasis to periods of formal instruction and discussion. Weekend retreats have also been organised in recent years to deal with important issues in lay training, such as sexuality, homosexuality and work. Alongside its retreat programme, the priory has also developed a residential training programme, enabling lay trainees to stay there outside of scheduled times and share in its contemplative life. As well as being vital to the spiritual development of the laity, retreat periods are also considered important from the perspective of monastic growth and development, since they provide monks with 'an excellent opportunity to share our understanding and explain the Buddha's teaching to others'.[52] Throssel Hole Priory will thus continue to function as the main retreat centre for the OBC in Britain, even though the creation of new priories, with the facilities to offer retreats at a regional level, will enable it to develop a more monastic focus.

Lay trainees have found it helpful to practise with others and, towards this end, have organised themselves into local meditation groups. During the early period, such groups did not always affiliate themselves exclusively with the ZMS's style of practice; whilst including *Sōtō* Zen meditation in their religious repertoire, they often represented 'a wide range of Buddhist and non-Buddhist points of view'.[53] Kennett's call for a more exclusive form of practice and commitment during the Lotus Blossom period, however, prompted more focused guidelines, the 'true meditation group' now being defined as a group

> comprised of people who look to one Teacher or church for their spiritual guidance – who are, in other words, past the point of 'shopping around' and are getting down to the hard work of training in one discipline.[54]

This emphasis on exclusive affiliation hardened and, with the formulation of the *Bylaws of the* OBC, became official policy for the Order. In Britain, the question of meditation group affiliation has since been clarified further. Two kinds of group are now recognised by Throssel Hole Priory: official affiliates, which consist of experienced meditators and at least one Lay Minister; and 'stage one groups', which are newer to the practice and require further grounding and experience before affiliation proper can be considered. Meditation groups usually meet weekly, either in members' homes or in rented rooms (often in Quaker Meeting Houses), and include periods of formal religious practice and informal social interaction. Whilst the format may differ slightly between groups, 'thus reflecting the natural evolution of groups in diverse settings',[55] in the main there is considerable uniformity in the structure of group meetings.

Meditation groups have always enjoyed a close and reciprocal relationship with Throssel Hole, sharing in the organisation of outside retreats and teaching ventures, and supporting the monks in a variety of financial and practical ways. Of particular importance during the Lotus Blossom period, for example, was the organisation of 'work days', whereby groups would labour alongside the priory's severely depleted resident community upon its various building projects. The successful return and continuing growth of the British monastic community nevertheless required a parallel process of growth and development within the lay congregation. The introduction of the Lay Ministry programme proved to be the key factor behind this process. Meditation groups had, until this time, operated largely independently of each other, concentrating on their individual relationships with the priory and the development of the lay congregation at a local level. Through the agency of Lay Ministers, previously disparate groups began to interact and practise with each other and organise regional and national lay events, thereby generating an awareness of how 'the Sangha exists throughout the country'.[56] The growing sense of cohesion and community within the lay congregation promoted the financial and material security of the monastic *Sangha*.

The Lay Ministry programme was started at Throssel Hole Priory in 1983, following the return of the monastic community, and the first British-trained Lay Ministers were certified a year later. The programme quickly became very popular and there are currently over fifty Lay Ministers in Britain. The Lay Ministry thus represents a sizeable segment of the British lay congregation, which, according to recent estimates, is over a thousand strong. Lay Ministers have, as we have seen, been vital to the growth and development of the British laity, facilitating an increasing connectivity within the lay congregation and between laity and monks, and contributing greatly to the emergence of a sense of cohesion and community in the Order. Lay Ministers assume a position of responsibility within the priory's affiliated meditation groups, taking a leading role in their organisation, running and social development. Inter-group connections on a regional and national level are also fostered through the British Lay Ministry network. Lay Ministers liaise closely with the priory and represent an important bridge between the monastic centre and the wider lay congregation, for example by mediating news and information in both directions and by organising local events which bring monks and lay trainees together. They also take collective responsibility for organising larger-scale events that take place away from the priory. Events such as *Wesak* (festival of the Buddha's birth) and Congregation Day, which are held annually at an outside venue, are important not only because they allow the laity to meet and celebrate together, but also because they provide the lay congregation with an opportunity 'to play host to the monastic community in the traditional way'.[57] Other lay events – the Summer Family Camp, for example – are organised by, and held at, the priory. Their organisation, nevertheless, often involves a high degree of lay input; the meditation groups and Lay Ministers weekends, for example, are scheduled according to lay members' suggestions of topics to be addressed.

The OBC and the British Buddhist context

The openness displayed by Kennett towards alternative religious traditions, through her project of adapting Zen for the West and her perennial certainty that experience of the truth transcends external differences, has never furnished her followers with a licence for eclecticism. The opposite, in fact, has been the case; as we have seen, she has always expected her disciples to adopt an exclusiveness of faith, practice and institutional affiliation. The *Bylaws of the OBC* thus state that

No teachings of religions other than those of the Serene Reflection Meditation Church of Buddhism may be practised by members of the OBC or at any affiliated meditation group, parish church or training monastery.[58]

In this respect, the OBC resembles the FWBO, a movement which has, in a similar way, drawn upon multiple Buddhist and non-Buddhist sources in the construction of a distinctive and unique religious and institutional identity. The arguments offered by Kennett in defence of her exclusive policy are also strikingly reminiscent of the NKT. The following statement from the *Rules of the OBC* would not look out of place in a book by Geshe Kelsang:

Commitment to one form of religious practice is an important aspect of spiritual development. Mixing spiritual practices causes confusion and is potentially dangerous to the spiritual well-being of the person concerned.[59]

The OBC's exclusivism, however, has been 'softer' than that of the NKT. Whilst demanding wholehearted dedication to OBC practice, the *Rules* also state that it is 'both permissible and reasonable' for trainees to study the teachings of and visit 'other churches and religious groups, both Buddhist and non-Buddhist'. Kennett herself cultivated such connections throughout her career, engaging in dialogue with Christian monks and forging friendly links with religious teachers in California.[60]

The nature and degree of Kennett's exclusivism has, in reaction to certain contingencies and events, shifted and changed throughout the OBC's history. During the early period, she attempted to remove her American disciples from the 'guru-hopping' culture of California by moving the headquarters of the ZMS to Mount Shasta and by introducing measures to weed out 'dabblers'. In Britain, the perceived hostility of the Buddhist establishment led her to formulate a policy of non-participation in Buddhist Society events. She was also wary of the fact that a number of her early British followers were former disciples of Sangharakshita, of whom she was also critical. British trainees were thus discouraged from, and chastised for, cultivating connections with these groups. The forging of friendly links and associations with British *Theravāda* Buddhists and Roman Catholic priests was, however, fully endorsed and promoted.

During the Lotus Blossom period, the emphasis changed again. The catalyst this time was the crisis of authority that erupted within the ZMS following Kennett's controversial 'third *kenshō*'. In response to this, she strategically reinforced and strengthened her exclusivism, increasing her emphasis on obedience and commitment to the teacher and introducing measures to regulate religious experience. There was also an increasing tendency, from this period, to employ a rhetoric of 'purity' when defining OBC practice, and this provided the basis of her critique of, and her decision to distance herself from, both Japanese *Sōtō* and wider currents in American Zen. The OBC in America has thus been criticised, in recent years, for being insular and isolationist. The same charge cannot, however, be levelled against the Order in Britain. During the later period, Throssel Hole Priory has adopted a more enthusiastic approach towards interfaith and cross-Buddhist dialogue than Shasta Abbey. Linkages and connections have been developed with a variety of Buddhist and non-Buddhist groups, and on various levels of informal and formal dialogue.

Notwithstanding its early policy of selective exclusivism, Throssel Hole Priory has always fostered friendly and informal linkages. During the early and Lotus Blossom periods, monks from the priory helped to organise and run annual Zen-Catholic inter-religious retreats. Since their return from America, the British monks have participated in Christian-Buddhist monastic retreats and a Dominican priest has regularly visited the priory to lecture on Christian mysticism. On a domestic level of Buddhist activity, a particularly warm and reciprocal relationship has been cultivated with the British Forest Sangha. This has grown out of a perceived 'similarity between Zen and Theravāda practice',[61] and in particular a shared monastic ethos, although the geographical proximity between the priory and Harnham Buddhist monastery, also situated in Northumberland, has provided the necessary practical conditions for the relationship to develop. The priory has also fostered friendly connections with other Buddhist groups, including the Kagyu Samye Ling Tibetan Centre in Dumfriesshire, the *Theravāda* Birmingham Vihara, Plum Village in Bordeaux (the French headquarters of Thich Nhat Hanh's Order of Interbeing), and the non-sectarian Gaia House and Sharpham Community. Such informal links and connections are also cultivated at a local level of activity between the priory's affiliated meditation groups and groups of other traditions; the Aberdeen Serene Reflection Meditation Group, for example, participates in a joint annual celebration of the Buddha's enlightenment along with the local FWBO and Vajradhatu groups. Relations between the priory and the Buddhist Society have also markedly improved during the later period. The passing of Christmas Humphreys in 1983 was clearly an important factor here. The priory only began submitting material for the 'News' section of *The Middle Way* towards the end of that year, and since then has been represented at Buddhist Society events such as *Wesak*.

Besides these informal and individual connections, the OBC in Britain has also been active in broader, more formal contexts of interfaith activity and cross-Buddhist networking. During the later period, monks from the priory have attended a variety of interfaith meetings and conferences around the UK. The OBC in Britain has also been supportive and active in pan-Buddhist umbrella frameworks such as the European Buddhist Union and, in particular, the Network of Buddhist Organisations (NBO) (UK). The priory, on behalf of the OBC in Britain, was one of the NBO's initial participating organisations, contributing an article to the opening issue of its journal, *Roots and Branches* (Autumn 1994), and attending the first NBO conference at Amaravati monastery. The decision to join the NBO marked the beginning of the OBC's formal dialogue with other Buddhist traditions in Britain, and it prompted an interesting process of internal discussion wherein 'the joys and hazards of dialogue with other Buddhists' have been explored. Dialogue and cooperation are viewed positively, both in terms of the specific development of the OBC and from a wider Buddhist perspective. Isolation from the rest of Buddhism is considered unhealthy and dangerous because it breeds a 'siege mentality' and a 'distorted view of others', hindering progress 'towards the development of a mutually supportive climate'. Enthusiasm towards dialogue, though, is hedged with caution and concern. The need 'to commit ourselves to a single practice' is reiterated, and the importance of being 'well grounded in your own faith' before entering into dialogue, and of taking care 'to not compromise the principles of the Order', is emphasised.[62]

The *Rules of the OBC* adopt a rather cautious stance towards 'engaged Buddhist' activities, stating that the exclusively *religious* purpose of the Order's priories 'must not be diluted by political or social action functions'.[63] This declaration does not reject engaged activity per se, but functions as an institutional guideline and safeguard, defining the significance and appropriate context of such activity (i.e. secondary to spiritual affairs and outside the monastery). The support of social welfare and even political causes has always, in fact, formed an important part of the presentation and identity of the OBC. Kennett considered herself part of the movement for sexual equality whilst training in Japan and also thought seriously, before returning to the West, of opening a school for illegitimate children. She has subsequently been outspoken on a number of social and politically charged issues, including abortion, euthanasia and the American presidential elections. She has been particularly concerned with animal rights and welfare, turning Shasta Abbey into a place of refuge for stray and condemned dogs and cats:

> it is the duty of every Buddhist and, I would imagine, Christian also, to offer a home to at least one animal: this is clearly the law of the Cosmic Buddha.[64]

Throssel Hole Priory has also, alongside its support of activities promoting fellowship, dialogue and exchange between Buddhist organisations, and in line with precedents set by Shasta Abbey, developed an 'engaged Buddhist' profile by supporting social welfare causes, both individually and in conjunction with other Buddhists. In this respect, it reflects a broader pattern within British Buddhism:

> Buddhism in Britain has moved beyond the initial stages of transmission and institutionalisation. Engagement with social and political realities reflects a new confidence and maturity. There is a determined

will to integrate Buddhism further into the mainstream of British society and to establish its presence as a moral force in the nation.

(Bell 2000a: 418)

Following the example of Shasta Abbey, the priory instigated a project in 1978 to take Zen Buddhism into British prisons, sending copies of its journal and other literature to prisoners so that they could learn about Zen and 'do something positive with their lives'.[65] This activity has continued in a cooperative way since 1985 through the priory's support of Angulimala (Buddhist Prison Chaplaincy Organisation), an organisation that unites various Buddhist groups in the provision of support, counselling and spiritual guidance for prisoners. One of Angulimala's prison chaplains is an OBC monk, and in recent years Lay Ministers have become more actively involved in its work. Other cooperative ventures supported by the priory include the Buddhist Hospice Trust, the Network of Engaged Buddhists, and its offshoot, the (now disbanded) Leeds Network of Engaged Buddhists.

On the subject of education, the priory has expressed its commitment to supporting the teaching of Buddhism in schools by offering courses and resources for primary and secondary school religious education teachers. Like Shasta Abbey, it has also provided a home for animals, and there is even a special animal cemetery on its grounds. The monastery has endeavoured to use its grounds in an ecologically sound and sustainable way, developing a tree-planting scheme in 1977 that was consciously modelled on E. F. Schumacher's outline of Buddhist economics (Schumacher 1973). This scheme began on a modest scale as a Buddhist tree sanctuary, but subsequently became a major project, receiving the financial backing of various trusts and the Forestry Commission. The priory has organised regular 'tree-planting days', which double up as social occasions for the laity, so that many thousands of trees, of various species, are now spread out over 18 acres of land.

Part IV

EPILOGUE AND CONCLUSION

8

EPILOGUE AND CONCLUSION

A number of scholarly ideas concerning the relationship between Buddhism and British culture and the nature of the transplantation process have been explored and subjected to critical scrutiny throughout this study. In this concluding chapter, I return to the framework adopted in the opening chapter to structure a comparative discussion of the NKT and OBC. Before doing this, though, our historical analysis of the NKT and OBC will be brought up to date with a discussion about recent developments within the organisations.

Recent developments in the NKT

Although the NKT's public image was undoubtedly damaged by media representations of the *Dorje Shugden* dispute, the organisation seemed to emerge from the turbulence of 1996 with a significant degree of internal stability and, in some ways, a clarified self-identity. Students remained philosophical about depictions of the NKT in the British press and maintained that, though generally negative, the articles nevertheless served a useful function by publicly and unambiguously stating that the movement is neither a follower of the Dalai Lama nor a 'Tibetan' organisation. The NKT's embrace of this increased public awareness seemed genuine in spite of the view held by some of its critics that the organisation's past success was attributable, in part, to the positive image of Tibetan Buddhism in the Western imagination, an image that is inextricably interwoven with the figure of the Dalai Lama. On a practical level, following the organisation's withdrawal from the *Dorje Shugden* dispute in 1996 it was, as predicted by the student mentioned earlier, 'back to normal' for the NKT. There have, however, been a couple of notable developments in recent years, the most significant being the organisation's re-entry into the *Dorje Shugden* dispute towards the close of 1997 and its decision to join the Network of Buddhist Organisations (NBO) (UK) in 1998.

The NKT's involvement in the 1996 *Dorje Shugden* controversy underlined the difficulties new religious movements (NRMs) face as they seek to maintain a coherent and consistent public-level identity whilst simultaneously responding to shifting contingencies and events in the world around them. At the time of the campaign, the NKT maintained that its participation did not compromise its self-proclaimed separation and independence from the degenerate religio-political world of Tibetan Buddhism, and the temporary and expedient nature of the alliances forged with *Dorje Shugden* devotees in India and around the world were emphasised. This point was subsequently borne out by the organisation's rather abrupt and complete withdrawal from the dispute later that year. The oracle's renunciation of the NKT during the dispute, and the media's portrayal of the organisation as a movement that is critical of the Dalai Lama, also ensured that at the close of 1996, the NKT's self-identity as a separate and independent organisation was not only in tact but reinforced and strengthened.

The organisation's withdrawal from the *Dorje Shugden* dispute, however, did not last. Towards the end of 1997, the NKT re-entered the campaign when the secretary of the organisation released a booklet entitled *A Report on the Dalai Lama's Abuses of Human Rights and Religious Freedom*. This document chronicled the alleged abuses by the Dalai Lama and his government of human rights and religious freedom within the Tibetan community-in-exile since 1996. It appears to have been provoked, in particular, by allegations made against *Dorje Shugden* devotees during 1997 following the murder in February of that year of Venerable Lobsang Gyatso (b. 1928), the Principal of the Buddhist Dialectics School in Dharamsala, and two of his students.[1] Venerable Lobsang Gyatso was, like the Dalai Lama, religiously and politically progressive and was outspoken in his criticism both of the conservative elements within Tibetan society and of the *Dorje Shugden* cult. The subsequent investigation by the Indian police linked the murders to the *Dorje Shugden* faction of the exiled Tibetan community. A number of high-profile members of the Dorje Shugdan Devotees Charitable and Religious Society were questioned but later cleared of any connection with the murders.

In 1998, the *Dorje Shugden* dispute was reignited in the West when the Dorje Shugden International Coalition was created by Western devotees 'to engage in peaceful actions which put pressure on the Dalai Lama to lift the ban on the worship of Dorje Shugden'.[2] The campaign orchestrated by this pressure group followed precisely the same format as that of the Shugden Supporters Community of 1996. Media coverage of the Dalai Lama's alleged human rights abuses was generated through the issuing of a number of news releases and press packs. These served as a prelude to a number of public protests, petitions and demonstrations that were staged during the Dalai Lama's visit to America in the spring of 1998. Although the Coalition's directory of representatives indicated a support base that was much broader than the NKT, including Tibetan *Gelug* teachers and their students living both in India and in the West, disciples of Geshe Kelsang were heavily represented and clearly played a leading role in the campaign. The ideological continuities that exist between the NKT and other *Gelug* Buddhists with an allegiance to *Dorje Shugden* were thus once again underlined by this latest episode in the controversy. This time, however, the identity issues raised by the NKT's organisational alliance with non-NKT teachers and groups appear to have been anticipated and reconciled within the mission statement of the Coalition itself, which maintained that 'the coalition will dissolve upon the lifting of the ban by the Dalai Lama and the Tibetan government-in-exile'.[3]

In the spring of 1998, the NKT made a request to join the NBO and, following a meeting of its member groups, its request was accepted. This was a significant event, raising issues both for the NBO and its participating organisations as well as for the self-identity of the NKT. The NBO arose out of an initial meeting of Buddhist groups, convened by Jamyang Centre in 1993, for the purpose of jointly inviting the Dalai Lama to teach in Britain. It quickly expanded beyond this original purpose, though, developing its own identity in 1994 'as a forum for communication and co-operation between the diverse Buddhist organisations around the UK'.[4] Thus, when the Dalai Lama eventually came to Britain in the summer of 1996, only twenty-seven of the forty-three member organisations were signatories to the visit. This lack of internal unanimity with respect to the activities of the NBO is evidence of the enduring diversity and dividedness of British Buddhism. The diversity of British Buddhism notwithstanding, Scott's observation that 'there has been a discernible convergence or moving closer together between Buddhist groupings in this country' (Scott 1995b) is accurate. In light of the fact that over half of the NBO's members supported the visit of the Dalai Lama, Scott's comment that 'the Dalai Lama has been instrumental in fostering closer ties across British Buddhist traditions' is also sound.

The founding principles of the NBO state that participation in the organisation 'is open to all UK Buddhist organisations' and that one of its purposes is to 'ensure the diversity of Buddhist views is expressed',[5] irrespective of the specific beliefs and practices held by particular groups. Nevertheless, as a group widely perceived to have sown conflict and disharmony by publicly protesting against the Dalai Lama, the NKT's request for membership posed a challenge to the NBO. A number of its member groups regarded the NKT's activities as incompatible with the NBO's commitment to promoting fellowship, dialogue and harmony, and with the high esteem in which the Dalai Lama is held by many. Consequently, a number of groups severed their connection with the NBO when the NKT opted in. According to Waterhouse, the NKT's affiliation with the NBO prompted about 30 per cent of the groups identifying themselves with Tibetan traditions to leave (Waterhouse 2000: 154).

The decision to join the NBO also had implications for the NKT's self-identity, which, for the first seven years of its existence, was firmly predicated upon ideas of purity, exclusivism and separatism. This uncharacteristic move towards the British Buddhist mainstream seemed to represent a reversal of its self-proclaimed separation from other Western Buddhist groups, and a softening of its hardline approach towards maintaining the purity of its lineage-tradition. On the surface, this development also appears to support Scott's prediction that the NKT may, like the Friends of the Western Buddhist Order, 're-emerge into wider active Buddhist settings' (Scott 1995a) once it has passed through an initial stage of retrenchment, distancing and identity-building. It is too early to tell at this stage, however, whether there have been any significant shifts in the NKT's self-understanding resulting from its willingness to enter a forum of Buddhist dialogue and fellowship. Indeed, the organisation's decision to join the NBO may have had a primarily pragmatic and expedient, rather than ideological, motivation. When seen against the backdrop of the 1996 *Dorje Shugden* dispute, it can be understood as an attempt to reclaim some of the credibility that had been lost during the campaign, particularly at the hands of the British media, which presented the movement as inward-looking, mind-controlling and 'cultish'. By entering into pan-Buddhist settings, the NKT may be seeking to rebuild and redefine its public face in a way that is acceptable to the moral mainstream. This move also suggests a realisation amongst the organisation's leadership that separation from wider Buddhist currents may create more problems than it solves. At the cost of preserving its purity, the organisation has often been viewed with suspicion, criticism and even hostility by other Buddhist groups, and the recent media explosion demonstrated how damaging such external criticism can be. The decision to join the NBO thus illustrates Lifton's observation that in order to function and succeed, movements which disseminate 'fundamentalist' principles need to cater to varied interests, become more compromising and assimilable, and generally interact 'with the protean currents of the larger society' (Lifton 1993: 165). There may not have been any substantive shift in the NKT's self-identity as a pure tradition in a world of degeneration, or in its view that this purity must be preserved through a radically exclusive form of practice. Nor is its participation necessarily indicative of a new, more positive, attitude towards the value of cross-Buddhist dialogue, discussion and fellowship. What this move does indicate, though, is an awareness that a more working relationship with wider currents on the British Buddhist landscape is required. Within the NBO, the NKT has a forum in which it can represent itself to others, and thereby reduce the potential for future misunderstanding and misrepresentation.

In light of the traditional basis of *Gelug* clericalism and exclusivism underpinning Geshe Kelsang's thought, and the gradual hardening of his exclusive orientation over time in reaction to both indigenous Tibetan and modern Western forces, any significant reversals or overhauls in the NKT's self-identity seem, at least for the foreseeable future, unlikely. The organisation's participation in the *Dorje Shugden* dispute and its more recent decision to join the NBO do indicate, however, that the NKT is prepared to respond reflexively to the changing circumstances in which it finds itself, and this quality will be essential to its future growth. Whether or not the latter development has any substantial implications on an ideological level, only time will tell. It is not unfeasible, though, that through participating in broader pan-Buddhist settings, the excesses of NKT exclusivism may gradually soften until its initially pragmatic motivation is replaced with an increasingly ideological one.

Recent developments in the OBC

On 6 November 1996, at the age of 72, Rev. Master Jiyu-Kennett died of complications from diabetes, from which she had been suffering for many years. The monks at Shasta Abbey and Throssel Hole Priory observed the traditional week-long meditation vigil 'that follows the death of a Great Master and Abbess'[6] and performed weekly memorials during the following seven weeks 'so everyone who wished to could formally say farewell'.[7] Meditating with her body prior to performing the traditional funeral ceremonies left a deep impression on the monks, many of whom testified to her *parinirvāṇa*, or entry into 'eternal meditation'.

In his study of the emergence and evolution of the Radhasoami tradition in India, Juergensmeyer observes that in the life cycle of NRMs, 'the death of the original central figure usually signals the beginning of a critical stage, and often spells the end of the movement itself' (Juergensmeyer 1991: 33). The main point of crisis at this crucial juncture is that of leadership succession, since the 'crux for the continuance of any kind of institutional religion' is the continuity of religious specialism and authority:

> it is only because of succession that a religious movement can become institutionalised.
>
> (Minney 1975: 146)

The presence of clear lines of authority and continuity minimises the potential for disunity and fragmentation, promoting the stability and solidity required for further growth, expansion and institutionalisation.

Juergensmeyer also points out that once agreement has been reached on the 'heir to the collective memory', other challenges present themselves: namely the content of the memory itself or 'the need to sort out orthodox from heterodox interpretations of the past'; and 'the challenge of keeping pace with history by assimilating new pasts into the collective memory' (Juergensmeyer 1991: 33). These challenges must be successfully negotiated if a religious group is to make the transition from being a *movement* – that is, 'a community not yet fully formed' and in 'a state of transition from an old worldview to a new one' – into a *tradition* – that is, 'a culturally transmitted view of reality' which is characterised by 'diversity, identity and endurance' (Juergensmeyer 1991: 8).

In the light of these considerations, it will be useful to consider the OBC's responses to the critical stage ushered in by Kennett's death. As we shall see, during the years following Kennett's death, the Order's leadership successfully negotiated the challenges of succession and authority, ideological continuity, and the need for continuing reflexivity and adaptability. These problems were largely alleviated, in fact, by the guidelines and structures that had been formulated by Kennett herself during her lifetime and, in Juergensmeyer's terms, 'the expansive view' (1991: 33) she took of her movement. The later period, as we have seen, was a time of considerable routinisation; clear structures of authority, organisation and ideology were devised to stabilise and consolidate the Order and to guarantee its future continuity and integrity. In the event of the charismatic founder's death, the potential for disagreement in the OBC over succession, identity and doctrine was thus successfully bypassed. Institutional mechanisms came into play immediately as, according to procedures laid down in the *Bylaws of the OBC*, elections were held to appoint a new abbot for Shasta Abbey and a new Head of the Order. Kennett had already nominated a successor to her abbacy 'pending his election by the monastic community after her death', and the new Head of the OBC, 'elected with a substantial majority by the members of the monastic Sangha who formed the electorate',[8] was Rev. Master Daizui MacPhillamy, one of her closest disciples and co-author of *The Book of Life* (1979).

Having assumed their positions of responsibility and leadership, the first action of the Order's main figures of authority and influence was to declare their unity and to collectively vow to preserve, protect and promote Kennett's teachings and religious order. An article in a special memorial issue of the Order's journal entitled 'Where do we go from here?', to which the Head of the Order and the abbots of Shasta Abbey and Throssel Hole Priory were signatories, stated that

> The Abbey and priories will continue to operate as they have before; the practice remains unchanged; the teaching will have new voices, but its Sound will be the same.[9]

At the same time, though, the dangers of becoming too conservative and rigid were recognised, and an additional vow was made to meet the third of the challenges outlined by Juergensmeyer; namely to keep the Order alive and vital by remaining responsive to new stimuli and open to further development, change and adaptation:

> In putting this into practice, we realize that the spirit of a teaching requires a form in order that it be seen and passed on, and we are mindful that this form can either vitalize or kill the spirit. It can kill it quickly if sweeping and unnecessary changes of form are made, if one chases after the trendy religious fashion of the moment. But it can also kill it slowly if, in the sincere attempt to stay true to the spirit, one holds on so tightly to the form exactly as it existed at the time of the teacher's death that the preservation of the form becomes an end in itself, thus causing it to 'fossilize' for all time and slowly strangle the spirit which it was meant to embody.[10]

During the immediate years following Kennett's death, a number of strategies were employed by the leadership in the interests of promoting unity and stability and strengthening the foundations of the Order. The first of these was the highly public manner in which the Head assumed authority and the very deliberate transparency characterising his early running of the Order. This is best illustrated by an article that appeared in the *Journal of Throssel Hole Buddhist Abbey* entitled 'How the OBC works'.[11] This explained that whereas the operation of the Order previously went unnoticed due to the informal and ad hoc way in which Kennett (because of ill-health) had to make decisions, his own good health and mobility 'permits these things to be done more publicly'. By reiterating that the Order's structures of authority and organisation were formulated and implemented by Kennett herself, he also reinforced them with the weight of her charismatic authority. Furthermore, a spirit of confidence and trust was promoted through his assurance that, in the interests of staying 'true to the source', authority will never be exercised arbitrarily or in isolation, but always through 'mutually interlocking links of refuge-taking' and 'the natural checks and balances implied in the division of responsibilities between the various officers of the Order and its communities'.

The second strategy of promoting unity and stability was that of centralisation. In the years following Kennett's death, the leadership introduced various measures aimed at strengthening the connections between the constituent parts of the Order and keeping the channels of communication between the centre and the periphery open and well lubricated. The relationship between Shasta Abbey and the OBC in Britain and Europe was, predictably, the focal point of these efforts. Without the compelling and unifying authority of its charismatic founder, and with the onset of an authority structure based more upon legal-rational principles,[12] the distance between the American and European congregations might have become a weak link had steps not been taken to bridge it. An awareness of the role played by distance in accentuating earlier periods of conflict and disagreement may also have made the urge to centralise even more keenly felt. The introduction of centralising measures, however, was not only a 'negative' strategy aimed at minimising the potential for fragmentation and breakdown; it was also a way of asserting the equality and partnership of the American and European branches in the furtherance of the aims and purposes of the Order.

Three main centralising measures can be discerned. First, the leadership of the Order attempted to bring the American and European congregations closer together by encouraging an increase in the mutual visits and exchanges between senior monks at Throssel Hole Priory and Shasta Abbey. In the summer of 1997, the Head himself visited Britain to provide 'an opportunity for those of us who did not already know him to be able to become acquainted' and thereby 'help foster mutual trust and harmony within the Sangha'.[13] Secondly, and during his visit to Britain, the Head formally conferred upon Throssel Hole Priory the title and status of an 'abbey'. In light of the fact that the priory had, for many years, already been functioning as a full training monastery and sub-registry of the OBC, the significance of this event must be seen mainly in symbolic terms as a public declaration of confidence, unity and partnership.

The third centralising measure was the decision to merge the two main journals of the Order – *The Journal of the Order of Buddhist Contemplatives* and *The Journal of Throssel Hole Buddhist Abbey* – into one. There were many sound spiritual and practical reasons for doing this; a greater variety of articles on Buddhist practice, for example, could now be made available. The central motivation, though, was to promote unity within the Order by bringing the OBC's scattered trainees 'from all of our corners [of the globe] into one meeting place':[14]

> 'One Journal for One Order' is how the Head of the Order, Rev. Master Daizui MacPhillamy describes the importance of this event.[15]

It is too early in the Order's post-Kennett development to assess the continuity, or otherwise, of its identity, doctrine and practice. Suffice it to say that all the evidence at this early stage, both from journals and from personal communications, is that the spirit of conservation and caution underpinning the mission statement of the OBC's leadership has been carefully fostered and assimilated throughout the organisation. At the time of writing, the Order is still in a period of mourning, and is more concerned with celebrating and preserving the memory and legacy of its founder and figurehead than with exploring new areas of growth, adaptation and development.[16] The future development of the Order will undoubtedly bring new challenges and difficulties. One of these, I suspect, will be the problem of retaining its unity and stability in the face of competing interpretations of Kennett's teachings. As we have seen, even during her lifetime there were considerable differences of opinion, within the OBC's membership, concerning such issues as the use of theistic terminology and the importance of ceremonial observance. These differences could, over time, become more accentuated, thereby increasing the risk of a similar kind of splintering and fragmentation that has characterised the development of other Zen groups in the West.[17]

Buddhism and British culture

The subtle interaction between Buddhism and British culture, a phenomenon described by Mellor (1991) as 'cultural translation', has been a major preoccupation of scholars of contemporary British Buddhism, and it has also featured strongly in this study. The theory that contemporary Buddhist practice displays continuities with both Protestant Christianity and the conditions of modernity has been explored and tested throughout. In particular, the view that British Buddhism can be understood as 'broadly Protestant' in character has been subjected to critical scrutiny. Whilst the NKT and OBC both give much emphasis to the value of lay religiosity, and in this respect could be deemed as displaying 'broadly Protestant' tendencies, I have argued for a more cautious application of the Protestant Buddhism thesis than has been evident elsewhere. Waterhouse, whilst accepting the Protestant Buddhism thesis as axiomatic, nevertheless states in a footnote that 'none of the ideological features of "Protestant Buddhism" are absent altogether from traditional forms of Buddhism' (Waterhouse 1997: 24). By placing the traditional forms of Buddhism firmly at the centre of this study, it has become apparent that features of Buddhist practice which seem to have emerged from cultural translation may in fact have been transplanted as part of the traditional package. This point has been demonstrated most forcefully through my analysis of the OBC, an organisation that displays in abundance the features that Mellor identified as suggestive of Protestant Christian influences. When contextualised against its traditional Japanese Sōtō Zen background, the supposedly 'Protestant' features of OBC belief and practice – such as its emphasis on lay religiosity and its personalistic view of religious form – also turn out to have very traditional Eastern precedents. This clearly problematises the application of the 'Protestant Buddhist' designation in this case. This study therefore underlines the importance of adopting a genuinely cross-cultural approach in the study of Buddhist traditions in transition. The theoretical bias within the study of British Buddhism that places the analytical centre of gravity on British culture must be replaced by a more balanced perspective, one that incorporates the study of traditional Buddhist precedents and influences alongside cultural translation theory.

With respect to the second main strand of cultural translation theory – the widely accepted argument that the conditions of modernity are reflected in contemporary Buddhist practice – this study has again yielded interesting results. First, it is clear that the modern emphasis on individual authority and personal experience, and the concomitant reflexivity of identity, have indeed been reflected in many aspects of NKT and OBC identity, belief and practice, at both the institutional and the individual levels. These processes have been most clearly exemplified during times of internal conflict and crisis. During periods of conflict, the authority sources called upon to legitimate Buddhist practice, both by individual practitioners and by group leaders, have been challenged, tested and renegotiated. The Lotus Blossom period of the OBC's development, for instance, prompted a number of shifts, in both individual and group identities, as opposing positions on the legitimacy of Kennett's religious experiences were adopted and defended through recourse to the same authority sources differently interpreted. The reflexivity of this process was evident, both in the different assessments of individual practitioners about which authority sources should be primary, and in the responses of the OBC's leadership to internal conflict and dissension. Individual differences notwithstanding, the authority of personal experience remained central to the decision-making process of all practitioners within the OBC. Similarly, whilst the Lotus Blossom period witnessed an increase in Kennett's dependence on the legitimate authorities of lineage-tradition and scripture, personal experience nevertheless remained at the forefront of her presentation.

This study has acknowledged that the conditions of modernity are also reflected within the NKT, both in the importance of personal authority to individual practitioners, and in the reflexive manner in which Geshe Kelsang's thought has developed in response to the orientations of his Western disciples. I have also argued, however, that an acknowledgement of the NKT's 'fit' with modernity only partially explains the nature of this organisation. Aspects of the NKT's organisational and ideological structure suggest that the movement may actually represent a more critical and reactionary response to the forces of modernity. Geshe Kelsang's concern to establish a uniformity of belief and prac-tice throughout the NKT, his emphasis on following one pure tradition exclusively and his critique of the protean inclusivism of Western practitioners are all suggestive of a response to modernity that has been characterised by Lifton as 'fundamentalist' (1993: 10). Whereas the 'protean' mode of being embraces historical dislocation and social restlessness in a spirit of exploration, experimentation and improvisation, 'fundamentalism' reacts against uncertainty by creating all-encompassing systems of belief and practice which reject pluralism and unpredictability and offer their members certainty and security. A survey of the organisation's membership has indicated that for many practi-tioners, NKT Buddhism does indeed represent a favourable alternative to the fragmented and uncertain nature of modern society and, in particular, has heralded an end to their protean quest for spiritual fulfilment.

The transplantation process

Whilst cultural translation theory should be central to any study of the develop-ment of Buddhist traditions in Britain, an appreciation of religious and cultural relationships does not explain the total transplantation process. A major aim of this study has been to shed light on the various factors and conditions that, alongside cultural translation, shape the transplantation process as a whole. Three main conditions affecting the successful transplantation of Buddhist traditions in Britain were outlined in the opening chapter – material condi-tions, trans-cultural processes and the nature of the incoming tradition – and these have been explored throughout with reference to the NKT and OBC.

As with other Buddhist groups in Britain, the importance of material condi-tions to the successful emergence of the NKT and OBC has manifested itself through the struggle for control of institutional sites and the creation of effi-cient legal, organisational, administrative and financial structures. The early development of both the NKT and the OBC witnessed disputes over institu-tional sites for the dissemination of Buddhist discourse. The control and appropriation of existing institutional sites and the successful creation of alter-native sites of discourse became central to the unfolding ideological vision of both groups. In the case of the NKT, the effects of the early institutional conflict over Manjushri Institute were far-reaching. As we have seen, repressed memories of institutional conflict returned later to influence the way in which the NKT understood and articulated itself organisationally through a rhetoric of decentralisation. With respect to the legal, organisational and administrative structure of the OBC, the turbulent Lotus Blossom period was much more important than the earlier disputes over who controlled Throssel Hole Priory. The creation by Kennett of clear structures of authority and organisation was part of a deliberate and systematic attempt to routinise and restore equilibrium to a movement rocked by conflict and instability.

The importance of trans-cultural processes – that is, processes resulting from the prior transformation of Buddhist traditions in indigenous Asian contexts due to the impact of Western cultural, political and ideological forces – to the transplantation of Buddhist traditions in Britain has been explored throughout this study. These processes have not been a factor in the growth and development of the NKT because Tibetan forms of Buddhism did not generally develop in a modernist direction prior to their transplantation in the West. The impact of Western and modernist forces on Japanese Zen Buddhism, by contrast, ensured that the transplantation of the OBC in Britain involved trans-cultural constituents. In particular, Kennett's emphasis upon the spiritual experience of *kenshō* and her personalistic or 'utilitarian' view of religious form reflected the modern – or, in Sharf's terms, 'Protestant' (1995c: 250) – reconstruction of Zen as an essentially meditative and mystical tradition. It is necessary to restate here, however, that the 'Protestant Buddhism' designation must be used with caution. The 'irrepressible multivocality' of the Zen tradition that Faure (1991: 285) points to reminds us that the mystical, demythologising and anti-ritual interpretations of modern Zen apologists all have deeply traditional precedents. It has thus been necessary to counterbalance our discussion of trans-cultural processes in the transplantation of the OBC with an examination of the traditional Buddhist precedents underpinning Kennett's thought.

The importance of understanding how the shape and nature of incoming traditions – that is, the traditionally Buddhist forms and structures that have developed quite independently of Western cultural contact – influence and affect the transplantation and development of Buddhism in Britain has been underlined consistently. By situating the OBC within a genuinely cross-cultural context, and by eschewing the theoretical bias that places the analytical centre of gravity firmly upon Western culture, a more theoretically balanced perspective has been brought to bear upon the development of Zen in the West and a long-overdue critique of the Protestant Buddhism thesis has been provided. The importance of adopting a theoretically balanced approach has been argued most forcefully with respect to the transplantation and development of Tibetan Buddhist traditions in Britain. By situating the development and self-identity of the NKT within its appropriate historical, cultural and ideological contexts, the importance of understanding how broader oriental contexts continue to exert a normative influence on the development of Buddhist traditions in the Occident has been demonstrated. This study has argued that the emergence of the NKT onto the British religious landscape represents the manifestation, in a Western context, of classical and contemporary divisions within the *Gelug* tradition with regard to policies about inter-traditional relations and the related issue of *Dorje*

Shugden reliance. These divisions have been dwelt upon at length because of their relevance not only to the study of the NKT, but also to the wider fields of contemporary Tibetan religious, cultural and political studies. When this historical and cross-cultural approach to the development of Tibetan Buddhism in Britain is coupled with the findings of cultural translation theory, the NKT emerges as a contemporary Buddhist movement that is rooted firmly within traditional *Gelug* exclusivism but which simultaneously reflects and reacts against the conditions of modernity.

Policies and patterns of adaptation

An appreciation of the policies and patterns of adaptation at work within Buddhist groups is central to our understanding of the successful transplantation of those traditions in Britain and so has featured strongly in this study. Both the NKT and the OBC have been sensitive to the manner of their insertion into Western society and have each devised, in Mellor's terms, 'significant perspectives on culture' (1989: 21) to facilitate their transplantation. An analysis of NKT and OBC policies and strategies of adaptation has indicated a number of similarities in their approaches. Both groups, for example, adopt an essentialist perspective towards the project of adaptation; each claim to have stripped the 'essence' of Buddhism away from Eastern cultural accretions and to have presented it in forms that are meaningful and accessible to Western practitioners. The adaptations and innovations made by both Geshe Kelsang and Jiyu-Kennett have been legitimated through recourse to the traditional authority structures within their schools. Tibetan and Zen forms of Buddhism, as noted in the opening chapter, share a similar emphasis upon the authority of the spiritual guide as a living representative of the ultimate truth that has been handed down via an unbroken lineage. The policy of adaptation within both the NKT and the OBC can thus be characterised as an essentialism that combines both traditional and charismatic elements.

Whilst the skilful adaptation of Buddhism by Geshe Kelsang forms an integral part of the NKT's self-identity and claim to centrality in the Western Buddhist world, this study has revealed that the organisation places an equal, if not greater, emphasis upon conserving the pure tradition of *Tsong Khapa*. This is rooted in the perception that both the contemporary *Gelug* sect of Tibetan Buddhism and the eclectic style of practice adopted by many Western Buddhists represent a serious threat to the continuation of *Tsong Khapa*'s pure tradition in the modern world. Geshe Kelsang's emphasis upon preserving and protecting this pure tradition ensures that the project of adapting Buddhism for the West is treated with a degree of caution within the NKT, and it has led some practitioners to criticise other Buddhist groups for over-adapting, and thereby destroying the purity of, their respective traditions. This study has argued that the NKT's claim to represent a 'Western' form of Buddhism thus reflects two aspects of its self-identity: on the one hand, it reflects the belief that Geshe

Kelsang has adapted Buddhism in an accessible way for Western practitioners; on the other, it expresses his concern to preserve and conserve the pure tradition by separating from the degenerate religio-political world of 'Tibetan' *Gelug* Buddhism. It has also been argued that alongside his wish to make Buddhism more accessible to westerners, a key motivation behind Geshe Kelsang's main adaptations of traditional forms is conservation and preservation. By requiring an exclusive commitment to one teacher and by limiting the field of Highest Yoga Tantra to one main *yidam*, for example, the NKT study programmes have placed a boundary around the practice of NKT disciples, and in this way they protect the tradition of *Tsong Khapa* from external contaminants. The dynamic of *conservation through adaptation* is a special feature of the NKT's identity that may well accompany the transplantation of other conservative and clerical forms of Buddhism, Tibetan or otherwise, in Western societies.

The adaptation of *Sōtō* Zen for the West was from the outset a major preoccupation of Kennett's, whose intimate awareness of the subtle ways in which Buddhism and Western culture interact, and whose ability to empathise with Western Buddhist practitioners, made her a highly skilled cultural negotiator. As a disaffected Christian, Kennett understood the wider 'reactionary' appeal of Buddhism, and she catered to this by elucidating key Buddhist concepts in terms of their fundamental differences to those of Christianity. At the same time, she understood that many Western Buddhists, like herself, have deeply ambivalent attitudes towards their indigenous Christian backgrounds and seek, in Tweed's terms, to be cultural *consenters* as well as dissenters (1992: xxi–xxii). Consequently, the main strategy she used for the adaptation of Zen for the West was the appropriation of Christian religious forms. The OBC thus developed as a Zen Buddhist movement that organisationally, ritually and doctrinally reflected the Western religious background both of its founder and of its members.

Whilst Kennett's essentialist policy and main strategies of adaptation remained unchanged throughout her spiritual career, the project of adaptation within the OBC nevertheless underwent a number of interesting shifts during the Lotus Blossom and later periods. The visionary experiences that constituted Kennett's 'third *kenshō*' prompted, as we have seen, a number of doctrinal developments and innovations. Of particular interest was her rather unconventional interpretation of karma and past-life experiences and her intensified employment of Christian terminology, imagery and symbolism. At times during the Lotus Blossom period, Kennett was no longer simply *borrowing* Christian religious forms to make Buddhism more acceptable and accessible to westerners: she was asserting the deep and essential *identity* of the two traditions. She retracted from this position later by tempering her use of explicitly theistic terminology and by abandoning a number of early adaptations that were now considered to be 'straying from the source', such as the utilisation of Christian religious holidays for the celebration of key Buddhist festivals. A final noteworthy development in Kennett's thought during the later period was her increasing tendency, when discussing adaptation, to make sectarian statements about the state of *Sōtō* Zen in Japan, which, unlike the OBC, had deviated from the source, that is the essential principles of *Dōgen*. Having weathered the storm of the Lotus Blossom period, during which the legitimating sanction of the official arbiters of *Sōtō* orthodoxy was actively sought and courted, Kennett was now in a much stronger position to publicly articulate her critique of the Japanese sect.

Constructing history and resolving conflict

This study has not only been concerned with examining the historical emergence and ideological development of significant Buddhist organisations on the British Buddhist landscape. The dynamics of history and identity construction in NRMs have also been explored throughout. The NKT and OBC are two contemporary religious movements in which the dynamics of history construction, as outlined by Coney (1997), are well exemplified. Each group contains a diverse set of 'histories' ranging across the individual, small group and public levels of the organisation. Individual accounts diverge widely over points of historical detail and the same events are often interpreted in very different ways, reflecting a wide range of experience, bias, opinion and group loyalty. At the level of public discourse, shifts and developments in the self-identity and world-view of the NKT and OBC have been accompanied always by the leadership's revision and conscious 'forgetfulness' of earlier narratives. Coney's observation that the dynamics of history and identity construction in NRMs are best exemplified within groups that have undergone periods of conflict and disunity has also been borne out by this study. The leaderships of the NKT and OBC have striven to erase unwelcome memories of the internal conflicts that have rocked both organisations by constructing simplified group histories which iron out discontinuities in favour of strong, continuous storylines. For both organisations, the changing of group names has been an important technique of burying unwelcome memories and promoting the creation of new ones in their place. The project of deliberately excluding unwanted histories, however, has not been completely successful in either organisation. Memories that have been repressed at the level of public discourse not only live on at the level of individual group members but can also, as we have seen within the NKT, return to haunt the margins of public discourse, influencing its structure.

The manner in which the respective leaderships of the NKT and OBC have responded to periods of conflict, discontinuity and instability has been an area of considerable interest in this study. Whilst both groups have displayed similar patterns of history and identity construction through their ordering of social memory and forgetfulness, the immediate strategies they have adopted for dealing with internal conflict and instability have often been quite different. The main difference concerns the degree of dialogue that has taken place between the leadership and membership of each group, and the channels through which such dialogue has occurred.

The NKT's allegiance to the controversial protective deity *Dorje Shugden* has been the main source of potential and actual instability within this group. Prior to the recent public outbreak of this dispute, awareness of the contentious dimensions of the practice within the NKT was extremely limited due to a policy of silence adopted by the group's leadership following a dispute in the mid-1980s between Geshe Kelsang and the Office of the Dalai Lama. This policy of non-discussion resumed following the NKT's withdrawal from its brief, and uncharacteristically proactive, involvement in the *Dorje Shugden* supporters campaign of 1996. During the campaign itself, as in the general running of the group, the minimal amount of dialogue between the group's leadership and wider membership was mediated by NKT centre directors. At no point in the NKT's development has Geshe Kelsang used either his texts or the group's periodical publications as a vehicle for directly addressing and allaying the concerns of the wider membership.

This manner of dealing with conflict and instability is very different from the preferred style of the OBC's leadership. Throughout the development of her Order, and especially during periods of conflict and instability, Kennett engaged in regular and direct dialogue with her wider following. Her publications and, in particular, the Order's quarterly journals have always functioned as a channel of communication between the centre and the periphery. This has ensured that, in times of conflict, the leadership of the OBC has been able to skilfully utilise its publications as a vehicle for negotiating, mediating and restoring stability to the organisation. The manner in which the journals were utilised following Kennett's death to facilitate the transition from her charismatic leadership of the Order to the legal-rational leadership of her successors is the most recent example of the dynamic role played by publications within the organisation. Within the OBC, in contrast to the NKT, the interplay between text and context has therefore been much more conspicuous, dynamic and vital to the group's stability and growth.

Conclusion

This study situated the historical and ideological development of the NKT and OBC within their broader British, and specifically Tibetan and Japanese Zen, Buddhist contexts. Their emergence and growth was also analysed against the processes and trends that have characterised the development of other forms of Buddhism in Britain and the West. Scholarly perspectives on the subtle interactions between Buddhism and British culture, and the various other factors and conditions affecting the transplantation process, were explored, tested and, in some cases, challenged by the data. A wider range of theories concerning the internal dynamics of NRMs were also utilised to make sense of the inner patterns and processes at work within the NKT and OBC. It is therefore anticipated that the present study will have relevance and application not only to the field of contemporary Western Buddhism, but also to the study of contemporary religion generally.

Tibetan and Zen forms of Buddhism have been a significantly neglected area within the study of British Buddhism. It is my hope that by taking the largest Tibetan and Zen organisations on the British Buddhist landscape as the focus of research, this study has gone some way towards filling a gap in the literature. Studies of British Buddhism have also tended to concentrate upon the shape and nature of Buddhist organisations at the point of time in which they are studied. This study, by contrast, has provided a detailed historical analysis of the complex organisational and ideological development of two Buddhist movements. It has not been my aim to make broad generalisations about the shape and nature of Tibetan and Zen Buddhism in Britain. The aim, rather, has been to reveal the complex nature of the transplantation of Tibetan and Zen traditions of Buddhism in Britain, and to explore the development and diversity of identity, belief and practice within British Buddhist groups.

The problem of overlooking diversity within British Buddhism by analysing Buddhist groups only at the level of public discourse has been raised by Waterhouse (1997), and this study has shared her concern to also take account of the attitudes of the 'ordinary member'. However, to establish a dichotomy between, on the one hand, the ordinary members of Buddhist organisations and, on the other, the group leaders would also lead to a misrepresentation of the nature of Buddhism's development in Britain. The detailed analysis of the NKT and OBC presented here has revealed that the emergence and growth of Buddhist organisations involves a dialectical relationship between group leadership and group membership. The amount of rejection or reinforcement that Geshe Kelsang and Jiyu-Kennett received from their followers acted as a constraining or facilitating force on the shape and nature of their Buddhist discourse and ensured that an intimate relationship between text and context developed. This study has argued that an understanding of Buddhist organisations requires an analysis not only of group identity at the public level and of the attitudes, beliefs and practices of ordinary group members, but also of the subtle and complex interaction that takes place between the two.

NOTES

1 Buddhism in Britain: review and contextualisation

1 She refers, for example, to the philosopher Jacob Needleman, the scientists Fritjof Capra and David Bohm, and the psychologists Erich Fromm and Abraham Maslow.

2 Whether Buddhism actually offers this or not is another matter. The point is that many people perceive it in this way.

3 For comparative purposes, see Tweed (1992). Tweed argues that, whilst Americans during this period were often opposed to the dominant political, economic and social forms, their attraction to the 'alien intellectual landscape' of Buddhism did not lead to unqualified dissent. They had, rather, 'an ambivalent relation to the prevailing religion and dominant culture' and should be seen as 'cultural consenters as well as cultural dissenters' (1992: xxi–xxii).

4 A cursory glance through the catalogue of Wisdom Books, one of the world's largest suppliers of Buddhist books in English, reveals the ongoing concern of Buddhist writers to present Buddhism as a religion that embodies an environmental ethic and which anticipates the findings of modern psychology and science.

5 The 'pure' religion mentioned here refers to the Buddhist tradition as it exists in its indigenous context before it is transformed by the values and attitudes of the Western Buddhist convert. Chryssides is not making a value judgement about pure or impure forms of Buddhism.

6 Similar arguments are advanced by Welbon (1968), Clausen (1975) and Brear (1975).

7 This view of the FWBO's stance on ritual has also been refuted directly by Sangharakshita, founder of the FWBO, in his critique of Mellor's thesis, *The FWBO and 'Protestant Buddhism'* (1992).

8 Bell relies here on the theories of Anthony Giddens as found in his *Modernity and Self-identity: Self and Society in the Late Modern Age* (1991).

9 In a similar vein, but with reference to the practise of Japanese Zen Buddhism by westerners, Brian Victoria has commented upon 'the resistance on the part of Westerners to confront the dark side of their tradition', such as the use of Zen teachings to promote Japanese nationalism, military endeavour and anti-Semitism (Victoria *et al.*, 1999: 62).

10 However, it is unlikely that the financial assistance received by the British Forest Sangha from its Thai patrons is as extensive as that received by the SGI-UK from Japan.

11 The Buddhist groups at the centre of this study have all created their own publishing companies: Tharpa Publications (created by the NKT), Wisdom Publications (created by the Foundation for the Preservation of the Mahayana Tradition) and Shasta Abbey Press (created by the OBC).

12 The term 'Protestant Buddhism' was first coined by Gananath Obeyeskere (1970) but has since been adopted by other scholars with reference to modern Buddhist movements in Eastern contexts, and by Mellor with reference to Buddhism in Britain. Mellor maintains that the emergence of Buddhism in a Protestant shape is a development that has taken place primarily upon British shores through the process of 'cultural translation'. Bell's research into the British Forest Sangha indicates that Mellor's understanding of this *Theravāda* movement is one-sided. Although she does not refer to developments in South-East Asian countries as 'Protestant' in nature, she does argue that the successful transplantation of *Theravāda* Buddhism in Britain has involved not only its 'cultural translation' into a British context, but also important trans-cultural processes that are rooted in Asian Buddhist modernist movements.

13 See, for example, William James's *The Varieties of Religious Experience* (1902) and Rudolf Otto's conception of the 'numinous' experience in *Idea of the Holy* (1917).

14 Mellor's article 'Protestant Buddhism? The cultural translation of Buddhism in England' (1991), which characterised the FWBO as a form of Buddhism that reflects strongly 'Protestant' tendencies, was criticised in the subsequent issue of *Religion* by the FWBO's liaison officer and later by Sangharakshita's *The FWBO and 'Protestant Buddhism'* (1992).

15 Numerous studies on the cross-cultural diffusion of Buddhism could be mentioned here, but by way of illustration I will mention only two: the study of the establishment of Indian Buddhism in Tibet by David L. Snellgrove (1987) and the study of the diffusion of Chinese Buddhism, via Korea, to Japan by J. H. Kamstra (1967).

16 Mellor's assessment of the FWBO as a movement that regards tradition as peripheral is not accepted by members of the movement who argue that there are many 'traditional' features to FWBO organisation and practice, such as its use of Buddhist scriptures. Furthermore, it is also claimed that Sangharakshita's authority is based on his ordinations and links with tradition, whilst he regards charismatic leadership with suspicion (Sangharakshita 1992: 136). Mellor's characterisation of the FWBO as an individualistic movement has also been forcefully refuted by Sangharakshita (1992: 112–124).

17 The issues raised by transplanting the practice of *guru*-devotion from a Tibetan into a Western context have been examined by Stephen T. Butterfield (1994) and June Campbell (1996).

18 See, for example, Shenpen Hookham's essay 'In search of the guru' (1992).

19 Pye's 'scientific' assessment of *Aum Shinrikyō* is not shared by Robert J. Lifton, who has been conducting research into *Aum Shinrikyō* since 1995. In a recent interview about the movement, he defended its 'Buddhist' credentials, which 'were largely taken from the Tibetan tradition', and maintained that 'it's not Buddhist compassion, certainly – but you can't say it's not Buddhism' (Lifton 1997: 56, 97).

20 See, for example, Werner (1973).

21 Ken Jones, the British representative of the International Network of Engaged Buddhists, recently wrote an article about the three movements entitled 'Many bodies, one mind: movements in British Buddhism' (1996), which appeared in the journal *New Ch'an Forum*. This is critical of their alleged ideological uniformity, their ambitious evangelicalism and their exclusivism.

22 These figures are based mainly on Buddhist Society listings.

23 Humphreys' works on Zen are replete with quotes taken from H. P. Blavatsky's works, thus reflecting his lifelong commitment to theosophy.

24 Taken from 'An introduction to Genpo Roshi' on the Kanzeon Sangha International website (www.neis.net/kanzeon/genpo.html). For a detailed 'insider's' account of Maezumi Roshi's Zen Centre of Los Angeles, see Preston (1988).

25 'Thich Nhat Hanh', in *The Community of Interbeing Manual of Practice*, Section E (June 1996).

26 Taken from 'What is Amida Trust?' on the Amida Trust website (www.cyberus.ca/vellino/amida/home.html).

27 There are no purpose-built temples or centres in Britain that function as religio-cultural focal points for the ethnic Tibetan community. The Tibetan community in Britain is very small in comparison to the ethnic communities and temples that include Zen or *Ch'an* teachings and practices within their self-definition and religious repertoire.

28 See, for example, the work of Knott (1986) on Hinduism in Britain.

29 Events at the Chinese Fa Yue Buddhist Monastery (West Midlands) and the Vietnamese Linh-Son Temple (London and Birmingham), for example, can attract up to 3,000 participants. It is highly unlikely that any British-based Zen grouping could, as the landscape presently stands, attract anything like this number to a single event.

2 The New Kadampa Tradition: background and cross-cultural context

1 Recent research, such as Waterhouse (1997), has endeavoured to adopt a more balanced, cross-cultural perspective, suggesting that this situation may be changing.

2 I am using Samuel's definition of the 'pre-modern' period here, which refers to the period prior to 1950 'when the status of most Tibetan societies was changed drastically as a result of Chinese military intervention and occupation' (1993: 3).

3 The *Kadam* order, it should be noted, was important not only to the emergence of the *Gelug* tradition, but 'has had profound influence – mainly monastic – on all subsequent Tibetan orders' (Snellgrove 1987: 485).

4 Dreyfus himself, for example, seems to reject out of hand any religious persuasion that is not of the open and ecumenical atmosphere of the fourteenth century, blaming intellectual stagnation within the Tibetan traditions upon the hardening of their boundaries in relation to each other.

5 Samuel is not saying that *Tsong Khapa* himself was exclusively orientated or sectarian, but rather that his systematisation of the religious path lent itself to these perspectives.

6 The Fifth Dalai Lama's orientation was generally inclusive, but, as Dreyfus observes, he 'nevertheless agreed to a number of measures aimed at curbing the influence of the groups that had opposed the Ge-luk school most openly. The Jo-nang-ba were directly suppressed' (1997: 37).

7 The inclusive faction within the *Gelug*, of course, has never been restricted to the Dalai Lamas, as Samuel's discussion of 'shamanic' *Gelug lamas* illustrates.

8 From the unpublished transcript 'An anthology of talks given by H.H. the Dalai Lama concerning reliance upon the Dharma protectors' (Dalai Lama 1983: 14). In a manner that is reminiscent of the *Rimed* approach, the Dalai Lama encourages individuals to practise the teachings of different traditions whilst seeking 'to maintain purely the terminology exclusive to each tradition' (Dalai Lama 1983: 14).

9 As noted, the generally inclusive perspective of the Fifth Dalai Lama needs some qualification due to certain exclusive policies implemented by him following the victory of the *Gelugpa*-patronising Mongol forces of Central Tibet over the *Karma-Kagyupa* rulers of *Tsang*. This illustrates how the exclusive and inclusive orientations of *lamas* are not absolute and immutable but can be influenced by political circumstance. The inclusivism of the Fourteenth Dalai Lama provides another illustrative example of this. The Dalai Lama, of course, stands within a long tradition of *Gelug*

inclusivism, but his attempts to foster unity and openness between the different Tibetan traditions in exile must also be seen as a politically expedient policy.

10 According to Smith, the suppressive tendencies of the tradition functioned so thoroughly that a number of *Gelug* works synthesising *Gelug*, *Nyingma* and *Kagyu* teachings are as yet uninvestigated.

11 Kapstein describes how Phabongkha's visions of *Dorje Shugden* 'seem to have entailed a commitment to oppose actively the other schools of Tibetan Buddhism and the Bon-po' (Kapstein 1989: 231). Samuel also describes how Phabongkha, a strict purist and conservative, adopted an attitude of sectarian intolerance and 'instituted a campaign to convert non-Gelugpa *gompa* in K'am to the Gelugpa school, by force where necessary' (Samuel 1993: 52).

12 There are actually conflicting views concerning the extent of Phabongkha's exclusivism, and it is important to acknowledge that a different picture is painted by others who maintain that he was not as actively sectarian as is widely claimed. The image presented here is gleaned from Kapstein (1989), Samuel (1993), Dreyfus (1998) and Beyer (1978), as well as from personal discussions with *Gelug* Buddhists.

13 *Ngatrul Dragpa Gyaltsen*, a hardline *Gelug* adherent who was critical of the Fifth Dalai Lama's eclecticism, was the latest in a series of high-status reincarnate *lamas* beginning with *Panchen Sonam Dragpa*, the first reincarnation of a disciple of *Tsong Khapa's* called *Duldzin Dragpa Gyaltsen*. Devotees who regard *Dorje Shugden* as a Buddha believe that *Duldzin Dragpa Gyaltsen* himself was but the latest in a series of human incarnations of the Buddha *Mañjuśrī*, which stretches all the way back to the time of Buddha *Śākyamuni*.

14 This claim is widely refuted by *Sakya lamas* themselves. Lama Jampa Thaye, an English teacher within both the *Sakya* and the *Kagyu* traditions and founder of the Dechen Community, maintains that 'The Sakyas generally have been ambivalent about *Shugden* [...] The usual *Sakya* view about *Shugden* is that he is controlled by a particular *Mahākāla*, the *Mahākāla* known as "Four-Faced *Mahākāla*". So he is a *'jig rten pa'i srung ma*, a worldly deity, or demon, who is no harm to the *Sakya* tradition because he is under the influence of this particular *Mahākāla*' (interview, July 1996).

15 Examples of such *lamas*, who have taught in the West, include Geshe Rabten, Gonsar Rinpoche, Geshe Ngawang Dhargyey, Lama Thubten Yeshe, Lama Zopa Rinpoche, Geshe Thubten Loden, Geshe Lobsang Tharchin, Lama Gangchen and Geshe Lhundup Sopa. It should be remembered that their association with this particular lineage-tradition does not necessarily mean that they are exclusive in orientation or devotees of *Dorje Shugden*. Some *lamas*, like Geshe Kelsang and the late Geshe Rabten, *have* combined these elements, whereas others, like Lamas Yeshe and Zopa Rinpoche and Lama Gangchen, came into exile with a commitment to the protector practice but not to its associated exclusivism.

16 However, it is not so categorical in its declarations of how *Dragpa Gyaltsen* died. According to this view, his death – which was by suffocation – may have been by suicide or assassination.

17 Scholarly discussions of the various legends behind the emergence of the *Dorje Shugden* cult can be found in Nebesky-Wojkowitz (1956), Chime Radha Rinpoche (1981), and Mumford (1989). All of these accounts narrate the latter of the two positions, in which the deity is defined as a worldly protector. The fact that these scholars reveal no awareness of an alternative view suggests that the position which defines *Dorje Shugden* as an enlightened being is both a marginal viewpoint and one of recent provenance.

18 Since the time of the Fifth Dalai Lama, *Pehar* has served as the traditional Dharma-protector of the Tibetan state. *Pehar* has been, and continues to be, consulted by the Dalai Lama and his government on affairs of state through the protector's chief

medium, who is known as the *Nechung* (*gNas chung*) Oracle. The importance of oracle-priests in the processes of political decision-making may provide a context for understanding the claim that *Dorje Shugden* should replace *Pehar* as the state protector. According to ex-monk and popular Buddhist author Stephen Batchelor, such a shift in Dharma-protector allegiance would have given supporters of *Dorje Shugden* a degree of political influence (interview, June 1994). If the view that he was the chief Dharma-protector in Central Tibet had gained a wider acceptance, it would have been '*Rdo-Rje-Sugs-Ldan* rather than *Pe Har* himself who functions as the State Oracle at Nechung' (Chime Radha Rinpoche, 1981: 31). According to some commentators, *Dorje Shugden* worshippers within the *Gelug* continue to harbour aspirations for political power. The most recent declaration of the Dalai Lama regarding *Dorje Shugden* propitiation has thus been interpreted by some as an essentially political statement.

19 *Palden Lhamo* is seen not only as the chief guardian goddess of the *Gelug* tradition, but also as the patron-deity of Tibet who is 'very much connected with the cause of Tibetan independence and the protection of Tibet from foreign invaders' (Schwartz 1994: 131).

20 The full Tibetan title of Zimey Rinpoche's text translates as 'Account of the Protective Deity Dorje Shugden, Chief Guardian of the Gelug Sect, and of the Punishments meted out to Religious and Lay Leaders who incurred His Wrath'. The book was published in 1973 but not circulated publicly until 1975.

21 The main participants in this exchange were a *Gelug* disciple of Zimey Rinpoche called Yonten Gyaltso and the *Sakya* scholar T. G. Dhongthog, who composed at least three rejoinders to Zimey Rinpoche's position, one of which was entitled *The Rain of Adamant Fire: A Holy Discourse Based Upon Scriptures and Reason, Annihilating the Poisonous Seeds of the Wicked Speech of Dzeme Trulku Lobsang Palden* (1979). Full bibliographical details of this dispute can be gleaned from Kapstein (1989: 231).

22 'An anthology of talks' (Dalai Lama 1983: 11–13).

23 From the unpublished transcript 'Advice concerning the Dharma protectors' (Dalai Lama 1986: 1).

24 'An anthology of talks' (Dalai Lama 1983: 12–14).

25 'An anthology of talks' (Dalai Lama 1983: 42, 21).

26 *Ganden* monastery has two main colleges, *Jangtse* (*bYang rtse*) and *Shartse* (*Shar rtse*), both of which have been re-established in South India. In Tibet, *Dorje Shugden* reliance was traditionally associated with *Shartse* college, and this association has continued in exile. This practice was also very popular in the *Je* (*bYes*) college of *Sera*, which is where Geshe Kelsang Gyatso studied as a monk prior to coming into exile in 1959.

27 The furore created by the Dalai Lama's pronouncements was not confined to the major monastic centres of the *Gelug* tradition, but impacted also upon the lives of many lay devotees. For an account of the reactions of Tibetan villagers living in Nepal to the statement as it filtered up the Himalayan trail, see Mumford (1989: 135).

28 'Advice concerning the Dharma protectors' (Dalai Lama 1986: 3).

29 For a clear discussion of the traditional role played by the *Gelug* monastic leadership of the three main monasteries in the Tibetan religio-political process, see Goldstein (1989). Goldstein argues that intra-religious conflict between the *Gelug* monastic system and the Dalai Lama's government, at varying levels, contributed to the ultimate downfall of the twentieth-century Tibetan religio-political state. Sparham is interpreting the recent *Dorje Shugden* dispute in similar terms: that is, as a religio-political confrontation between traditionalists and modernists.

3 The emergence of the NKT in Britain

1 Geshe Rabten (1920–86) is also a very well-known *Gelug lama* in the West who, besides writing a number of popular books, founded the Tharpa Choeling Centre for Higher Buddhist Studies (now known as Rabten Choeling) in 1977 as a focal point for Tibetan refugees in Switzerland and as a monastery for Western Buddhists, the first of its kind in Europe.

2 The Manjushri Institute, charity registration no. 271873, Trust Deed, July 1976, 1.

3 These tended to be *geshes* from *Sera* monastery who were old friends and classmates of Lama Yeshe. In more recent years, the FPMT has employed younger *geshes* who have been brought up within, and have graduated from, the re-established monastic institutions-in-exile.

4 The yearly exams were conducted by the Gelugpa Society, the organisation responsible for examining students in Tibetan monasteries and granting the *geshe* degree. No one, to my knowledge, ever completed the FPMT Geshe Studies Programme. The programme never ran its full course in any of the centres where it was taught. It had more success at Manjushri Institute than anywhere else, however, both in terms of numbers (upwards of fifty students took part in the early years of the programme) and in terms of duration (it ran until the late 1980s, making it the longest-running Geshe Programme in the FPMT).

5 Empowerment ceremonies forge a close and powerful bond between the *lama*, as Tantric master, and his students. The particularly close relationship that developed between Geshe Kelsang and his disciples at the Institute strongly influenced how the later dispute with the FPMT unfolded.

6 Taken from the larger FPMT report upon which 'A report on recent events at Manjushri Institute' (discussed in detail below) was based.

7 These texts, like most of his subsequent works, are edited transcripts of oral teachings delivered at Manjushri Institute.

8 Taken from 'Eradicating wrong views' (dated 27 October 1983), a letter written in response to an FPMT report concerning the deteriorating situation at Manjushri Institute called 'A report on recent events at Manjushri Institute' (dated 1 October 1983). Both of these documents were sent to all FPMT centres around the world, as well as to the Office of the Dalai Lama in Dharamsala.

9 *Wisdom: Magazine of the FPMT* 2 (1984): 49.

10 The first draft of the FPMT handbook appeared in February 1987.

11 'Eradicating wrong views'. It appears that the other resident *geshe* at the Institute, Geshe Jampa Tekchog, was also unwilling to sign the contract. In light of what close students of his have told me about him and his relationship with the FPMT, it is quite likely that Geshe Konchog Tsewang did not sign one either.

12 Personal communication, July 1997.

13 *Wisdom: Magazine of the FPMT* 2 (1984): 19.

14 'Eradicating wrong views'.

15 Of the two monastic institutions where *Dorje Shugden* reliance was prominent, *Ganden Shartse* seems to have had the strongest allegiance. Trijang Rinpoche, Song Rinpoche and Zimey Rinpoche all had strong connections with *Ganden Shartse* as students and, later, in exile, as resident teachers. *Ganden Shartse* has also been the monastic base-in-exile for the main oracle of *Dorje Shugden*, Venerable Choyang Duldzin Kuten Lama. Consequently, when the dispute erupted in 1996, the main resistance to the Dalai Lama's pronouncements came from *Ganden Shartse* rather than *Sera Je*.

16 It should be remembered that *Dorje Shugden* reliance need not *necessarily* entail a commitment to an exclusive interpretation of *Gelug* Buddhism. The role of protective deities can be interpreted in different ways depending upon the context, and *Dorje Shugden* has no doubt been seen as a powerful Dharma-protector by both inclu-

sively and exclusively orientated Buddhists, as well as by the most 'sectarian' practitioners within the *Gelug* tradition. I am arguing here that *Dorje Shugden* reliance, as presented by Geshe Kelsang, is bound up with his exclusive interpretation of *Gelug* Buddhism. Other *lamas* may have understood the practice differently.

17 The information about Kuten Lama is taken from the booklet *Autobiography of Venerable Choyang Duldzin Kuten Lama*, printed by Manjushri Institute in 1988.

18 *The Middle Way* 63(4) (1989): 244.

19 For a discussion of the importance of 'continuity' as a structural principle of Tibetan societies, see Samuel (1993).

20 Of the nineteen books Geshe Kelsang has, to date, published, fourteen have appeared since the time of his retreat.

21 Not only were the transcripts of the Dalai Lama's talks on *Dorje Shugden* becoming more widely available to westerners (by this time they could be obtained through the FPMT's Manjushri Centre, London, or from the Office of Tibet), but his views were also published in 1988 in Cabezon's *Bodh Gaya Interviews*.

22 Some disaffiliated students also maintain that Geshe Kelsang's teachings had at this time started to speak out explicitly against *Nyingma*, and especially *Dzogchen*, practices. This is denied by current NKT students who are sensitive to the charge of 'sectarianism'.

23 James Belither, 'The New Kadampa Tradition: a new development', *Full Moon* 3 (1991): 1. *Full Moon* (FM) was renamed as *Full Moon Journal* (FMJ) in 1997.

24 *FMJ* 1(1) (1997): 61.

25 According to NKT sources, 'Gen' is a respectful title that is often used with reference to resident NKT teachers.

26 The New Kadampa Tradition, charity registration no. 2758093, Memorandum and Articles of Association, October 1992, clause 3. The Foundation Programme (FP) and TTP are courses designed for students to deepen their knowledge and experience of Geshe Kelsang's presentation of Buddhism and to train as NKT teachers. They involve attending classes for the study and memorisation of his texts, knowledge of which is formally examined, and also entail a commitment to undertake meditational retreats. The General Programme (GP) refers to teachings that occur outside the FP and TTP and which require no real commitment from students. GP teachings that are delivered within NKT weekly meditation groups represent a first point of contact for many with NKT Buddhism.

27 'Over the moon', FM 6 (Winter 1992): 46.

4 The identity of the NKT

1 Taken from personal communications with FPMT members between May and September 1995.

2 The question of gender within the NKT has been more fully examined by Waterhouse (1997, 2001). She found that since the majority of male and female NKT monastics receive only the lower form of *gets'ul* ordination, the issues raised by the absence of an available equivalent of the *gelong* (full monastic ordination) for women do not arise and hence 'nuns are not discriminated against at this time' (1997: 175).

3 'Over the moon', *Full Moon* [FM] 7 (Spring 1993): 46.

4 Taken from personal communications with NKT disciples.

5 FM 4 (April 1992): 1.

6 The Dalai Lama has even rejected the idea that we are living in a time of decline altogether, affirming that this is 'an epoch of virtue, of mutual aid, of better observance of the Scriptures, a fortunate period' (as quoted in Carriere 1996: 7).

7 Samten Kelsang, 'The Kadampa way of studying', FM 10 (Summer 1994): 8.

8 'Tara makes everyone gentle', FM 5 (Summer 1992): 7.

9 Personal communication, September 1995. The Panchen Lama is revered as the second greatest and most influential incarnate *lama* within the *Gelug* school after the Dalai Lama. For a discussion of the conflict between the Ninth Panchen Lama and the government of the Thirteenth Dalai Lama during the early twentieth century, see Goldstein (1989).

10 I am again indebted to Paul Williams and Stephen Batchelor for their helpful insights regarding the possible reasons behind these textual revisions.

11 'On training as a teacher', FM 9 (Spring 1994): 28–31.

12 FM 12 (Spring 1995): 46.

13 'Go west young man', FM 7 (Spring 1993): 45.

14 Kelsang Gyatso, 'Wisdom', FM 14 (Winter 1995): 7. This exclusivity of texts even extends to English-language translations of Phabongkha Rinpoche's teachings. According to one NKT student, Phabongkha's published discourse on the *Lamrim* teachings, *Liberation in the Palm of Your Hand* (1991), is not used within the NKT because 'the translation of one of the verses of the root text is not correct and so the value of the book is limited' (personal communication, March 1994).

15 FM 14 (Winter 1995): 41.

16 Gen Thubten Gyatso, *Notes on Teaching Skills* (1992: 5).

17 'On training as a teacher', FM 9 (Spring 1994): 31.

18 'A day in the life of Kelsang Lhamo', FM 9 (Spring 1994): 15.

19 'Over the moon', FM 8 (Autumn 1993): 46.

20 'Over the moon', FM 6 (Winter 1992): 46.

21 'Tharpa Publications: a rising sun of the NKT', FM 7 (Spring 1993): 33.

22 Taken from an unpublished paper written by a disaffected disciple of Geshe Kelsang entitled 'The New Kadampa Tradition' (1995).

23 From a document dated 9 June 1995.

24 FM 9 (Spring 1994): 41.

25 'Putting Dharma into practice – for 100 aeons?', FM 13 (Summer 1995): 38.

26 FM 14 (Winter 1995): 43.

27 During 1998, the NKT's policy on inter-Buddhist dialogue changed when the organisation made an application to join the Network of Buddhist Organisations (UK). This development will be discussed later.

28 Geshe Kelsang, 'Wisdom', FM 14 (Winter 1995): 7.

29 Geshe Kelsang teaching at the NKT Spring Festival at Manjushri Centre, 27 May 1995.

30 Hookham's review of the Dalai Lama's *Kindness, Clarity and Insight* appeared in *The Middle Way* 60(1) (1985): 46–47.

31 This debate took place on Usenet between May and June 1995.

32 The story was covered both by the *Hindustan Times* and by the *Times of India* during May and June of 1996.

33 The SSC alleged, for example, that under the order of the Dalai Lama and his administration, the houses of *Dorje Shugden* devotees were searched and images destroyed; that Tibetan government employees had been dismissed because of their religious persuasions; and that a forced signature campaign declaring renunciation of the practice had been instigated within monasteries and government departments. These allegations were all strenuously denied by the Kashag, the cabinet of the Tibetan government-in-exile.

34 It was even suggested by some that the NKT was being supported in its activities by the Chinese government, a charge that the organisation strenuously denied and for which I myself have never seen any supporting evidence.

35 In support of the NKT, the SSC's directory of supporters (listed in the second press pack released on 10 July 1996) does include monasteries in India *and* other non-

NKT Western-based centres, such as those associated with Gonsar Rinpoche, Gelek Rinpoche and Lama Gangchen (the 'Healing Buddha'). The listing of Western-based groups may, however, have been misleading. Contact details were not provided and it is not clear that all of the groups consented to being represented. British disciples of Lama Gangchen informed me, for example, that although he remained a committed devotee of *Dorje Shugden*, he did not express his support for the campaign and was shocked to hear that he had been listed as a supporter.

36 Taken from '22 points of clarification', released on the internet discussion group alt.religion.buddhism.tibetan on 23 July 1996. The figure of 4 million adherents is considered, by academic observers, to be a gross exaggeration.

37 I have not been able to discover from NKT sources the reasons behind Gen Thubten Gyatso's resignation from the NKT, although non-NKT sources have suggested that he was forcibly removed due to a breach of his monastic vows. Whatever the reason, the important role he played in the growth and development of the NKT, and the affection and respect for him amongst NKT students, made his departure a very important event.

38 Taken from an interview with Geshe Kelsang posted on the Internet site BUDDHA-L, 24 November 1996.

39 'Over the moon', FM 7 (Spring 1993): 46.

40 'Why community?', FM 7 (Spring 1993): 8.

41 FM 8 (Autumn 1993): 33.

42 'From dilettante to disciple', FM 14 (Winter 1995): 17.

43 Unfortunately, I do not have accurate figures for the numbers of FPMT and NKT Buddhists in Britain. From conversations with NKT and FPMT representatives, and from comparing the representation of the organisations in terms of centre numbers and types, I would estimate that there are roughly 300 to 400 FPMT Buddhists compared to over 2,000 NKT Buddhists active in Britain.

5 The Order of Buddhist Contemplatives: background and early development

1 See Boucher (1985), Friedman (1987) and Rawlinson (1997).

2 Kennett refers to Kōho Chisan throughout her diaries as 'Zenji Sama'. She did not actually receive the certificate giving her the right to do *sanzen* (give instruction as a Zen master) until September 1968. Copies of the various certificates Kennett received during her time in Japan – including certification of her transmission and status as a priest and teacher of Buddhism – have been made available to me by Shasta Abbey.

3 Copies of letters sent to Kennett from the *Sōtō* Zen headquarters in Japan and North America that address her as 'Jiyu Kennett *Rōshi*' have been made available to me by Shasta Abbey as evidence of her standing within the Japanese sect.

4 Kodo Sawaki was the teacher of the Japanese teacher Taisen Deshimaru (1914–82), founder of the Association Zen Internationale. Kodo Sawaki's image as an 'enlightened' Zen master has recently been reappraised by Brian Victoria in *Zen at War* (1997). According to this account, Sawaki was a fierce Japanese nationalist who supported, and indeed fought in, the Russo-Japanese war.

5 It should be noted that alongside his personal views and his fear of being upstaged within the British Zen scene, Humphreys was also assessing Kennett against a *Rinzai* framework, at that time the predominant form of Zen in Britain, and according to this her status as a '*Rōshi*' would indeed be questionable. Differences between *Sōtō* and *Rinzai* Zen on the title '*Rōshi*' will be discussed later.

6 Personal communication with Maurice Walshe, November 1994.

7 Taken from a letter to a British disciple dated April 1969.

8 Jiyu-Kennett, 'The goose at rest: 1969–1978', *Journal of Shasta Abbey* [JSA] 9(5–7) (1978): 18.
9 This includes Daishin Morgan, the current abbot of Throssel Hole Buddhist Abbey, who remembers Humphreys' approach to Zen as being 'largely intellectual with little emphasis on the practice of meditation' (Morgan 1994: 139).
10 As indicated by a letter written by a senior American disciple of Kennett's and distributed amongst her main disciples in Britain, dated 16 January 1976.
11 Taken from a letter written by Kennett to a British disciple, dated 6 June 1974.
12 The 'three regalia of transmission' refer to three transmission documents: the 'inheritance certificate' (*shiho*), the 'great matter' (*odaiji*) and the 'bloodline of the authentic transmission' (*shoden kechimyaku*). Within the context of Sōtō Zen, Dharma transmission (*denbō*) is an institutional prerequisite to becoming the head priest of an affiliated temple, and consequently 'virtually all Sōtō priests meet this ritual requirement at a relatively early stage in their careers' (Foulk 1988: 173).
13 For a discussion of *Manzan*'s reforms to the rules to be observed in Dharma transmission, see Bodiford (1991), Mohr (1994) and Faure (1996).
14 Unlike some Buddhist movements, such as the FWBO that successfully distributes its magazine *Dharma Life* beyond its internal membership, the production of journals within the OBC is essentially an internal affair.
15 'Sange Jūkai Lecture', *Journal of the Zen Mission Society* [JZMS] 5(2) (1974): 9.
16 'The Zen view of dying [part 2]', *Journal of the Throssel Hole Priory* [JTHP] 5(3) (1977): 2.
17 Taken from her opening address in *Throssel Hole Priory Newsletter* [THPN] 1(1) (1973): 4.
18 'The Zen view of dying [part 1]', *JTHP* 5(2) (1977): 3.
19 Though attributed to *Dōgen*, the *Shushōgi* is actually a highly selective compilation and reinterpretation of his writings that was first published in 1881. For an extended discussion of the creation of the *Shushōgi*, see Reader (1983).
20 'The Zen view of dying [part 1]', *JTHP* 5(2) (1977): 4.
21 It is important not to overstate the differences between ZMS/OBC priests and their Japanese counterparts. From the outset, the ZMS emphasised that its affiliated priories were to be seen as 'parish churches' which, in addition to meditation and spiritual instruction, offered their congregations priestly functions such as private spiritual counselling, the solemnization of marriages, naming ceremonies, funerals and memorial ceremonies.
22 'The Zen view of dying [part 1]', *JTHP* 5(2) (1977): 3.
23 Taken from her opening address in *THPN* 1(1) (1973): 5.
24 I say 'from Kennett's perspective' because whilst her texts and articles are littered with references to and criticisms of the 'British Buddhist establishment', there is no evidence that the Buddhist Society responded to these or participated, either privately or publicly, in any 'dispute' with Kennett.
25 'Do women have the Buddha Nature?', *JSA* (July–August 1981): 13 (reprint of an article that originally appeared in *JSA* (January–February 1976)).
26 'Women in religion', *JZMS* 7(5) (1976): 2.
27 'Women in religion', *JZMS* 7(5) (1976): 3.
28 Taken from her opening address in *THPN* 1(1) (1973): 5.
29 Jiyu-Kennett, 'The goose at rest, part 2: 1969–1978', *JSA* 9(8–10) (1978): 5.
30 Taken from a letter from Kennett to a member of her British congregation, dated September 1968.
31 *Zen is Eternal Life* (1976) appeared as the second and revised edition of *Selling Water*.
32 The transformation of Buddhism in its indigenous Japanese context under the influence of Western, and particularly Christian, values is discussed by Kashima (1977).
33 'Women in religion', *JZMS* 7(5) (1976): 5.

34 See Leighton and Okumara (1996: 15).

6 The Lotus Blossom period, 1976–83

1 For example, Yamada Kōun (1907–89), Phillip Kapleau (b. 1912), Robert Aitken (b. 1917), Maezumi Taizan (1930–96) and Eido Tai Shimano (b. 1932).
2 Both Reader (1986) and Foulk (1988) have called for a reappraisal of the images of Zen that abound in Western scholarship, and Buswell has also examined the discrepancies 'between Western portrayals of Zen and the testimony of its living tradition' (Buswell 1992: 8).
3 'The two forms of visions', *Journal of Shasta Abbey* [*JSA*] (September–October 1980): 6–11.
4 Tanabe also argues that dreams and visions 'are central to the East Asian Buddhist experience' (Tanabe 1992: 13).
5 For a more detailed account of these stages, see Cox (1986).
6 Although the practice outlined in *The Book of Life* is largely an innovation drawing upon multiple sources, there are traditional precedents for this threefold typology of illness. East Asian medicine understands health and ill health in terms of the movement and flow of *ki*, and divides ill health into three major types: illnesses of a physical, psychological and psychotic kind (see Lock 1980: 84–85).
7 'Compassion for the abbot', *JSA* (May–July 1978): 38.
8 See, for example, Morgan (1994: 141).
9 For an excellent overview of the pantheon of Buddhas and *Bodhisattvas* in *Mahāyāna* Buddhism, see Williams (1991).
10 'Letter to a Christian monk', *JSA* (March–April 1979): 6.
11 'More correspondence with a Christian monk', *JSA* (March–April 1980): 5.
12 The scenes from Kennett's *kenshō*, for example, were depicted at Shasta Abbey using stained-glass windows in the meditation hall.
13 'Udonge: "The flower of an udambara tree"', *Journal of Throssel Hole Priory* [*JTHP*] 9(4) (1982): 8–9.
14 For example, see Kapleau (1980: 239).
15 Kennett's interest in the oriental healing arts also coincided with the rise in the West in the late twentieth century of non-medical, holistic health and psychic healing movements, for a discussion of which see Fuller (1989).
16 See Lock (1980).
17 For example, the Diamond Mudra and the Spiritual Defense Mudra are protection *mudrās* to be used 'against influence by evil or disturbing external events' (Kennett and MacPhillamy 1979: 264).
18 The years 1977 to 1982 were the most prolific of Kennett's life. In addition to *How to Grow a Lotus Blossom* and *The Book of Life*, she released her two-volume diary of training in Japan, *The Wild, White Goose*, and composed over forty journal articles.
19 Taken from a letter from a senior American disciple to a British trainee, dated 9 March 1977.
20 *JTHP* 5(1) (May 1977): 8, 4.
21 'Training in the world', *JTHP* 7(7–9) (1980): 2.
22 Homyo Brazier, 'Editorial: the Kōan of Heaven and Earth', *JTHP* 5(8) (1978): 2. British monk Homyo Brazier was a resident trainee during Isan Sacco's stint as prior of Throssel Hole Priory. He quickly became dissatisfied with the teachings and practices Sacco had brought with him from the US, particularly the emphasis on harmonising *mudrās* and past-life experiences, and this ultimately resulted in Brazier leaving the priory. Having disrobed and severed his connections with Kennett's organization, Brazier later went on to found the Amida Trust, an organisation specialising in the interface between Zen and psychotherapy.

23 Taken from an open letter written by Kennett to the British congregation, dated 18 September 1977.

24 Jiyu-Kennett, 'The goose at rest: 1969–1978', *JSA* 9(5–7) (1978): 21.

25 The Trust was renamed as the 'Whitecross Buddhist Meditation Centre' in 1992, and now embraces *Theravāda* Buddhism as well as Zen.

26 Taken from a letter sent to some British monks in England in early 1980 to help them in their process of disaffiliation from Kennett's organisation.

27 J. I. Ford, 'On the arrangement of shoes: a memory of Jiyu Kennett *Rōshi*', *Still Point* 22(3–4) (1997): 1.

28 I. Sacco, 'Memories of Jiyu Kennett *Rōshi*', *Still Point* 22(3–4) (1997): 2.

29 See note 26, above.

30 J. I. Ford, 'On the arrangement of shoes: a memory of Jiyu Kennett *Rōshi*', *Still Point* 22(3–4) (1997): 1.

31 See note 26, above.

32 Letter dated February 1978.

33 See note 26, above.

34 K. Larson, 'A flashback', *Still Point* 22(3–4) (1997): 3.

35 Taken from a letter written by a British disciple to Kennett in February 1977.

36 See note 26, above.

37 I will hereafter refer to Kennett's movement as the OBC.

38 Taken from a letter dated 2 April 1977.

39 The first letter appeared in *JTHP* 4(6) (April 1977) and the second, longer letter was sent out on 18 September 1977.

40 *JTHP* 5(6) (February–March 1978): 11.

41 Taken from a letter sent by Kennett to a British trainee, dated 16 January 1977.

42 Taken from a letter dated 9 March 1977.

43 'A note from Rōshi Kennett', *JTHP* 5(6) (1978): 20.

44 Jisho Perry, 'Blessed are they that have not seen, yet have believed', *JTHP* 5(4) (1977): 3–8.

45 'Taking refuge in the Sangha', *JTHP* 6(4–6) (1979): 2.

46 'More correspondence with a Christian monk', *JSA* (March–April 1980): 6.

47 Letter dated 18 September 1977.

48 Jisho Perry, 'Blessed are they that have not seen, yet have believed', *JTHP* 5(4) (1977): 8.

49 This was first stated in Kennett's letter to the British congregation dated 18 September 1977, and then in her article 'The goose at rest: 1969–1978', *JSA* 9(5–7) (1978): 20. Whilst no formal, written endorsement was received from Japan, Kennett claims that the authorities at *Sōjiji* were satisfied with the content of *How to Grow a Lotus Blossom*.

50 'Disclaimer', *JTHP* 6(1–3) (1979): 15.

51 Taken from a letter dated 9 March 1977.

52 Homyo Brazier, 'Editorial: contemplative life', *JTHP* 5(7) (1978): 2.

53 The main figures Finney refers to as representatives of 'the American Zen Reformation', for example, are Japanese modernist thinkers and their disciples, including Shaku Sōen, D. T. Suzuki, Hakuun Yasutani, Taizan Maezumi and John Daido Loori.

54 'To all our members and friends', *JTHP* 9(4) (1982): 3.

7 The later period: routinisation and consolidation

1 The *Articles of Incorporation of the OBC* and the *Bylaws of the OBC*, dated January 1983, are the governing instruments of the OBC. The *Rules of the OBC* were initially

formulated in January 1982, although they have been adapted and added to in subsequent years.

2 'What we teach and what we practice', *Journal of the Order of Buddhist Contemplatives* [*JOBC*] 1(2–3) (1986): 2.

3 *Rules of the OBC*, 1982, Section 6.

4 Daizui MacPhillamy, 'How the O.B.C. works', *The Journal of Throssel Hole Buddhist Abbey* [*JTHBA*] 24(1) (1997): 21. Throssel Hole's change in status, from a priory to an abbey, will be discussed later.

5 *Rules of the OBC*, Appendix 1: Rules for the Lay Ministry, Rule 1.

6 For a discussion of which, see Reader (1983).

7 *Bylaws of the OBC*, Article 17, Sections 2–5.

8 '...And to the source kept true: part 9', *Journal of the Throssel Hole Priory* [*JTHP*] 18(1) (1991): 4.

9 Such as the ten-million-dollar lawsuit brought against Sogyal Rinpoche in 1995 by a former student.

10 The family name received by all disciples of Kennett is 'Houn', which translates as 'Dharma Cloud'. In addition to this, ordainees receive a new individual name. During the early and Lotus Blossom periods, new ordainees received traditional Japanese or Buddhist names. During the later period, in line with the Order's policy of adapting foreign names and terms, it has been more common for them to receive Western names such as Edmund, Alfred, Adelin and Olwen.

11 *JTHP* 14(2) (1987): 33.

12 *JTHP* 6(4–6) (1979): 15.

13 *JTHP* 12(2) (1985): 33.

14 *JTHP* 8.1 (1981): 24. The Order started to use 'Rev. Master' instead of '*Rōshi*' in 1983.

15 Daizui MacPhillamy, 'A note on transmission and priestly rank', *JTHP* (July 1978): 10.

16 Daishin Morgan, 'The Lay Ministry', *JTHP* 18(3) (1991): 24.

17 'The Lay Ministry programme', *JTHP* 9(4) (1982): 22.

18 Daishin Morgan, 'The Lay Ministry', *JTHP* 18(3) (1991): 25. Certified Lay Ministers receive a turquoise *rakhusu* and a copy of the *Lay Minister Manual*, which includes sections on organising, financing and running meditation groups.

19 Namely *The Liturgy of the Order of Buddhist Contemplatives for the Laity* (1987b), *The Monastic Office* (1993b), *The Denkōroku or The Record of the Transmission of the Light by Keizan Zenji* (1993c) and *Buddhist Writings* (1994).

20 'The qualifications of a Zen Master', *JOBC* 2(1–4) (1987): 2–4.

21 'The great heresies, 1', *JOBC* 1(1) (1986): 4. During this period, Kennett was increasingly intolerant of those who sought guidance from multiple masters, and demanded greater exclusivism from her disciples.

22 'News from the tiger's lair', *JSA* (October–December 1985): 1.

23 'The qualifications of a Zen Master', *JOBC* 2(1–4) (1987): 5.

24 The glossary to the second edition, for example, included terms like 'Cosmic Buddha', 'the Lord' and 'the Lord of the House' (Kennett 1976: 379, 403).

25 'To our readers', *JTHP* 10(2) (Summer 1983): 3.

26 '...And to the source kept true: part 6: concerning what I shall, hereafter, call the Eternal', *JTHP* 17(4) (1990): 2.

27 *JTHP* 14(4) (1987): 34.

28 '...And to the source kept true: part 2', *JTHP* 16(3) (1989): 5–6.

29 '...And to the source kept true: part 11: concerning beatings, killings and war', *JOBC* 6(1–2) (1991): 7.

30 '...And to the source kept true: part 2', *JTHP* 16(3) (1989): 7–8. Kennett may have had the sexual scandals involving Richard Baker *Rōshi* at the San Francisco Zen Center in the early 1980s in mind here.

31 'The visit of two officials from the Head Office in Japan on 1st. October, 1987', *JOBC* 2(1–4): 6–8.

32 'And, at dawn, no light shines', *JTHP* 22(4) (1995): 17.

33 'The truth holds true for beings all', *JTHP* 23(3) (1996): 36.

34 Chushin Passmore, 'The Bodhisattva vows', *JTHP* 11(3–4) (1984): 54.

35 *Rules of the OBC*, Appendix 1: Rules for the Lay Ministry, Rule 19.

36 Jimyo Krasner, 'Right vision', *JTHP* 11(1) (1984): 25.

37 Haryo Young, 'The truth of being', *JTHP* 23(2) (1996): 24.

38 Myoho Harris, 'Trust', *JTHP* 12(3) (1985): 12.

39 Daishin Morgan, 'Bonds of doubt', *JTHP* 19(4) (1992): 10–16.

40 Daishin Morgan, 'Adoration of the Buddha's relics', *JTHP* 12(4) and 13(1) (1985–86): 8.

41 Haryo Young, 'Why monasticism?', *JTHP* 15(1) (1988): 31.

42 'A Layman's Kōan', *JTHP* 14(2) (1987): 30.

43 'The value of a meditation group', *JTHP* 11(2) (1984): 27.

44 Daishin Morgan, 'No abiding place', *JTHP* 16(2) (1989): 15.

45 Daishin Morgan, 'The birth of the Buddha', *JTHP* 23(2) (1996): 5.

46 'This truth holds for beings all', *JTHP* 23(3) (1996): 25.

47 From 1985, the Order's journals have included a clarificatory statement for those who 'may consider the use of the word "He" inappropriate', part of which reads 'Whenever "He" is used, please understand that this is meant as He/She/It.'

48 'The begging bowl', *JTHP* 11(3–4) (1984): 16.

49 'Important public announcement', *JTHP* 5(4) (1977): 10.

50 *JTHP* 11(2) (1984): 34.

51 'Groups weekend 1996', *JTHP* 23(4) (1996–97): 21.

52 *JTHP* 10(2) (1983): 12.

53 *Throssel Hole Priory Newsletter* 1(4) (1974): 5.

54 'On retreats', *JTHP* (November–December 1978): 11–12.

55 'Groups weekend 1996', *JTHP* 23(4) (1996–97): 22.

56 *JTHP* 12(1) (1985): 39.

57 *JTHP* 12(4) and 13(1) (1985–86): 48.

58 Article 17, Section 1.

59 Appendix 1: Rules for the Lay Ministry of the OBC, Article 3.

60 She became a good friend, for example, of the Western Sufi teacher Samuel Lewis (Murshid Sam).

61 *JTHP* 6(11–12) (1979): 18.

62 Daishin Morgan, 'The joys and hazards of dialogue with other Buddhists', *JTHP* 22(1) (1995): 5–8.

63 *Rules of the OBC*, Section 15.

64 'The Buddhist's responsibility to animals', *Journal of Shasta Abbey* (July–August 1980): 10.

65 'Zen project to prisons', *JTHP* (June 1978): 3.

8 Epilogue and conclusion

1 An obituary of Venerable Geshe Lobsang Gyatso can be found in *Tibetan Review*, 32(4) (April 1997): 22–23.

2 'Dorje Shugden International Coalition', undated pamphlet.

3 'Dorje Shugden International Coalition', undated pamphlet.

4 *Roots and Branches*, 1 (Autumn 1994): inside cover.

5 *Roots and Branches*, 1 (Autumn 1994): inside cover.

6 Taken from a letter by Daishin Morgan to the congregation and friends of Throssel Hole Priory announcing Kennett's death (November 1996).

7 Jisho Perry, 'The funeral ceremonies for Rev. Master Jiyu-Kennett', *Special Memorial Issue of the Journal of the Order of Buddhist Contemplatives* [JOBC] 11(4) and 12(1) (1996–97): 82.

8 *Journal of Throssel Hole Priory* 23(4) (1996–97): 18.

9 *Special Memorial Issue of the JOBC* 11(4) and 12(1) (1996–97): 132–133.

10 *Special Memorial Issue of the JOBC* 11(4) and 12(1) (1996–97): 132.

11 Daizui MacPhillamy, *Journal of Throssel Hole Buddhist Abbey* [JTHBA] 24(1) (1997): 16–23.

12 Although this structure is sanctified by Kennett's charismatic authority, it is the office, rather than the person, that now commands respect.

13 'Visit by the Head of the Order', *JTHBA* 24(1) (1997): 10.

14 'To our readers', *JOBC* 13(1) (1998): 5.

15 *JTHBA* 24(2) (1997): 2.

16 The first volume of Kennett's recorded and transcribed lectures thus appeared in 2000 as *Roar of the Tigress: The Oral Teachings of Rev. Master Jiyu-Kennett: Western Woman and Zen Master*.

17 The International Zen Association, for example, which has, since the death of its founder Taisen Deshimaru in 1982, splintered into a number of different factions and groups.

BIBLIOGRAPHY

Almond, Philip C. (1988) *The British Discovery of Buddhism*, Cambridge: Cambridge University Press.

Arai, Paula (1994) 'Monastic women in cultural and historical context', *Seeds of Peace* 10(1): 17–19.

Asai, Senryo and Williams, Duncan Ryuken (1999) 'Japanese American Zen temples: cultural identity and economics', in Duncan Ryuken Williams and Christopher S. Queen (eds) *American Buddhism: Methods and Findings in Recent Scholarship*, Richmond, Surrey: Curzon Press, pp. 20–35.

Barnes, Nancy J. (1996) 'Buddhist women and the Nuns' Order in Asia', in Christopher S. Queen and Sallie B. King (eds) *Engaged Buddhism: Buddhist Liberation Movements in Asia*, Albany, NY: State University of New York Press, pp. 259–294.

Batchelor, Stephen (1994) *The Awakening of the West: The Encounter of Buddhism and Western Culture*, London: Aquarian.

—— (1996) 'Special report: trouble in Shangri-La', *Tricycle: The Buddhist Review* 6(1): 119–120.

Baumann, Martin (1994) 'The transplantation of Buddhism to Germany: processive modes and strategies of adaptation', *Method and Theory in the Study of Religion* 6(1): 35–61.

—— (1995) 'Creating a European path to Nirvāṇa: historical and contemporary developments of Buddhism in Europe', *Journal of Contemporary Religion* 10: 55–70.

—— (1997) 'Culture contact and valuation: early German Buddhists and the creation of a "Buddhism in Protestant shape"', *Numen* 44: 270–295.

Baxter, John (1986) 'The *Sangha* comes West', *Theology* 89: 173–178.

Bell, Sandra (1991) 'Buddhism in Britain: development and adaptation', unpublished doctoral thesis, University of Durham.

—— (1996) 'Change and identity in the Friends of the Western Buddhist Order', *Scottish Journal of Religious Studies* 17: 87–107.

—— (1997) 'British Buddhism and the negotiation of tradition' (original draft version of Bell (2000b)).

—— (1998) '"Crazy wisdom", charisma and the transmission of Buddhism in the United States', *Nova Religio*: 55–75.

—— (2000a) 'A survey of engaged Buddhism in Britain', in Christopher S. Queen (ed.) *Engaged Buddhism in the West*, Boston: Wisdom Publications, pp. 397–422.

—— (2000b) 'Being creative with tradition: rooting Theravaada Buddhism in Britain', *Journal of Global Buddhism* 1: 1–23.

Beyer, Stephan (1978) *The Cult of Tara: Magic and Ritual in Tibet*, Berkeley: University of California Press.

Bishop, Peter (1993) *Dreams of Power: Tibetan Buddhism and the Western Imagination*, London: The Athlone Press.

Bodiford, William M. (1991) 'Dharma transmission in Sōtō Zen: Manzan Dōhaku's reform movement', *Monumenta Nipponica* 46: 423–451.

Borelli, J. (1985) 'Jung's criticism of yoga spirituality', in Harold Coward (ed.) *Jung and Eastern Thought*, Albany, NY: State University of New York Press, pp. 79–92.

Boucher, Sandy (1985) *Turning the Wheel: American Women Creating New Buddhism*, London: Harper & Row.

Brear, Douglas (1975) 'Early assumptions in Western Buddhist studies', *Religion* 5: 136–159.

Buswell, Robert E. (1992) *The Zen Monastic Experience: Buddhist Practice in Contemporary Korea*, Princeton, NJ: Princeton University Press.

Butterfield, Stephen T. (1994) *The Double Mirror: A Skeptical Journey into Buddhist Tantra*, Berkeley, CA: North Atlantic Books.

Cabezon, Jose Ignatius (1988) *Bodh Gaya Interviews: His Holiness the Dalai Lama*, Ithaca, NY: Snow Lion Publications.

Campbell, June (1996) *Traveller in Space: In Search of Female Identity in Tibetan Buddhism*, London: Athlone Press.

Carriere, Jean-Claude (1996) *Violence and Compassion: His Holiness the Dalai Lama and Jean-Claude Carriere*, New York: Doubleday.

Chime Radha Rinpoche (1981) 'Tibet', in M. Loewe and C. Blacker (eds) *Divination and Oracles*, London: George Allen & Unwin, pp. 3–37.

Chryssides, George (1994) 'Britain's changing faiths: adaptation in a new environment', in Gerald Parsons (ed.) *The Growth of Religious Diversity: Britain from 1945*, London: Routledge, pp. 55–84.

Church, Alison M. (1982) 'Buddhist groups in Britain: adaptation and development of traditional religious forms within a Western environment', unpublished master's thesis, University of Manchester.

Clarke, J. J. (1997) *Oriental Enlightenment: The Encounter Between Asian and Western Thought*, London: Routledge.

Clarke, P. B. (1993) 'The appeal of non-Christian religions in contemporary Britain: Part II', *Religion Today* 8(2): 1–4.

Clausen, Christopher (1975) 'Victorian Buddhism and the origins of comparative religion', *Religion* 5(1): 1–15.

Coleman, Graham (1993) *A Handbook of Tibetan Culture: A Guide to Tibetan Centres and Resources throughout the World*, London: Rider.

Collcutt, Martin (1988) 'Epilogue: problems of authority in Western Zen', in Kenneth Kraft (ed.) *Zen: Tradition and Transition*, London: Rider, pp. 199–207.

Coney, Judith (1997) 'Making history: memory and forgetfulness in new religious movements', unpublished paper.

Connelly, Peter (1985) 'Buddhism in Britain', *Religion Today* 2(2): 3–6.

Cox, Michael (1986) *A Handbook of Christian Mysticism*, Great Britain: Aquarian Press.

Dalai Lama, H. H. the 14th (1983) 'An anthology of talks given by H.H. the Dalai Lama concerning reliance upon the Dharma protectors', trans. and ed. Tsepak Rigzin *et al.*, Library of Tibetan Works and Archives, Dharamsala, 1–46.

—— (1986) 'Advice concerning the Dharma protectors', trans. and ed. Tsepak Rigzin *et al.*, Library of Tibetan Works and Archives, Dharamsala, 1–7.

Dalai Lama, H. H. the 14th and Berzin, Alexander (1997) *The Gelug/Kagyu Tradition of Mahamudra*, Ithaca, NY: Snow Lion Publications.

Deshimaru, Taisen (1991) *Questions to a Zen Master*, London: Arkana.

Dhondup, K. (1984) *The Water-Horse and Other Years: A History of 17th and 18th Century Tibet*, Dharamsala: Library of Tibetan Works and Archives.

—— (1986) *The Water-Bird and Other Years: A History of the 13th Dalai Lama and After*, New Delhi: Rangwang Publishers.

Dhongthog, T. G. (1979) *The Rain of Adamant Fire: A Holy Discourse Based Upon Scriptures and Reason, Annihilating the Poisonous Seeds of the Wicked Speech of Dzeme Trulku Lobsang Palden*, Gangtok: Sherab Gyaltsen.

Dreyfus, Georges B. J. (1997) *Recognising Reality: Dharmakirti's Philosophy and its Tibetan Interpretations*, Albany, NY: State University of New York Press.

—— (1998) 'The Shuk-den affair: the history and nature of a quarrel', *Journal of the International Association of Buddhist Studies* 21: 227–270.

Earhart, H. Byron (1989) *Gedatsu-kai and Religion in Contemporary Japan: Returning to the Center*, Bloomington and Indianapolis: Indiana University Press.

Ellwood, Robert S., Jr (1979) *Alternative Altars: Unconventional and Eastern Spirituality in America*, Chicago: University of Chicago Press.

Faure, Bernard (1991) *The Rhetoric of Immediacy: A Cultural Critique of Chan/Zen Buddhism*, Princeton: Princeton University Press.

—— (1996) *Visions of Power: Imagining Medieval Japanese Buddhism*, Princeton: Princeton University Press.

Fields, Rick (1992) *How the Swans Came to the Lake: A Narrative History of Buddhism in America*, London: Shambhala Publications Inc.

Finney, Henry C. (1991) 'American Zen's "Japan connection": a critical case study of Zen Buddhism's diffusion to the West', *Sociological Analysis* 52: 379–396.

Foulk, T. Griffith (1988) 'The Zen institution in modern Japan', in Kenneth Kraft (ed.) *Zen: Tradition and Transition*, London: Rider, pp. 157–177.

Friedman, Lenore (1987) *Meetings with Remarkable Women: Buddhist Teachers in America*, Boston, MA: Shambhala.

Fuller, Robert C. (1989) *Alternative Medicine and American Religious Life*, New York: Oxford University Press.

Furlong, Monica (1987) *Genuine Fake: A Biography of Alan Watts*, 2nd edn, London: Unwin Hyman Ltd.

Giddens, Anthony (1991) *Modernity and Self-identity: Self and Society in the Late Modern Age*, Stanford, CA: Stanford University Press.

Goldstein, Melvyn C. (1989) *A History of Modern Tibet, 1913–1951: The Demise of the Lamaist State*, Berkeley and Los Angeles, CA: University of California Press.

—— (1990) 'Religious conflict in the traditional Tibetan state', in L. Epstein and R. F. Sherbourne (eds) *Reflections on Tibetan Culture: Essays in Memory of Turrell V. Wylie*, Lewiston and Queenston: Edwin Mellen Press, pp. 231–247.

Graef, Hilda (1966) *The Story of Mysticism*, London: Peter Davies.

Green, Dierdre (1989) 'Buddhism in Britain: skilful means or selling out?', in P. Badham (ed.) *Religion, State and Society in Modern Britain*, Lewiston: Edwin Mellen Press, pp. 277–291.

Gross, Rita M. (1993) *Buddhism After Patriarchy: A Feminist History, Analysis and Recon-struction of Buddhism*, Albany, NY: State University of New York Press.

Gusdorf, Georges (1980) 'Conditions and limits of autobiography', in J. Olney (ed.) *Autobiography: Essays Theoretical and Critical*, Princeton, NJ: Princeton University Press, pp. 28–48.

Hardy, Friedhelm (1984) 'How "Indian" are the new Indian religions of the West?', *Religion Today* 1(2/3): 15–18.

Harvey, Peter (1991) *An Introduction to Buddhism: Teachings, History and Practices*, Cambridge: Cambridge University Press.

Hookham, Shenpen (1992) 'In search of the guru', in John Snelling (ed.) *Sharpham Miscellany: Essays in Spirituality and Ecology*, Totnes: The Sharpham Trust, pp. 99–112.

Humphreys, Christmas (1962) *Zen*, Aylesbury, Bucks: English Universities Press Ltd.

Jones, Ken (1996) 'Many bodies, one mind: movements in British Buddhism', *New Ch'an Forum* 13.

Juergensmeyer, Mark (1991) *Radhasoami Reality: The Logic of a Modern Faith*, Princeton: Princeton University Press.

Kamstra, J. H (1967) *Encounter or Syncretism: The Initial Growth of Japanese Buddhism*, Leiden: E. J. Brill.

—— (1980) 'Skilful means as a "germinative principle"' [review of Pye's *Skilful Means* (1978)], *Numen* 27: 270–277.

Kapleau, Phillip (1980) *The Three Pillars of Zen*, London: Rider.

Kapstein, Matthew (1989) 'The purificatory gem and its cleansing: a late Tibetan polem-ical discussion of apocryphal texts', *History of Religions: An International Journal for Comparative Historical Studies* 28: 217–244.

Kashima, Tetsuden (1977) *Buddhism in America: The Social Organization of an Ethnic Reli-gious Institution*, Westport, CT: Greenwood Press.

Kay, David (1997) 'The New Kadampa Tradition and the continuity of Tibetan Buddhism in transition', *Journal of Contemporary Religion* 12: 277–293.

Kelsang Gyatso, Geshe (1980) *Meaningful to Behold*, Ulverston: Wisdom Publications (3rd edn, London: Tharpa Publications, 1989).

—— (1982) *Clear Light of Bliss*, London: Wisdom Publications (2nd edn, London: Tharpa Publications, 1992)

—— (1984) *Buddhism in the Tibetan Tradition: A Guide*, London: Routledge and Kegan Paul Ltd.

—— (1986) *Heart of Wisdom: A Commentary to the Heart Sutra*, London: Tharpa Publi-cations.

—— (1988) *Universal Compassion: A Commentary to Bodhisattva Chekhawa's Training the Mind in Seven Points*, London: Tharpa Publications.

—— (1991a) *Heart Jewel: A Commentary to the Essential Practice of the New Kadampa Tradition of Mahayana Buddhism*, London: Tharpa Publications.

—— (1991b) *Guide to Dakini Land*, London: Tharpa Publications.

—— (1992) *Great Treasury of Merit*, London, Tharpa Publications.

—— (1993a) *Understanding the Mind*, London: Tharpa Publications.

—— (1993b) *A Meditation Handbook*, 2nd edn, London: Tharpa Publications.

—— (1993c) *Introduction to Buddhism*, 2nd edn, London: Tharpa Publications.

—— (1993d) *Melodious Drum Victorious in All Directions: The Extensive Fulfilling and Restoring Ritual of the Dharma Protector, the Great King Dorje Shugdan, in Conjunction with Mahakala, Kalarupa, Kalindewi and Other Dharma Protectors*, London: Tharpa Publications.

Kennett, Jiyu (1972) *Selling Water by the River: A Manual of Zen Training*, New York: Random House Inc.

—— (1976) *Zen is Eternal Life*, 2nd edn, Emeryville, CA: Dharma Publishing.

—— (1977a and 1978) *The Wild, White Goose*, 2 vols, Mt Shasta, CA: Shasta Abbey Press.

—— (1977b) *How to Grow a Lotus Blossom or How a Zen Buddhist Prepares for Death*, Mt Shasta, CA: Shasta Abbey Press.

—— (1987a) *Zen is Eternal Life*, 3rd edn, Emeryville, CA: Dharma Publishing.

—— (1987b) *The Liturgy of the Order of Buddhist Contemplatives for the Laity*, Mt Shasta, CA: Shasta Abbey Press (2nd edn, 1990).

—— (1993a) *How to Grow a Lotus Blossom or How a Zen Buddhist Prepares for Death*, 2nd edn, Mt Shasta, CA: Shasta Abbey Press.

—— (1993b) *The Monastic Office*, Mt Shasta, CA: Shasta Abbey Press.

—— (1993c) *The Denkōroku or The Record of the Transmission of the Light by Keizan Zenji*, Mt Shasta, CA: Shasta Abbey Press.

—— (1994) *Buddhist Writings*, Mt Shasta, CA: Shasta Abbey Press.

—— (2000) *Roar of the Tigress: The Oral Teachings of Rev. Master Jiyu-Kennett: Western Woman and Zen Master*, Mt Shasta, CA: Shasta Abbey Press.

Kennett, Rōshi Jiyu and MacPhillamy, Rev. Daizui (1979) *The Book of Life*, Mt Shasta, CA: Shasta Abbey Press.

Knott, K. (1986) *Hinduism in Leeds: A Study of Religious Practices in the Indian Hindu Community and in Hindu Related Groups*, Leeds: Community Religions Project Monograph Series, University of Leeds.

Kulananda, Dharmachari (1992) 'Protestant Buddhism', *Religion* 22: 101–103

Kurtz, Lester R. (1995) *Gods in the Global Village: The World's Religions in Sociological Perspective*, Thousand Oaks, CA: Pine Forge Press.

Layman, Emma McCloy (1976) *Buddhism in America*, Chicago: Nelson-Hall Inc.

Leighton, Taigen Daniel and Okumara, Shohaku (ed. and trans.) (1996) *Dōgen's Pure Standards for the Zen Community*, Albany, NY: State University of New York Press.

Lifton, Robert J. (1993) *The Protean Self: Human Resilience in an Age of Fragmentation*, New York: Basic Books.

—— (1997) 'From mysticism to murder', *Tricycle: The Buddhist Review* 7(2): 54–59, 90–97.

Lock, Margaret M. (1980) *East Asian Medicine in Urban Japan: Varieties of Medical Experience*, Berkeley and Los Angeles, CA: University of California Press.

Mackenzie, Vicki (1988) *Reincarnation: The Boy Lama*, London: Bloomsbury Publishing Ltd.

—— (1997) *Reborn in the West: The Story of Western Men and Women Reincarnated as Tibetan Lamas*, London: Thorsons.

Mandel, Barrett J. (1980) 'Full of life now', in J. Olney (ed.) *Autobiography: Essays Theoretical and Critical*, Princeton, NJ: Princeton University Press, pp. 49–72.

Mellor, Philip (1989) 'The cultural translation of Buddhism: problems of theory and method arising in the study of Buddhism in England', unpublished doctoral thesis, University of Manchester.

—— (1991) 'Protestant Buddhism? The cultural translation of Buddhism in England', *Religion* 21: 73–92.

Melton, J. Gordon and Jones, Constance A. (1994) 'New Japanese religions in the United States', in Peter B. Clarke and Jeffrey Somers (eds) *Japanese New Religions in the West*, Folkestone, Kent: Japan Library, pp. 33–53.

Minney, Robin (1975) *Of Many Mouths and Eyes: A Study of the Forms of Religious Expression*, London: Hodder & Stoughton.

Mohr, Michel (1994) 'Zen Buddhism during the Tokugawa period: the challenge to go beyond sectarian consciousness', *Japanese Journal of Religious Studies* 21: 341–372.

Morgan, Reverend Daishin (1994) 'Sōtō Zen Buddhism in Britain', in Peter B. Clarke and Jeffrey Somers (eds) *Japanese New Religions in the West*, Folkestone, Kent: Japan Library, pp. 132–148.

Mumford, Stan Royal (1989) *Himalayan Dialogue: Tibetan Lamas and Gurung Shamans in Nepal*, Madison: University of Wisconsin Press.

Nattier, Jan (1991) *Once Upon a Future Time: Studies in a Buddhist Prophecy of Decline*, Berkeley, CA: Asian Humanities Press.

Nebesky-Wojkowitz, Rene de (1956) *Oracles and Demons of Tibet: The Cult and Iconography of the Tibetan Protective Deities*, Oxford: Oxford University Press.

Nishiyama, Kosen and Stevens, John (1975–77) *A Complete English Translation of Dōgen Zenji's Shōbōgenzō (The Eye and Treasury of the True Law)*, 2 vols, Tokyo, Japan: Nakayama Shobo.

Numrich, P. D. (1992) 'Americanization in immigrant Theravāda temples', unpublished doctoral thesis, University of Michigan.

Obeyeskere, Gananath (1970) 'Religious symbolism and political change in Ceylon', *Modern Ceylon Studies* 1: 43–63.

Oliver, Ian. P. (1979) *Buddhism in Britain*, London: Rider.

Olney, James (1980) 'Autobiography and the cultural moment: a thematic, historical, and biographical introduction', in J. Olney (ed.) *Autobiography: Essays Theoretical and Critical*, Princeton, NJ: Princeton University Press, pp. 3–27.

Phabongka Rinpoche (1991) *Liberation in the Palm of Your Hand*, ed. Trijang Rinpoche and trans. Michael Richards, Boston, MA: Wisdom Publications.

Preston, David L. (1988) *The Social Organization of Zen Practice: Constructing Transcultural Reality*, Cambridge: Cambridge University Press.

Puttick, Elizabeth (1993) ' "Why has Boddhidharma left for the West?" The growth and appeal of Buddhism in Britain', *Religion Today* 8(2): 5–10.

Pye, E. M. (1969) 'The transplantation of religions', *Numen* 16: 234–239.

—— (1973) 'Comparative hermeneutics in religion', in Michael Pye and Robert Morgan (eds) *The Cardinal Meaning: Essays in Comparative Hermeneutics: Buddhism and Christianity*, The Hague: Mouton and Co., pp. 9–58.

—— (1978) *Skilful Means: A Concept in Mahayana Buddhism*, London: Duckworth.

—— (1996) 'Aum Shinrikyō. Can religious studies cope?', *Religion* 26: 261–270.

Rabten, Geshe and Ngawang Dhargyey, Geshe (1977) *Advice from a Spiritual Friend: Buddhist Thought Transformation*, New Delhi: Wisdom Publications.

Rawlinson, Andrew (1997) *The Book of Enlightened Masters*, Chicago and La Salle, IL: Open Court.

Reader, Ian (1983) 'Contemporary thought in Sōtō Zen Buddhism: an investigation of the publications and teachings of the Sōtō sect in the light of their cultural and historical context', unpublished doctoral thesis, University of Leeds.

—— (1986) 'Zazenless Zen? The position of Zazen in institutional Zen Buddhism', *Japanese Religions* 14(3): 7–27.

Richardson, James T. (1996) 'Journalistic bias towards new religious movements in Australia', *Journal of Contemporary Religion* 11: 289–302.

Said, Edward W. (1978) *Orientalism*, London: Routledge and Kegan Paul Ltd.

Samuel, Geoffrey (1993) *Civilized Shamans: Buddhism in Tibetan Societies*, Washington, DC: Smithsonian Institution Press.

—— (1996) 'Tibetan Buddhism as a world religion: global networking and its consequences', unpublished paper, http://users.hunterlink.net.au/~mbbgbs/geoffrey/global.html (last updated 3 March 2002; date of access 10 November 2002).

Sangharakshita (1992) *The FWBO and 'Protestant Buddhism'*, Glasgow: Windhorse.

Saunders, E. Dale (1960) *Mudrā: A Study of Symbolic Gestures in Japanese Buddhist Sculpture*, London: Routledge and Kegan Paul Ltd.

Schumacher, E. F. (1973) *Small is Beautiful: A Study of Economics as if People Mattered*, London: Blond and Briggs Ltd.

Schwartz, Ronald D. (1994) *Circle of Protest: Political Ritual in the Tibetan Uprising*, London: Hurst.

Scott, David (1995a) 'Modern British Buddhism: patterns and directions', unpublished paper.

—— (1995b) 'Ecumenical convergence across modern British Buddhism: fact or fiction?', unpublished paper.

Sharf, Robert H. (1995a) 'The Zen of Japanese nationalism', in Donald S. Lopez Jr (ed.) *Curators of the Buddha: The Study of Buddhism Under Colonialism*, Chicago: University of Chicago Press, pp. 107–160.

—— (1995b) 'Whose Zen? Zen nationalism re-visited', in James W. Heisig and John C. Maraldo (eds) *Rude Awakenings: Zen, the Kyoto School and the Question of Nationalism*, Honolulu: University of Hawai Press, pp. 40–51.

—— (1995c) 'Buddhist modernism and the rhetoric of meditative experience', *Numen* 42: 228–283.

—— (1995d) 'Sanbōkyōdan: Zen and the way of the new religions', *Japanese Journal of Religious Studies* 22: 417–458.

Smart, Ninian (1995) *Worldviews: Cross-cultural Explorations of Human Beliefs*, Englewood Cliffs, NJ: Prentice-Hall Inc.

Smith, E. Gene (1970) 'Introduction', in Lokesh Chandra (ed.) *Kongtrul's Encyclopaedia of Indo-Tibetan Culture: Parts 1–3*, New Delhi: International Academy of Indian Culture, pp. 1–87.

Smith, Simon G. (1996) 'Western Buddhism: tradition and modernity', *Religion* 25: 311–321.

Snellgrove, David L. (1987) *Indo-Tibetan Buddhism: Indian Buddhists and their Tibetan Successors*, London: Serindia Publications.

Somers, Jeffrey (1991) 'Tibetan Buddhism in Britain', *Religion Today* 6(3): 1–3.

Sparham, Gareth (1996) 'Why the Dalai Lama rejects Shugden', *Tibetan Review* 31(6): 11–13.

Stark, Rodney (1992) 'How sane people talk to the gods: a rational theory of revelations', in Michael A. Williams, Collett Cox and Martin S. Jaffee (eds) *Innovation in Religious Traditions: Essays in the Interpretation of Religious Change*, Berlin: Mouton de Gruyter, pp. 19–34.

Suzuki, Daisetsu Teitaro (1988) *Mysticism: Christian and Buddhist*, 2nd edn, London: Unwin Hyman Ltd.

Tanabe, George J. (1992) *Myōe the Dreamkeeper: Fantasy and Knowledge in Early Kamakura Buddhism*, Cambridge, MA: Harvard University Press.

Thubten Yeshe, Lama (1978) *Silent Mind, Holy Mind*, Ulverston: Publications for Wisdom Culture.

—— (1979) *Wisdom Energy 2*, Ulverston: Publications for Wisdom Culture.

Tucker, Hilary Claire (1983) 'Opening the mind to a closed alternative: a sociological study of Western commitment to a Tibetan Buddhist group', unpublished M.Litt. thesis, Lancaster University.

Tweed, Thomas A. (1992) *The American Encounter with Buddhism 1844–1912: Victorian Culture and the Limits of Dissent*, Indiana: Indiana University Press.

Uchino, Kumiko (1983) 'The status elevation process of Sōtō sect nuns in modern Japan', *Japanese Journal of Religious Studies* 10: 177–194.

Victoria, Brian (1997) *Zen at War*, New York: Weatherhill Inc.

Victoria, Brian *et al.* (1999) 'Yasutani Roshi: the hardest koan', *Tricycle: The Buddhist Review* Fall: 60–75.

Volinn, Ernest (1985) 'Eastern meditation groups: why join?', *Sociological Analysis* 46: 147–156.

Waldman, Marilyn Robinson and Baum, Robert M. (1992) 'Innovation and renovation: the "prophet" as an agent of change', in Michael A. Williams, Collett Cox and Martin S. Jaffee (eds) *Innovation in Religious Traditions: Essays in the Interpretation of Religious Change*, Berlin: Mouton de Gruyter, pp. 241–284.

Waterhouse, Helen (1995) 'Who is the Karmapa? Western Buddhist responses to a challenge to traditional religious authority', *DISKUS* 3(2): 59–73.

—— (1997) *Buddhism in Bath: Authority and Adaptation*, Leeds: Community Religions Project Monograph Series, University of Leeds.

—— (1999) 'Who says so? Legitimacy and authenticity in British Buddhism', *Scottish Journal of Religious Studies* 20(1): 19–36.

—— (2001) 'Representing Western Buddhism: a United Kingdom focus', in Gwilym Beckerlegge (ed.) *Religion Today: Tradition, Modernity and Change*, Aldershot: Ashgate Publishing Ltd, pp. 117–160.

Watts, Alan W. (1958) 'Beat Zen, Square Zen and Zen', *Chicago Review* 12(2): 3–11.

Welbon, Guy Richard (1968) *The Buddhist Nirvāṇa and its Western Interpreters*, Chicago and London: University of Chicago Press.

Weller, P. (2001) *Religions in the UK 2001–2003*, Derby: University of Derby Press.

Werner, Karel (1973) 'Authenticity in the interpretation of Buddhism', in M. Pye and R. Morgan (eds) *The Cardinal Meaning: Essays in Comparative Hermeneutics: Buddhism and Christianity*, The Hague: Mouton and Co., pp. 161–193.

Williams, Michael A., Cox, Collett and Jaffee, Martin S. (1992) 'Religious innovation: an introductory essay', in Michael A. Williams, Collett Cox and Martin S. Jaffee (eds) *Innovation in Religious Traditions: Essays in the Interpretation of Religious Change*, Berlin: Mouton de Gruyter, pp. 1–17.

Williams, Paul (1991) *Mahāyāna Buddhism: The Doctrinal Foundations*, London: Routledge.

—— (1996) 'Dorje Shugden', *The Middle Way* 71: 130–132.

Wilson, Martin (1987) *Rebirth and the Western Buddhist*, London: Wisdom Publications.

Yandell, Keith E. (1993) *The Epistemology of Religious Experience*, Cambridge: Cambridge University Press.

INDEX